KING TROLLEY AND THE SUBURBAN QUEENS

BY

JAMES F. BAKER

COPYRIGHT 2005

MERAMEC HIGHLANDS BOOKS
1015 Barberry Lane
Kirkwood, MO 63122

KING TROLLEY AND THE SUBURBAN QUEENS

TABLE OF CONTENTS

KING TROLLEY AND THE SUBURBAN QUEENS

Then and Now: Maplewood's Sutton Avenue Streetcar Loop circa 1915. Same location used as a Bi-State bus loop circa 2000. Bregstone postcard courtesy of Maplewood Public Library. Bus loop photo by author.

KING TROLLEY AND THE SUBURBAN QUEENS:

INTRODUCTION

In the early 1890s, electrification of streetcar lines was a nationwide phenomenon already well underway in the city of St. Louis, Missouri. The streetcar lines were rapidly expanding in the city but leaving the rural county sparsely served, thus fueling the desire of the populace of St. Louis County towns to have their own electric street railway lines which would connect them with the city and each other. At the time, most county residents traveled to St. Louis by horse drawn vehicles, or more efficiently by steam train, if they were fortunate enough to live near a rail line. Though some steam railroad lines connected county towns with the city, no cross county steam or street rail lines connected county towns to each other or to Clayton, the county seat.

Throughout the years since the mid 1890s, two St. Louis County towns, Webster Groves and Kirkwood, have claimed the title, "Queen of the Suburbs." The friendly argument continues to this day, but for the purposes of this book, both cities are deserving of the title. By the turn of the century, the trolley lines were "King" of urban mass transit. A historical look at the service to the "Queens of the St. Louis Suburbs" by electric street rail, then the reigning "King" of mass transit, gives rise to the title, *King Trolley and the St. Louis Suburban Queens.* Not to be ignored in this work, small settlements which in 1890 consisted mainly of woods and fields, Maplewood, Brentwood, Glendale, and Oakland grew into thriving communities due in part to the influence of "King Trolley." In 1900, four years after Kirkwood and Webster Groves were connected by electric streetcar lines to St. Louis, the influence of "King Trolley" expanded when it joined the county's "Queen Mother," (Clayton) to the "Suburban Queens" and to points north and east.

This book tells the story of streetcar service provided by the St. Louis and Kirkwood Railroad, the St. Louis and Meramec River Railroad, and the successors to those two lines. Its narrative progresses from local entrepreneurs' and residents' desire for streetcar lines in the early 1890s to the last St. Louis streetcar run. It blends the history of the streetcar companies with anecdotes illustrating the strong influence of the trolley lines on the lives of residents of the Suburban Queens: their excitement and frustrations resulting from their patronage of the streetcars for work, play and routine travel.

KING TROLLEY: INTRODUCTION

At the turn of the century, the streetcar was undisputed "King" of urban transit, but by 1940, it was just a pretender to the transit throne. First the motor bus and then the automobile assumed mass transit supremacy. By May, 1966, "King Trolley" was dead in the St. Louis area except for remnants of track and vacant right-of-ways. However, what remained behind in many of those who had patronized and operated the streetcars, unable to be dismantled or discarded, was a set of beliefs about the viability of streetcar transit and a set of nostalgic memories of streetcar days.

In the 1990s, with the advent of Metro-Link, interest turned toward the original street rail systems which many believe efficiently served the populace of the St. Louis metropolitan area. Though additional Metro-Link routes and extensions will be constructed, it is doubtful that modern light rail will ever assume the level of dominance in the St. Louis area that the streetcar system enjoyed at the end of the nineteenth century and in the first couple of decades of the twentieth century. This story is timely because of the renewed interest in electric rail service and because of recent centennials marking milestones in streetcar service on the lines serving St. Louis County.

On occasion, errors creep into historical accounts. The author would be happy to hear from anyone who has corrections, photographs, or additional information which will help to complete an accurate historical record of the lines that served St. Louis County. Some pieces of streetcar history are elusive, such as photographs of streetcars at the Meramec Highlands loop. It would be satisfying to see such elusive pieces added to the collections of the Museum of Transport or county historical societies to make the public record more complete.

An impetus for writing this book was the wealth of fascinating material about the early days of the St. Louis and Kirkwood Railroad and the St. Louis and Meramec River Railroad compiled while doing research for an earlier book, *Glimpses of Meramec Highlands: St. Louis' Only Exclusive Health and Pleasure Resort*. The information about streetcars and their connection to the growth of the towns they served proved irresistible. I was compelled to write the history before it was lost, as those who rode the streetcars in the county are passing away with the inevitable march of time.

Thanks are due to my family who supported me through the long process of finishing this book, and to all those who shared encouragement, information, photographs, and memories of streetcar service. A special thanks is due to F. Travers Burgess and Charles Hamman who reviewed the content of the *King Trolley* manuscript for inaccuracies and shared their expertise and material from their personal archives; to Willis Goldschmidt for his support in finding information and photographs in the Museum of Transportation reference library; to Wayne Leeman for sharing photographs from his collection; to Francis Bud Barnes for his encouragement; to the Kirkwood Historical Society for photographs and source material; to the Glendale Historical Society for use of photographs and source material; to the Ferguson Historical Society

KING TROLLEY: INTRODUCTION

for use of photographs; to the Missouri Historical Society for use of their archives; to Francis Scheidegger for sharing memories and photographs; and to the Museum of Transportation and their volunteers for their efforts in saving and organizing streetcar photographs, electric railway company records and streetcar rolling stock.

Now step aboard, and enjoy the ride!

Intro-1. Sign on the side of a spliced Lindell car reads, *"Webster & Kirkwood & Meramec Highlands."* **It advertises the connection to those locations via the St. Louis and Kirkwood Railroad. Below the advertised connections, is painted the Lindell Railroad name. The end of the car bore a sign that announced, "Kirkwood Connection." The second car, a Lindell Company Chouteau Avenue car, also carried the name of the St. Louis and Kirkwood connection on its side. The photograph was taken in the southeast corner of Forest Park shortly after the cars left the Lindell loop there and headed for the private right-of-way which bordered the south edge of the park. It was included in the souvenir program of the 1896 National Convention of the Street Railway Association.**

Chapter 1

THE TIMES OF "KING TROLLEY" - A CONTEXT

By the mid 1890s, prior to the advent of their streetcar service, the Missouri towns of Kirkwood and Webster Groves had become well established primarily due to railroad service connecting them with St. Louis. Kirkwood began in 1853, developed and designed as a suburb served by the Missouri Pacific Railroad. It received its charter as an incorporated town in 1865, well before Webster Groves, which incorporated in 1896 after combining several settlements and real estate developments. Both towns, each of which fancied itself, the "Queen of St. Louis Suburbs," were already well served by the Missouri Pacific Railroad and the St. Louis and San Francisco Railroad. However, both towns eagerly anticipated the arrival of electric street rail service.

Formation of new electric street rail companies multiplied rapidly all over the world after the successful introduction of electric trolley service in Richmond, Virginia in 1889. Most already existing transit companies switched from horse drawn streetcars to the new electric trolley cars. Cable car service often lasted a bit longer, but by 1900 most cable railways had been converted to electric operation. The last decade of the 19th century was a boom time for the development of electric railroads in St. Louis area, just as it was in the rest of the United States.

On the national front in 1895 and 1896, the presidential race was front page news. Populist and well known orator William Jennings Bryan stopped in St. Louis and Kirkwood to make two of his 600 "Cross of Gold" speeches on his 18,000 mile campaign trip extolling Free Silver. The front porch campaign of Republican candidate William McKinley was bankrolled by a $7,000,000 war chest. Most of that money was spent on mailings supporting hard money, high tariffs to protect American industry, and other conservative policies which captured the urban vote and swept McKinley to the Presidency.

The "separate but equal" doctrine was upheld by the U.S. Supreme Court in Plessy v. Ferguson; the modern Olympic games started in Athens Greece; literary types read the new novel, *The Red Badge of Courage*; Charles Dana Gibson's illustrations of the "perfect" American man and woman swept the country; rural free postal delivery was established; newspapers entertained with new features such as captioned cartoons as well as columns and personal interest stories; pulpit thumping evangelism thrived; the first Ford automobile was assembled; use of bicycles became a craze; gold was discovered in the Yukon Territory; and speculative promotions in real estate, telephone service, electric service, water service, and electric railroads were rampant. Despite all the national and international events of the time, important news in 1895 and 1896 for many citizens of Webster Groves and Kirkwood, was the progress of two electric railroads, the St. Louis and Kirkwood Railroad and the St. Louis and Meramec River Railroad. Construction had started and would soon connect the "Suburban Queens" as well as numerous small villages and the newly constructed Meramec Highlands "Health and Pleasure Resort" to the city of St. Louis.

The arrival of the streetcar service was desired because it was expected to free area residents from the "expensive" fares[1] of the steam railroads and to substantially boost property values all along the streetcar lines. The cost of commuting on steam railroads was high compared with the typical 5 cent streetcar fare, and the frequency of the steam railroads' commuter service was generally limited to morning and evening rush-hour times. An exception was during the summers when extra accommodation trains, up to nine trains each way, ran to Meramec Highlands Resort situated on the Frisco line west of Kirkwood and to Valley Park and its Meramec River attractions. In 1895, the Kirkwood *Suburban Leader* newspaper predicted success for electric rail service to Kirkwood, "...the time between St. Louis and Kirkwood, is as yet undeterminable..., but electricity has proven a worthy opponent if not superior to steam throughout the east and the same results will doubtless obtain here."[2]

Streetcar lines were perceived as a very desirable commodity for the communities served because of increased access to businesses and services within the metropolitan area. Both city and county residents paid homage to "King Trolley," believing that streetcar service was a profitable investment and would provide a boon to the local economy. Rural areas were opened to residential development when blessed with a streetcar connection to St. Louis, so real estate promoters were especially vocal in favor of the new streetcar lines. By 1906, ten years after the arrival of the first St. Louis and Kirkwood streetcar, the population of the county had increased by 50% and taxable wealth had increased by 100%. Though the streetcars lines were not the sole reason for the growth, they had a significant effect.

The development of Glendale and Brentwood illustrates how quickly arrival of a streetcar line can change a rural area. When the St. Louis and Kirkwood Railroad purchased private right-of-way and constructed its road in 1896 through what is now Glendale,[3] the area roughly between Kirkwood and Webster Groves, no town existed. Collins Road (now Sappington) was a dirt road running from the village of Sappington north to Manchester Road. Most of the property in the area that is now Glendale and Oakland was owned by well-to-do farmers or city people who owned country estates. A scattering of houses existed, but no business district or subdivisions had yet been developed along the new streetcar route. Passengers on the line experienced a beautiful ride on private right-of-way through the woods and fields of the area.

---

[1] Suburban Leader, 18 December 1895. 20 cents per single round trip from Kirkwood to Union Station.
[2] Ibid.
[3] The Glendale name came from two railroad stations of the same name, one on the Missouri Pacific and one on the St. Louis and San Francisco Railway, located where each railroad crossed Berry Road.

KING TROLLEY: A CONTEXT

The St. Louis and Meramec River Railroad (the Manchester line) arrived in the Glendale area in 1897. It followed Lockwood Avenue west to Collins Road, where it continued west on a private right-of-way, joined Adams Avenue, and entered Kirkwood. The new streetcar line effectively separated the Glendale area into two sections, which later politically separated into two towns, Glendale to the north of the streetcar line, and Oakland to the south.

Glendale's subdivisions quickly followed the arrival of the streetcars. The first was built next to the St. Louis and Meramec River line. The subdivision plot consisting of two streets just east of Collins Road, Elm and Maple (now Parkland) avenues, was filed and recorded by E. P. Dickson Jr. in November of 1896. Each street was one block long, running north to Zoetta (now Hawbrook). In 1897, Glendale's second subdivision plot was filed by Annie Albright, and by Dr. John Pitman and his wife and was recorded as the Chelsea subdivision. It bordered the St. Louis and Kirkwood Railroad. Pitman had been president of the St. Louis and Kirkwood Railroad and was instrumental in bringing the line through the area. The Chelsea subdivision dedicated Dwyer Avenue, Brownell Avenue, and on the east side of Collins Road, Chelsea Avenue. Moreland Place was developed by E. P. Dickson in 1901. It dedicated Moreland Avenue which ran from Collins Road about 1000 feet west to the St. Louis and Kirkwood streetcar tracks and then turned south and ran up the hill to Scott (Essex).

Three more subdivisions were filed in 1905. Elsea Place dedicated Edwin Avenue, a street one block east of Collins Road running south from Zoetta (Hawbrook) to Lockwood and the Manchester streetcar line. Bonita Park adjoined the earlier subdivisions situated near the Manchester line, running north from Zoetta on the east side of Collins Road. Glendale Terrace was situated east of the other Glendale subdivisions. It was located west of Berry Road and immediately north of the Manchester tracks and included Trevilian, Cornelia, Austin, and Beverley avenues. These early subdivisions located near the streetcar lines were the start of continual development in Glendale sparked by the streetcar access to the city of St. Louis and to other parts of the county. At Collins Road on the St. Louis and Kirkwood line, a small cluster of Glendale businesses developed at the streetcar stop. Within 15 years, the rural area had become a town.

Brentwood's history with streetcars, like Glendale's, is older than the town. In 1895, Tom Madden a Brentwood area businessman and property owner sold to the St. Louis and Kirkwood Railroad Company a parcel of property adjacent to the Creve Coeur branch of the Missouri Pacific Railroad near what is now Brentwood Boulevard. Prior to the arrival of the streetcar line, Brentwood consisted of farms, woods, and a small group of business operators on Manchester Road. Madden was a savvy businessman who took advantage of the impending streetcar connection with the city by subdividing a large parcel of his property immediately north of the St. Louis and Kirkwood property. He named the subdivision Maddenville. Because of easy access to work in the city via the St. Louis and Kirkwood line and on Missouri-Pacific commuter trains, combined with a lower cost of property than in the city, a number of streetcar employees settled on and around the Brazeau hill area of Maddenville. Madden, Bompart and Dr. Berry built over a dozen houses in the area which they rented or sold to streetcar and railway employees. They also sold lots to others who built their own homes, thus creating a hub for the development of the community that was to become Brentwood.

The *St. Louis County Watchman* newspaper recognized the predominant support of the populace for the streetcar lines and the desire to have the lines connect not only to the city but across the county as well. In December 1899, the paper printed a witty paean in verse form to "King Trolley"[4] which concluded with a cautionary note:

KING TROLLEY

> *Trolley is King, King of the county,*
> *   To him do we bow, be we rich, be we poor;*
> *For a nickel we all partake of his bounty,*
> *   The trolley will take you right to your door.*
>
> *Trolley is King, don't you hear his bell clanging?*
> *   Up the hill, down the dale by day and by night;*
> *The platform is crowded, by straps we are hanging,*
> *   Whilst electricity puts forth its strength and its might.*
>
> *Rock roads or dirt roads, what careth King Trolley?*
> *   Out of the way, or o'er you he'll run;*
> *To resist his majesty, oh, what a folly!*
> *   To condemn rights of way to him it is fun.*
>
> *Trolley is King; He has set us all crazy,*
> *   The rails and the wires his ministers are;*
> *The folks that loved work once, all now are lazy,*
> *   No walking nor driving now; all ride on the car.*
>
> *Trolley is King; He ruleth by power;*
> *   Lightning he shows you, and light by the night;*
> *His dynamos work always, not by the hour,*
> *   His motors and motormen for him will fight.*
>
> *Hail to King Trolley; We submit to our fate.*
> *   O King, rule us wisely, and never be late;*
> *If you are always on time, our love you will win,*
> *   We'll sing to your praise, as thro' space you us spin.*

---

[4]M. B. Greensfelder, "King Trolley," SLCW, 8 December 1899, p. 1.

KING TROLLEY: A CONTEXT

Yet, Court of the County, watch ye the King,
Regulations and laws he must mind and obey;
If the King proves a Tyrant, no Blessing he'll bring,
Oh, Court of the County, be watchful, we pray.

M. B. GREENSFELDER[5]

The belief that electric railways could provide almost constant availability of travel to the city for a fraction of the cost to the consumer, made the idea of street rail very exciting to the county residents. Real estate and streetcar promoters of the day fed the prevailing belief that the property around an electric rail line which connected to St. Louis would multiply exponentially in value. They promoted the idea that residents could not lose by investing in a streetcar line. Profit was "guaranteed." In reality, most streetcar lines serving the sparsely populated county never made money because of capital expenses which were extremely high for county lines because of the long distances involved. All lines of the day faced the expense of frequent relaying of stronger rails as cars became too large and heavy for the existing tracks. A fare of 5 cents or less was expected by the populace. Fares were not raised above that in the St. Louis County for many years, though an additional 5 cent fare was charged when the county passenger traveled into the city. Unchanging fare structures caused constant money flow problems as the lines' expenses rose faster than the income. The scattered population of the county with its small concentration of residents in far flung county towns was inadequate to provide consistent streetcar ridership throughout the day. For much of the typical weekday, with the exception of rush hour, streetcars in the county ran almost empty. Without county attractions, such as Meramec Highlands Resort, Ramona Lake and Park, Suburban Gardens, Delmar Gardens, and Creve Coeur Lake to attract city riders, the lines operating in the county would have immediately been in dire financial straits.

How did the arrival of streetcar lines change the suburbs and county towns? Once the lines were established in an area, population increases were noted. Vacant houses were rented, most often by commuters to the city. Sections of the towns not adjacent to the steam rail lines were opened up by the new electric railways. Subdivisions were developed in proximity to the lines, and shopping districts began to grow along the streetcar routes. The Maplewood shopping area near the Sutton Avenue loop became very robust with residents of Kirkwood and Webster riding the streetcar to Maplewood to go shopping. Because the city fare zone ended, and the county fare zone started at the Maplewood loop, commuters returning home from work in the city could get off, do their shopping, and then continue on home.

The Manchester line through Webster Groves traversed several shopping districts, such as one at the corner of Marshall and Summit, where prior to the construction of the streetcar line a grocery and confectionery operated. After the line came through, the area soon sprouted stores on the north side of Marshall Avenue. A tavern then set up shop in the area to serve the thirsty

---

[5]Greensfelder was from a prominent and politically active St. Louis County family after which the Greensfelder County Park is named.

streetcar riders returning home. The street railroad company built a wooden shelter with wicker seats for its riders at that corner and later provided shelters for Webster Groves residents at Tuxedo, Lockwood, and Newport. A paper boy sold newspapers to patrons of the line at Marshall and Summit.[6] Paper vendors were commonly found at most major stops on the line. The main Webster Groves business district served by the Manchester line was located at Lockwood and Gore, though residents of Old Orchard and Tuxedo Park often found it more convenient to use the streetcars to travel to Maplewood to shop. Businesses in Webster Groves sprang up at the corner of Lockwood and Summit, near the current Old Orchard shopping district as well as along Lockwood.

In Kirkwood, the lines were carefully routed by the town board to serve the downtown business district. Because that district was well established, less business development followed the route of the line, except where loops were constructed. The Magnolia loop, often known as the Kirkwood-Ferguson loop, and the Meramec Highlands/Osage Hills loop stimulated the development of nearby businesses which catered to a thirsty and hungry crowd of travelers and streetcar crews. Today a small business district exists just west of the former Magnolia loop even though streetcar service to the area was dropped more fifty-five years ago.

The streetcar lines to the Meramec Highlands provided moneymaking opportunities for a variety of area entrepreneurs. Anticipated income from streetcar tourists was a major factor in the development of the Meramec Highlands as a place to play. The resort became a wildly popular streetcar destination during the summers of the late 1890s and early decades of the 1900s. Paradoxically, it is possible that without the streetcar connections, the resort may have retained its exclusive appeal for the well-to-do and thus maintained financial stability.[7] Opening in 1905, near the Meramec Highlands loop, Ben Groth operated a livery stable where farmers left their teams of horses and wagons while they rode the streetcars into St. Louis to shop. He also operated a saloon to assuage the thirst of streetcar riders and local residents. Two dance halls, each with their own restaurant and saloon, operated near the loop. The various live bands drew customers from all over the St. Louis area, most riding the streetcars to the popular nightspot. On the south side of Quinette Road (Big Bend Road), the Meramec Highlands Dance Hall was operated by Arthur L. Autenrieth, and on the north side of the road, Eden Amusement Park was operated by Peter Gouness. Both had expansive picnic grounds. To maximize use of the dance floors, the owners also used them as roller skating rinks.

The streetcar line at Meramec Highlands offered the nearest walking access to the Meramec River where Guyol, Hance, Stites, McConnell, Jackson and others, at various times, operated boat and canoe rentals, swimming beaches complete with bathhouses, ball fields, and provided live music and entertainment events. Food and drink was available from restaurants and refreshment stands at the river. The Meramec Highlands Inn, which opened in 1894, was located

---

[6] Ann Morris, "History Tracked Along Manchester Streetcar Line -Old Tracks Stir Memories of Webster - Kirkwood Link to St. Louis," Webster-Kirkwood Times, 9 October 1987.

[7] An extensive treatment of Meramec Highlands by James Baker is found in Glimpses of Meramec Highlands, St. Louis' Only Exclusive Health and Pleasure Resort, Kirkwood, Meramec Highlands Books, 1995.

just east of the streetcar loop. During the warm months, it offered fine dining, billiards, ten pins, theater, dancing and other amusements until it closed after the 1904 season. Most resort bound streetcar riders only cut through its grounds on their way to other pleasures. The hotel's exclusive nature and high prices tended to discourage the streetcar crowd from patronage. Many picnickers exited the streetcars at the Meramec Highlands Store to purchase food for their stay in the Highlands or on the Meramec River beaches. Despite cooling off at the Meramec, most were hot and sweaty by the time they had trudged back up the bluffs to return home, so the general store and saloons near the loop did a brisk business in cold drinks. All the businesses near the former Meramec Highlands loop have closed or were converted to residential use over fifty years ago with the exception of the Greenbriar Country Club.

The streetcar lines running through the "Suburban Queens" provided their own set of negatives such as opportunities for pickpockets and robbers, causing many streetcar conductors to carry weapons in order to protect themselves and their passengers. The rough element of society at times ensured that the marshals were kept busy. The Kirkwood marshal had to periodically break up fights at the Meramec Highlands and on the streetcars. Members of neighborhood gangs often rode out to the Highlands dance halls where they started fights with young men from other gangs. Those fights on occasion spilled over into the streetcars. When called out to the Highlands to break up a fight or track down robbers, the lawmen rode out from Kirkwood on the first available streetcar. The loop at the Meramec Highlands was considered, the "end of the line," by some passengers, creating extra business for the coroner and undertakers in the area. The streetcar line provided a means to flee from the harsh realities of a personal "hell" to a peaceful rural place with many secluded spots where an individual could commit suicide unobserved

In the early years of the twentieth century, roads were so bad that automobiles and motor buses were neither speedy or reliable due to frequent flat tires and breakdowns, so most residents were dependent on streetcars or horse drawn conveyances. The obvious advantage of not having to make arrangements for the horses at the end destination made streetcar service convenient - IF one lived near a line. Only during streetcar strikes or disruption of service by natural forces like flood or extreme cold, did large numbers of patrons switch back to the steam railroads. The existence of the Meramec Highlands Frisco Depot close to the streetcar terminus gave a sense of security to the streetcar riders who frequented the resort. If the streetcar line was shut down due to a wreck, track problem, power failure etc., the resort patrons could always return to the city via steam train. Though the Missouri Pacific station was about two miles away, it was still within walking distance and was at times used as a backup for stranded streetcar riders. Despite the immediate popularity of the streetcar lines, the rail lines retained a core of loyal commuters. Most of the loyal riders had no close access to the streetcar lines, could get closer to their desired destination by riding commuter trains, or they believed that the trains were more comfortable, safe, and reliable.

Town boosters pointed with pride to their streetcar lines, touting the existence of their modern conveyances which demonstrated the progressive nature of their towns. The arrival of streetcar lines reinforced an already strong sense of civic pride in Webster Groves and Kirkwood, while also giving a focal point for development of civic pride in the more undeveloped areas such as Maplewood, Brentwood and Glendale.

Residents have shared their memories from the early part of this century in the *Glendale Historical Society Bulletin* since its inception in 1986. A persistent thread in many of the remembrances was the use of the streetcar lines for transportation to school, work, church, shopping and entertainment. As a result of the importance of the streetcar lines in the development of Glendale, the Glendale Historical Society selected a streetcar design for its logo. For its 75th anniversary, Maplewood selected a streetcar logo for its special postmark to represent its 75 years of progress. Ironically, by that time, all Maplewood's streetcars were but a memory, though the Sutton Avenue loop was still used as a transfer point for Bi-State bus riders. Brentwood recognized the importance of the streetcar in its history by incorporating a streetcar into the graphic design used for the cover of its 50th anniversary publication. Maplewood provides a classic illustration of how important streetcar lines were to the development and health of a city. With the departure of streetcar service and the advent of an automobile owning population that preferred new shopping malls, Maplewood's business district began to suffer. It has never regained the robust health of its streetcar days.

On the negative side, the streetcar lines brought unsightly poles and tracks to beautiful residential and rural areas. The noise of metal grinding on metal, clanging bells, the snap and crackle of sparks from the overhead wires as the trolley wheel rolled along them, and of squealing brakes changed the atmosphere in quiet residential areas. Congestion on shared roads and the unaccustomed speed of streetcars in the streets of the Suburban Queens resulted in physical danger to passengers and crew of the streetcars, other vehicles, pedestrians, and animals.

Adding to financial woes of the lines was frequent litigation against the electric railway companies, a negative factor not anticipated by investors. Accidents were a common occurrence, and so were the resulting lawsuits. Streetcar companies faced additional litigation as a result of violations of the various franchises awarded to them by the county and its towns. Company attorneys were kept quite busy defending the lines. Many of the suits were dismissed or settled out of court, but others ended with the courts giving large settlements (by the standards of the day) to the injured parties. There was merit in many of the suits against the lines. However, many others were fraudulent attempts to, "milk the cash cow."

Aldermen received complaints that the streetcars were speeding in violation of their franchises, that cars blocked traffic when receiving and discharging passengers, that there was no service after midnight, and that streetcar motormen were dumping cinders from the cars' stoves on the streets. Town officials in the still rural suburbs had to concern themselves with keeping animals off the streets so that the streetcars would not be interrupted. The streetcar lines provided an convenient way for unsavory characters to come into the communities to fight, steal, or perpetuate "cons" on the populace and then leave quickly on one of the frequently scheduled cars. Equally disconcerting to the "Drys," electric railroads provided residents of towns with hard won bans on the sale of liquor easy access to drink and the "illicit pleasures" found in the city or resorts such as Meramec Highlands. Perhaps the most disturbing use of the streetcars to present day sensibilities was as a result of the school segregation that occurred at the time. For example, high schoolers of African-American descent were not allowed to attend high school in Kirkwood, so families deprived themselves in order to pay the cost of daily streetcar fare to and from St. Louis city schools.

While the streetcars created problems for the residents of Kirkwood, the youth of Webster, Glendale, Kirkwood and Osage Hills created vexation for the streetcar motormen. Soaped rails, dislodged trolley poles and large rocks on the rails were frequent pranks, often fondly remembered by older adults many years later.

Of the two streetcar lines, some residents of Glendale believed that the Kirkwood-Ferguson was more intimately associated with the development of the town because it ran through the business district past city hall and ran through the middle of Glendale's residential area. The Manchester line ran along the south edge of the current town boundary. Fond memories of both lines are still maintained by those who rode the streetcars. Without streetcars Maplewood, Brentwood, Glendale, and Oakland would have developed at a much slower pace. but their eventual development was inevitable as the population moved west from the city. Would Webster Groves, Kirkwood, and nearby areas have developed in the same way without the arrival of streetcar lines? Perhaps. They may not have grown quite as quickly, but they already had good anchors with the rail lines connecting them to St. Louis.

In the early part of the twentieth century, the majority of St. Louis area residents came to depend on the streetcar for transportation, but as roads became better and automobiles and motor buses became more prevalent, a shift away from streetcar use was obvious. One limitation of streetcars which boosted the appeal of automobiles in Kirkwood and points west was fact that Kirkwood was the end of the line. To go further west for any reason, another form of transit was required.

If streetcars were not required for the development of the "Suburban Queens," why is there a sense of loss caused by the demise of streetcar service, and why is there the desire for successful expansion of modern-day Metro-Link? Time has a way of fading memories of the little irritations: the cold, the swaying of the cars causing motion sickness, the crowded conditions at rush hour with standing room only, the dirty or shabby cars, inconsiderate riders spitting on the floor of the streetcar, delays due to track problems, tardiness caused by youthful pranks, and frequent accidents. Despite the income produced in their towns by streetcar riders, and despite the dependence of much of the populace on streetcars for transportation, streetcars were truly a mixed blessing for the "Suburban Queens."

At the same time, memories of the good times glow brighter as the years pass; the all day Sunday excursions, riding to the end of the line and back just for fun, riding to events such as school picnics at Forest Park or baseball games at Sportsman's Park with high-spirited friends, riding to meaningful places such as work, school and church, or going on family excursions for shopping or entertainment. Many older residents don't think of yesteryear's streetcar travel without memories of the Maplewood loop, paying the extra fare, waiting for their right connection, transferring, shopping, and dating.

Anything that becomes routine in our lives leaves some kind of gap, a sense of loss, when it is gone. That sense of loss is poignant, especially when the lost item is replaced by something that has its own set of negatives, such as exhaust belching buses with less frequent service or traffic jams and parking problems caused by a glut of automobiles. The memory of the earlier form of transit becomes a bit brighter as the later form proves to have its own problems.

This book helps preserve streetcar history and memories of residents of the "Suburban Queens" and others who experienced the pleasures and irritants of riding the St. Louis County streetcar lines at the end of the 19th century and during the first half of the 20th century. For those who haven't experienced "King Trolley" and for former streetcar riders, "Welcome aboard!"

1-1. Ben Groth's bar and livery stable operated across Quinette Road from the Meramec Highlands loop. Cold motormen and conductors left their cars while they purchased steaming mugs of coffee at Groth's establishment. The structure still stands as a residence, minus the porches, on the north side of Big Bend Road near the Greenbriar Country Club entrance. Photograph courtesy of Bill Groth.

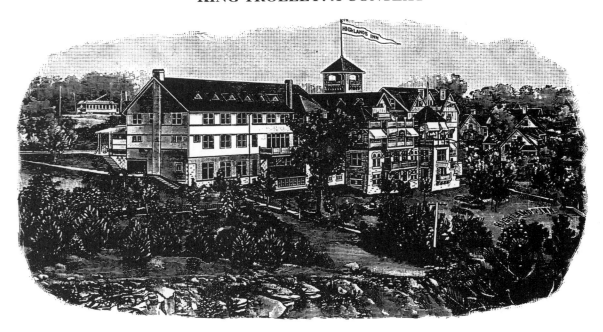

1-2. 1899 illustration from *Reedy's Mirror* showing the Meramec Highlands Resort, complete with streetcars serving the Highlands Inn.

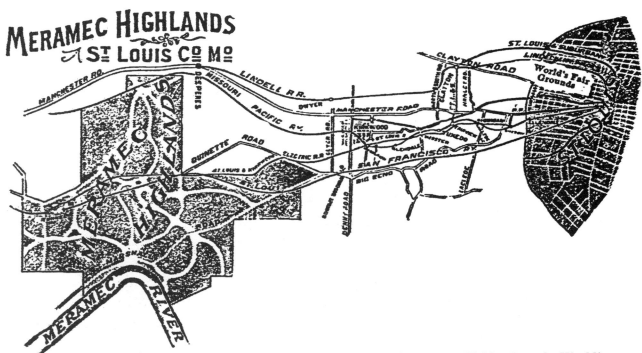

1-3. Map showing the close and "speedy" proximity of Meramec Highlands to the World's Fair via streetcar. The map was included in an advertisement booklet designed to entice fair visitors to stay at the resort.

AS THE LADIES SEE IT.

1-4. This front page cartoon featured in the March 15, 1900 *St. Louis Post-Dispatch* **decried the pig like behavior of many male streetcar riders who did not rise to give a lady a seat, smoked in the cars, and spat upon the floors.**

1-5. Charles Delbridge concurred with the above opinion in his tract *Move Forward Please*. **His illustration shows the "vile unsanitary" condition of the St. Louis streetcars of the day with "gentlemen" spitting on the floor of the car.**

Nagg: The motormen and conductors on
this line are going to put on an opera.
Nigg: What opera?
Nagg: "Carmen."

1-6. Illustrative of how pervasive the influence of the streetcar was in the early 1900s, streetcar humor appeared often in newspapers. "The Sunny Side of Life" was printed in the September 8, 1904 *St. Louis Post-Dispatch*.

1-7. Mural on the side of the Hanneke's Westwood Market, at 190 North Sappington Road. The market, built in 1914, is situated between Glendale's two former streetcar lines. The mural, which depicts the Kirkwood-Ferguson car at the Sappington Road crossing, attests to the importance of the streetcar line to the development of Glendale. Photograph by the author.

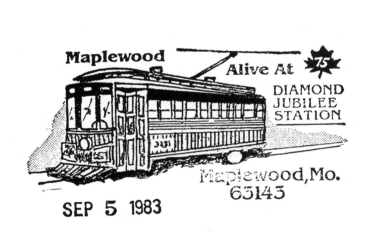

1-8. Illustrating the importance of the streetcars to the communities they served are three logos: the Glendale Historical Society, the Maplewood 75th Anniversary postmark, and the Brentwood Anniversary - 50 Years booklet cover.

Chapter 2

PROMOTION, TALK, AND MORE PROMOTION

After false starts by several street railroad companies desiring to serve Kirkwood and Webster Groves, the St. Louis and Kirkwood Railroad was the first to begin construction in 1895.

An early proposal for a streetcar line from St. Louis to Kirkwood and Webster Groves was submitted to the County Court in 1891. The proposal called for a street railroad along Manchester Road to Kirkwood and Webster Groves. It asked for a 50 year franchise to construct and maintain an elevated or surface road to be operated by horse or electricity, for passenger traffic only. The proposed route was from Chouteau and Manchester in the city, west on Manchester to Denny Road (now Lindbergh Boulevard on the north side of Manchester Road), and south on Denny (now Kirkwood Road) to Kirkwood. A branch was to be constructed south from Manchester Road to Webster Groves at Rock Hill Road. The work was to be completed within three years.[1] Among the petitioners was Dr. John Pitman of Kirkwood. Though the Manchester Line venture failed, Pitman remained interested in bringing a streetcar line to Kirkwood, so he joined the rival St. Louis and Kirkwood Railroad Company effort to obtain a franchise. Nearly six years after the Manchester Road proposal, the St. Louis and Meramec River Railroad utilized a five mile stretch of the earlier proposed route along Manchester Road from Sarah street in the city to Sutton Avenue in Ellendale (Maplewood). However, a street rail line was never extended out Manchester Road to Rock Hill Road and Denny Road as proposed in 1891.

The St. Louis and Kirkwood Rapid Transit Company funded in part by Kirkwood resident Edward Dickson proposed a line from St. Louis to Kirkwood which also failed to start construction. A franchise was awarded by the County Court on April 25, 1892, to the St. Louis and Kirkwood Rapid Transit Company. In an interview reported in August, 1893, Dickson stated that the venture was being abandoned because of the opposition encountered with the "Howard people."[2] The Howard line, officially known as the St. Louis and Meramec River Railroad, had

---

[1] An Electric Road to Kirkwood and Webster Groves," St. Louis County Real Estate column, SLCW, 15 May 1891.
[2] An Elephant on Their Hands," SLCW, 4 August 1893.

secured an option from the County Court for a line over great parts of the same streets targeted for Dickson's line. Dickson's Rapid Transit Co. line was to have run from the city limits on Manchester Road to Sutton Avenue in Maplewood, then south to Lockwood Avenue in the Webster area, west to Berry Road, where the road was to run over private property to Sappington Road, north past Dickson's property to the first public street, and west to its terminus at Woodland Avenue in Kirkwood. Because his proposal called for a delay of two years before construction was to start, residents along the proposed route opposed it. They felt two years was too long to wait. They were also opposed to any operation of a steam dummy on the line and believed, "erroneously," said Dickson, that the line would operate one. An additional reason, and perhaps the most valid, given by Dickson for the company's withdrawal was the lack of funds due to the stringency of the money market at the time.[3]

The withdrawal of Dickson's Rapid Transit Company left the Howard group's St. Louis, Kirkwood and Meramec River Railroad in full possession of the rights to disputed sections of the route, including portions of private right-of-way and public roads adjacent to the Missouri Pacific Railroad. On February 20, 1893, Rapid Transit's route was officially transferred to the St. Louis, Kirkwood and Meramec River Railroad. The County Court tightened some of the requirements of the previous agreement such as requiring the railroad to macadamize[4] 16 feet in width from the outside rail of each track. The court stipulated that rails were to be laid even with the surface of the highways so they would not interfere with the normal flow of traffic.

Though it was left as the only active competitor to the Houseman group's proposed St. Louis and Kirkwood Railroad, the Howard line had already petitioned the County Court for an extension less than a year after approval, causing residents to express doubts that it would ever be built. Doubts were calmed, on June 7, 1895, when the *Watchman* reported that the company backing the St. Louis and Meramec River Railroad had reorganized and increased its capital stock from $500,000 to $750,000. Major stockholders, Thomas Howard, J. B. Case, John A. Holmes, M. C. Orton, and James P. Dawson were given all franchises, rights-of-way, etc. that had been granted before the restructuring. The contract for construction of the line was reported, "about to be finalized with work on the road bed to commence immediately."[5]

The St. Louis and Meramec River Railroad had long held the franchise rights for the city section of the route, but not until September 3, 1895, was the final franchise for the county section of the route issued by the County Court. A *Watchman* reporter in June had optimistically informed readers, "that the new line would connect with John Scullin's electric line at Sarah and Manchester Road, and would pass through Webster Groves, Webster Park, Kirkwood, and Meramec Highlands on its way to the Meramec River."[6] Property owners along the proposed route were "more than anxious" that the road be completed as soon as possible.

---

[3] Ibid.

[4] Macadamizing was a method of paving, a forerunner of blacktop, done by compacting broken stone with asphalt or tar.

[5] "St. Louis - Meramec River Railroad," SLCW, 7 June 1895, p. 4.

[6] Ibid. The projected section connecting the Meramec Highlands to the Meramec River was never constructed.

Hundreds of acres were ready to "throw on the market" as soon as the long-wished-for connection with the city was completed.[7]

Despite the optimism voiced by the *Watchman*, financial problems continued to plague the venture, leading a Webster Groves correspondent to state on October 25th, 1895, "The Manchester-Howard scheme seems to have swallowed itself whole."[8] The line became a subsidiary of the St. Louis and Suburban Railroad Company in 1896, but in the meantime, Houseman's St. Louis and Kirkwood Railroad gained a head start on construction.

James D. Houseman Jr. was both the promoter and general manager of the St. Louis and Kirkwood Railroad. He was so involved with the line that most people referred to the franchise as the "Houseman Air Line." The "Air Line" designation had been commonly used as part of the corporate name of numerous main line railroads such as the Seaboard Air Line Railway prior to the advent of electric railroads, but the "Air Line" name also became attached to a number of electric railroad companies in the late 1800s, possibly because the electric power lines that were "hung in air" above the streetcar tracks. The "Air Line" term may also have been also used by Houseman as a subtle form of advertising, to imply the most direct route or to induce city residents to use the line to enjoy the pure air of Webster Groves, Kirkwood, and the Meramec Highlands at a time when the city was covered by a cloud of soft-coal smoke. No matter what its origin, the "Houseman Air Line" name was commonly used by area residents rather than the formal St. Louis and Kirkwood Railroad name. Others who knew Houseman and had watched construction of the line, dropped "Air" and always referred to it as the "Houseman Line," no matter what other electric railroad company operated on the tracks.[9]

Prior to promotion and operation of electric railroads, Houseman's experience was in promotion of an early telephone company in St. Louis and in real estate. The jump to promotion of streetcar lines was a natural for him. What better way to open up an area for a real estate development boom than to connect it to the city via streetcar? Houseman recognized the profits to be made on promoting streetcar lines to those who desperately desired a convenient link from rural county towns to the city. He understood and played upon the land holders' belief that their property would become more valuable when accessible from the city. Though he undertook study of various lines in nearby states and drew up his plans according to what he believed was the best use of current technology, including telephones on the cars, he was not an experienced street-rail man. Andrew Young, author of *The St. Louis Streetcar Story*, describes Houseman as an outsider, "a maverick with no connections to the St. Louis power elite and few financial resources to back up his schemes."[10]

Though Houseman was briefly involved in promoting the Howard Line proposal before he had a falling out with other principals in the company, the Air Line was the first of many

---

[7]Ibid.

[8]"Webster Groves," SLCW, 25 October 1895.

[9]Travers Burgess related that his grandfather, despite several name changes for the line, always called it the Houseman Line.

[10]Young, Andrew D. (1988). St. Louis Streetcar Story. Glendale, CA: Interurban Press, p. 109.

streetcar line franchises (and failed proposals for new franchises) in the St. Louis metropolitan area in which he was the promoter or manager. At the same time he was meeting with property owners to gain right-of-way for the Air Line through their properties, he was promoting development of a Kirkwood and Des Peres line, a separate venture. It was pitched as a way to allow Des Peres residents a connection to Kirkwood and St. Louis via a street rail line to the Kirkwood rail stations. The proposed Kirkwood and Des Peres line was to be "entirely independent"[11] of the Houseman Air Line, though several investors were interested in both. However, despite reported interest the Kirkwood and Des Peres line was never financed or constructed.

Another promotion of Houseman's, a line that was to begin at the Air Line's Brentwood power house and extend westward nearly forty miles to Pacific, Missouri, was reported in the October 18, 1895 *Watchman*. Houseman proposed innovations on the line due to the distance:

> One of these will be the generation of electrical current by water power instead of steam. The operation of fifty miles of electric railway would be too severe a draft on our power plant at Brentwood, so I purpose to erect a power plant on the banks of the Meramec River, a short distance west of Pacific, where I have secured land for that purpose, and my engineers who have been prospecting in that neighborhood, report that the supply is sufficient to produce water power of 2000 horse capacity net.[12]

Despite Houseman's claims of support from the farmers of the outlying areas, the project was never approved, nor would it have been profitable due to the distance and sparse population served.

Since Houseman's electric railway required a power house to generate electric current for operation of the streetcars, he tried to sell electric power to the towns to be served by the Air Line. On February 21, 1896, the *Watchman* reported his offer to Kirkwood, to provide 125 incandescent 32 candle power lights for a period of 10 years at a cost of $1500 a year with $10 charged for each additional light. The lights were to burn from dark to daylight.[13] Both Kirkwood and Webster Groves rejected his offers to power streetlights with electricity from the Air Line's power house.

By summer of 1893, Kirkwood and Webster Groves residents had begun to believe that Houseman's St. Louis and Kirkwood Railroad promotion was going to be one more abandoned attempt to start an electric railroad to their towns. However, they were encouraged on September 29, 1893, by a *Watchman* article headed, "AFTER A RIGHT-OF-WAY   The St. Louis and Kirkwood Means Business in the Construction of Their Road."[14]   The paper informed readers that the line had been surveyed by B. E. Johnson in June, and that during the summer the

---

[11]"After a Right-of-way, "SLCW, 29 September 1893, p. 4.
[12]SLCW, 18 October 1895.
[13]SLCW, 21 February 1896, p. 8.
[14]"After a Right-of-way," SLCW, 29 September 1893, p. 4.

company had received incorporation papers from the Missouri Secretary of State, had elected officers, and had begun meeting with property owners to obtain right-of-way deeds.

The company announced that it did not plan to begin construction in 1893, because of the need to complete preliminaries, but assured the public that it intended to put large forces of men to work in the Spring of 1894 in order to complete the road by 1895.[15] It was fortunate that the extra year for preliminaries was added to the deadline, because Houseman's timelines proved to be overly optimistic.

Powerful backers, primarily from Kirkwood, with proper political connections and financial resources joined forces with Houseman. Several were elected as officers of the company after its incorporation: Dr. John Pitman, president, George L. Edwards, vice-president, George W. Taussig, secretary and treasurer, Jeremiah Fruin and J. D. Houseman as directors. Houseman was an excellent promoter, and soon had many of the area residents placing their money into the company. The *Watchman* reported that the capital for the project was assured, "with several prominent capitalists" having committed to assist in the enterprise.[16]

The request for a franchise to construct and operate an electric road through Kirkwood was presented to Kirkwood Board of Trustees by Dr. John Pitman on behalf of the St. Louis and Kirkwood Electric Railroad Company on December 18, 1893. Pitman was both a Kirkwood trustee and the President of the fledgling electric railway company. Three months later, after much spirited discussion and after weighing all sides of the question, the Board of Trustees granted permission to build an electric railway through Kirkwood. Newspaper headlines on May 11, 1894 reported:

> KIRKWOOD - The Beautiful Suburban Town is Happy - St. Louis, Kirkwood and Meramec Heights Electric Railway Now Certain.

Kirkwood was so happy that, as the *Watchman* reported, it granted, "a liberal franchise covering the best streets of the town through which (the line) passes westward, to Meramec Highlands, one of the most beautiful suburbs in the county."[17]

St. Louis and Kirkwood Railroad Company officials issued a prospectus in May 1894, which was circulated among property owners along the line. It called for them to subscribe the $75,000 required for a bond which had to be paid to the trust company before a contractor could begin work. The *Watchman* reporter in turn provided editorial comment most pleasing to the promoters:

> The amount which property owners are asked to subscribe toward making the enterprise a success… is a mere bagatelle, compared with the benefits which they are

---

[15] Ibid.
[16] Ibid.
[17] "Kirkwood, The Beautiful Suburban Town is Happy, The St. Louis, Kirkwood and Meramec Heights Electric Railway Now Certain," SLCW, 11 May 1894, p. 1.

to receive in return, even if it was given as a bonus: but the company proposes to make each subscriber a stockholder in the enterprise, which will undoubtedly at one distant day prove a most profitable investment... When completed, this road will be an incomparable benefit to the county, and especially to the property along the route which will be thereby largely increased in value, by being made directly accessible by rapid transit to the city.[18]

For civic boosters, J. D. Houseman was the man of the hour. The *Watchman* reporter encouraged further support for Houseman's Air Line:

> In view of the successful consummation of the most laudable enterprise, it is only justly due the energy, perseverance and pluck of the promoter, Mr. J. D. Houseman Jr., to say that he deserves the hearty cooperation of the citizens of the county, most especially the people of Kirkwood and the territory lying between that suburb and the city limits who will be so largely benefited by the building of this railway.[19]

The initial St. Louis and Kirkwood Electric Railway stock offering was successful, allowing for a contract to be awarded for $150,000 to George Baumhoff's Suburban Construction Company for, "grading, filling, construction of all bridges and culverts, the furnishing and laying of ties and rails throughout the entire line and everything, including the construction of a power house, preparatory for electrical equipment."[20] The contract stipulated that the holder of the $150,000 bond, Union Trust Company of St. Louis, would pay the contractor in three installments; one third when grading, filling and culverts were completed; one third when the materials for tracks and bridges were delivered and on the ground ready for use; and one third when the entire road was completed ready for electrical equipment. The contract required that the workmanship and materials had to be first class and that payment would be based on the approval of a disinterested expert engineer reporting to the trust company.

George Baumhoff, the manager of the Lindell Railroad Company and an experienced electric railroad man, was in charge of the construction contract. For the acquisition of cars, electric motors and other required equipment, he was to receive another $100,000 upon delivery.

Costs mounted. In June, 1895, a required $75,000 "bonus" so that construction could begin was announced. Contractor Baumhoff explained to a meeting of "public spirited citizens" assembled in Kirkwood's Iowa Hall, the nature of his contract with the Houseman line and the reason why the bonus was asked. The *Watchman* reported results of the meeting:

> The following gentlemen were appointed on committees: Mr. Marcus Bernheimer to solicit subscriptions on the road between Kirkwood and Meramec Highlands, Messrs. B. White, W. Bryant and M. Nevins for Kirkwood and vicinity, Mr. Merrill for

---

[18]Ibid.
[19]SLCW, 11 May 1894.
[20]SLCW, 11 May 1894.

Webster Groves, and Messrs. Rannells and Sterritt for the section west of Forest Park. These several committees are expected to begin at work at once and will report at as early a date as possible.[21]

One committee member, Marcus Bernheimer, the president of the Meramec Highlands Company, was banking on the success of the electric railways and was anxious for completion of both the Howard and the Houseman lines. In May, 1895, he advertised the benefits of streetcar lines for his real estate and resort development at the Highlands:

> Remember that all Electric Roads now projected in St. Louis County toward its western limits have Meramec Highlands as their objective point, and it is safe to assume that two of these at least will be built and in running order ere another season is at hand; and when this is accomplished every foot of ground of Meramec Highlands will be worth three times the amount at which we are now offering it.[22]

In July, 1895, due to insufficient subscriptions from the general public, a mass meeting of residents and property owners was held at Bartold's Grove (near the current intersection of Manchester and Hanley roads) to secure additional investors and stockholders for the Houseman Air Line. The *Watchman* reported that St. Louis and Kirkwood Railroad officials and stockholders urged the property owners attending the meeting to subscribe to the company's stock and thus secure an early completion of the road. Not all were convinced to part with their money,[23] but enough was generated to meet the immediate needs.

The proposed route through Kirkwood which had been approved, was later found to be unsatisfactory by the Kirkwood Board of Trustees, so in July of 1895, they approved a revised route. On October 3, 1895, the Board of Trustees approved yet another revision of the route which was the actual route constructed. It began at a point on the eastern boundary of Kirkwood, 600 feet north of Gill Avenue. It crossed Woodlawn Avenue running west parallel to Gill Avenue, to a northern projection of Fillmore, then turned south on Fillmore to Washington Avenue where it turned west. At Clay, it turned and headed south. The Houseman line was given two options, one of turning the route west at Main Street (Argonne) to Harrison Avenue, then turning and running south on Harrison. At Woodbine, it turned and headed west until it hit the city limits. The second option was to cross the Missouri Pacific tracks over the Clay Avenue bridge and continue south to Woodbine. If the company had selected the Harrison Avenue route, it would have been required to construct and maintain a bridge across the Missouri Pacific tracks wide enough for, "one railroad car to pass one wagon,"[24] with the bridge not to be less than 20 feet in width. Whichever route was chosen by the company, the other route was waived, "ipso facto."[25] Houseman officials selected the Clay Avenue route, obviously the cheaper alternative.

---

[21]SLCW, 14 June 1895.

[22]Nicholls-Ritter Realty, Meramec Highlands fold out advertisement, April 1895.

[23]SLCW, 20 July 1895. F. Travers Burgess relates that both of his grandfathers, who lived in the area, attended the meeting but neither invested in the line.

[24]Kirkwood Board of Aldermen Minutes, 3 October 1895, p. 27.

[25]Ibid., p. 28.

KING TROLLEY: PROMOTION, TALK, AND MORE PROMOTION

The company was also given the right to extend the route north from Washington on Clay to Essex Avenue. However, that option was never utilized.

Despite uncertainty about the route through Kirkwood, the St. Louis and Kirkwood Railroad in June of 1895 moved forward with its agreement with Lindell Railroad general manager, George Baumhoff, to build the line. Because of Baumhoff's connection with the Lindell Company, rumors were rampant that the Lindell had, "purchased or absorbed," the St. Louis and Kirkwood Company. Houseman stated to the newspapers that no contract had been entered into between the two lines, even though the Houseman Air Line in the county would connect with the Lindell Railway at the St. Louis city limits. He assured, "We will in no sense be part of that system."[26]

With solid political and financial backing, the company obtained approval from the County Court to construct a street rail line from the St. Louis city limits through Webster Groves to Kirkwood. To gain approval was not terribly difficult because government officials believed the county needed streetcar connections with the city. The rural county had about 50 to 60,000 residents at that time, most of whom were farmers. County boosters believed that the presence of the streetcar lines would stimulate development, so they were inclined to agree with proposals without being overly critical or too closely perusing the details of financial backing. Approved franchises were required to post guarantee bonds and were given timelines to complete their construction, though extensions were routinely granted. Not until 1899, did the County Court come under fire by numerous residents for the free and easy practice of approving franchises.

In a June 28, 1895, *Watchman* piece headed, "CLAYTON-KIRKWOOD-ST .LOUIS, Houseman's Efforts Crowned With Success, Brains, Pluck and Perseverance Win After a Prolonged Struggle," readers learned that company officials and Chief Engineer E. A. Guill spent the day on June 24th in Clayton arranging the final details of their legal preparations to begin work on the electric line. A few complications in fulfilling the rules of the court required that they return on the following Monday with a $5000 bond to, "indemnify the county against injury or loss,"[27] and to provide a complete map of their right of way through the county. That done, they received approval of the court to begin construction.

While in Clayton, company officials closed a deal with Thomas Madden, a large land owner in the Brentwood area, for a parcel of land situated on the Creve Coeur branch of the Missouri-Pacific Railroad. The two and a half acre lot three miles from the line's eastern terminus was purchased for $3000 as the site, "upon which an immense power house is to be erected, of capacity sufficient to supply the whole system." The power house was to be constructed of iron and brick, fireproof throughout and equipped with, "the very latest and most highly improved electrical appliances."[28] The Houseman company offices were to be located in the new building. Also to be located on the grounds were a a frame depot and a solidly

[26]SLCW, 7 June 1895, p. 8.
[27]"Clayton-Kirkwood-St.Louis, Houseman's Efforts Crowned With Success," SLCW, 28 June 1895, p. 1.
[28]Ibid.

constructed brick car shed large enough to hold 15 streetcars. A loop was constructed around the powerhouse so that cars not proceeding on to Kirkwood could turn around and return to West End Heights. Due to the name of a new subdivision being developed by Madden on the north border of the site, the frame station constructed there was called "Maddenville" instead of Brentwood.

In the early years of the line, the Maddenville depot was a busy place. Mary Hilke (deceased in May 1993) a longtime Brentwood resident shared her "Musings From Memory" in publications celebrating both the 50th and 75th anniversary of her hometown. She recalled the depot at Maddenville:

> Also built was a large depot. This frame building had a separate room for coal, supplies, and accommodation of motormen and conductors of the line. The waiting room had seats along the walls, a pot bellied stove, and a counter with attendant who sold newspapers, cigars, and candy. There were also men's rooms and ladies' rooms. The depot was at the foot of Brazeau Avenue and was a transfer point for the Brentwood and Kirkwood lines...[29]

In an interview with Brentwood historian Robert Eastin, Edwin Vogelsang, a retired employee of United Railways and Public Service Company, recalled residents of Brazeau Hill wearing their heavy boots when they walked down the muddy road to the station. They stored their mud-caked boots for the day in lockers under the long station benches. [30]

Brentwood and Madden had another close connection to the early county street railroads. At the site approximately where the Syms store stands today on the south side of Manchester road, Tom Madden operated a quarry, selling rock and gravel. One of his major customers was the St. Louis and Kirkwood Railroad Company. It purchased the ballast for its roadbed from Madden's quarry. Eventually, nearby residents filed lawsuits over indiscriminate blasting which rained rock upon them, so the site was sold to United Railways which used it as a source of ballast for its streetcar roadbeds throughout the city and county. The Public Service Company later imported Mexican laborers to work the quarry. Each family was allowed one room in a barracks style building. Once the quarry became too deep and began to fill with water, it was sold for use as a dump. It was filled, and the site is now used for commercial purposes.[31]

In June, 1895, the Houseman line purchased land at Meramec Highlands for the terminal buildings. Contracts for rails and materials had already been signed, so Chief Engineer Guill indicated that construction would start as soon as the last paper was filed. He estimated the line would be completed by October 1, 1895, but was off in his prediction by four months. The *Watchman* reporter was excited by the news:

---

[29]Mary Hilke, "Musings From Memory," *Pulse* Brentwood 75th Anniversary Special Edition, 20 September 1994 , in Brentwood Public Library files.

[30]Robert Eastin, "Interview with Edwin Vogelsang," Brentwood Anniversary - 50 Years, 1969.

[31]Lillian Klersch and Mary Madden Sadlier, A History of Brentwood, Missouri, Brentwood Public Library, 1951.

KING TROLLEY: PROMOTION, TALK, AND MORE PROMOTION

At last Clayton, Kirkwood and St. Louis are to be connected by ribbons of glittering steel. The three great centers of population will be brought into closer relationship by the omnipotent power of electricity.[32]

The St. Louis and Kirkwood was not the first line that had been approved to serve Kirkwood and Webster Groves, but it was first to put together necessary approvals, required finances, and acquisition of needed property and right-of-ways. The right-of-way deeds called for a strip of land 50 feet wide which would revert to the owner if the electric road was not built by 1896. If in the future the line was discontinued, each private right-of-way would revert to its owner. In fact, today one cannot walk the route of the Houseman line by street from Fillmore in Kirkwood to Kirkham in Webster Groves because the property reverted to private owners after the Kirkwood 01 streetcar line was discontinued. Numerous property owners in Kirkwood, Glendale, Webster Groves, and Brentwood are proud of the fact that the streetcar line used to run through their back yards.

On October 21, 1895, The St. Louis and Kirkwood Railroad accepted the terms of the Kirkwood ordinance, paid a $5000 bond and submitted John Pitman, G. L. Edwards and George W. Taussig as bond sureties.[33]

The agreement was binding for fifty years from July 16, 1894, "to construct, maintain and operate a single or double track on, over, and along," the designated route through Kirkwood.[34] The town stipulated that the Air Line keep its road in complete repair and good condition: the tracks, the rails, the space in-between the rails and 12 inches outside of each rail. It was required to pave with the same material as found on the adjoining street, and to have the paving done within 60 days of notice. The town would give 10 days notice if repairs were needed, and, "on failure of said company to make the same, said repairs may be made by the Town Board at the cost and expense of the said company."[35] Girder rail, commonly known as "T" rail, was designated to be used on all Kirkwood streets on the route except at curves where "U" rail was to be used. The Board also passed a stipulation that it had the right to designate the type of rail to be used for a second track or for renewed rails.

The proposed line was to run in a "direct" southwest line from St. Louis city limits at the southwest corner of Forest Park through Forest Park Heights (later known as West End Heights), Bartold's Valley, Maddenville (Brentwood), Tuxedo Park, North Webster, Glendale, Woodlawn, and Kirkwood, then turn west to the Meramec Highlands Resort and subdivision.

To add to the high expectations, a solution to the city connection puzzle was announced. Property owners on the south side of Forest Park had united to secure an extension of a Lindell electric line which connected to major city routes. The group donated a strip of land 100 feet

---

[32]"Clayton-Kirkwood-St.Louis, Houseman's Efforts Crowned With Success," SLCW, 28 June 1895, p. 1. .

[33]SLCW, 21 October 1895, p. 30.

[34]SLCW, 3 October 1895, p. 27.

[35]SLCW, 21 October 1895, p. 30.

wide (now Oakland Avenue) and reached agreement with the Lindell Railway Company to build a line from the western city limits, the southwest corner of Forest Park, along the south border of the park east to Kingshighway where it connected with other city routes. The *Watchman* stated, "This gives the Houseman Line a complete city connection, through the most desirable section of the city, avoiding the dust, smoke and traffic of the Manchester road and other proposed city connections."[36] Once the new Lindell and the St. Louis and Kirkwood lines were completed, a traveler would be able to take connecting streetcars for the fifteen mile ride from Eads Bridge in St. Louis to the Meramec Highlands Resort. Of course, additional fares at transfer points would be required.

At last, all was in place for construction work to proceed.

2-1. James D. Houseman, promoter and driving force behind the St. Louis and Kirkwood Railroad, known as the "Houseman Air Line."

---

[36]Ibid.

2-2. George Baumhoff, known for his street railway expertise, was hired by the St. Louis and Kirkwood Railroad Company as the contractor in charge of the construction of the line. At the time, most observers believed that the new road would become part of Baumhoff's Lindell lines. The sketch of Baumhoff was printed in St. Louis papers during the Transit strike of 1900.

2-3. The Brentwood power house for the St. Louis and Kirkwood line has been converted to industrial use as a plastics factory. The plant is located a block east of the Missouri Pacific crossing at Brentwood Boulevard. Though the Maddenville streetcar barns are long gone, the nearby Brentwood Bi-State bus garage, continues the tradition, started by Houseman's St. Louis and Kirkwood Railroad, of Brentwood being a county site for storage and service for mass transit vehicles.

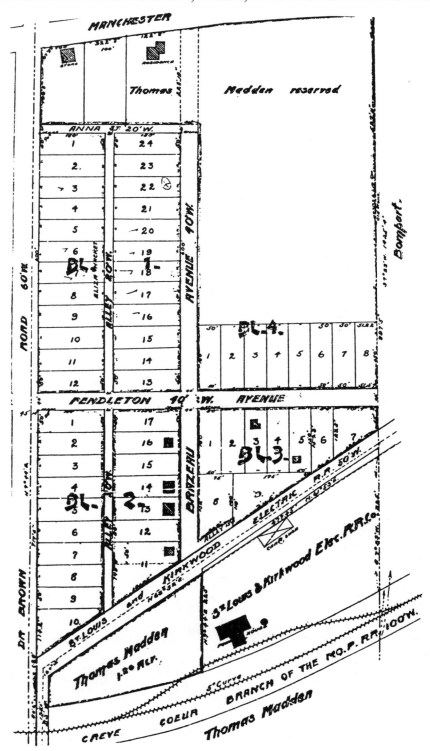

2-4. 1896 plat map of Maddenville, now part of Brentwood. Note that the line from Brentwood to Clayton which became part of the Kirkwood-Ferguson had not yet made its appearance. The St. Louis and Kirkwood, from the point where the map starts on the lower left to West End Heights, later became the Brentwood "Dinky" line.

Chapter 3

CONSTRUCTION MOVES FORWARD

Clearing work began on the Houseman Air Line right-of-way on July 9, 1895, after years of talk and paper work. Meramec Highlands residents were cheered by the beginning efforts. Their *St. Louis County Watchman* correspondent stated, "We are glad to know that the street car line between St. Louis and the Highlands is a settled fact and that work was begun today."[1] Preliminary work on the Brentwood location for the powerhouse commenced two weeks later on July 25th, and at long last, on August 8th, 1895, George Baumhoff and his crew officially started construction of the St. Louis and Kirkwood Railroad.

William Essex, a prominent Kirkwood resident, on September 23, 1895, wrote about the progress and the route of the new line to his friend William Vincent Byars, a well known newspaperman and former resident:

> The "Electric R Road" is being built very fast. The whole line is now underway. Graders and trolley men are pushing it along. The trolley rails are all set from Haight's Corner through Mrs. Gratz's and Armstrongs and so on to Webster.... The line will run from McEnnis and Haight's[2] corner up Washington Avenue to Clay Ave. corner of last named street at Methodist church then south over the (Clay Ave.) bridge to the southern limits of the town (Woodbine) then west to Geyer Road at "Catlin's" place then across Geyer road toward the back part of the old Spaulding place and in front of Couch's place, direct to Meramec Highlands. They are making some awful tall fills near Couch's and some very fine stone culvert work. The cross ties are laid along the side of the whole road.[3]

The Webster Groves and Kirkwood residents were very interested in the progress of the construction so frequent updates were included in the *County Watchman*:

> [9/13/1895] The Houseman Air Line is breaking the record in the matter of rapid railway construction. Fully two thirds of the road bed is already completed. The large car sheds, water tank, artesian well and switch track at Brentwood were completed

[1]"Meramec Highlands," SLCW, 12 July 1895.
[2]Colonel Haight ran the Kirkwood Military Academy at the NW corner of Fillmore and Washington.31
[3]William Essex to William Vincent Byars, 23 September 1895, Byars collection, MHS.

two weeks ago and the immense power station at the same point will be under roof in a few days. The ties and rails have been delivered along almost the entire route, and the poles have been set in position over a considerable portion of the line. Work is progressing rapidly on all the culverts, and the bridge work will begin in a few days. An immense stone crusher is grinding out the ballast at Madden's quarry near Brentwood, and every branch of this construction is being pushed as fast as men and money can push them, and the prospect for completion of this line within the specified time is to say the least, exceedingly bright.[4]

[10/4/1895] Mr. J. D. Houseman… informed a *Watchman* reporter that there are employed at present 250 men and 125 teams on his line and that it is graded and the ties placed in position from Brentwood to Forest Park. With good weather, he says the road will be completed… by December 1st. Tis good, if true.[5]

[10/11/1895] A large gang of men are employed in the laying of track for the Electric Railroad on Clay Avenue. An admiring throng of small boys look on.[6]

[11/8/1895] All the grading on the electric road between Kirkwood and the Highlands has been finished, and the contractor has seven teams hauling macadam from the quarry here (Meramec Highlands Quarry).[7]

[11/8/1895] Work is progressing rapidly on the St. Louis and Kirkwood Electric Railway,… The tracks have been laid between the east end of the road and Brentwood, and large forces of men are employed laying tracks in Kirkwood and the west terminus, Meramec Highlands… The managers of the company promise to have the road in operation before January 1, 1896.[8]

[12/13/1895] The tracks of the Houseman Air Line from Kirkwood to Meramec Highlands were tested Thursday by Superintendent Baumhoff and a party of citizens from Kirkwood. The run was made in good time both ways, and the track found to be in excellent condition. The top ballast will be put on in a few days, and as soon as one or two bridges and the power house at Brentwood are completed, the road will be open to travel.[9]

[12/13/1895 - There has been a trap built at the end of the electric road here where macadam will be loaded on cars for distribution along the tracks. In this way long hauls over bad roads will be avoided and the work done much quicker.[10]

---

[4]"Kirkwood," SLCW, 13 September 1895, p. 1.
[5]"The Air Line," SLCW, 4 October 1895, p. 4.
[6]Ibid.
[7]"Meramec Highlands," SLCW, 8 November 1895.
[8]SLCW, 8 November 1895, p. 8.
[9]"The Houseman Line," SLCW 13 December 1895.
[10]"Meramec Highlands," SLCW, 13 December 1895.

KING TROLLEY: CONSTRUCTION MOVES FORWARD

Real estate speculation geared up immediately as a result of the construction. A 40 acre tract of land near the Houseman line was purchased in mid October by a Kirkwood group of investors for $20,000 and sold the next week to a St. Louis group for $25,000. The new owners announced, in the *Watchman*, their intention to subdivide the entire forty acres for housing and to put improvements (roads) on the property.[11]

As the work moved along more slowly than residents were led to expect by early optimistic projections and reports, some of the local enthusiasm for the project waned. Residents of Kirkwood began complaining to their trustees that construction crews left unrepaired damage to the streets. A Webster Groves subscriber to the *Watchman* complained in a letter to the editor about the conditions in which the Houseman Air Line left the Webster streets:

> ...Shady Avenue (Kirkham) is so badly cut up and strewn with material between the bridge at Fairview and the Rock Hill road that it is impossible to travel on the same after dark; also people who tried to pass the tracks at the intersection of Rock Hill road last Saturday were surprised to find a car which is used to haul ballast across the track, completely obstructing sidewalk and street. It is true there was a lantern on the same… The minions who are working on the road drive all over our places when it is more convenient for them, and if remonstrated with, property owners only receive some of their lip….[12]

Despite residents' concerns, the project moved on. Just after Christmas 1895, the line was tested. The December 27th *Watchman* reported that a moving electric car through the streets of Kirkwood, "gladdened the eyes of Kirkwoodians."[13] The car was reported to have been followed by a procession of small boys.

Even though construction was nearly on schedule, James Houseman was impatient for the line to begin operation. He wanted to capture the electric railroad business before the St. Louis and Meramec River Railroad was completed. His sense of urgency was heightened by articles in the *Watchman* on November 1st and November 22nd reporting the progress of the "Howard Electric Line." It was projected to be completed to Webster Groves by June 1, 1896, and to Kirkwood by August 15, 1896.

Future patrons and residents were also anxious for construction to be completed. Hopes were raised again late in January 1896, when a double deck streetcar arrived in Kirkwood, but residents were disappointed to find that it was only another test. "We are tired of waiting," declared the Kirkwood correspondent to the *Watchman*.[14] The paper had earlier reported on the

---

[11]SLCW, 25 October 1895.
[12]"How Is This?", letter to the editor, SLCW, 13 December 1895.
[13]"Kirkwood," SLCW, 27 December 1895.
[14]"Kirkwood," SLCW, 31 January 1896.

17th of January that, "a bright red and very new car (bearing the colors of the new line) electrified Kirkwood on Sunday last, making rapid headway for the Highlands."[15]

Though streetcars were not yet running except for tests, electric work cars were using the line for construction purposes, giving hope that the end was near:

> [1/24/1896] The electric car still attracts attention in passing to and fro with its load of rejected ties or freight trailer of ballast, and the anxious inquirer is told that it will stop for passengers on the 23rd by some and Feb. 1st by others. The 5 cent fare to city limits will prevail for big and little. No children's half fare rate, which is considered proper by citizens generally. Cheap enough, all exclaim.[16]

Approval by the County Court was granted to the Houseman Air Line on February 3rd, 1896, to extend the franchise from a terminus on Quinette Road through the Meramec Highlands Resort to a new terminus on Sunset Hill close to the resort's hotel and dance pavilion.[17]

As the opening of the line became imminent, the Kirkwood *Watchman* correspondent optimistically echoed the hopes of area residents about the effects of the line on the town: "Some of the vacant houses here are being occupied, and it is hoped that the starting of the electric railroad will prove a drawing card for the town."[18]

No resident was more impatient for the line to begin operation than General Manager J. D. Houseman Jr. A completion date of February 8th was announced. At that time the electric railroad was to be turned over by George Baumhauff to the St. Louis and Kirkwood Railroad Company. However, a dispute between Houseman and the contractor, George Baumhoff, arose over the completeness of the work. Houseman would not allow payment, as stipulated in the contract, until grading and ballasting of tracks and streets through Kirkwood and on Shady Avenue in Webster Groves were completed to his satisfaction. Baumhoff refused to turn over the line and planned to remain in control of the line and the powerhouse until he was paid.

Meanwhile, Mrs. Anna Sneed Cairns, President of Forest Park University and a long time booster of the Houseman line because it would make her university more accessible to residents all over St. Louis, issued invitation cards to a February 8th program of celebration at her university. The *Watchman* reporter speculated that the cars would run only as far as the university on the first day of operation.[19] Despite the fact that no cars ran due to the delay in turning over the railroad, Cairns' event took place with more than 1000 persons present. The celebration featured addresses by numerous "Reverend Doctors" as well as one by Mrs. Cairns.

---

[15]"Kirkwood," SLCW, 17 January 1896.
[16]"Kirkwood," SLCW, 24 January 1896, p. 1.
[17]SLCW, 7 February 1896.
[18]SLCW, 14 February 1896.
[19]"Kirkwood," SLCW, 7 February 1896, p. 1.

Her young lady students sang, "a number of songs rejoicing over the acquisition of this road (the Houseman Air Line)."[20]

The *Watchman* reporter, on February 14th, optimistically characterized the dispute as a, "little disagreement." He stated that the line, would probably be opened to the public in a few days, and continued, "The road bed still requires a little work on it that will take a few days to finish, but it will not interfere with the operation of the road."[21] On the same day, the paper reported that the "Varsity" railroad, which was the new two mile extension of the Lindell line, opened for service.[22] The all important city linkage was in place, providing high speed private right-of-way from Kirkwood to Kingshighway in the city, yet Houseman's company was unable to take advantage of it.

The disagreement stretched on for more than a week with Houseman becoming more and more frustrated by the day. The line had been nearly complete for a month, but the dispute was preventing it from beginning operation. On February 15th the frustration boiled over causing Houseman and company officials to take drastic action!

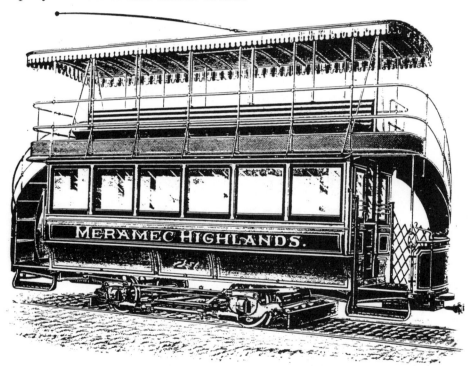

3-1. "A fine new double decked car came out on the electric railway lately, but alas, not for passengers." (January 31, 1896 *County Watchman* - Kirkwood correspondent)
The only documented double-decker that ran on the St. Louis and Kirkwood Electric Railroad was a loaner on a trial run to test the tracks prior to the line's opening. The American Car Company proposed that the line buy double-decker cars as presented in the builder's engraving shown. None were purchased.

---

[20]SLCW, 14 February 1896.
[21]Ibid.
[22]Ibid.

WEBSTER GROVES.

A Flower-Strewn Garden Of The Gods.

AN IDEAL RESIDENCE PLACE.

Queen of The Western Suburbs of a Wonderful Metropolis.

MODERN CITY OF THE FOURTH CLASS.

A STORY THAT READS LIKE A PAGE TORN FROM ARABIAN NIGHTS. YET A LIVING TRUTH AND SHINING REALITY.

Historical And Commercial Review of a Thoroughly Progressive And Modern Suburban District.

Like the chrysanthemum, "Queen of the Autumn," with its regal plumes of white and gold and bronze and purple, Webster is in the zenith of its splendid reign. By the addition of its electric street railway lines it has unfolded new avenues of trade which have attracted new votaries to its shrine. It has revealed new charms wherewith to compete for the crown which has so long been claimed by rivals in other towns.

3-2. This printed salvo in the battle over the rights to be "Queen of the Suburbs" appeared in the Saturday, October 10, 1896 article in the *Webster Times*. Courtesy of The Webster Groves Public Library microfilm archive.

Chapter 4

DRASTIC ACTION AND HEADY SUCCESS

On February 15, 1896, a frustrated and angry, J. D. Houseman and two company officers, President John Pitman and Secretary George Taussig, seized the power house and took forcible possession of the electric rail line. They dismissed Baumhoff's watchman and started the generating plant. By 5:00 p.m., the power house was in operation, with a few cars running; passengers were offered rides; and their fares were collected. Houseman announced to the press his intention to operate the line fully on the 16th and to, "hold possession at all hazards."[1]

The Houseman Air Line was a ten mile single track line with seven (once reported as six by Houseman when interviewed) turn-outs or side switches so that cars could pass. Each car was fitted with a portable telephone, which could be connected to an overhead telephone wire every thousand feet, so the conductor could call the office for orders. At no place on the line would a conductor need to travel more than 2000 feet in order to call for assistance in case of a breakdown or for instructions in case of an extraordinary delay. Before leaving the switches, motormen were to receive orders via telephone. Houseman felt that there was no need for a dispatcher with the use of telephones.

Even though few Kirkwoodians knew of the start, the first two cars that were operated carried enough passengers to bring in an income of $25.00. On the second day of operation, three cars ran: four cars ran on the third day. A *Watchman* dispatch stated, "Good time was made and many enjoyed the trip."[2]

By *Watchman* accounts, the road was operated with fair regularity on the second day, though there was a shortage of equipment. Some cars had been delivered without brake handles, so Houseman had his employees fabricate, "rough but serviceable," brake handles so the cars could be used until the new handles arrived. Despite equipment problems, over 1000 passengers were transported to Meramec Highlands on the first full day of operation.[3]

---

[1]"Captured the Power House," GD, 16 February 1896.
[2]"Kirkwood," SLCW, 21 February 1896, p. 1.
[3]SLCW, 21 February 1896.

Baumhoff was busy running the Lindell line, and was not present when the line was seized. He elected not to take any physical action to regain the line. He instead filed a $280,000 mechanic lien against the St. Louis and Kirkwood Railroad Company in the St. Louis County Circuit Court, for work and labor done, materials, rolling stock, equipment, power house, station house, car sheds, water tank, reservoirs, bridges, culverts, road bed, poles, wire, rails, ties, etc. furnished under the contract dated June 1, 1895. Baumhoff stated that the work was completed on February 14, 1896. He listed for the court the prices he charged:

> Power and engine house, building engines, electrical generators, boilers, pumps, heaters, pipe fittings, and electrical attachments and apparatus, $32,500; car shed and building, $1500; water tank, $1500; deep well for water supply, $1300; pond or basin for water supply, $600; five motor cars, $15,000; salt car, $350; poles for trolley wire, trolley wire and feed wire, $11,500; road bed, including grading, ballasting, rails, ties, bridges and culverts, $212,340.[4]

At the time the line was seized, Baumhoff was holding $250,000 of St. Louis and Kirkwood Railroad Company first mortgage bonds that St. Louis Trust Company had delivered as his payment. When Houseman and company attorney Taussig learned that the trust company had delivered the railroad bonds to contractor Baumhoff without advising or consulting St. Louis and Kirkwood Railroad officers, they claimed that because the bonds were illegally delivered they were worthless. Attorney Taussig, also Secretary of the company, explained to news reporters that in December 1895, the St. Louis Union Trust Company had:

> … delivered to Mr. Baumhoff 100 bonds, to the value of $100,000, and they delivered the remaining 150 bonds of the value of $150,000 in the same secret manner February 14, 1896, before Mr. Baumhoff had delivered us a single car, and before a large part of the work of construction had been completed.[5]

On February 15th, when Houseman's group seized the line, he was unaware that Baumhoff had been given the bonds for completion of the road. When he found out, he was furious. The St. Louis and Kirkwood Company then quickly filed a petition to the County Court to remove St. Louis Trust Company as the trustee in the contract between the St. Louis and Kirkwood Railroad and George Baumhoff. On February 19, Houseman's company filed a damage suit against the St. Louis Trust Company for $250,000. On March 2nd, the petition was denied and dismissed by Judge Hirzel of the County Circuit Court.[6]

Because of the conflicts between Houseman and Baumhoff, the St. Louis and Kirkwood Railroad, which many observers believed was going to become an extension of Baumhoff's Lindell Line, instead became an independent.

---

[4]"Mechanics Lien Filed," SLCW, 15 May 1896.
[5]"Sues for a Big Amount," SLCW, 21 January 1896.
[6]"SLCW, 6 March 1896.

KING TROLLEY: DRASTIC ACTION AND HEADY SUCCESS

Even though Houseman had gained possession of the line, he refused to complete the work that he felt was the responsibility of George Baumhoff. Street conditions were almost impassable in places in Kirkwood and Webster Groves. A *Watchman* editorial in the February 21, 1896 edition, urged the county court not to grant any more franchises to the St. Louis and Kirkwood Railroad Company until Shady Avenue in Webster Groves was put in passable shape:

> If the railroad company has any grievance against the contractor, it may sue him on his bond, but not allow the public to suffer. Let it take all necessary steps without delay… and put itself into proper position to ask further favors at the hands of the people.[7]

Despite the controversy, citizens in St. Louis and along the electric route were delighted. At last there was an inexpensive link between the city and the Meramec Highlands Resort which benefited all points in-between. The Kirkwood-Meramec Highlands cars, required a five cent fare. They operated between Meramec Highlands and the corner of Woodbine and Clay avenues in Kirkwood, a distance of about two miles. For ten cents, passengers from Kirkwood could reach downtown St. Louis by transferring from the St. Louis and Kirkwood cars to the Lindell Railway cars at Forest Park. The fare was a nickel between Kirkwood and Forest Park.

Speaking for the Meramec Highlands residents, the *Watchman* correspondent expressed relief that the cars were at last in operation:

> After long waiting and weary watching, our eyes have been gladdened by the sight of electric cars, which have been running since last Sunday. Although a regular time table has not yet put on, we are thankful for small favors, and live in the hopes that sometime soon we will be able to go the city with a reasonable certainty of not having to come back on the [steam] railroad.[8]

Once the cars began to run on a regular schedule, they were filled to capacity. The *Watchman*'s Kirkwood correspondent commented:

> The electric road had a wonderful week of traffic. Saturday being a holiday, many city people spent it in a ride over the new road. The sunshine of Sunday drew out a still greater throng. Cars came and went through our town with passengers packed in like sardines in a box. Some contained 145, 125, 135, 90, etc… Kirkwoodians stood on street corners, anxious to get to the Highlands or the city, but [were] unable to get a footing.[9]

---

[7]Editorial, SLCW, 21 February 1896.
[8]"Meramec Highlands," SLCW, 21 February 1896.
[9]"Kirkwood," SLCW, 28 February 1896.

KING TROLLEY: DRASTIC ACTION AND HEADY SUCCESS

On the same day the Old Orchard (a section of Webster Groves) correspondent expressed a desire that since the electric road connected Kirkwood and Webster Groves, that, "residents in both Webster and Kirkwood will be more sociable." She suggested that residents from both places list their planned events ahead of time in the *Watchman*, so that the opportunities to enjoy each other's events could be made possible by the easy access of the streetcar line.[10]

As predicted, residents took advantage of the low streetcar fares, which had an immediate effect on ridership on the Missouri-Pacific and St. Louis and San Francisco railroads. Rumors began circulating that the railroads' accommodation trains were no longer profitable and would be discontinued. Local residents speculated that when night streetcars (owl cars) began to run, the Missouri Pacific and the Frisco would lose even more traffic. As a result of competition from the streetcar line, the Missouri Pacific Railroad made the first of many reductions in service on March 6th by taking a coach off each of its suburban trains.

Even though the new streetcar line had problems, such as the trolley frequently slipping off the wire and causing delays, and some near collisions, the public was still enamored with the Houseman Air Line:

> No timetable is published for the electric, and many delays and long stops have been met by a humorous and good natured public. One lady who waited an hour for a car said she knew of no other way to save forty cents.[11] … The electric road collected 5,200 fares on Sunday and some came free, and many either went back to Vandeventer Station and took the Missouri Pacific or went home, tired of waiting for a county car.[12]

Not all were happy with the delays. A party of ladies took "the electric" to attend a choral concert in the city. The younger ladies took the delays as a "huge joke", but the matrons were reported to protest most gravely over "tenting" [waiting at switches] on the way.[13]

The five new state of the art cars in active service since the opening of the line were bigger than those in use at the time on the Lindell or the Scullin systems. A Kirkwood paper, the *Suburban Leader* in December 1985, described the cars as, "held to be the finest run in the west, if not in the country, being fifty feet in length, beautifully finished and commodious."[14] They were built to seat 38 people, but in the early days of the line, they often carried more than one hundred people on a car. The cars were furnished with 100 horsepower, more power than provided by the double truck motors used on the Lindell or Scullin systems.[15]

---

[10] "Old Orchard," SLCW, 28 February 1896.

[11] "Kirkwood," SLCW, 28 February 1896.

[12] Ibid.

[13] "Kirkwood," SLCW, 6 March 1896.

[14] Suburban Leader, Kirkwood, MO, December 1895.

[15] Travers Burgess, an authority on streetcar trucks, stated that the power was probably provided by four 25-hp. motors - one motor per axle or two per truck and that a 100 hp. motor would have been too large for streetcar use.

KING TROLLEY: DRASTIC ACTION AND HEADY SUCCESS

The tracks from St. Louis to Kirkwood were designed to accommodate cars traveling at speeds up to forty miles an hour. However, frequent stops and numerous curves prevented the cars from making that kind of speed.

Houseman was not about to rest on his laurels after gaining control of the St. Louis and Kirkwood line. On February 17, 1896, the St. Louis and Kirkwood Railroad made application in St. Louis County Court for an extension one mile in length from, "a point on the New Manchester road, where it intersects with the St. Louis and Kirkwood Railroad, 300 feet west of the River Des Peres, and extending eastwardly along the Manchester road through Bartolds and Sutton, to Marshall Avenue, where it will connect with the new county extension of the St. Louis and Suburban Railroad, which is now in the course of construction and is almost completed to that point."[16] Houseman's action, even though the extension was never constructed, gave rise to conjecture in the major papers such as the *St. Louis Globe-Democrat*:

> In view of present strained relations between [Houseman and] George W. Baumhoff, Superintendent of the Lindell Railway, with which their line connects at city limits, the action of Houseman… is of more than ordinary significance.[17]

Houseman admitted to reporters that the purpose of the application was to connect with the Suburban, thus giving the St. Louis and Kirkwood a double city connection. However, he would not admit that any arrangements for the connection had already been made. The *Globe-Democrat* reporter further speculated:

> The well known antagonism between the Howard line which has been absorbed by the Suburban, and the Houseman line, makes this action all the more significant and gives color to the rumors… to the effect that a consolidation of the two lines in the near future might be expected.[18]

At that point everything looked rosy for the Houseman Air Line, but that was soon to change. In order to meet the overwhelming demand, Houseman's streetcar crews had to follow a complex schedule. Overcrowded cars, cars heading in opposite directions on a single track, the need for motormen to use switches to allow cars to pass, human error, the lack of dispatchers, and equipment malfunctions made the line ripe for catastrophe.

Disaster struck on March 8, 1896, the 22nd day of operation. In the late afternoon, two electric cars carrying more than 100 people on each car, fatally collided on a curve between Kirkwood and the Meramec Highlands.

---

[16]"Ask For a New Franchise - St. Louis and Kirkwood Railroad Wishes to Extend its Line," GD, 18 February 1896.
[17]Ibid.
[18]Ibid.

4-1. Houseman Air Line cars were often overcrowded on weekends, as the lure of Meramec Highlands and a beautiful ride through the country, not to mention the novelty of the new streetcar line, drew passengers to ride the cars. Though not one of the "Air Line" cars, the car illustrated in the *Post-Dispatch* is representative of the crowded conditions on the weekend cars to Meramec Highlands.

4-2. In a tranquil and scenic wooded area near the Meramec Highlands, where a single set of Houseman Air Line tracks curved and ran down a hill, the tracks crossed a stone culvert, which allowed streetcar passengers a nice view of the stream below. The illustration of the site of the, "Air Line Disaster," appeared in the March 9, 1896 *St. Louis Republic*.

Chapter 5

DISASTER ON THE "AIR LINE"

Sunday, March 8th, 1896, was a beautiful sunny day. The novelty of the ride out through the wooded and rural countryside to Meramec Highlands and the opportunity for a breath of fresh clean air drew unusually large crowds from early that morning until late in the afternoon. Crowds of over 100 people rode each of the available streetcars, with passengers filling every seat, all standing space inside, and spilling out onto the end platforms of the Houseman Air Line's cars.

Cars 3 and 4 of the St. Louis and Kirkwood Electric Railway were assigned to the Meramec Highlands Line that day. Shortly after four p.m., car number 3, an eastbound car, left Meramec Highlands with 130 passengers aboard. It was seven or eight minutes behind schedule with motorman Robert Aiken at the controls and G. L. Peasley as conductor. A westbound car, under control of motorman Sam Smith with John M. Edwards as conductor, was five minutes behind schedule. Smith was speeding in an effort to make up lost time. His car left Kirkwood at 4:15 p.m.

Under the rules of the single track road as stated by General Manager John Houseman to reporters, "The right of way is given to morning trains going east, in order that businessmen may not be delayed in going to their places of business, and to afternoon trains going west, in order that our patrons returning home may not be delayed."[1] Under that system, Smith's westbound car number 4 had the right-of-way.

Aiken's car soon approached Taussig's Switch which was located west of Geyer Road midway between Kirkwood city limits and Meramec Highlands. Craig Road currently occupies the stretch of streetcar route that included Taussig's Switch. By Houseman's stated rules, motorman Aiken was supposed to wait at Taussig's Switch until the westbound car had passed or until given permission via the telephone to proceed. Instead of following the rules, Aiken in the eastbound car decided to make up time by, "stealing a switch" .By some passenger accounts, Conductor Peasley remonstrated with him, but Aiken believed that he could make the next switch before the westbound car arrived.

---

[1]PD, GD, and Republic, 9 March 1896, p. 1.

KING TROLLEY: DISASTER ON THE "AIR LINE"

A collision had been narrowly averted near Taussig's switch earlier that morning. When the approaching eastbound car was sighted, the motorman applied the brakes in haste. Fortunately the westbound car was running at a slower speed than usual. The two cars stopped within 10 feet of each other. The westbound car then backed 300 yards to a siding and proceeded on its way after the eastbound car passed. The incident would have been forgotten had it not been for the later disaster at the same spot.[2]

A passenger on that earlier westbound car, Mr. A. F. Rodman, a bookkeeper for Rice, Stix and Company, stated to the *Globe-Democrat*:

> On our trip out, the car we were in at one time had to back a considerable distance to a switch, as we met an eastbound car on the same track.... I know any number of remarks were made at the time we had to go back, that if the road did not exercise more care in arranging the switching schedule, an accident would be inevitable.[3]

Taking advantage of a downhill grade, Aiken ran his eastbound car at speeds around 35 MPH past Taussig's Switch. A curve in the track caused his view to be blocked by trees. The approaching westbound car had gained momentum on a downhill slope and had started uphill and around the curve when the two motormen each saw the imminent danger. Both remained in their exposed positions, immediately reversed the streetcar motors, and applied the brakes. Their actions lessened the speed, but the cars were too close and speeding too fast to be stopped. The two cars packed with lighthearted pleasure seekers met head-on. The presumed time of the crash was fixed at 4:20 p.m. by a terrific power surge that was noticed at the Brentwood powerhouse at the instant the two motormen reversed the motors.

Hustling *Globe-Democrat*, *Republic*, and *Post-Dispatch* reporters interviewed numerous survivors of the crash. The *Globe-Democrat* featured the, "Thrilling Stories of Their Experiences in the Wreck," across the front page of its next day's editions. Of particular interest to the *Globe* reporter were statements from survivors about the moments leading to the crash:

> The car was crowded going out and as two of us had to stand all the way, we determined not to get off the car at Meramec Highlands, but to come right back. We secured seats in the rear of the car, but the people were packed in so thickly that it was very uncomfortable. A few seconds before the collision occurred a woman or girl in the front end of the car jumped up and screamed that there was going to be a collision. Before any of us had time to realize the meaning of her words, the crash came.[4]

Another passenger recounted:

---

[2]"Electric Cars Collide," GD, 9 March 1896.
[3]Ibid.
[4]Ibid.

I was right up in the front seat on the right hand side. The first thing I knew, the other car came dashing around the curve. Somebody cried, "Break the windows and jump." Just then the crash came.[5]

All the newspapers interviewed numerous victims of the crash, and printed their stories. The *Globe-Democrat* reporter interviewed injured passenger Henry Floerke at his home as he was being taken from an ambulance. He had been on the westbound car. Floerke stated that when the car reached the top of a hill near Meramec Highlands, the motorman slowed up and looked back as though he desired instructions. A man who Floerke claimed was in authority as a superintendent of the division, said, "Oh, go ahead, these people want to get back tonight." Floerke continued:

> We were going down the hill and, although I am not an expert, I am certain that the speed was far in excess of twelve miles an hour. Every second added increased speed, and when we reached the foot of the hill, where the curve commences, we were going at a rate which would do justice to a railway (steam) train. At the foot of the hill, a man on the forward platform yelled out, "There is a car!" and our motorman did all in his power to stop the car. The cars were then probably 800 feet apart and going like fury… At the signal of the approach of another car, all the passengers sprang from their seats and consternation reigned. Some attempted to gain an exit by way of the windows and others sprang for the back door, and jammed into such a mass that the door could not be opened.[6]

Conductor John Edwards of the westbound car testified about the events leading up to the moment of the crash at the coroner's inquest. He disputed statements presented by some of the passengers who indicated that his car was running twenty-five miles an hour, "faster at that time than at any other point on the trip." Edwards stated that his car had started upgrade at a rate of from four to six miles an hour. He also disputed claims of the number of passengers over 100 on the car, stating that he registered 115 passengers on the whole trip and had let off twenty-five in Webster Groves. He indicated that about twelve passengers were riding on the front platform, which was allowed on most St. Louis lines. Edwards disagreed with the 4:20 p.m. stated time of the accident, as reported in the March 11th *Post-Dispatch*:

> My car was two minutes late when we reached Kirkwood at 4:22 p.m. Sunday. We were due there at 4:20, and should have met car 3 at that point. We waited there three minutes, according to rules, and then proceeded on westward, according to the schedule. I did not telephone, as it was not my duty. I was running by the schedule. It was not an extra schedule for that day, but the same that had been in use on the previous day. I had an extra man to look after the trolley. We always have an extra

---

[5]Ibid.
[6]Ibid.

man to watch the trolley when traffic is very heavy. The conductor directs the running of the car, and the motorman does not start the car until he gets a signal from the conductor to do so. We were five minutes late when we left Kirkwood, and the other car was not in sight. I did not see the other car until it was nearly on us, and did not have time to do anything before we came together.[7]

People were tossed about inside the cars and many of the about thirty people standing on the platforms at the front of the cars, including the motormen, were seriously hurt. Motorman Aiken suffered both arms and both legs broken as well as a broken jaw and fatal internal injuries. Motorman Smith was expected to die from his multiple injuries. The reporter from the *St. Louis Globe-Democrat* described the result of the impact:

The scene when the two swift moving cars collided was awful. Cries of horror rent the air, and the shrieks of the injured followed in quick succession, as the two relentless forces came together… The panic stricken passengers who were not too badly injured to move, tried to extricate themselves. Men trampled over their fellows, women screamed and fainted and children gasped for air as the terror stricken people tried to get through the doors. Some few got out but the doors were soon jammed full of struggling humanity. Strong men pushed others aside and literally crawled out over the heads of their fellow passengers. There was no jollity, no good nature; it was a grim, horrible fight for liberty… When egress through the doors was found impossible, window sashes were torn out and, men, women and children crawled out to liberty, heedless of broken glass or anything else that stood in the way.[8]

Neither car left the tracks, but the westbound car was driven from 100 to 600 feet (depending on the news account) backwards down the grade. It was fortunate that the cars did not leave the tracks as the collision occurred over a culvert spanning a ravine with an embankment thirty feet high. Had the cars fallen into the ravine, there would have been many more injuries and deaths among the passengers and crew.

The *Watchman* described the scene following the crash in an article titled, "A SUNDAY HORROR!"

The wounded wandered about the track, many lay on the ground unable to move, and the more seriously injured were freed from the wreck and laid beside the rails until relief should come.[9]

Three men died the next day as a result of the wreck: motorman Aiken, E. J. Jones, an MKT claims agent, and Richard Lanigan, an insurance agent. Nearly 50 passengers had injuries

---

[7]"Progress of the Inquest," PD, 11 March 1896.
[8]"Electric Cars Collide," GD, 9 March 1896.
[9]"A Sunday Horror," SLCW, 13 March 1896, p. 1.

of note, serious enough to be listed in newspaper accounts the next day. Twenty had limbs broken or serious internal injuries. More than twenty others were cut by glass or were badly bruised during the accident. Others with only minor scrapes, cuts and bruises were not listed.

Passengers who were fortunate to escape with only slight bruises, set to work at once to help the injured. Others started for Kirkwood to give the alarm. The alarm was first raised by Edwards, the conductor of the westbound car, who had the presence of mind to use his telephone to notify General Manager Houseman at the Brentwood powerhouse. Houseman notified authorities, sent a relief car at once, and called doctors from Kirkwood and the surrounding area to provide emergency aid to the injured.

Within minutes, Doctor Pitman, the President of the line, and Doctor C. A. Dunnavant arrived with George Taussig on a relief car to try to bring order out of chaos. Many of the passengers with only slight cuts and bruises were treated at the scene and left without giving their names. Some passengers, who were only slightly injured, were treated at the scene and walked back to Meramec Highlands Frisco Depot to take the steam railroad back to the city. Many vowed never to ride the electric line again. Other uninjured passengers walked to the Mo-Pac station in Kirkwood. Missouri-Pacific records showed 140 tickets sold from Kirkwood to St. Louis on the day of the accident when only two had been sold the previous day.

Within an hour of the accident, half of the wounded had their wounds dressed and were on their way home. More seriously injured were retained and made as comfortable as possible. Several of the wounded were taken to residences nearby, while the very badly injured were placed in the relief car and taken to the Northside Inn in Kirkwood where a quickly assembled corps of physicians from Kirkwood, Webster Groves, Glendale and Old Orchard, and over 50 local women volunteers had converged to care for the injured.

A special Lindell ambulance car was brought out from the city which took injured city residents home or to city hospitals. Several trips of the special ambulance car were necessary to handle the large number of injured.

Anxious parents, friends and loved ones feared the worst when news of the wreck spread. They besieged Houseman's office and the Lindell Railway Company car sheds at Chouteau and Jefferson avenues where many of the less seriously injured passengers were taken before they were removed to hospitals in the city or taken to their homes. The scene at the car sheds was "heart-rending." A silent anxious crowd awaited the first car which did not arrive until three hours after the news of the accident had spread. Only with difficulty were relatives and friends kept back as they surged forward to look to see who was being transferred to ambulances. Officials at the Lindell offices could not satisfy the worried crowds for they had only sketchy details of the wreck. From time to time during the night other relief cars arrived. City ambulances were lined up waiting for the injured.

KING TROLLEY: DISASTER ON THE "AIR LINE"

The Northside Inn on Monday was more like a hospital than a hotel. Its entire second floor was set aside for accommodation of the wounded. That day, Motorman Robert Aiken was the first to die. J. Jones who had internal injuries as well as both legs broken, died near noon. Richard Lanigan lapsed into unconsciousness and died about an hour later. Aiken's and Lanigan's wives were at the side of their husbands till the end. Motorman Sam Smith defied the odds, and survived though he was reported to be in pitiful shape:

> The unfortunate motorman was a terrible sight as he lay upon the bed, his face about completely covered with bandages. He is badly crushed, and besides internally injured, and though conscious is still unable to speak without great effort and evident pain… at best the poor fellow has months of suffering before him.[10]

By the Wednesday following the wreck, only Smith and one other man remained at the Northside Inn. As soon as they were able to withstand travel, they were moved to a hospital. On March 15th, Sam Smith left the hospital for his home in St. Louis under the care of relatives and friends, however he was not safe yet. Within a week of returning home, he contracted a serious case of pneumonia. He ultimately fended off the illness and recovered from his injuries.

The wrecked cars were quickly removed, and the debris from the wreck was cleaned up by the next day. The line was running as usual the next day, but the wreck and the resulting suits for damages were the beginning of line's unrelenting financial woes.

5-1. Illustration of the fatal streetcar collision which appeared on the front page of the March 9, 1896 *St. Louis Republic*.

---

[10]"Three Are Now Dead," GD, 10 March 1896, p. 1.

ESPONSIBILITY for an awful disaster on the recently-built route of the St. Louis and Kirkwood Electric Railroad Company, commonly called the Houseman Air Line, last Sunday afternoon, in which 8 persons were fatally injured, many others seriously hurt, and a still large number bruised or maimed, will be with difficulty ascertained. The accident was a frightful one in all particulars.

5-2. Illustration of the Houseman Air Line disaster and front page headlines were printed in the Friday, March 13, 1896 *St. Louis County Watchman*. The time lag in reporting the accident was due to the weekly nature of the publication. The paper reported that most of the injured were city residents, but Kirkwood and Webster residents were injured in the crash: Mrs. Lou Spencer of Webster Groves, right leg broken in two places and foot crushed, James McGrath of Kirkwood, broken leg, Richard Williams of Webster Groves, both feet crushed, John and James McKelvey of Kirkwood and Walter Reid and William Wilson of Webster Groves, unspecified injuries.

5-3. The car number of the St. Louis and Kirkwood car matches that of one of the wrecked cars. However, the trucks resemble Lindell trucks. Perhaps this is a replacement car borrowed from the Lindell line until the wrecked car was repaired. Photo from the Museum of Transportation.

5-4. St. Louis and Kirkwood Railroad power plant at Brentwood serves as a backdrop for a Houseman car heading west to Meramec Highlands. Streetcar historian Charles Hamman verified the accuracy of the *Republic*'s artwork by comparing the sign atop the car in this little seen photograph with the one in the crash illustration. An enlargement of the car and a portion of the illustration are provided for the reader to make a comparison. Note the motorman in the exposed position on the vestibule and the sign on front of the car that reads Lindell Railroad Connection. Circa 1896 photo is from the Charles Hamman collection.

Chapter 6

ASSIGNING BLAME

Editorial opinion following the crash was harsh toward Houseman and his single track line. A *St. Louis County Watchman* editorial stated:

> No street railroad should be allowed to run cars both ways on the same track. This is the lesson of the deplorable accident on the Houseman Air Line, and is the only lesson there is to it. Such accidents will always be possible on a single track road. In the end there will be no economy in a single track. The capital saved in construction will be more than lost in paying for accidents.[1]

The *Watchman* had other unkind things to say about Houseman's operation of a single track line but indicated a single line could be as safe as any if managed properly: "Baumhoff and other experienced men in rapid transit methods will substantiate this averment if Brother Houseman desires. They believe in dispatchers and use them on their busy lines."[2]

The *Watchman* further questioned Houseman's knowledge:

> It was an easy task to capture a railroad, but to manage it successfully is something in which knowledge supported by years of experience rather than "spunk wrapped up in a horse blanket" is an absolute necessity.[3]

The king of yellow journalism, the *St. Louis Post-Dispatch*, had perhaps the most disparaging editorials of all the local papers:

> The wreck that occurred Sunday on the Kirkwood Electric Railway surprises no one who has ridden on that line. It seems to have been planned on the theory that electric cars can almost fly through the air, and that brakes, motormen, and conductors are all

---

[1]Editorial, SLCW, 13 March 1896.
[2]Ibid.
[3]Ibid.

perfect.... But even if switches were properly maintained, with such curves and grades as are found on this line, frequent accidents may be confidently expected.[4]

The dreadful collision between electric cars on the St. Louis and Kirkwood line yesterday shows how foolish and reckless was the attempt to manage a single track electric railway in the country in the same happy-go-lucky way as a double track city railway.... The failure to provide an experienced train dispatcher leaves the company without any defense against suits which will be brought for damages.... It is absurd for the managers to lay the whole blame upon the motormen and conductors.... A train dispatcher should be provided immediately and an adequate means of signaling provided.[5]

The Post-Dispatch continued editorials regarding the operation of the Houseman line for most of the following week. The editor suggested that the damages that the line would have to pay from the "accident" would pay an experienced train dispatcher and signal men for years. The reporter covering the story pilloried Houseman, indicating that he had no experience in moving trains. "He was simply a real estate man, who promoted the enterprise and after the road was completed had himself named as general manager, a title that had a good rich sound."[6] Houseman came under fire for the competence of his employees whom he asserted that he had personally selected. George Baumhoff, Houseman's recent adversary, stated to the papers that prior to Houseman's hiring of Aiken, the Lindell line had discharged him for having been mixed up in a number of collisions. Smith had previously been in the employ of the Lindell line as a transfer man. Baumhoff indicated that when Smith had applied to the Lindell to move up to be a motorman, he was found to be deaf and near sighted, so he was fired.[7]

In an interview printed in the *St. Louis Republic* on March 10, 1896, Houseman's operation was reported to be haphazard. One section of the article was headed, "Lax Rules and Regulations." In it the reporter opined, "The road has no printed set of rules. J. D. Houseman the general manager runs the road as he thinks proper..." In the interview, Houseman admitted that he had no set of printed rules but simply wrote to each man telling them what he wanted done.[8]

When questioned about the rules pertaining to the "Right of the Road," Houseman complicated the picture by justifying switch-stealing:

Well, some of the motormen try to steal a switch. If they think they can make the next switch before the opposite train gets there, they use their judgment and run for it.

---

[4]"The Kirkwood Electric," PD, 10 March 1896.
[5]"That Electric Railway `Accident,'" PD, 9 March 1896.
[6]"A Defective Trolley Wire," PD, 12 March 1896.
[7]Ibid.
[8]"Three Lives Sacrificed to the Collision," St. Louis Republic, 10 March 1896.

Now there's a man (pointing) sitting there; he steals switches right along, only he does it carefully.[9]

At that point in the interview, Houseman was asked if his motormen had to obey the rule to wait at the meeting point until the opposite train arrived - if they could steal a switch, regardless of the rules, if they thought they could make it? He replied that they could, but they were, "not supposed to go faster than a walk."[10] When queried about the rapid speeds of the cars, Houseman stated that the reported 35 mile per hour speed was wrong, that the actual running speed was 20 miles per hour. He stated that the reporter in order to get high speeds had timed cars on short downhill sections, showing unusual speeds up to 40 MPH.

The *Republic*, printed mixed messages about the roadbed, calling it one of the, "crookedest pieces of track running out of St. Louis. In fact, it resembles a great crawling serpent, stretched across the hills and dales. The track, however, is first class being of solid rock ballast and laid with heavy T rails."[11] Though the paper exaggerated the layout of the track, it credited the line's well built rolling stock with saving lives.

> The cars are strong and staunch, and it is due to the strength of these cars that more people were not killed. Had they been of the light pattern, they (passengers) would have been crushed like eggshells so terrific was the crash.[12]

Even more graphic than print editorial comment was a cartoon on the front page of the March 10th *Post-Dispatch* showing a Kirkwood Electric R.R. car barreling along with terrified passengers losing their hats and screaming, a farmer running to escape getting hit by the streetcar and a dog hit and sliced in two. A brutish looking motorman was shown operating the car. The cartoon was captioned, "Stealing a Switch on the Kirkwood Electric Line."[13]

Houseman testily responded to the pervasive media criticism in a statement to the newspapers. He consistently maintained the accident was the fault of motorman Robert Aiken:

> According to the rules of the company, Aiken should have held his car at Taussig's switch on the return trip. Those were his orders, and they were never countermanded. I feel badly over Aiken's death, but I cannot allow the blame to rest on another when I know he was guilty. Our system is perfect as long as the men obey orders. With our system of telephones, we do not need a dispatcher. I have devoted all my time to this road for the past three years and I believe our system is safer than that used by steam railroads, and I would not change to the dispatcher system if I could.... The accident

---

[9]Ibid.
[10]Ibid.
[11]Ibid.
[12]Ibid.
[13]"Stealing a Switch on the Kirkwood Electric Line," PD, 10 March 1896.

is such as might happen on the best road in the world, and is attributable to one man's negligence and not to any fault in the system or equipment.[14]

Company attorney Taussig stated that the company could prove that the blame in disobeying rules rested on Aiken and that a jury would not award a large amount in Jones' death because he was a young man without dependents. Taussig assessed the company's potential liability: "Besides these (Aiken and Jones) there are not more than seven or eight persons that are so severely injured as to have claims for any considerable amount even if we were held responsible."[15]

On March 11, 1896, the St. Louis County Coroner began an inquest into the deaths of the three people killed as a result of the crash. Newspaper reporters covered the proceedings closely. The *Republic* speculated that the jury was split three for the company and three for action, a possible hung jury. On March 18th, the jury debated long over the verdict. Only one member held out for a finding of criminal conduct on the part of the railway. At last he wore down and agreed to sign any verdict the others could agree upon. A unanimous verdict was returned late in the day:

> We the jury find that the deceased… died in the above said accident and that said accident was caused by electric car number three on said St. Louis and Kirkwood Railway leaving Meramec Highlands by a mistake and no criminal intent on the part of those parties in charge of said car number three is found.[16]

The newspaper articles about the accident and its aftermath were followed closely by the victims and their relatives as well as by the residents of Kirkwood and Webster Groves. Many were not happy with the verdict. The *Watchman* reporter stated:

> The verdict, would no doubt be pleasing to the management of the railway company, as it holds no one responsible for the most deplorable accident that has occurred in the county since electricity has been brought into use as a motive power… There are none who believe this accident and the lives sacrificed by it were caused by "criminal intent" but there are some who believe it was caused by criminal carelessness or negligence and if the matter is ever turned over to the grand jury, evidence enough may be provided to establish that fact.[17]

Though Doctor Pitman and company attorney George Taussig spent the 16th and 17th of March in the city visiting victims recovering from the accident,[18] less than two weeks after the

---

[14]"A Sunday Horror," SLCW, 13 March 1896, p. 1.
[15]PD, 12 March 1896.
[16]"The Kirkwood Collision - Verdict of the Coroners Jury," SLCW, 20 March 1896.
[17]Ibid.
[18]"Kirkwood," SLCW, 20 March 1896, p. 1.

accident, four damage suits had already been filed against the St. Louis and Kirkwood Railroad. The most notable was a suit filed three days after the accident by Dr. M. C. Marshall, a dentist who had suffered a broken leg during the collision. He was asking for $25,000 in damages. The fourth suit was brought by plaintiff Theresa Lanigan, the wife of Dick Lanigan who died from his injuries the day following the wreck. She sued for $5,000.

The *Globe-Democrat* speculated that the matter of faulty equipment would be used largely in evidence by the plaintiffs. George Baumhoff, was reportedly going to be the principal witness as to the inefficiency of the equipment:

> The charges which it is said will be made are that the St. Louis and Kirkwood Company practically nullified the efficiency of its motors by improvising handle bars (controller handles) and reverse levers, which were never intended to be used on such motors as used by the company.[19]

The lack of the correct handles was the result of Houseman's seizure of the cars from Baumhoff. Due to a misunderstanding, the Westinghouse Company had not turned over the "handle bars" to Baumhoff for three of the cars. Houseman was then forced to improvise handles in order to operate the cars. When questioned, Houseman agreed that the "handle bars" in use were not intended for use on Westinghouse motors and were crude in appearance. However, he maintained that they were effective in stopping or reversing a car, and that the reverse levers had worked well in previous use.[20]

Another *Post-Dispatch* front page expose' on March 12th laid the blame for the original delay, on a defective trolley wire, which caused the need for switch stealing to make up time:

> A mistake was made in the construction of the wire and it was found that it was almost impossible to keep the trolley pole in place. It was for this reason that an extra conductor was placed on each car. The duty of this man was to guard the trolley pole and whenever it jumped from the wire he was to see that it was immediately put back in position.[21]

Houseman and Taussig immediately met with a local car building company representative to discuss securing cars to replace those that were badly damaged. When reporters suggested that the attorney and Houseman were discussing how to avert possible lawsuits, Houseman denied that they had discussed damage suits at all.

Though cleared by the Coroner's Jury, the operation of the Houseman Air Line gained a public image of an inefficient and unsafe operation. Streetcar passengers in Webster Groves and

---

[19]"First Damage Suit Filed," GD, 11 March 1896.
[20]Ibid.
[21]"A Defective Trolley Wire," PD, 12 March 1896.

Kirkwood hoped for safer transit when the new double track Suburban owned line was completed, but continued to ride the Houseman Air Line, still the sole streetcar line operating in the area.

STEALING A SWITCH ON THE KIRKWOOD ELECTRIC LINE.

6-1. Attention grabbing editorial cartoon featured on the front page of the March 10, 1896 *St. Louis Post-Dispatch.*

Chapter 7

THE AIR LINE BOUNCES BACK - BRIEFLY

Even though newspapers sensationalized the Houseman Air Line wreck, the reports and disparaging editorials initially did little to dampen the public's enthusiasm for riding Houseman's streetcars. Despite the disaster, the line's streetcars were fully loaded the day after the accident. Many were curiosity seekers who rode out to view the spot where the accident occurred. Others rode to Kirkwood to visit the injured who were being cared for at the North Side Inn. Still others, who may have been justifiably leery of the line, rode because they had little choice. They were dependent on the line for travel to work and other daily travel needs.

The continuing heavy patronage created its own set of problems some of which were described by the Kirkwood correspondent to the *St. Louis County Watchman*: "Sunday's rain did not decrease electric travel… At West Forest Park Station a man was kept busy all Sunday afternoon keeping people from overcrowding the Kirkwood electric cars. Some say he had a shotgun to deter them."[1] "… Numbers on the houses are badly needed, since the electric brings so many seeking board and furnished houses."[2]

A mere three weeks after the wreck, one of the cars was repaired and back in service, replacing a car borrowed from the Lindell Railway. American Car Company of St. Louis completed the repairs of the wrecked cars at a cost of $864.90.[3] In an attempt to turn aside negative publicity, Houseman promised that eight new cars would be purchased to help handle the heavy summer traffic.

Because of the fatal accident and to accommodate heavy traffic, the St. Louis and Kirkwood Railroad changed the locations of some switches and constructed additional switches. Work was completed by the end of April. Houseman announced that one of the first steps taken by the railroad would be to double-track the line and put on more cars. Even with changes in the switches and procedures, the *Watchman* pronounced that the line was, "entirely inadequate for the Sunday traffic."[4] However, on a more positive note, the Kirkwood correspondent reported

---

[1]"Kirkwood," SLCW, 3 April 1896.
[2]"Kirkwood," SLCW, 24 April 1896.
[3]SLCW, 24 July 1896, p. 8. Documented in a mechanics lien for costs of materials and labor which was filed in St. Louis County Circuit Court in July 1896.
[4]"Kirkwood," SLCW, 8 May 1896, p. 1.

that the town's residents were pleased with the prospect of a double track which would eliminate the danger of head on collisions.

The Houseman electric road tried to resolve the problem of riders crowding and pushing at the Forest Park connection by arranging a gangway. "Single file prevails," noted the Kirkwood correspondent. She stated that, though the weekend had been big for the Houseman line, employees were not allowed to say how many riders passed in and out of the new gangway.[5]

The heavy traffic on the Houseman line was damaging to the steam railroads. On May 15th, the *Watchman* reported an effort by the Missouri Pacific to combat the shift of traffic to the electric lines:

> On Saturday the 9th, timetables were freely distributed on the Missouri Pacific cars showing a 10 cent fare from here to St. Louis. Had this been done before the electric cars started, more than four trains would have been needed to carry the crowd... No other ticket than 10 for $1.00 is sold.[6]

Despite its decrease in commuter patronage, the Missouri Pacific railroad remained in the commuter business into the 1960s and ultimately outlived streetcar service to Webster Groves and Kirkwood.

Houseman wanted more control of the Air Line. In May 1896, he worked out a twenty-five year lease arrangement with the St. Louis and Kirkwood Electric Railroad which put him in absolute control of the road. He applied for and received a certificate of incorporation from the Missouri Secretary of State for the Highland Scenic Railroad Company. It was based in Brentwood, funded with a capital stock of $150,000. Houseman, Ernest Marshall, J. I. Broderick, L. B. Jones, and W. F. Richards were listed as members of the company. The Highland Scenic Railroad company was given authorization by the state to operate the existing streetcar line from St. Louis to Meramec Highlands and to build an extension of about two miles from a point near Manchester Road in Brentwood to the St. Louis and Meramec River Railroad, joining that road where it crossed the city limits of St. Louis. The proposed new extension linking Houseman's line with the Manchester line was to be built entirely over a private right of way through the Rannells farm.[7]

The May 22nd *Watchman* reported details of Houseman's lease agreement with the St. Louis and Kirkwood Railroad Company:

> The road is valued at $650,000, upon which valuation Mr. Houseman agrees to pay 3 percent, and 5 percent of the net earnings per year during the terms of the lease, less two years, the rental for them to be used in constructing an additional track. The leasing of the road will in no wise affect the litigation for which the company is now

---

[5]"Kirkwood," SLCW, 15 May 1896, p. 1.
[6]Ibid.
[7]"Houseman's New Line," SLCW, 15 May 1896. The extension was never built.

involved for damages to persons injured in the recent collision, although steps are being taken toward a compromise with most of the parties who have filed suit against it.[8]

In June, following the deal with Houseman, new officers were elected by the St. Louis and Kirkwood Electric Railway. Both president John Pitman and Vice-president F. E. Niesen had resigned. Edgar A. B. Haynes was elected President, Edgar S. Rannells, Vice-president, George L. Edwards, Treasurer, and George W. Taussig, Secretary. Taussig and Edwards were reelected. The election had no effect on the management of the streetcar line since it was by that time under lease to the Highlands Scenic Railway Company.[9]

In June of 1896, a disastrous tornado struck St. Louis. It was devastating in the city and also created hardship in the county. The *Watchman* described its effects on one group of Kirkwood residents riding the Houseman Air Line:

> Perhaps no more trying experience of detention in the storm was that of a carload of passengers on an electric car that had the power cut off alongside Frank Sterrett's pretty home near the eastern terminus of the Kirkwood line. One lady became ill, and a gentleman offered to seek shelter for her alone at the Sterretts. This the host (Sterrett) refused. At daylight, Mrs. William Ross of Kirkwood, went on the platform of the car and begged for a cup of coffee. This too was denied.[10]

The unflattering picture of Sterrett's lack of hospitality in the face of a natural disaster was hotly contested the following week in a letter to the editor from W. S. Fleming, Mayor of Webster Groves. He contended that Judge Sterrett had been in the company of several other prominent citizens of Webster Groves and left St. Louis in a carriage, not arriving at home until 1:30 a.m. on the night of the tornado. Fleming continued:

> We found his wife almost distracted and his home badly damaged. At early dawn, while a lady who had sought shelter in Mr. Sterrett's house was leaving, one of the passengers requested of her to ascertain if coffee could be obtained. This lady immediately returned to the house and informed the cook (the only person awake at that time), who knowing her employer's generous disposition, immediately prepared to accommodate the unfortunates. In a few minutes word was sent to the passengers, but when the messenger arrived the occupants of the car had all departed. That gross injustice has been done to one of our leading families will be recognized by all who have come into contact with them or have partaken of their kind hospitality.[11]

Did Republican and Democrat rivalries or Kirkwood and Webster Groves rivalries come into play in the reported differences? The only thing that was agreed upon in the two newspaper

---

[8]"New Railroad Deal," SLCW, 22 May 1896.
[9]"The Kirkwood Road Elects Officers," SLCW, 19 June 1896.
[10]"Kirkwood," SLCW, 5 June 1896.
[11]"A Correction," letter to the editor, SLCW, 12 June 1896.

items was that a group of passengers was stranded overnight in the streetcar as the result of the tornado.

Though patronage of the line was good during the spring and summer, all was not well. Suits for damages were rapidly multiplying in Circuit Court as a result of the wreck in March. Most plaintiffs were asking for $5000.00 for injuries. Some asked for compensation to the parent for loss of labor of a minor child in addition to compensation to the minor for expenses incurred in the treatment of the injuries received. For example, William Gildehaus, 18 years old, who suffered a fractured knee sued for $10,000 in damages. His father, Frank Gildehaus, sued for $5000 for medical services and the loss of his son's labor while still a minor. Other accident victims like Webster Groves resident Robert Willams, who sued for $15,000, asked for large settlements.

Despite the legal restructuring of the operation and continued heavy patronage of the line, Houseman still refused to repair Shady Avenue in Webster Groves. He considered that job to be contractor Baumhoff's responsibility. The July 3rd *Watchman* reported the people of Webster Groves were anxious to have the road "put in repair."[12] After their complaints mounted at the County Court, on July 6th, County Clerk Helmering was ordered by the court to notify Houseman that he had ten days to repair Shady Avenue or the court would use the company's deposit to return the street to good condition.[13]

Company officials weren't the only financial targets. Because the streetcars were a source of ready cash, streetcar crews were targeted by robbers. A man boarded a Highland Scenic Railroad car at Meramec Highlands planning to commit a robbery. As he entered, he stumbled and fell against a woman, knocking her to the floor. At the same time, he tried to take her purse which she held in her hand. Conductor P. H. Gunning saw the incident and ordered the man off the car, but his order only enraged the robber, named Mr. Bryan:

> Bryan took the opportunity when Gunning's back was turned to plunge a knife into his side. As soon as he did this, Bryan fled, and several hundred persons joined in his pursuit. He was finally run down and captured and locked up in the Kirkwood jail. Conductor Gunning received medical attention as soon as possible, and it was found that his injury was quite serious.[14]

The incident caused Houseman's streetcar motormen and conductors to arm themselves. The revolver was their weapon of choice.

On a more positive note, the *Watchman* reported that on the Fourth of July the electric cars were "profusely decorated with flags," and ran on schedule even though all cars were

---

[12]SLCW, 3 July 1896.
[13]SLCW, 10 July 1896, p. 8.
[14]"A Bad Man," SLCW, 17 July 1896.

crowded.[15] Later in the month, Kirkwood resident William Essex wrote a letter to his friend, William Vincent Byars, and updated him on the progress of the Houseman line:

> The Road is doing a fine business — have put on more cars and run every 15 minutes, two cars following one another. The road is now finished to Sunset Hill and has a loop where cars turn around and come back with the same end of the car forward.[16]

Houseman, ever the promoter, sponsored a trolley party on his new palace car, the "Rambler," for many of those from whom support for his promotions was desired. The *Watchman* chronicled the event in a piece titled, "EXCURSION TO THE HIGHLANDS - A Handsome Entertainment Provided for Prominent Citizens of the County:" [17]

> President J. D. Houseman of the Highlands Scenic Railroad Company, covered himself with glory last Saturday, by adding to his reputation as a railroad projector and promoter, that of a prince of entertainers. At his solicitation, a distinguished group of county officials and representatives of press and bar, enjoyed a delightful excursion and banquet on his new palace dining and drawing-room trolley car, "The Rambler." Those who enjoyed the hospitalities of the "pioneer and king promoter of electric railways in St. Louis County" were Judge Rudolph Hirzel of the St. Louis County Circuit Court… (followed by a listing of judges, government officials, lawyers, newspaper editors, and men of wealth, including Dr. John Pitman of Kirkwood, the ex-president of the St. Louis and Kirkwood R.R. Co.).[18]

The group stopped at the Brentwood powerhouse where Highlands Scenic Railway Superintendent McClelland escorted them on a tour to observe the machinery which furnished the power for the entire line. After leaving the powerhouse, they headed for Meramec Highlands, enjoying a dinner that was served in the car en route. Speeches and congratulations were delivered by the guests and host. Upon reaching Meramec Highlands, guest Marcus Bernheimer of the Meramec Highlands Improvement Company, hosted a visit to the Pagoda on Sunset Hill where the group viewed the beautiful Meramec River scenery from the observation deck atop the Pagoda. They were entertained for an hour or so at the Highlands Inn by Mr. Bernheimer before returning to their starting point at the east end of the line.

A toast was made to Houseman after the guests were in a "happy mood," presumably fueled by good food and drink. He responded, referring to the wonderful improvements in St. Louis County in the last few years, and classified his road as being one of the most important. He optimistically prophesied a network system of electric roads in the county in the near future.[19]

---

[15] "Kirkwood," SLCW, 10 July 1896, p. 1.

[16] William Essex, Letter to William Vincent Byars, 21 July 1896, Byar's Papers, MHS.

[17] "Excursion to the Highlands," SLCW, 24 July 1896.

[18] Ibid.

[19] Ibid.

THE AIR LINE BOUNCES BACK - BRIEFLY

Unexpected costs as a result of a tremendous storm that roared through the county on August 15th, buffeted the financially beleaguered line. Several *Watchman* correspondents commented in the August 21st edition, about the effect of the storm on the Houseman line. A flood of the River Des Peres caused complete washouts of track in some sections between Brentwood and Bartold. The Brentwood powerhouse was submerged by the flood. Not only did the line have to pay for repairs, it also lost passengers to the new St. Louis and Meramec River Railroad which had reached Webster Groves. The Kirkwood correspondent stated, "It gave the good people of Kirkwood an opportunity of trying the Howard electric line, and starting from the Highlands end of the Kirkwood line, changing at Rock Hill road in Webster to the Howard road, one had ample opportunity to realize that "falling around the curves" is the only way of expressing the rapidity with which the Highlands road moves."[20] At Rock Hill Road, the two lines came within two blocks of each other, so passengers could get off the Kirkwood line and easily walk up to Lockwood to catch the Howard line. Within two days the line was repaired, and cars again ran as usual on the Houseman line.

On August 22nd, William Essex again wrote to Byars updating him on the progress of the electric line:

> All the dwellings have been filled since the trolley line commenced to run. They are carrying an immense number of people every day and especially on Sundays. One day it went up to 8000, the Highlands are doing great business, boating parties or dances at the "Inn" and at the "Pagoda" on Sunset Hill. My wife and I go up there frequently. It is cool and delightful on the cars and only twelve minutes to the Pagoda from our street.[21]

The editor of the *Webster Times* expressed a somewhat negative point of view toward Houseman's line in the August 29th edition. After reporting that a Kirkwood family moved to Webster Groves to be near the new Manchester line, he stated, "Kirkwood has not the excellent electric car accommodations that Webster has, and the removal of some of the Missouri-Pacific trains makes the daily trip to the city a serious matter."[22] As if to bolster his point, the Missouri Pacific announced in September that the trains serving Kirkwood in the middle of the day were being discontinued, leaving trains only in the morning and evening.

Even though Kirkwood citizens had looked forward to the advent of streetcars, they were to find that the Kirkwood streets were not well maintained after the electric line construction. In 1896, Kirkwood trustees initiated legal action against the St. Louis and Kirkwood line for failure to maintain its tracks within the town in a safe and satisfactory manner. After almost two years of wrangling and litigation, Kirkwood officials agreed that the work done on the streets by the St. Louis and Kirkwood line was at last satisfactory. However, the disagreement over the

---

[20]"Kirkwood," SLCW, 21 August 1896, p. 1.
[21]William Essex, Letter to William Vincent Byars, 22 August 1896, MHS.
[22]Webster Times, 29 August 1896.

condition of the streets was just the first of many long legal battles between the town of Kirkwood and the electric railway companies.

The American Street Railway Association met in St. Louis in October 1896. Its *Official Souvenir of the Local Committee of Arrangements of the American Street Railway Association*, summarized the operation of the St. Louis and Kirkwood road to that date, reporting that it was operated by lessees (Houseman's group) who paid a rental of 3% per annum on the cost of the road and 5% of the earnings. The summary continued:

> The business has grown beyond expectation during the few months since the road was open for travel and it is frequently necessary to run two cars together to accommodate the travel. Arrangements are reported to have been made for double-tracking the road throughout its entire length. The feature of a dining car has been introduced on this road... The Southwest terminal is Sunset Hill, a section of Meramec Highlands, a very popular and high-class summer resort. The road runs through a very attractive stretch of county. On its route it passes through the newly incorporated town of Webster Groves and also the much older city of Kirkwood.[23]

The summary made no mention of the March crash, perhaps wishing to put St. Louis lines in the best possible light, or perhaps because accidents and collisions with pedestrians and horse drawn vehicles were common occurrences in the industry.

Adding to the Houseman line's mounting economic uncertainty was the continuing progress of the St. Louis and Meramec River Railroad's Manchester line, which had by summer of 1896 reached the western section of Webster Groves. The County Court granted the company an extension of one year to complete its line to Kirkwood, thus preventing any penalty against it for late completion. The only good news for Houseman's line was that it would operate without competition in Kirkwood and Meramec Highlands for nearly a year longer than was first projected.

Approval of a cross county line was asked of County Court, in February 1897. It was projected to run north from Big Bend where it intersected Gore in Webster Groves. It was to cross the Missouri Pacific Railroad, the St. Louis and Meramec River Railroad, the St. Louis and Kirkwood Railroad, the Clayton and Forest Park line and numerous roads, private properties and railroads till it reached its terminus north of St. Cyr Road (in the Jennings/Belfountain Neighbors area). The construction of that line might have made countywide streetcar traffic, earlier predicted by Houseman, more viable. However, it was a nonstarter.

An unwelcome though expected piece of news for backers of the Houseman line was the final authorization by Kirkwood trustees, in January 1897, for the St. Louis and Meramec River Railroad Company, to operate on right-of-ways through the town. That allowed the line the right

---

[23]Robert Mc Cullough for the American Street Railway Association (1896), <u>Official Souvenir of the Local Committee of Arrangements of the American Street Railway Association</u>. St. Louis.

to complete a connection from downtown St. Louis to the Meramec Highlands and to compete with the Houseman line for Kirkwood and resort traffic.

The St. Louis and Meramec River line had features which made it more attractive than Houseman's Highlands Scenic Railway to many riders. It was planned and built as a double-track system. People felt safer without the possibility of a repeat of the Houseman single-track "switch stealing" disaster. The new line carried passengers to downtown St. Louis without a change in cars, as required on Houseman's line. "It is a great improvement on the old plan of changing at the city limits and having to wait for a car to get the rest of the way," reported the *Watchman*'s Meramec Highlands correspondent.[24]

The Houseman electric railroad's financial problems resulted in frequent litigation for, "payment on account." In September most of the law suits over injuries sustained in the March crash were settled in, "some way satisfactory to all concerned," but one particular claim by Mrs.. Gussie C. Spencer of Webster Groves for $20,000 was diligently pursued by her attorney, resulting in a $5000 judgment in her favor. Because the company did not have enough cash to pay her, it was placed in receivership. The *Watchman* remained optimistic about the future of the line despite receivership:

> The property and franchise of the St. Louis and Kirkwood road are very valuable, and there is no doubt that in due time it will pay off all judgments and indebtedness and become the best paying property of its kind in the country.[25]

On September 5, 1896, the *Webster Times* reported that the Judge Hirzel of the County Court appointed State Senator G. A. Wurdeman as receiver for the line. The receiver's job was to help the company put its financial house in order. Houseman objected but was forced by the court to allow Wurdeman to assume financial control. Two weeks later the *Times* reported, "Receiver Wurdeman of the Houseman electric road, after some difficulties, gained possession of the power house last Saturday and is now operating the line."[26] Ironically, Judge Hirzel, who appointed the receiver, and Wurdeman had been Houseman's guests only two months earlier on the "Rambler" for his private party car junket to Meramec Highlands. No sooner than he was appointed, Wurdeman was named as codefendant in two new suits against the Houseman line by a father and his son, each of whom had "an arm crushed" in the March crash.

Because of a default on the bonds already in George Baumhoff's possession as collateral for his construction of the line, the Houseman and the Lindell lines became closely linked in late 1896. Some of the service on the line was from cars on loan from the Lindell line, with the name of the new line painted over the Lindell name. Baumhoff was still actively litigating for a cash settlement. The legal issues ultimately were settled in Baumhoff's favor by the Missouri

---

[24]"Meramec Highlands," SLCW, 24 September 1897.

[25]SLCW, 4 September 1897.

[26]Webster Times, 19 September 1897.

THE AIR LINE BOUNCES BACK - BRIEFLY

 Supreme Court in 1907 after more than ten years of attempts to collect full payment from the St. Louis and Kirkwood Railroad and the Highlands Scenic Railroad.

Attorney George Taussig, the troubled line's secretary, resigned. He was upset with the lack of payment for his legal services from September 1893 to June 1896. Houseman maintained that since Taussig was an officer of the company, he could not expect to be paid for his legal work. Taussig's dispute with Houseman was so bitter that he lodged complaints with the Kirkwood trustees about the excessive rate of speed of Houseman's streetcars on Clay Avenue. In October 1896, Taussig sued the St. Louis and Kirkwood Railroad for payment. That legal battle made its way through the courts with the case finally reaching the Missouri Supreme Court in 1904. The court ruled that Taussig was acting as an attorney when performing legal services, and was entitled to $4,500 for his work even though he was an officer of the company at the time the work was completed. The largest portion of the bill was for, "legal services in connection with settlement of claims for damages for personal injuries by accident of March 8, 1896....$1,500." Other legal duties he had performed included preparation of articles of incorporation, preparation of ordinances for right-of-way through St. Louis County and Kirkwood, preparation of contracts regarding the power house and the loop at Meramec Highlands, examination of titles in securing rights-of-way, procuring increased capital stock, preparing first mortgage bonds and deeds of mortgage, preparing bonus subscriptions, litigating against St. Louis Trust Company for removal as trustee, and preparing George Baumhoff's contract.[27]

Consolidated Coal, which had provided coal for the Brentwood powerhouse, and the St. Louis Trust Company had litigation pending against the line. In addition, the County Court docket on Wednesday October the 21st listed 9 cases against the St. Louis and Kirkwood Railroad, and the docket on the 22nd showed eight additional damage suits against the line. Several other cases were being prepared but were not yet on the docket.[28]

On October 23rd, the *Watchman* indicated that Houseman had met with damage suit claimants to "consider a proposition for an amicable settlement of the claims." Houseman reported a lack of money to pay claims, stating that capital stock of the company, $300,000, was tied up in bonded indebtedness of $300,000 in 20 year 6 percent bonds. According to Houseman, the company had no assets except bonus subscriptions. Due to limited resources, he offered small settlements to the claimants:

> The suits filed against the company (through the first two weeks in October) aggregate $216,983, of which $31,983 are lien suits, and $185,000 are damage suits. Three judgments have been entered against the company for a total of $7,308, and suits have been brought for sundry small bills amounting to $2,700.[29]

---

[27]"Taussig v. Railroad," Reports of Cases Determined in the Supreme Court of Missouri, (October Term 1904), Vol. 186, Columbia, MO: E. W. Stephens.
[28]"County Court," SLCW, 23 October 1897.
[29]"Probable Settlement of Damage Suits," SLCW, 23 October 1897.

THE AIR LINE BOUNCES BACK - BRIEFLY

Despite financial problems, the Houseman line, as long as the weather was nice, still carried large numbers of passengers, especially on weekends. After a train wreck on the Frisco line near Meramec Highlands, thousands jammed the streetcars to travel out to Kirkwood to view the wreckage of the two Frisco trains involved. The Kirkwood correspondent to the *Watchman* reported in the October 30, 1896 edition:

> All afternoon the electric cars ran in pairs, and then could not carry all who attempted to come. Fully 10,000 people visited the scene of the collision on Sunday, and quite a number were there on Monday.[30]

In November 1896, numerous plaintiffs from St. Louis, frustrated with the prior results and delays in the county courts, asked for a change of venue to the St. Louis Circuit Court for their suits against the Houseman line. Contractor George Baumhoff's mechanic lien suit was the most prominent of those pending cases.

On January 19th, the St. Louis and Kirkwood road reduced its frequency of runs as a cost saving measure. The *Watchman*'s Meramec Highlands correspondent complained that electric cars running at only half hour intervals were "quite a source of regret," to travelers on the line.[31]

Houseman was briefly able to regain control of the line. Early in December, he received a "congratulatory testimonial" in honor of his reappointment as manager.[32] But his return was cut short in the last week of January 1897, when one of the St. Louis and Kirkwood Railroad bondholders asked that a receiver be appointed. Judge Hirzel reappointed Senator Wurdeman. When the Senator again took charge, he appointed W. H. McClelland superintendent and general manager. The *Watchman* on February 5th stated, "Messrs. Wurdeman and McClelland are still in charge of the road and operating it to the best advantage of all concerned."[33]

By February 1897, the Houseman line was in even deeper financial trouble. The Circuit Court on February 2nd still listed on the docket seven different suits against the St. Louis and Kirkwood Railroad Company. The St. Louis Car Company, which built streetcars for the line, was one of the most prominent litigants for payment. The *Watchman*'s Kirkwood correspondent summarized Kirkwoodians' opinion about the troubled line in the February 5, 1897, edition:

> The various litigation over the Houseman electric road attracts much attention and interest here. The outcome is closely watched for, and few feel that Kirkwood would be bettered by its change in ownership. Last month it was said to have fallen $500 short of paying expenses.[34]

---

[30]"Head End Collision," SLCW, 30 October 1896.
[31]"Meramec Highlands," SLCW, 22 January 1897.
[32]SLCW, 11 December 1896, p. 8.
[33]"Again in Receiver's Hands," SLCW, 5 February 1897, p. 4.
[34]"Kirkwood," SLCW, 5 February 1897.

THE AIR LINE BOUNCES BACK - BRIEFLY

By mid-February, a number of the claims against the line were settled, in the county for a total of $2865, and in the city Circuit Court for a total of $3200. However, four more damage suits were filed in Clayton that week. The good news for Houseman was that he was able to keep the judgments small in many of the cases. On February 19th, the *Watchman* reported compromise had been reached in 8 more suits against the company which were before Justice of the Peace Coggeshall of Webster Groves. Judgments ranged from a low of $8.00 to a high of $41.65.

Houseman approached operation of his line as if he could not fail despite temporary financial shortfalls. He hosted a "merry party of gentlemen" for a Saturday afternoon trolley party and liberally dispensed cigars and liquor. The Kirkwood correspondent in the March 26th *Watchman* sniffed disapprovingly: "It was not a temperance party, either, from the number of decanters and wine glasses displayed. Cigars too were in evidence."[35]

The same *Watchman* edition noted a positive development for the Houseman line. Crowds on the previous Sunday had been so heavy that the streetcars were run double out to Meramec Highlands. The "Refreshment Season" was due to open at the resort April 1st, ushering in a period of high traffic.[36] Unfortunately, as revenues increased, so did expenses. In the first week of April, heavy rains washed out areas of roadbed near the Highlands causing "cave ins" which prevented the cars from reaching the resort.

Houseman believed in the potential of his line and was still trying to make the Meramec Highlands Scenic Railroad line more efficient and profitable in spite of financial problems. In May 1897, he was seen by Kirkwood residents taking "views" with his camera at Kirkwood's Clay Avenue bridge with the stated intention of improving it by straightening the walks on the side in order to make the bridge safer for both pedestrians and riders.[37] New switches were added to the line, with service increased to ten minute intervals.[38] Houseman was reported to be, "well pleased with the turn of affairs in his pet scheme."[39] The *Watchman* reported cars running every ten minutes for Saturday afternoon traffic on May 22nd, and 5,900 people visiting on Sunday, May 23rd, with "picnics galore" at the Highlands.[40] With the advent of spring weather and large crowds, an enterprising young man from Fenton, Louis Gnauck, began operating a steam boat from Fenton to Meramec Highlands for passengers who wanted to make connections with the Houseman electric line or the Frisco steam railroad. His enterprise was not long lived, for inconsistent demand and winter ice posed problems.[41]

June and July proved to be a good months for the line. In addition to regular service, various organizations and church groups utilized the cars for special events: "The Methodists

---

[35]"Kirkwood," SLCW, 26 March 1897, p. 1.

[36]"Meramec Highlands," SLCW, 26 March 1897.

[37]"Meramec Highlands"SLCW, 7 May 1897.

[38]"Meramec Highlands," SLCW, 4 June 1897 p. 1.

[39]Ibid., 28 May 1897.

[40]SLCW, 28 May 1897.

[41]SLCW, 14 May 1897, p. 8.

chartered cars to take their Sunday School to Meramec Highlands Thursday last and filled the same with a jolly crowd, well supplied with picnic refreshments."[42] The 4th of July weekend saw 12,000 to 13,000 visitors per day, the vast majority of which traveled to the resort via Houseman's line.[43]

Houseman was still pursuing County Court agreement for an extension of the line connecting his line with the St. Louis and Meramec River Railroad. The extension plan had been accepted by the Secretary of State when granting the Highlands Scenic Railway incorporation, but in reality only gave approval to be in business. Approval for construction had to come from county and local jurisdictions. In February 1897, Houseman applied to the court for permission to extend his line, but it was not until November 12, 1897, that the petition for an extension of the St. Louis and Kirkwood Railroad was ordered received and filed by the County Court.

A problem of thieves cutting and removing the copper ground bonds connecting the rails along the Houseman line became so common that Houseman was forced to employ men to patrol sections of the track most often hit. The June 11, 1897 *Watchman* reported one patrol's gun battle which narrowly escaped being tragic.

> There are at least two young men in Webster Groves who... will not soon again, in the still watches of night, order a trio of strangers to throw up their hands without first somehow making a show of authority for so doing. For by neglecting this, these same young men are carrying about with them perforations in their anatomies which, luckily will only temporarily, it is hoped, incapacitate them for business.[44]

The three Webster youth, when patrolling, ran into three Dundeck brothers who were returning from Meramec Highlands. When the last car for the night turned in at the Brentwood power house, the brothers were required to walk to their home in Maplewood near the city limits. They chose to follow the tracks. They were suddenly confronted by the patrol who ordered them to halt and throw up their hands. They were so surprised that they were slow in complying, so one of the patrol members fired a shot which struck a suspender buckle, inflicting a slight flesh wound on one of the brothers. At that point one of the Dundecks pulled out his revolver and immediately began shooting back, lodging bullets in the right breast of one patrol member and in the leg of another. The third patrol member escaped by dropping into a brush pile.[45]

The attorney for The Houseman line was kept busy. Beside damage suits and payment on account suits, the line was faced with other litigation such as that brought by Edward Dickson, a Kirkwood resident and former investor in the failed Kirkwood Rapid Transit Company. He filed two suits against the electric railroad in July 1897 to have the railroad ejected from its right of way on his property near Collins Road (Sappington Road). His case eventually reached the

---

[42] "Kirkwood," SLCW, 2 July 1897.
[43] "Kirkwood," SLCW, 9 July 1897.
[44] "Bad Enough, But Might Have Been Worse," SLCW, 11 June 1897.
[45] Ibid.

THE AIR LINE BOUNCES BACK - BRIEFLY

 Missouri Supreme Court which ruled that the railroad had in essence complied with requirements. Where they had made minor deviations in their right of way, it was with his knowledge and without complaint at the time.[46]

 By October 1897, as a result of financial problems and the loss of traffic due to the arrival of the St. Louis and Meramec River Railroad line in Kirkwood, the Houseman line was running only three cars, forty minutes apart. The infrequent trips of the electric cars to the Meramec Highlands was a matter of much complaint by residents of the area:

> Mr. Leopold Marquitz of Meramec Highlands, paid the *Watchman* a friendly visit Wednesday. He and many of his neighbors have a large-sized kick to register against the Houseman electric line since the Inn at the Highlands has closed for the season, as since that event the railway company doesn't seem to care how they run their cars; that at times they were an hour apart, and then did not run nearer the Highlands than the store, which is quite a distance to walk for patrons of the line.[47]

 Not all litigation against the Houseman line was successful. The December 24, 1897 *Watchman*, reported an accident on the Houseman line which resulted in litigation against the line:

> William Yeager, an old citizen of the county, residing at Webster Groves, was a victim of a serious accident last Friday evening, while traveling from Clayton to his home. He was driving along Shady Avenue, when a car of the Houseman line ran into the rear part of his buggy, smashing the vehicle and throwing Mr. Yeager to the side of the road, severely cutting and bruising him. Beside wrecking his buggy, the horse was killed. The old gentleman had several cuts in the back of his head, and his upper lip was split open, necessitating three stitches. We learn that he was also hurt internally.[48]

 In April, Yeager filed suit against the St. Louis and Kirkwood Railroad for $5000 in damages. Before the case came to trial on July 1, 1898, the St. Louis and Suburban had assumed ownership of the Houseman line. The *Watchman* reported the results of the Yeager suit: "Mr. Yeager got lots of sympathy for his hurts, but no consoling ducats."[49]

 In April 1898, a double tracking contract was let for the electric line from Geyer Road to Meramec Highlands, the area in which the earlier disaster had occurred. Work was expected to be completed before the summer season began for the resort.[50] Other work on the Houseman line

---

[46]"Dickson v. St. Louis and Kirkwood Ry. Co.," Reports...Supreme Court of Missouri, (October Term, 1901) Vol. 168, Columbia: Stevens
[47]SLCW, 5 November 1897.
[48]SLCW, 24 December 1897.
[49]"Webster Groves," SLCW, 8 July 1898.
[50]SLCW, 29 April 1898.

was ordered by the County Court, "to put its right of way at Berry and Collins (Sappington) roads in proper and passable condition, the same being dangerous to public travel."[51]

After nearly two years of economic difficulties, the St. Louis and Kirkwood Railway was taken over by the St. Louis and Suburban Railway System. Though the Suburban won the struggle for supremacy against the St. Louis and Kirkwood line, it was soon embroiled in its own problems.

7-1. Streetcars were seen as a money maker for the newspaper companies, who hired newsboys to sell papers to the passengers. However after 9 a.m. and 7 p.m. the newsboys stopped selling papers. The August 8, 1897 *St. Louis Post-Dispatch* **reported a new paper vending machine designed for streetcars which was invented by Robert Schlegal of St. Louis. It would allow a newspaper to be obtained at any hour, "with no danger of infectious diseases, for street car companies are particular about the character and cleanliness of their employees."**

[51]"County Court," SLCW, 15 April 1898.

7-2. Former Houseman car taken over by the St. Louis and Suburban was photographed at the DeHodiamont sheds. The double end car had a closed vestibule on each end for the protection of the motormen. After the Suburban takeover, the car was painted a dark olive drab color. Photograph from the collection of Charles Hamman.

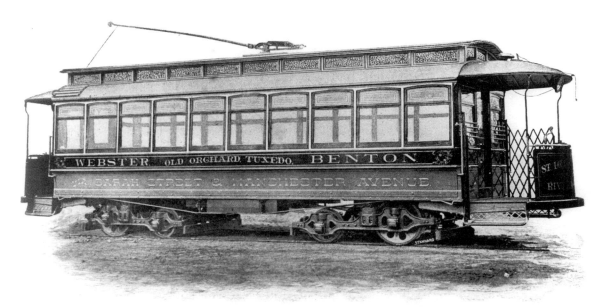

7-3. St. Louis Car Company engraving of a Manchester line car that was in competition with Houseman's cars. The end of the car reads St. Louis and Meramec River Railroad. Though it advertised that connection, it mainly ran on Sarah and Manchester, going no farther than Webster Groves.

Chapter 8

ST. LOUIS AND MERAMEC RIVER RAILROAD
ARRIVES IN WEBSTER GROVES

On February 20, 1893, St. Louis County Court granted a franchise to the St. Louis, Kirkwood and Meramec Railroad Company. However that company was unable to fulfill the requirements of its franchise. The company was reorganized and was renamed the St. Louis and Meramec River Railroad in 1895. Once the reorganization was recognized by the Secretary of State of Missouri, the new company presented its Articles of Association and Incorporation to the County Court. On July 15, 1895, St. Louis County Court assigned to the St. Louis and Meramec River Railroad Company, "all rights and privileges heretofore granted by this Court to the St. Louis, Kirkwood and Meramec River railroad Company."[1] The Court ordered that the cash bond be reduced to $1000, to be received before work could commence. The penalty from the 1893 franchise was reduced to $5000 from $25,000, thus leaving the court with a total of $6000 bond from the company to cover potential damage caused by the company. Otherwise the granted route and other provisions remained the same as granted in 1893.

Less than a month later, the St. Louis and Meramec River Railroad requested and received approval from the court to modify its route:

> Leaving original line on Sutton avenue 1300 feet more or less south of Manchester road; thence westwardly over Flora Avenue and private property crossing Big Bend road and Laclede Station road to a point in the center of Bartold avenue 1015 feet more or less north of the Missouri Pacific Railroad; thence southwardly... over private property crossing Missouri Pacific Railroad and Marshall road to a point in Laclede boulevard just south of Marshall road...[2]

The revised route continued south along Laclede Boulevard and private property to Tuxedo Park where it ran south along Summit Avenue and over private property to Lockwood Avenue. There it turned and ran westwardly along Lockwood Avenue and continued to Berry Road.

---

[1]"St. Louis County Court, 15 July 1895," Franchises of United Railways and Constituent Companies, (1913) p. 780. St. Louis: United Railways. Found in Museum of Transportation (MOT).
[2]Franchises of United Railways ... (1913), pp. 781-782, in MOT.

KING TROLLEY: ST. LOUIS AND MERAMEC RIVER RAILROAD ARRIVES

On August 19, 1895, the St. Louis and Meramec River Railroad Company paid its cash bond and gave the court written notification to County court that it had started construction. Despite initial delays, the company, still commonly known in Webster Groves and Kirkwood as the "Howard Line," began construction in earnest by September. The progress was closely watched. On November 1, 1895, the *St. Louis County Watchman* reported:

"And Still Another"

> The Howard Electric Line, whose promoters are chiefly gentlemen of Webster Groves, (James B. Case, Samuel M. Kennard, and Lucien R. Blackmer) is "getting a move on it," and will soon be in as advanced state as any of the lines so far started in the county. Already considerable amount of work has been done on it, and we understand grading was begun on the Manchester road at Clifton Heights last Friday. Under the terms of their franchise, the road must be completed from its eastern terminus, Sarah Street, to the city limits by December 20th, and as that time is rapidly approaching the company will have to do some hustling…[3]

Three weeks later the paper reported that a large force of men were working seven days a week with "every energy" to complete the work within St. Louis city limits by the time deadline, January 1, 1896. The new double track line, the first to be constructed in the county, was projected to reach Webster Groves on June 1, 1896, and Kirkwood on August 15, 1896. Additional details about the Howard operation were included in the article:

> The patrons of the Howard line will be deposited at Sixth and Locust streets in the city by the Suburban road, which will connect with the Howard at Sarah street. A 10 cent fare[4] will be charged from Kirkwood and Webster Groves. Mr.. J. B. Case is the president of the Howard line, and as he is known to be a gentleman who accomplishes what he undertakes, those who build their hopes upon early completion of the road will not be disappointed.[5]

Despite such high hopes, controversy immediately centered on the route through Webster Groves. Residents were "up in arms" about the proposed route from Old Orchard through Webster Groves on Lockwood Avenue, "a most beautiful thoroughfare and the pride of both municipalities."[6]

The residents of Webster Grove who lived in the vicinity of Lockwood Avenue, in an effort to maintain its beauty, petitioned the County Court to allow the St. Louis and Meramec River Railroad Company to use iron center poles between its tracks on

---

[3]"And Still Another," SLCW, 1 November 1895, p. 4.
[4]Five cents from Kirkwood and Webster Groves to Maplewood and 5 cents from Maplewood to St. Louis.
[5]SLCW, 22 November 1895.
[6]SLCW, 10 January 1896, p. 8.

Lockwood Avenue, instead of wooden poles erected on the sides of the street. The court on March 16th, granted their wish with the requirement that the railroad company keep Lockwood Avenue lighted at night so the poles could be seen. A week later the provision was amended by the court to be more specific:

> ...the said railroad company shall maintain at least twelve electric lights of at least 20 candle power between the point where said railroad enters upon said Lockwood Avenue east of the Bompart Road, and the western end of said Lockwood avenue where it runs into Jefferson Barracks Road.[7]

The St. Louis and Suburban Railroad had taken control of the Howard Line by March 1896. Forty new cars were being built by a St. Louis car manufacturing plant for the new company. The cars were reported to be the largest, finest, costliest and fastest in the country, having wide aisles, 5 foot platforms, capacious seats, and two 50 horsepower G.E. 1200 electric motors per car. The *Watchman* reporter continued:

> Although the cars are intended for the use of the Manchester Road Electric Railway Company, the patrons of the St. Louis and Suburban Railroad can make use of them as the cars will run from Sixth and Locust streets over the Suburban tracks to Morgan and Sarah streets, where the cars will go south on Sarah street to Manchester road.... the Manchester road electric will be ready for business by April 15. That is the road will be completed to Webster... By placing forty additional cars the people living along the Suburban will have an elegant and fast service, as a car will leave every two minutes and move swiftly.[8]

Due to quick action from county commissioners appointed to assess damages in requested condemnation hearings for right-of-way between the city limits and Webster Groves, 45 days were shaved from earlier projections for completion to Webster Groves. However, the projected date of completion to Kirkwood remained the same.[9]

In the Spring of 1896, a number of construction related suits were brought against the St. Louis and Meramec River Railroad. A Mr. Dolan complained that the railroad was set too high in front of his house. The railroad company lowered one of the tracks which was agreeable to Dolan who then settled with the company with no further complaint. About the same time a Webster resident, Mrs. Reber, filed suit because the road was not properly graded on Lockwood avenue. The Circuit Court ruled against Mrs. Reber's claim. Despite the court's support for the company in some issues, in others it required the railroad to revise its construction where it did not meet the terms of the franchise agreement. Due to complaints about how the company was grading the roads it encountered, the County Court requested grade profiles and maps from the company.

---

[7] "County Court Orders, 23 March, 1896," <u>Franchises of United Railways...</u> (1913) p. 782, in MOT.
[8] "The Manchester Electric Line," SLCW, 6 March 1896.
[9] Ibid.

On March 30, 1896, the Court authorized the company to proceed with its construction on public roads with the requirement that it change the established grade of the roads to conform to the newly approved profiles.[10] Such construction challenges were minor compared to the monumental task facing the construction contractor, the Edgebrook Bridge.

Edgebrook Bridge

A major obstacle to the construction of the Howard line was located between Webster Groves and Maplewood. A long bridge had to be built above Deer Creek, a tributary of the River Des Peres, and above the right-of-way of the Missouri Pacific main line. The project required "some skillful engineering" as the street railroad was not allowed to touch the right-of-way.[11] The Kohen Iron Works Company of Detroit, Michigan was engaged as the bridge builder.

By March 20th, the St. Louis and Meramec River "electric railway" double tracks were laid to Big Bend road, three-quarters of a mile east of the Edgebrook bridge,[12] and the work on the bridge was being pushed along with "great rapidity." The piers and columns were completed, and the steel roadway was being laid.[13] Nearly 400 tons of steel were used in the construction of the bridge.

The Edgebrook bridge was a monumental engineering task at the time. Hyde's 1899 *Encyclopedia of the History of St. Louis* Street Railways section described the "$50,000 viaduct" as being "a thousand feet from end to end" which established "a record in steel railway construction."[14]

The 903 foot long bridge ran from Bartold Avenue on the Maplewood side, spanned a ravine, Deer Creek, and the Missouri Pacific tracks and then connected with land near Marshall Avenue on the Webster Groves side. Hyde's description indicated that the company's initial estimates for completion of the 60 foot high steel bridge, which were reported as $35,000,[15] were $15,000 under the eventual cost. The bridge with its "handsome six foot railing on either side" was "tested at 720,000 pounds."[16]

---

[10] Franchises of United Railways, p. 784.

[11] "Kirkwood," SLCW, 6 March 1896.

[12] Though called by many, "the Edgebrook trestle," the Edgebrook bridge was not a "trestle." It was a multi-span steel truss bridge with a through truss over the Missouri Pacific tracks and under deck trusses from there to the Webster end.

[13] SLCW, 20 March 1896, p. 8.

[14] Hyde, (1899). "Street Railways," Encyclopedia of the History of St. Louis, vol. 4, p. 2160.

[15] "The Manchester Road Electric Line," SLCW, 6 March 1896.

[16] Official Souvenir ..Convention of the American Street Railway Association, (1896) p. 44.

KING TROLLEY: ST. LOUIS AND MERAMEC RIVER RAILROAD ARRIVES

A dangerous moment occurred on a nearby wooden trestle at Edgebrook in 1904. While a cut was being blasted for the Terminal Belt Line during its construction, an extra large blast caused an upheaval of earth and rock which covered the Manchester streetcar tracks. The trestle was nearly destroyed when the pilings supporting it were damaged by the blast.

The *Watchman* reported on the damage to the "Edgebrook trestle," causing some to mistakenly believe the Edgebrook bridge was unsafe. The two section wooden Edgebrook trestle was constructed east of Bartold Avenue, about a half mile northeast of the Edgebrook bridge. The south section was so badly damaged by the blast that the superstructure was hanging to the end supports and had sagged five feet. The other section was held in place by the earth, but was so weakened that motormen made no attempt to run their cars over it. Until it could be rebuilt, passengers were compelled to get off the streetcars and walk across to board streetcars on the opposite side.[17]

The Edgebrook bridge long outlived the St. Louis and Meramec River Railroad. In fact, it outlived St. Louis streetcar travel. When the Manchester streetcar lines were closed in 1949, the bridge was modified and used for bus operation. It was still in use long after streetcars stopped serving Webster Groves and Kirkwood. The Edgebrook bridge was closed in 1968 and torn down in December 1974. The paving on the right-of-way that led from the bridge to Summit Avenue was removed and covered with dirt in 1980 in a $50,000 beautification project that made the stretch part of Webster Groves' Deer Creek Park. Today, unless one knows where to look, it is nearly impossible to tell where the "world's longest steel streetcar bridge" once stood.

******

A St. Louis portion of the "Manchester Road Extension" was opened to the public on May 7, 1896, with six cars operating from the intersection of Sarah Street to Clifton Heights. The *Watchman* reported that cars would be running as far as Maplewood by the 10th of May with intervals of 10 minutes between cars. Streetcar service to Webster Groves was still reported to be two weeks away.[18]

Delays occurred, so two weeks later, on May 22nd, the paper reported that the residents of Webster Groves were "rejoicing" that the "Manchester Electric road" would start service to Tuxedo and Webster Groves in 9 days.[19]

Completion of construction to Lockwood Avenue took longer than expected. By June 1896, the new street railroad had reached northeastern Webster Groves, providing the town with its second streetcar connection to St. Louis. Old Orchard's *Watchman* correspondent was complimentary when discussing the "fine road given to Webster

---

[17] Dynamite Wrecks Belt Line Trestle. Meramec Highlands and Kirkwood Cars Blocked by Accident at Edgebrook," SLCW, 15 April 1904.

[18] SLCW, 8 May 1896.

[19] SLCW, 22 May 1896, p. 8.

Groves" on Lockwood Avenue by the Manchester line. The correspondent also expressed a number of misgivings about the new line's service:

> We are glad to have the new electric road through our town. The cars are welcome, and we ought not complain, perhaps, but it does seem with a double track road, it is absolutely child's play to transfer to other cars at Sutton or Sarah street. We can make allowances for slow time until the wires, etc. are completed, but there is no sense in making passengers "change cars for downtown." Again Sunday being a day for sightseers, the cars ran only every twenty minutes, and crowded at that… With ladies standing up, when it could be easily averted, seems to me a fair way to avoid traveling on such a line. We hope it is temporary, but at all events, do away with this abominable, everlasting transfer business.[20]

The correspondent also opined that despite the number of visitors that came out to "our beautiful suburb" on the electric line, Webster Groves would not boom until accommodations were provided.[21] Stations and shelters had not yet been completed.

The new line experienced occasional difficulties until the motormen learned the dangerous curves, hills, and crossings. On June 14th, a car sped down a steep incline about a mile east of Webster Groves, and wrecked against a sharp curve at the bottom of the hill. Four ladies and one man were "severely injured" in the car filled with passengers. The cause of the accident was attributed to a defective brake.[22]

By June 26th, the line was completed to Jackson Park, about half a mile west of Webster Groves. However, a week later, the line still was not operating to the "new park, or picnic grounds," but was expected "in a day or so."[23] Finally, on July 10th, the *Watchman* announced that the Jackson Park Resort was to open the next day. The resort was described as a "temperance resort" and was considered to be the terminus of the "Lockwood Avenue Road."[24] Service on Lockwood had started prior to the resort's opening, cars running every five minutes on Sundays. On July 13th, the cars were scheduled to run 10 minutes apart on weekdays.[25]

The opening of the new line brought danger to the streets of Webster Groves. Within two weeks, two men had been killed in accidents on the line. The July 10th *Watchman* reported the death of Herman Kramer, an employee of the Polar Wave Ice Company, at a spot, "not far from where Harry Newbold was killed last week."[26]

---

[20]"Old Orchard," SLCW, 12 June 1896, p. 1.
[21]Ibid.
[22]"Old Orchard," SLCW, 19 June 1896, p. 8.
[23]"Webster Groves," SLCW, 5 July 1896.
[24]"Webster Groves," SLCW, 10 July 1896.
[25]Ibid.
[26]SLCW, 10 July 1896, p. 8.

Kramer was struck by Manchester car #16 and died of injuries and accompanying shock. The railroad was held blameless by the coroner's investigation.

A third accident quickly occurred. Jacob Giardina,[27] who had been visiting his brother, was standing on the tracks at Howard's Station[28] waiting for an eastbound Webster electric car at ten o'clock in the evening. While watching the westbound car take on passengers, he failed to notice the approach of the east-bound car, was struck and knocked under the car. When rescued from under the car, he was unconscious with scalp lacerations and a mangled right leg which later required amputation. Giardina sued for damages but was found negligent in relying solely on the sound of the gong to tell if streetcar was coming from the opposite direction. He could have easily looked to see if it was safe to stand on the tracks or to cross the tracks. The streetcar crew was found not to have properly sounded the gong, but no damages were awarded. Giardina appealed. The case was heard in front of the Missouri Supreme Court on December 22, 1904. The original ruling in favor of the St. Louis and Meramec River Railroad was upheld by the high court. It found that the plaintiff was negligent, so the company was not held accountable for his injuries.[29]

Work remained to be completed on the new line. In July, John Bellairs, a Webster Groves contractor, received the contract from the "Suburban electric line" for building the depots and platforms on the Webster division of the street railroad from Webster Groves to Sutton (Maplewood).[30] The Old Orchard correspondent would soon have her "accommodations."

Residents in Kirkwood closely followed the progress of the new line. Among them was William Essex who in July wrote, "The Suburban Trolley which comes out by Tuxedo and Webster is double track and well built, runs now as far as the Jackson road which crosses the Missouri Pacific this side of Webster."[31]

Deterred by a crossing of the Missouri Pacific Railroad west of Webster Groves, a shortage of ready cash, and a lack of agreement with city fathers about a route through Kirkwood, the St. Louis and Meramec River Railroad requested and was granted a time extension. It was given until August 14, 1897, to complete the line to Kirkwood.[32]

It wasn't long before the Old Orchard correspondent aired more complaints about the operation of the new line. She wrote:

---

[27]"Another Railroad Accident," SLCW, 10 July 1896, p. 8. Giardina's name was misspelled *Gardena*.

[28]Named for the nearby Evans and Howard brick yard a few blocks west of Kingshighway. The car line occupied the south side of Manchester Avenue immediately adjacent to the Missouri Pacific right-of-way.

[29]"Giardina v. St. Louis and Meramec River Railroad Company," Reports... Supreme Court of Missouri, (October Term, 1904) Vol. 185, pp. 330-335, Columbia: Stevens.

[30]SLCW, 10 July 1896. Perhaps the depots and platforms were the missing accommodations wished for by the Old Orchard correspondent on the 12th of June.

[31]Essex to Byars, 21 July 1896, Byars papers, MHS.

[32]Franchises of United Railways.., (1913) p. 774.

KING TROLLEY: ST. LOUIS AND MERAMEC RIVER RAILROAD ARRIVES

> The Meramec River Electric R. R. will soon have to put on more cars. It is almost impossible to obtain a seat at any time. Why not run all the cars through to Jackson Park during the week, as they do on Sunday?[33]

Steam rail traffic was immediately hurt as a result of the arrival of the Manchester line in Webster Groves. The *Webster Times* reported, "The Missouri Pacific has taken off 10 passenger cars daily; as a result, an avalanche of travel has set to our two electric lines… passenger travel by steam between Webster and St. Louis is well nigh stopped."[34]

Despite successful passenger traffic, the editor indicated that an express car on the Meramec River road would, "do a big business and would be greatly appreciated by Webster Groves people."[35]

In October 1896, the Street Railway Association convention "Official Souvenir" publication reported on the progress of the St. Louis and Meramec River Railroad:

> In the spring of 1896 the St. Louis and Meramec River Road was opened for traffic as far as Webster Groves. This company was chartered in 1894,[36] and is operated by the Suburban Company, whose line track it joins at Sarah street, about three and a half miles from the down-town terminus. It has eighteen miles of electric track in operation or authorized. Forty motor cars were especially built for the road which is equipped in the highest style, and is operated in the county as well as in the city with very full service at short intervals. This branch of the Suburban Road, as it is generally regarded, runs through some of the most populous residence sections of the southwestern portions of the twentieth ward, including many subdivisions hitherto obtained entirely on suburban service on steam railways.[37]

The publication reported the line had the first double track in St. Louis County and that it was shortly to be extended several miles further into the county (to Kirkwood) from Webster Groves.

In November 1896, a rumored consolidation of the Suburban with the Southern Electric lines was reported. With the consolidation, a rider would be able to ride 26 miles from Florissant to Jefferson Barracks. The Webster Groves division of the Suburban was reported to be part of the deal. As a result of the rumors, the reporter envisioned a unified transit system:

---

[33]"Old Orchard," SLCW, 1 September 1896.

[34]Webster Times, 5 September 1896.

[35]Ibid.

[36]The 1894 charter date is questionable since no change in franchise was requested by the company from County Court until 1895. The date may be for a charter from the state of Missouri.

[37]American Street Railway Association, Official Souvenir, (1896) p. 44.

It is only a question of time, we think, when a system of transfers will be inaugurated which will embrace all the lines in the city and their country extensions as well, and it will prove, we think as great a benefit to the companies as to their patrons.[38]

Though the rumor was wrong, the reporter was correct. By 1907, one could transfer to most lines in the St. Louis area. However, many transfers still required payment of a separate fare.

A major barrier to the St. Louis and Meramec River Railroad's connection with Kirkwood was removed on June 1, 1897, by Webster Groves Ordinance No. 65. It vacated part of Jackson Road and authorized the company to operate a double track railroad on a new street, upon its completion. The new street section would provide a crossing at least forty feet wide *under* the tracks of the Missouri Pacific Railroad approximately 450 feet south of the then existing Jackson Road crossing. The ordinance allowed the company to construct and operate its railroad on the new street from the terminus of the tracks at the end of Lockwood "southwardly and westwardly, under the said Missouri Pacific Railroad" to a point about 120 feet west of the railroad's tracks.[39]

On November 30th, 1897, the St. Louis and Meramec River Railroad suffered a minor setback, when the County Court found the company to be in violation of its franchise. It had placed its trolley poles less than 25 feet from the center of Manchester Road. The company was ordered to remove and reset the poles, located in Maplewood from Sutton Road to the St. Louis city limits. The company attorney appeared in court and agreed that the railroad would conform to the terms of the franchise and move its poles so that they would no longer impede traffic.[40]

Webster Groves residents read with anticipation an item in the December 18th *Watchman* which indicated that two new mail cars were in the course of construction and were to be put into commission on the St. Louis and Meramec River extension of the Suburban on January 1, 1897.[41] However, it wasn't until January 25th that a mail car was run over the Suburban tracks to Sarah Street where it was "taken up" by the St. Louis and Meramec River Railroad and sent via Maplewood to Webster Groves.[42]

During 1897, most of the press attention was focused on the extension of the electric railroad to Kirkwood. In 1898, the line again became a hot topic of conversation and controversy in Webster Groves. An issue was brewing as to whether the town should pay to have Lockwood Avenue widened. A resident expressed both his frustrations from the effects of the electric road on Lockwood as well as his appreciation for the service provided, in a letter to the editor printed in the February 26, 1898 *Webster Times*.

---

[38]"Street Car Consolidation," SLCW, 27 November 1896. p. 4.

[39] "Webster Groves Ordinances," Franchises of United Railways.., (1913) pp. 774-775.

[40]SLCW, 11 December 1896, p. 8.

[41]SLCW, 18 December 1896, p. 8.

[42]SLCW, 29 January 1897.

… the road has not been widened and is still only thirty feet wide, 20 feet of that occupied by the Suburban electric road… the Suburban road has got our street. I don't know if we could oust them if we wanted to — I like to see the cars go by. It is no annoyance to me. I like the convenience and cheapness of riding thereon… The black trolley posts occupy the middle of the street, the unsightly telephone poles occupy the sides, making it dangerous for horses and vehicles. Put the wires underground. Remove the posts and poles, put the tracks closer together, macadamize the street from gutter to gutter and that would leave a road of fifteen feet wide on each side of the railroad tracks without poles or posts to dodge or run against.[43]

On a lighter note, an eerie article by Maxwell Hewitt was found starting on the front page of the April 2, 1898 *Webster Times* and concluding in the next week's issue. It had the feel of fiction, yet it contained many of the details of a winter ride on a St. Louis and Meramec River Railroad owl car and included mention of an actual notable of the area, Webster's Marshal Nace.

THE SPECTER PASSENGER [44]

It was a drizzly, disagreeable night, the whimsical weather seeming to vacillate between rain and sleet and snow, driven along the sloppy street by a cold river wind.

After waiting in vain under a dripping umbrella for a Kirkwood car, I determined to board the first Suburban car which passed, it happened to be a Benton,[45] and, for the lateness of the hour, was tolerably well filled with passengers. The electric lights burned dim and the electric heaters[46] were equally as generous; all the passengers seemed cross, making the inside conditions little better than the raging storm without. I dropped into a seat about the center of the car, the other end of which was occupied by a pious looking corpulent old gentleman who blew his nose hard occasionally and once or twice tried to engage me in conversation.

I was not in the mood however and only answered him in monosyllables, attempting the while to read an evening paper. As not unfrequently happens while taking a long streetcar ride, I fell fast asleep. At Boyle avenue, I was awakened by my seatmate trying to get out and sat up to notice that only a few of my fellow passengers remained. These dropped off as the car splashed

---

[43]"Lockwood Avenue Extension," Webster Times, 26 February 1898.

[44]Maxwell Hewitt, "The Specter Passenger," Webster Times, 2 April and 9 April 1898.

[45]Benton cars ran no further west than the Maplewood loop at Sutton.

[46]While the Houseman line used stoves to heat its cars, the new Suburban cars featured electric heaters, apparently inadequate for the job of warming the cars.

through the mud along Manchester road and by the time Sutton avenue was reached, I was the only passenger.

I found a nice fire going at the station and after thawing out and starting a good cigar, began to forgive the world for its past hard treatment and have a softened feeling in my heart for all my fellow mortals.

The last Kirkwood car soon hove in sight around the corner and I walked out upon the platform in a considerably better state of mind than when I arrived. As the car slowed up I noticed but a single passenger. The face gazing out through the rain bespattered window struck me as being particularly beautiful; even in the brief time in passing from the station to the car, I noticed her large expressive eyes, even features though somewhat prominent, her lustrous black hair falling upon a pair of shapely shoulders which were covered in a light gray jacket, fur tipped, and a boa of the same color around her neck. A pair of ear rings depended from her delicately lobed ears, while a hat extravagantly covered with ostrich plumes adorned her head. In spite of the general air of aristocracy about the young lady there was an expression of undenyable sadness and evidence of recent weeping which left its impression upon me. I made up my mind to take an unobserved seat and while away the tedium of the remaining ride by studying the girl and speculating on her probable identity. "Well, how's everything," I idly asked of the conductor dropping the fare into his outstretched hand, and waiting on the platform to finish my cigar.

"Cold and lonesome," responded the man of brass and blue giving the register rope a vigorous pull. "This is a special car for you tonight." I looked at him wonderingly but said nothing. I finished my cigar and went inside; the car was just then turning off Flora avenue and the trolley slipping, filled the car with darkness a moment or two. After a few flashes however as the conductor wildly probed for the trolley wire, light was restored and the car went bounding on through the strip of woodland just off the Big Bend road, I looked and nothing could have been more complete than my surprise to see that I was the only passenger in the car.

I rubbed my eyes and gazed harder. There is no insanity in our family and none of us have been immoderate devotees of the cup that queers but I confess myself feeling rather nervous.

The conductor entered just then.
"Has this car stopped since leaving the Sutton ave. station?" I asked.

"It has not," replied the conductor.

"Then why did that young lady get off?"

"What young lady?"

"Why the one who sat there with dark hair, large eyes, gray jacket, boa and ostrich feathered hat?"

"Why there was such a lady on the car tonight, and sat in that seat. Sad looking woman; was crying part of the time. She got off at Prather avenue."

"Impossible," I cried. "I saw her when the car stopped at Sutton avenue."

The conductor looked at me queerly and I imagined he was thinking "bughouse." I subsided and asked no more questions but could not get the strange occurrence out of my mind. Who was the beautiful young woman? What was her trouble? And why was her ghost permitted to ride around on owl cars while she was still in the land of the living? And why above all was it sent to torment me?

The car by this time had switched around on Lockwood avenue and determining to shake off the uncanny fascination I arose, walked out on the platform, and lit a fresh cigar. The conductor still eyed me curiously but I engaged him on other topics, and to my gratification and vain glory I was soon getting control of my wits again.

At Gore avenue I left the car and ran plumb into the arms of Marshal Nace.

"What was the matter with the woman?" he asked me bluntly.

"What woman?" I gasped and instantly felt myself going back into that half hypnotic fantastical state.

"Why the lady in the car with the gray jacket and the ostrich plumed hat."

"With large eyes and dark hair, handsome features?"

"Yes."

"Then you saw her too?"

"Too!" echoed the officer, "why what was the matter with her?"

"Oh nothing," I replied recovering myself, "you see there wasn't any lady there; you've been dr---," but Nace raised his club and I did not dare to finish.

"Its deuced queer anyway," I said to myself as I picked my way through the muddy street, and to this day I have not been able to forget that midnight owl car ride or solve the mystery of the specter passenger.

*****

Perhaps the specter story was an April Fool's joke, or it may have been a tweaking of Marshal Nace. Either way, it caused some comment among the *Webster Times'* readers while giving today's reader the feel of a ride on the owl car.

Local papers as well as city papers found streetcar accidents of be of particular interest to its readers. Streetcar accidents often became front page headlines. Streetcar travel was not without hazards. On September 19th, the *Webster Times* reported a near fatal accident, caused by "an attempt to manage a streetcar, a fighting stallion and a quart of Old Rye."[47] A twenty-three year old man was driving along Lockwood Avenue near the Episcopal Church. According to the motorman, the intoxicated young man drove directly in front of the car. His horse was struck throwing it back on top of the young man, causing him severe internal injuries. The horse was so injured that it had to be killed. No mention was made of injuries to the streetcar riders, though they were shaken up by the event.

Headlines were especially lurid when a child was injured or killed. The Sunday April 11, 1898 edition of the *St. Louis Post-Dispatch* featured an illustration of a Suburban car running down a "flaxen haired" little girl. The headlines read, "UNDER CRUEL CAR WHEELS, Life Crushed Out of Little Florence Dierking. FIRST PICKED UP BY THE FENDER. THEN ROLLED OFF AND WAS KILLED..."[48]

Accidents were also big news in the Webster Groves' local paper and in the county paper. A 1898 edition of the *County Watchman* described an all too common type of accident involving a horse drawn cart:

> Last Saturday night a car on the Kirkwood electric line ran into a heavily loaded wagon on Lockwood Avenue, Webster Groves, driven by Mr. Roberts the expressman of that town, killing one of his horses and badly damaging his wagon. Roberts himself was badly bruised up.[49]

On July 23, 1898, an accident at Lockwood and Plant avenues resulted in a demolished seed company wagon, a dead horse, and a driver who miraculously escaped with only minor sprains. The *Webster Times* reporter pointedly blamed the street railway for the accident:

---

[47]"Injured by a Streetcar," Webster Times, 19 September 1896, p. 4.
[48]"Under Cruel Car Wheels," PD, 11 April 1898.
[49]SLCW, 6 May 1898.

The car was running through Webster at its highest speed, as usual, and the motorman was not ringing his gong, which is also usual.[50]

On the editorial page that day, the paper joined the political fray about the need to widen Lockwood for safety. The editor was free with his criticism of the operation of the St. Louis and Meramec River Railroad:

> … this thoroughfare easily accommodated the traffic until the county court gave 20 feet out of the center of the street to the electric railroad; today it can accommodate nothing. The 20 feet is gone; it can not be regained; there is but one remedy: widen the avenue ten feet on each side. Until this is done accidents are inevitable; they will increase as traffic increases. Already vehicles have been smashed, and horses killed; so far no human life has been lost… Another protection against accident is required. Reasonable diligence on the part of the railroad company is due the public. The carelessness of the motormen is to blame for more than one collision. Steps should be taken to end this dangerous recklessness and incapacity.[51]

A week later, the editor was still incensed about the speed of the streetcars in Webster Groves. A town board meeting that evening was scheduled to discuss the issue and to allow the company officers to present their views on the subject. The editor was sure the railroad would not advise the board to, "hamper them with restrictions and limitations upon the running of their road,"[52] which would cut into their profit. He was more concerned that some aldermen felt that since they had not received formal petitions or formal protests, that the issue was not of real concern to the populace:

> …formal protest there may not have been, but protests there have been, protests long and loud. What petition is necessary beyond the lengthy and growing list of accidents on Lockwood avenue? Smashed carriages, lame and crippled men, women and children are petition enough. What protest could be louder than that which filled the neighborhood of Plant and Lockwood Avenues for three days last week, the protest of a dead and decaying horse, whose stench was surely strong enough and formal enough to rouse the Board from its lethargy… If it is truly their idea that accidents, collisions and dead and stinking animals delight the souls of Webster's citizens; if it is believed that a constant menace to the life of children, to all pedestrians and all who drive is a satisfaction and joy to Webster, let that illusion be dispelled. Now is the time for Webster to air its views on this subject. The speed of streetcars must be limited by ordinance, and incidentally the same ordinance might provide that the motormen must ring their bells before every crossing.[53]

---

[50]"Collision on Electric Railroad," Webster Times, 23 July 1898.

[51]Webster Times, 23 July 1898.

[52]Webster Times, 30 July 1898.

[53]Ibid.

KING TROLLEY: ST. LOUIS AND MERAMEC RIVER RAILROAD ARRIVES

The campaign to force the aldermen to enact an ordinance governing the speed of streetcars in Webster Groves culminated successfully on August 31, 1898. The aldermen passed Ordinance No. 110 which specified that engines, cars and trains could not be lawfully run at a speed greater than fifteen miles per hour "upon and along" Lockwood Avenue and Shady Avenue. It also ordered that violation of the provisions of the ordinance would be considered a misdemeanor and imposed a penalty, if convicted, of not less than $25 and not more than $200.[54] Despite the ordinance, accidents were not eliminated. In November 1900, Miss Charlotte Petty, a vegetable vendor from Glencoe, Missouri, was driving along Plant Avenue in Webster Groves with her brother when their wagon was struck by a Suburban car, throwing them both "violently" to the ground and injuring them "seriously."[55] Miss Petty filed a $20,000 complaint against the St. Louis and Meramec River Railroad for injuries sustained in the accident.

The presence of the streetcar in front of a business could mean the difference between success or failure. It also opened up new possibilities such as the one discussed in an October 1, 1898 editorial in the *Webster Times*.

> There has been some talk of having a course of lectures this winter. Entertainments here can draw from the people all along the electric line from Maplewood to Kirkwood, for the cars stop in front of the hall and the fare is only five cents. The Bristol Music Hall is large enough to hold enough people to pay for first class talent… If a committee will take hold of the matter and will furnish, say a course of five entertainments for two dollars, good talent can be secured if done promptly.[56]

Despite accidents and other difficulties caused by the St. Louis and Meramec River division of the St. Louis and Suburban Railroad, Webster Groves town officials had a more amicable relationship with the line than did Kirkwood's government officials. Litigation between Kirkwood and the electric railways had become commonplace.

---

[54]"Webster Groves Ordinances," Franchises of United Transit Companies, (1913) p. 1145.
[55]SLCW, 27 November 1900.
[56]Webster Times, 1 October 1898.

8-1. Illustration in the April 11, 1898 *Post-Dispatch* showing a Suburban car with a Meramec Highlands connection running down a small child.

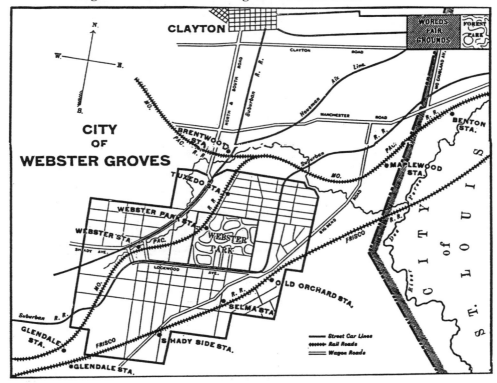

8-2. 1903-1904 inset from Map 6 of the Webster Park Realty Company shows both electric railway routes from the Worlds Fair grounds through Webster Groves.

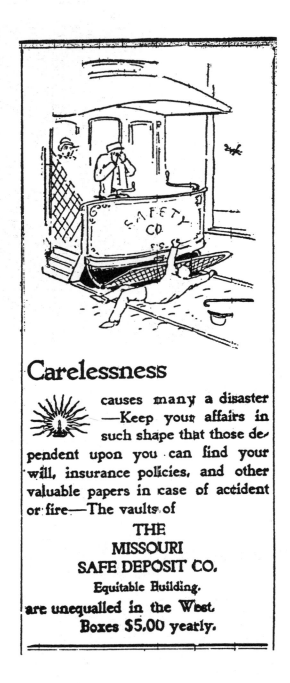

8-3. In 1897, the streetcar was a pervasive image used in advertising. This ad from the November 19, 1897 *St. Louis County Watchman* played on the fears caused by frequent streetcar accidents.

8-4. Construction of the Edgebrook bridge pictured in the 1896 Street Railway Association national convention souvenir booklet. At the time the 903 foot long bridge was the longest street railway bridge in the world. Photograph from the Charles Hamman collection.

8-5. Photograph from the 1940s shows the Edgebrook bridge still in use, no longer featuring wooden clad cars but used primarily by sleek modern steel PCC cars. The bridge remained in use by streetcars until the Manchester lines shut down in 1949. Photograph by Wayne Leeman.

Chapter 9

ST. LOUIS AND SUBURBAN ARRIVES IN KIRKWOOD

Kirkwood residents and officials were anxious to begin the Suburban service enjoyed by Webster Groves, their rival to the east. Frequent rumors of routes and route changes were reported and were a topic of much discussion by residents. For example, in the December 11, 1896 *Watchman*, the Kirkwood correspondent reported a rumored and later rejected route of the St. Louis and Meramec River Railroad through Kirkwood:

> Rumors have been frequent during the past week of the near approach of the Webster electric line. The president and attorney of the road were in Kirkwood trying to arrange right of way through Woodlawn. The route suggested was along Jackson road, and between the Forsyth and Morris homes, just back of Mrs. Laura Bodley's[1]

One Kirkwood resident, a Mr. Meyers, offered to give $2500 to the new road, and also offered to sacrifice a "beautiful row of trees" to make room for the roadway.[2]

In January, according to the *Watchman*, another route was accepted by the town council which granted a permit to the St. Louis and Suburban to enter Kirkwood on Adams Avenue to Taylor, lay tracks on Taylor to Jefferson Avenue to Harrison and then cross the Missouri-Pacific tracks by bridge. After five years, the company would pay Kirkwood $250 per year.[3] That route, while closer to the route eventually approved, was also rejected. A week later the *Watchman* backtracked, indicating that the Kirkwood council was still considering "right of way" without a decision having been reached.[4]

Residents of Adams Avenue were upset that they would lose their carriage road if a double track railroad was built down the center of their quiet street. Their opposition was noted in a piece in the *St. Louis Republic* in the first week of January 1897.

---

[1]"Kirkwood," SLCW, 11 December 1896.
[2]Ibid.
[3]"Kirkwood," SLCW, 8 January 1897.
[4]"Kirkwood," SLCW, 15 January 1897, p. 1.

KING TROLLEY: ST. LOUIS AND SUBURBAN ARRIVES IN KIRKWOOD

It characterized the issue as turning Kirkwoodians against each other. That claim in turn caused the Kirkwood *Watchman* correspondent to take issue with the piece:

> The sensational column in the "Republic" of last week, as to the animosities stirred in Kirkwood by the prospective entrance of the Webster electric railroad was a surprise to our citizens as none of them knew of "church being arrayed against church" and "neighbor against neighbor." On the contrary only good feelings and harmony exist - not even the Civil War could make strife here.[5]

The correspondent was either naive or ingenuous. The minutes of the town board made it very clear that the Adams Avenue route proposal was a hot issue. Perhaps because of the controversy, wishful thinking gave rise to report in the March 5th *Watchman*.

> It is rumored that from Glendale to the Highlands, the Suburban electric road has leased the Houseman track and will lay a second track and come in that way instead of Adams Avenue. It is a round about way to the city.[6]

During the debate on the route, the desire for the second connection to the city was satisfied for some by creative travel arrangements. The Kirkwood *Watchman* correspondent reported that a large group of Kirkwood residents attended the Damrosch Opera in the city, reaching home at its close via the Webster electric car to Rock Hill Road and then taking the Kirkwood car on the nearby Meramec Scenic Railway (the Houseman line) into Kirkwood.[7]

A route was eventually agreed upon after months of speculation and negotiation. Kirkwood ordinance 238 which was passed on May 21, 1897, governed operation of the Suburban line in Kirkwood. It stated in part:

> Authority is hereby given to the St. Louis and Meramec River Railroad Company… to construct, maintain and operate an electric railroad for the transportation of passengers, on, along, over and upon the following route within the Town of Kirkwood…[8]

---

[5]Ibid.
[6]"Kirkwood," SLCW, 5 March 1897, p. 2.
[7]"Kirkwood," SLCW, 26 February 1897.
[8]Minutes of the Kirkwood Town Board, pp. 151 to 169, Kirkwood City Hall, 21 May 1897.

KING TROLLEY: ST. LOUIS AND SUBURBAN ARRIVES IN KIRKWOOD

The route entered Kirkwood beginning in the center line of Woodlawn Avenue east of the property of Mrs. George Gill, then proceeded westwardly with a double track through Mrs. Gill's property to the east end of the center line of Adams Avenue. It then proceeded westwardly along Adams Avenue to Fillmore Avenue; then northwardly with a single track in the center of the street to Washington Avenue, then westwardly along Washington Avenue. At Washington Avenue, the company was given permission to connect with and to operate its cars on the tracks and route maintained by the St. Louis and Kirkwood Railroad - west on Washington to Clay, south on Clay to Woodbine Avenue, then west on Woodbine to the southwestern limits of Kirkwood. A new eastbound single track was granted on Adams from Clay to Fillmore. The ordinance stipulated that if the tracks of the St. Louis and Kirkwood Railroad Company were to be discontinued either by ouster of the Town of Kirkwood or other reason, the St. Louis and Meramec River Railroad would be authorized to construct, maintain and operate a single track railroad over the previous St. Louis and Kirkwood route.

Though the new line represented competition to the St. Louis and Kirkwood Railroad, it also represented a benefit because the Kirkwood ordinance stipulated that any other street railroad using the St. Louis and Kirkwood tracks would provide reasonable compensation.

In order to prevent use of steam engines or horse drawn cars, the ordinance stipulated that streetcars must be operated by electricity, "either by storage battery, the conduit underground, or by overhead wire system."[9]

Before the St. Louis and Meramec River Railroad was allowed to begin construction through Kirkwood, it was required to provide town officials with a duplicate set of plats or maps of the roadway showing the course of the railway and profiles showing the grade of the roadbed. The maps were to show the radius of all curves, the location of switches, curves, turnouts, sidings, crossovers, and connections.

Special attention was given to construction on Adams Avenue. It was to be macadamized for a width of sixteen feet each way from the center of the tracks in a manner common to the construction of the macadamized streets in Kirkwood. The special attention paid to Adams Avenue was in part due to the vocal opposition of many of the Adams Avenue residents to the construction of the railroad down their quiet residential street. As a result of Kirkwood's continuing disputes with the St. Louis and Kirkwood Railroad, the ordinance included the stipulation that the line, "shall ever thereafter maintain in good condition and repair," the part of the street lying inside the rails and for two feet outside each rail.

---

[9]Ibid.

KING TROLLEY: ST. LOUIS AND SUBURBAN ARRIVES IN KIRKWOOD

In order to ensure a minimum of disruption of travel by its citizens during construction, no more than four blocks of a street could be torn up at one time in such a way so as to be withdrawn from public use. Nor were two successive crossings on the same street to be rendered unfit for travel by the construction. A six month time limit was imposed to encourage prompt completion of construction. The road was to be in full operation through Kirkwood by October 1897.

The fare was set at five cents for a continuous passage from any point on the line between the Sutton Avenue Station in Maplewood and the southwestern limits of Kirkwood. No more than five cents could be charged for passage from any point on the streetcar line between the eastern limits of Kirkwood and the Meramec Highlands. The total fare from any point in Kirkwood to the eastern terminus of the railroad at Sixth and Locust streets was not to exceed ten cents.

The St. Louis and Meramec River Railroad was required by Kirkwood ordinance #238 to run its cars every day of the year at "regular intervals not greater than thirty minutes apart" between the hours of 6 A.M. and 12 o' clock midnight. However, the town officials conceded that "accidental derangement of machinery" and extraordinary accidents or emergencies would not be deemed a violation of the ordinance.[10]

When a patron in Kirkwood hailed a car, the car was to be stopped so that the rear platform would be over a crosswalk. Persons signaling in a "proper and usual way" were to stand near a crosswalk on the right side of the car. They were expected to signal in time for the car to be stopped at the crosswalk.[11]

The streetcar's rate of speed within Kirkwood city limits was limited to ten miles per hour with the motorman required at all times to "keep a vigilant watch along the track ahead of his car for persons (with special vigilance for children) or vehicles upon the track." At the first appearance of danger, the motorman was required to stop the car "in the shortest time and space possible."[12]

The streetcars were to be equipped with "modern and approved fenders and brakes" as well as gongs or bells which were to be rung to give warning of the approach of the streetcar as it neared a crossing.[13]

---

[10]Minutes of the Kirkwood Town Board, pp. 151 to 169, Kirkwood City Hall, 21 May 1897.
[11]Ibid.
[12]Ibid.
[13]Ibid.

KING TROLLEY: ST. LOUIS AND SUBURBAN ARRIVES IN KIRKWOOD

After five years of operation, the St. Louis and Meramec River Railroad would be required to pay a $250.00 per year fee to the town treasury for the privilege of operating in Kirkwood. After ten years, the fee was to be increased to $500.00.

Any successor or assignee of the new line was to be held to the terms of the ordinance and to *any ordinances enacted at a later date*[14] by the town of Kirkwood for the purpose of governing street railroads.

Work was to begin within 60 days after the acceptance of the agreement by the company. Before the town clerk would accept the agreement, the company was required to file a bond in the sum of $10,000 to protect the town from loss as a result of "any wrongful act, negligence, or default" in the construction, equipment, and operation of the railroad within the town of Kirkwood.[15]

If the road or its successors "willfully and persistently" violated any provisions of the streetcar ordinance, the franchise was to be forfeited and the ordinance allowing the company to operate would be considered "null and void."[16] The ordinance was written for a duration of 50 years, unless sooner forfeited for cause. Little did the town fathers dream of the effect of the automobile and motor bus, that would make the streetcar an endangered species in less than 50 years.

For the life of the franchise, the St. Louis and Meramec River Railroad Company and its successors were considered to own the tracks over its route under a lawful franchise granted by the town of Kirkwood. As the owner, the company was expected to properly maintain the tracks. Even though the tracks were "owned" by the company, any other company granted a franchise to own and operate a street railroad in Kirkwood would have the right to run its cars on the St. Louis and Meramec River Railroad tracks upon payment of a reasonable compensation to the owners for use of the tracks.[17] If the two companies were unable to agree on the amount of compensation, each company was to appoint one man to meet with a representative of the Town Board. The Board would act as commissioners to set a reasonable compensation, and their decision would be final. Though stipulated, this provision of the ordinance was never invoked.

Following the agreement with Kirkwood, the St. Louis and Meramec River Railroad Company's attorney, James P. Dawson of Webster Groves, petitioned County Court to amend its franchise. The change to section 10, bringing the language of the

---

[14]Within a couple of years, the "later date" stipulation led to a bitter legal battle between the town and the company.

[15]Minutes of the Kirkwood Town Board, pp.151 to 169.

[16]Ibid.

[17]Ibid.

county franchise charter and the Kirkwood franchise into agreement, was approved by the court on March 1, 1897. The change read:

> … the railroad may charge 5 cents for a continuous passage between Kirkwood and Sutton Avenue and intermediate points, so long as the total fare between Kirkwood and the eastern terminus of said road at Sixth and Locust streets in the City of St. Louis shall not exceed 10 cents… [18]

Minor adjustments to Ordinance 238 were made early in June, resulting in a new ordinance, #240. The provisions of 238 and 240 were accepted by the St. Louis and Meramec River Railroad on June 3, 1897. That evening, the company officials presented proof of a $10,000 bond with the Lincoln Trust Company. As town clerk, J. G. Hawken, noted in the Kirkwood Town Board minutes, the company also: "presented map, plans and profiles - showing the construction of their roadway. The same were considered approved and ordered filed."[19]

The approval of the franchise was most distressing to residents of Adams Avenue. They had presented their concerns to the Town Board and had aired their concerns in neighborhood meetings. Though they were a prominent group of citizens, the Board elected to go with the lure of income for the town and the promise of growth and prosperity represented by the additional street rail link to St. Louis.

Litigation against the St. Louis and Meramec Railroad was implemented by numerous parties over the condition of the properties and roads as a result of the track construction. One such case was the damage suit of Mr. Andreas Boenecke who sued for $500 in damages for the condition in which his property was left after grading. On the witness stand he was unable to make the jury understand the damage, so the judge allowed the jury to go as a body on a streetcar and investigate the damage in person. After returning and several more hours of arguments, the jury was given the case. The July 9th *Watchman* reported the verdict "for the plaintiff for one cent and costs."[20]

By mid August, Adams was closed between Taylor and Webster Avenue (Kirkwood Road) for the laying of the eastbound track and a wye, "making a noisy corner of Clay and Adams avenue as 8 bumps - loud ones - are noticed by the passage of each car."[21]

---

[18]Records of County Court, 1 March 1897.

[19]Minutes of the Kirkwood Town Board, 3 June 1897.

[20]"An Accommodating Jury," SLCW, 9 July 1897, p. 1.

[21]"Kirkwood," SLCW, 20 August 1897. On Adams from Clay to Fillmore, the line was single track. Westbound Manchester cars ran on single track from Fillmore to Washington to Clay. Double track resumed on Clay south of Adams.

By the end of August, all the wires were up, causing the Kirkwood *Watchman* correspondent to comment, "By next week the Suburban will be making dust fly."[22] Indeed, Suburban cars were run to Meramec Highlands on the following Sunday, though none were run during the week to allow for completion of the construction work.[23] A crew of 26 men "worked all day steadily in the dust and heat on the Suburban Railroad on the 8th finishing the roadbed."[24]

By September 1897, most of the construction work through Kirkwood was completed. Adams Avenue up to that time had been a short street without through traffic. It ended a little past Dickson when traveling east. After the construction, though the St. Louis and Meramec River line continued on, the street was not extended. The double tracks crossed a creek on a trestle and connected with Lockwood at Park Avenue in Glendale. From Dickson to Sappington Road, the line was on private right of way. From Sappington to Berry Road, the double track line bordered the south side of Lockwood.

As the Suburban was built through Kirkwood, some of the enthusiasm for the project waned. Adams was "totally disfigured" by the heavy grade of the line, and residents along the route were "sore indeed."[25] When the cars began running on September 9th, the noise was "excessive" until the Suburban added rock to its roadbed. That was done between the 10th and the 17th when "quite a force of men distributed Macadam on the track."[26] Much to the displeasure of local tongue wagging WCTU[27] members, resident males used the streetcar lines to leave Kirkwood or Webster for the Highlands or the city to partake of "evil" spirits. A *Watchman* correspondent on September 10, 1897, disapprovingly sniffed:

> Within the past week four of our well known citizens have returned from the city helplessly intoxicated — a sad spectacle — two at a time on the electric cars. Where is their self respect thus to expose themselves?[28]

Tempers in the Adams Avenue area were as hot as the Indian Summer weather. The Kirkwood columnist noted on September 24th, "Most of the property on Adams avenue could be bought cheap, the owners feeling that since the street is transformed into a canal and its trees killed by cutting the roots, it is no longer desirable."[29]

---

[22]"Kirkwood," SLCW, 27 August 1897.

[23]"Meramec Highlands," SLCW, 3 September 1897.

[24]"Kirkwood," SLCW, 17 September 1897.

[25]"Kirkwood," SLCW, 10 September 1897.

[26]"Kirkwood," SLCW, 17 September 1897.

[27]Women's Christian Temperance Union.

[28]"Kirkwood," SLCW, 10 September 1897, p. 1.

[29]"Kirkwood," SLCW, 24 September 1897.

KING TROLLEY: ST. LOUIS AND SUBURBAN ARRIVES IN KIRKWOOD

Not only were the residents of the street bombarded with clanging bells and mechanical noise from the cars, noisy high spirited passengers filled the cars, especially on normally quiet weekends. "Sunday was a big day for the new electric line. Each car was full to overflowing, and Adams avenue resounded with noise."[30] Large crowds filled the cars on Sunday, September 12th, as riders came from the city through Kirkwood on their way to Meramec Highlands and the beaches of the Meramec River to escape the heat. The noise was not only from the new line as the correspondent noted: "Adams avenue is a noisy street of late. For 10 days the Salvation Army band was heard… two squealing pigs in pens, and the Mo. Pac and electric trains at all hours."[31]

Frustrations of the residents were lessened in October when the muddy Adams Avenue was covered with Meramec gravel from Valley Park. To their chagrin, Kirkwood residents learned that the electric railway also provided an avenue for con men to hit the towns along the route. Shortly after the new line opened, three men set up a fake 10 cent show for children in Kirkwood's Armory Hall. The con men used the streetcar as their getaway car, running from the Armory Hall to the electric car twenty minutes after the show began, knowing that they would soon be in trouble with the law.

For many of the younger residents and for their romantic elders, moonlight trips to the river on the new streetcar line were quite in vogue. An aura of romance imbued the streetcars, even during the day, when used by couples for courting or entertainment. The electric railroad offered ideal inexpensive transportation to cool rural picnic areas such as Creve Coeur Lake and Meramec Highlands. An afternoon on the Meramec River complete with boating and bathing enticed many couples to board the Manchester or the Kirkwood cars. The night cars were filled with dancers and those who wished to enjoy the moonlight and solitude in a secluded spot by the river. Many couples just enjoyed the long rides with the cool breezes on hot summer days.

Patience was not a virtue of some Kirkwood residents. Complaints were being aired less than two weeks after the beginning of operation, that the Suburban had not yet delivered on its promise of a mail car to serve Kirkwood. Because mail took so long by conventional means to get to the city, it was common practice to go to the streetcar line and ask a waiting rider to drop letters off at a city mailbox.[32]

---

[30]"Kirkwood," SLCW, 10 September 1897.
[31]"Kirkwood," SLCW, 24 September 1897.
[32]Kirkwood mail was handled on the Missouri Pacific before the advent of the Railway Post Office on the Manchester line.

KING TROLLEY: ST. LOUIS AND SUBURBAN ARRIVES IN KIRKWOOD

The Suburban, wishing to keep its employees busy and the public happy, put conductors and motormen to work cleaning streetcars during a 15 minute wait in Kirkwood. "They do it well," stated a Kirkwood correspondent in December, 1897.[33]

Express companies used the St. Louis and Meramec River railroad daily to provide package and freight service. "Cheap, prompt, and reliable delivery of all goods direct to residence or stores," was proclaimed by a frequently appearing Walton-Knost Express Company ad on the front pages of the *Webster Times* in April of 1898.[34] A rival express company's advertisement, located just above Walton-Knost's, indicated that Central Electric Express made "TWO DAILY DELIVERIES to all points on the St. Louis & Meramec and St. Louis & Suburban Ry's." Central Electric Express stated arrival times in Webster of 10:30 a. m. and 2:30 p. m. The express car departed one half hour after arrival. In Webster Groves, the company's office was located in Kalb's store on Gore Avenue. The Walton-Knost Express offered, "One delivery to St. Louis and Return Daily," leaving Webster at 8 a. m. and St. Louis at 1 p. m. It also provided delivery service to Kirkwood. In Webster, the company office was located in the Grove Pharmacy "next to the Post Office." The Kirkwood office was at Armentrout's store. Cost of delivery was 15 or 25 cents depending on the size of the item.[35]

A disastrous fire destroyed a number of businesses in downtown Kirkwood, due to a lack of water and inadequate equipment. It caused the town board to seriously consider a fire fighting proposal from the St. Louis Fire Department and the Manchester Division of the Suburban. Fire engines would be transported to Kirkwood on specially constructed streetcars. Fire department officials estimated that it would take 20 minutes for an engine to get to the scene of a fire in Kirkwood, once the alarm had been received. Because only cisterns were available as the source of water, the water supply would still be a major problem. Kirkwood rejected the proposal.

By July 2, 1898, double track had been completed by the Suburban from Geyer Road, Kirkwood, to Meramec Highlands. The St. Louis and Meramec River Railroad company announced changes in the schedule as a result. Cars that had been turning back to the city at Sutton station in Maplewood began to run on through to Meramec Highlands, which doubled the number of runs on the western division and decreased them on the eastern division by the same proportions. As a result, points west of Sutton had a car every fifteen minutes instead of every half hour. The schedule was reported to be experimental, with the amount of service depending on customer demand.[36]

---

[33]"Kirkwood," SLCW, 31 December 1897, p. 1.
[34]Webster Times, 21 April 1898, p. 1.
[35]Ibid.
[36]"New Time Table," Webster Times, 2 July 1898.

KING TROLLEY: ST. LOUIS AND SUBURBAN ARRIVES IN KIRKWOOD

Like most streetcar companies of the day, the St. Louis and Suburban provided a clubhouse for its employees as well as a yearly picnic at a popular resort, usually reached via the line. For several years the company picnic had been held at Ramona Park, but in 1898, the location was changed to the Meramec Highlands Resort which had become available via Suburban tracks. The Kirkwood correspondent described the 1898 picnic:

> From 10 a.m. to 10 p.m., the employees of the Suburban line made merry at Meramec Highlands Wednesday, this occasion being their sixth annual picnic. A regular program of races and amusements was carried out, and dancing was indulged in the evening.[37]

In contrast to the fun and games of the company picnic, Suburban officials soon found themselves embroiled in a legal dispute with Kirkwood over the town's right to regulate the running of streetcars and express cars.

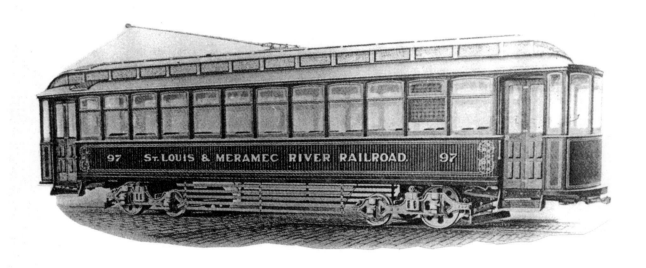

9-1. St. Louis Car Company engraving of St. Louis and Suburban Meramec Valley division car 97. Its specifications read: "Length over Bumpers, 45 feet. Length over Vestibules, 44 feet. Length over Corner Posts, 34 feet. Seating Capacity, 45 passengers."

---

[37]"Kirkwood," SLCW, 3 September 1898.

A MOTORMAN TO HIS MATE,
(Whom he is "breaking in.")

BY CHARLES L. DELBRIDGE.

Out and away, at the break of day;
  Clinkety. clang: let me speed away.
None to bar and none to stop;
  Watch me make that fellow hop.

9-2. Illustration and first stanza of *A Motorman to His Mate*. **Found in** Move Forward Please! **by Charles L. Delbridge, St. Louis, 1901.**

9-3. Stock certificate from a financial restructuring effort sometime between 1900 and 1910. The original shares in the company were sold in the 1890s.

Chapter 10

PARTY IN THE SUMMER - FREEZE IN THE WINTER

Kirkwood's William Essex and other county residents were impressed by the palatial "private party cars" that ran through Kirkwood to the Meramec Highlands, "[It is] a Palace buffet car in which parties are given at night, [passengers] having supper on board," wrote Essex in 1896.[1] Initially, for residents served by the Air Line, a private party car was available only from the Lindell line, but Houseman assured his customers that parlor cars would soon be constructed to accommodate private parties. Trolley parties were expected to be numerous at the Highlands in the spring and summer of 1896. Early that spring, the ladies of the Kirkwood Women's Christian Temperance Union (WCTU) had already begun arranging a trolley party with music, refreshments and decorations as attractive features.

Houseman's plans to build numerous private party cars did not come to fruition because of the mounting financial problems that his line faced as a result of litigation and the need to double track the line in order to compete with the new Suburban line. Instead, Lindell private parlor cars were utilized. The "Rover" was specially designed and constructed by the Lindell Railway for accommodation of trolley parties. A *St. Louis County Watchman* reporter who was invited to inspect the interior of the "Rover" described it in the February 28, 1896 issue, as "the finest street car built and operated in St. Louis."[2]

> The "Rover" is forty feet in length and about ten in width inside measurement, and has two compartments and a vestibule; each compartment is provided with ten large and roomy wicker arm chairs with heavy plush cushions, and handsome wicker stools are placed in the vestibule, which will accommodate four or five passengers. The inside work is of hard wood, oil finished, and the windows are of the best quality of French plate glass, as are the mirrors distributed throughout the car, with handsome hangings to conform to the inner coloring of the car and the cushions of the chairs. It has double end trucks, and is equipped with the Westinghouse latest improved motors, and is heated as well as propelled by electricity.[3]

---

[1] Essex to Byars, 21 July 1896, MHS.
[2] "Rover," SLCW, 28 February 1896, p. 7.
[3] Ibid.

KING TROLLEY: PARTY IN THE SUMMER - FREEZE IN THE WINTER

In July of 1896, the "Rambler" the first and only party car constructed for the St. Louis and Kirkwood Railroad made its inaugural appearance for a complimentary trolley party which was hosted by Miss Eliza Pitman, daughter of John Pitman, the former president of the company. She and thirty-five of her Kirkwood friends left Kirkwood on the "Rambler" at 9 o'clock p.m., and made a round trip over the line stopping at Meramec Highlands, where the party enjoyed a dance before returning to Kirkwood. A string orchestra accompanied the party on the entire trip. A *Watchman* reporter described the car for those not lucky enough to experience it:

> The car is provided with a complete buffet with the finest cut glass, silver and china service, and an attendant in a white duck uniform trimmed in gold lace and buttons, served refreshments en route on portable tables. The interior decorations of the car are a marvel of beauty in green and gold and the upholstery and hangings are of silk brocade, the whole being lighted by 30 incandescent lights of the same colors.[4]

The Houseman's used the private parlor car for both social and political reasons. One of the ploys to win friends and influence people was to invite the "movers and shakers" to parties in the company parlor car. Mrs. Houseman's parties, unlike James Houseman's, catered solely to women. Her parties were more likely to be "Temperance" parties without alcohol served, than those hosted by Mr. Houseman.

Others were able to charter the parlor car for private parties. A July 1897 parlor car party was chronicled in the *Watchman*:

> There was a pleasant trolley party over the Houseman line from St. Louis to Meramec Highlands last Friday evening, in which a number of ladies and gentlemen from St. Louis and Kirkwood participated. There were refreshments for all on board and at the Highlands, and to still further make the occasion enjoyable, a quartet of Negro jubilee singers were in attendance… All enjoyed the evening's outing splendidly and are ready to undertake the same trip again.[5]

In 1897, after the St. Louis and Meramec River Railway construction was completed by the St. Louis and Suburban, the parlor cars "Kinloch" and "Suburban" were frequent visitors to Meramec Highlands. The "Kinloch" was most often used for parties on the new line. Upon completion of the Suburban line's construction through Kirkwood, on September 10, 1897, the entire Kirkwood Board of Trustees and town officials were treated to a party on the "Kinloch" in appreciation of their support for the new line.[6]

The *Street Railway Journal* characterized the "Kinloch," built at a cost of $10,000, as "one of the finest private street cars ever operated on an electric road." The "Suburban" was merely described as "a handsome car, having cost more than $6,000."[7]

---

[4] "Rambler's Initial Trip," SLCW, 10 July 1896.
[5] SLCW, 27 July 1897.
[6] "Kirkwood," SLCW, 10 September 1897.
[7] Street Railway Journal, 14 March 1903.

The comings and goings of private parlor cars were of special interest to the *Watchman* corespondents. One reported in October, "a merry party of gents" rode out to the Highlands on the "Kinloch."[8] On Thanksgiving morning in 1897, the "Kinloch" carried guests from St. Louis to Kirkwood to the Rushcoe - Ryan wedding.[9] In March of 1898, even steady rain failed to dampen the spirits of a "merry party" aboard the "Kinloch."[10] By 1898, reports of the "Kinloch's" arrival at the Highlands were limited to unusual circumstances: "Nothing stops the *Kinloch*. On Sunday morning it took out a party of pleasure seekers in the pouring rain."[11] Of course, the Highlands was not the only destination for a party car. A principal of the St. Louis and Meramec River Railroad, J. B. Case, used the "Kinloch" to entertain the directors of his club at a "stag party." The gentlemen rode the Suburban's private car over the Houseman route to Webster Groves where they were driven to Case's "palatial" home at which they "enjoyed a delightful evening."[12]

The "Kinloch" was also used for political purposes. The mayor of Webster Groves on October 23, 1897, arranged for friends and power brokers from around the city and the county to be transported on the "Kinloch" to Meramec Highlands where they met at the Highlands Inn to hold a summit on water service for St. Louis County towns and villages.[13]

A private car party for the choir of Kirkwood Methodist Church was described by Mrs. Alfred Franklin Smith, wife of the pastor. Her memories of the struggle to get an organ for the church, circa 1903, are found in the September 1969 *Kirkwood Historical Review*:

> It was in the spring of this very year that Richard McCullough, president of the St. Louis Railways, graciously sent his private car out for my use to take the choir on a joy ride (not the modern so-called one). It was raining! It always rains for me but no matter, the choir with a few invited guests… boarded the car at the church, Clay and Washington Avenues, and we had some ride, going over the Suburban and city lines. After an evening spent in the most delightful fashion on wheels, games, mostly guessing, conversation and I must say that the lovely old Music Box which was aboard (for we had no Victrolas or radios in that day) was greatly enjoyed. Mr. McCullough also sent a chef with the car, and he served our sandwiches, cakes and hot coffee…. We had a wondrous evening! And I think the "populace" if they had heard the singing thought Gabriel's choir had arrived.[14]

Mrs. Smith probably surprised McCullough when she showed up at the De Hodiamont Railway offices with a large bunch of violets to show her appreciation for the courtesy and kindness that he had shown.

---

[8]"Kirkwood," SLCW, 29 October 1897.

[9]"Kirkwood," SLCW, 26 November 1897.

[10]"Meramec Highlands," SLCW, 18 March 1898.

[11]"Meramec Highlands," SLCW, 1 April 1898.

[12]"Webster Groves," SLCW, 8 July 1898.

[13]"Trolley Ride to the Highlands," SLCW, 29 October 1897, p. 8.

[14]Mrs. Alfred Franklin Smith, "The Traveler Who Returned," Kirkwood Historical Review, September 1969, pp. 146-147.

KING TROLLEY: PARTY IN THE SUMMER - FREEZE IN THE WINTER

One possible guessing game that the choir could have played during their party was found in *Bright Ideas for Entertaining* published in 1905 as a source book for the aspiring hostess. In the middle of the book (rescued by St. Louis writer Martha Baker from the floor of an aged drugstore in Thomaston, Maine) was a game for a Trolley Party. "A Trolley Ride — St. Louis to Kirkwood," was generated when a St. Louis area subscriber to the *Ladies Home Journal* wrote to the author and described her successful "trolley" party.

The party hostess gave each of her twenty guests a card with a pencil attached. She announced that the "conductor" would ring a bell to start and, a half-hour later, to finish. Clues for street names on the line were on printed on cards pinned throughout the room, on curtains, tablecloths etc. The hostess gave the person with the most correct guesses a carnation, while the one with the least correct answers was given a new penny.

The clues for the twenty streets follow. (Some of the streets no longer exist or their names have been changed.) Try to identify the streets. Can you beat the 1903 Kirkwood Methodist Church choir members?

A TROLLEY RIDE — ST. LOUIS TO KIRKWOOD[15]

1. Abraham's wife.
2. What idol's feet are made of.
3. Stop here when hungry.
4. Always owns a goose.
5. Dear to our hearts though sometimes a "Rip."
6. Brought lightning from the clouds.
7. A part of a door and what doors are usually made of.
8. A somber color.
9. Of cherry-tree fame.
10. A direction of the compass and a preacher.
11. The side of a tiny stream.
12. One of the discoverers of Pike's Peak.
13. A great turn.
14. Associated with the lower regions.
15. The highest point.
16. What most housewives do on Monday.
17. A famous summer resort.
18. What the preacher who lisped said to the sinner.
19. Green, and dear to girlish hearts.
20. Makes a quick fire.

To see how you did, check the answers at the end of the chapter. There is room to question the accuracy of the clues on a couple, but giving the benefit of the doubt to the hostess,

---

[15]Mrs. Herbert B. Linscott. (1905) <u>Bright Ideas for Entertaining</u>, 9th ed., Philadelphia, PA.

the game was a successful entertainment, or she would not have been moved to share it with others.

Even the splendid private parlor cars were not immune to the same types of accidents that were the bane of the streetcar industry. On September 7, 1900, president Jenkins of the St. Louis and Suburban and his wife were returning home to Florissant on the "Kinloch" from an evening at Ramona Park, the Suburban's amusement park. On the same track, heading in an opposite direction, was a well-filled passenger service car headed toward the city, with standing room only. The motorman of the "Kinloch," which was waiting at a switch, asked the motorman of what he assumed to be the last car traveling toward the city if he was, "the last one out?" The response was that there was one more car out there but that he didn't know if the "Kinloch" would meet it or not. Jenkins then directed the "Kinloch" motorman to go ahead, based on his interpretation of the information.

Because the president's car was a private car, there was no knowledge of it being on the track by the motorman in the oncoming car. The two cars were both operating at a rapid rate of speed. Witness accounts placed the speed from twenty to thirty-five miles an hour. The two Suburban cars collided on a curve in the track where underbrush and small trees were growing near the track, obstructing the view of both motormen. Neither knew prior to the instant of the collision that the other car was on the track. Numerous passengers in the public streetcar, especially those standing, were injured. Fortunately, no-one was killed. At least two of those seriously injured sued the railroad for damages and won large settlements for the day, $7000 and $3500. The Suburban's lawyers appealed the finding of negligence on the part of the company. Though the cases were eventually argued in front of the Missouri Supreme Court in 1902, the high court affirmed the decision of the circuit court in favor of the injured parties. The court found that the unregulated nature of the "Kinloch's" itinerary posed a threat to regularly scheduled streetcars. Therefore, it was critical for the motorman of the private car to use extreme caution when traveling on a single track section of the line.[16]

In 1903, the St. Louis Car Company built car 102 for the St. Louis and Suburban line. It was a Robertson sill palace car, one of five cars, from the order of 20 new cars for the World's Fair, to survive the De Hodiamont carhouse fire in 1903. Before car 102 entered service, it was refurbished and changed into a private car. In 1907, when the Suburban fleet was absorbed by United Railways, it continued service as a private car.

The "Kinloch" and the "Suburban" were used as passenger cars following the 1903 fire at the De Hodiamont car house which destroyed a large part of the Suburban's fleet. The cars were returned to service as private cars after replacement passenger cars were secured. Prior to the fire, the two private cars had been used to haul many of the distinguished guests of St. Louis and the World's Fair Company.

The private parlor cars operated on all the Suburban lines, not just the St. Louis and Kirkwood and the St. Louis and Meramec River lines, and after the merger with United

---

[16]A full discussion of Molloy v. St. Louis and Suburban Railway Company and Hennessy v. the same is found in Reports... Supreme Court of Missouri, (October Term, 1902) vol. 173, pages 75-86, Columbia, MO: Stevens

Railways they operated on most city and county lines. However, the parlor cars were never a financial success for the St. Louis and Kirkwood, the St. Louis and Suburban, or United Railways. The cars had limited use because of their extra cost for rental. Ed Vogelsang, a Brentwood resident, remembered joining a group of 24 couples who paid $5.00 a couple for use of a private party car with plush seats, food and drink, and a crew which ran the party car all over St. Louis for the evening.[17] In the early 1900s, $5.00 was a steep fee for the average citizen, limiting use by most residents of the city and county. Very few wanted the party cars for winter use. After a couple years of use, some owners already considered the private party cars to appear "shabby."

For a few years, the fashionable set considered the elaborate private cars a classy way to travel and entertain during the summer season, but the masses of St. Louis city and county residents never set foot on one of the four private party cars owned by the St. Louis and Suburban Company: "Suburban," "Kinloch," "Ramona," and the "Meramec." The "Ramona" was most likely Houseman's "Rambler," given a new name after the Houseman line merged with the Suburban.

Once the automobile became popular, demand for private cars diminished even further. In 1926, the "Meramec" was renumbered (#3010) and converted to a passenger car, running on the St. Charles line. The "Kinloch" was the last of the Suburban's private parlor cars to remain in service with its luxurious furnishings intact. It was refurbished in 1922 for continued use as a party car, then went into storage for a time and was ultimately scrapped in November 1939. The "Suburban" and the "Ramona" were scrapped about the same time.

Though they had a brief period of glory and popularity, the private parlor cars quickly faded from the scene.

****

Winter months added to the financial woes of the streetcar lines. Costs were higher because of the fuel required for the stoves in the cars. Income was depressed because patronage on the lines was lower due to the cold. The streetcar stoves were lighted in late October, usually before fires were established in area homes.[18] The lighting date was eagerly anticipated by both passengers and crew, though the heating was woefully inadequate, too hot for those next to the stove and too cold for the rest. Wait times were supposed to be short, but even so passengers suffered from the cold while waiting for the next car. In December of 1897, the St. Louis and Kirkwood Railroad placed a "much appreciated" car with a stove in it at the corner of Adams and Clay avenues in Kirkwood for use as a waiting room for passengers and employees.[19]

When it was extremely cold, no-one rode the streetcars unless they had to get somewhere and had no other option. Gone were the droves of pleasure seekers. Often only the lonely crew was found on the cars, braving the elements to keep service going. Late January of 1897 featured a particularly cold week which was a "rough week on local street car men" who were

---

[17]Robert Eastin, "Interview With Edwin Vogelsang," (1969) Brentwood 50 Yr. Anniversary 1919-1969, p. 32-33.
[18]"Kirkwood," SLCW, 29 October 1897.
[19]"Kirkwood," SLCW, 31 December 1897, p. 1.

characterized as "uncomplaining and courteous as ever."[20] The cold snap wasn't welcomed by Kirkwood residents, reported the Kirkwood *Watchman* correspondent: "Electric cars ran light on Sunday - too cold."[21]

Streetcars at that time had an open vestibule which left the motorman unprotected from the cold and wind. Motormen usually had two pairs of heavy fleece lined leather gloves. They wore one pair while the other was heating on top of the stove. A former Suburban conductor wrote about winter conditions in the *United Railways Bulletin* in May 1915:

> On the Suburban, every motorman wore Arctic overshoes, earmuffs, an enormous overcoat, nearly always fur, and carried two pairs of gloves. When the conductor was not collecting fares, he was warming the "other pair" of the motorman's gloves so his hands would not freeze.[22]

The superintendent of the St. Louis and Suburban Line kept big urns of steaming hot coffee at the DeHodiamont car sheds. As fast as cars came in he would exchange motormen to allow the "frozen" one to thaw out and have a chance to drink the hot coffee. Sometimes the conductors were envious because they were not given that opportunity, though few would have wished to trade places with the motorman on the exposed open-front platform.

The December 17, 1897 *Post-Dispatch* featured a front page expose' about the travails of St. Louis motormen: "FACES CUT AND EYES BLINDED BY A FURIOUS STORM OF SLEET, Suffering of Motormen Who Faced the Icy Blasts of Winter on St. Louis Street Car Lines." Under an illustration of a bundled up motorman facing the storm, a caption read, "There Is a State Law That Requires Companies to Protect the Motormen by Putting Vestibules on Their Cars, but It is Ignored." The reporter visited various company car sheds and described the sorry state of the motormen: "There were chapped cheeks and watery eyes in every gathering." He reported that one motorman wore woolen gloves, which "had caught and held particles of the relentless sleet, and the conductor's assistance was required to remove them."[23] The reporter's description of the suffering of the motormen would have applied equally to those working on the county lines operated by Houseman and the St. Louis and Suburban. "They certainly did (suffer)," Travers Burgess stated based on old family stories handed down from a great-uncle who worked in the St. Louis and Meramec River Railroad mechanical department at the Benton carhouse and who frequently served as a motorman on the Manchester line.[24]

A little over a year after the Post-Dispatch expose, the *Watchman* reported on the innovation of a car with a closed vestibule, with an additional editorial comment:

---

[20]"Kirkwood," SLCW , 29 January 1897.
[21]Ibid.
[22]United Railways Bulletin, May 1915.
[23]"Faces Cut and Eyes Blinded by a Furious Storm," PD, 17 December 1897, p. 1.
[24]Travers Burgess interview with author, May 1997.

The Lindell Railway last Sunday ran the first vestibule car in St. Louis. The line will have all motormen protected by next winter. Other lines should follow suit.[25]

Unfortunately, most did not immediately follow suit. It was not until May 1915, when the Missouri Public Service Commission required vestibules to be enclosed and forced air furnaces with blowers to be installed in passenger cars to distribute heat and provide ventilation, that the entire fleet of St. Louis cars was modified. At first, only front platforms on single end cars were enclosed. Rear platforms remained open for some time thereafter, but by 1916, most platforms and vestibules were enclosed, thus easing the life of the motorman.

Answers to: A TROLLEY GAME — ST. LOUIS TO KIRKWOOD

1. Sarah 2. Clay 3. Berry Road 4. Taylor 5. Jefferson 6. Franklin
7. Lockwood 8. Gray 9. Washington 10. Westminster 11. Edgebrook
12. Clark 13. Big Bend 14. Sulpher 15. Summit 16. Wash
17. Newport 18. Prather (Pray Sir!) 19. Olive 20. Pine.

---

[25]SLCW, 14 February 1898.

10-1. Photograph of the "Meramec," car 102, which was built in 1903 by the St. Louis Car Company for the St. Louis and Suburban Railway Company. As a private parlor car, it was used to entertain dignitaries as they were shuttled to and from the 1904 World's Fair. After popularity of private cars waned, the "Meramec" was refitted for regular passenger service. It was last used on the St. Charles line.

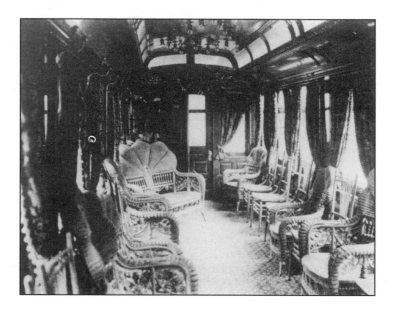

10-2. Opulent interior of St. Louis and Suburban car 102 after it was remodeled and made into the palatial private car "Meramec" in time for World's Fair service. Photographs courtesy of the Museum of Transportation.

"Special" Car Service in St. Louis

Private Parlor Cars of Former Days Now Rented for
Special Parties—Only One Retains Original
Luxurious Furnishings

10-3. Photographs published in 1922 of the last of a dying breed, private parlor cars. Only the "Kinloch" was left with its original sumptuous furnishings. Photographs from the May 6, 1922 Electric Railway Journal.[26]

REFRIGERATOR CARS.   ICE-COLD RIDE—5 CENTS.

10-4. Illustration showing riders' winter woes. From Charles Delbridge's Move Forward Please, a scathing attack on the St. Louis area streetcar industry.[27]

---

[26] "Special' Car Service in St. Louis - Private Parlor Cars of Former Days Now Rented for Special Parties — Only One Retains Original Furnishings," Electric Railway Journal, 6 May 1922, pp. 751-752.

[27] Charles Delbridge, Move Forward Please, St. Louis 1901, MHS.

FACES CUT AND EYES BLINDED BY A FURIOUS STORM OF SLEET.

Suffering of Motormen Who Faced the Icy Blasts of Winter on St. Louis Street Car Lines.

FACING THE STORM.

10-5. "How to dress for a car ride." Illustration from a Nov. 16, 1897 *St. Louis Post-Dispatch* editorial cartoon which highlighted the woes of the St. Louis streetcar customers.

10-6. Illustration appearing in the December 17, 1897 *Post-Dispatch* with an article advocating the use of enclosed vestibules to ease the lot of the motormen in the winter.

Chapter 11

KIRKWOOD VS. THE ST. LOUIS AND SUBURBAN

The optimism of the city government over the benefits that the St. Louis and Suburban could bring to Kirkwood collapsed in 1897. The relationship between the company and the town officials soon became combative about the issue of the company's compliance with the terms of the streetcar ordinance.

The company considered its charter received from the state of Missouri on May 31, 1895, to "construct, maintain and operate a standard gauge railroad for public use in the conveyance of persons and *property*"[1] to supersede the Kirkwood franchise granted on May 21, 1897. The franchise granted by Kirkwood stipulated that the railroad could "construct maintain and operate an electric railroad for the *transportation of passengers.*"[2] The words "conveyance of property" were conspicuous in their absence.

After construction was finished in September of 1897, the St. Louis and Meramec River Railroad conveyed only passengers in its cars through Kirkwood for a period of over six months. Then the company began to run a mail and freight car which carried no passengers but was used solely for traffic in mail, express baggage and freight. Though the car displayed signs identifying it as a "United Stated Mail Car," a partition separated the car into two totally unconnected compartments. One was for the Railway Post Office. The other was for the Walton-Knost Express Company which had purchased the exclusive right for shipping freight on the line.

The mail-express car made two trips a day, stopping to load and unload at the corner of Adams and Clay avenues. When it stopped to handle express matters, the car blocked the crosswalks on Adams and Clay, and it blocked half of the street for public use. At times when passenger cars passed the standing mail-express car, the street was totally blocked. The time spent in loading and unloading the car ranged from 10 to 40 minutes. At times when the car was not in use, it was often left standing there.[3]

Kirkwood officials were irritated; they believed that the company had not complied with terms of their franchise. On November 20, 1899, the Board of Aldermen directed the mayor to:

---

[1]*Reports of Cases Determined in the Supreme Court of the State of Missouri* (Columbia: E. W. Stevens Publisher, 1901), v. 159, pp. 239-256.
[2]Board Minutes, City of Kirkwood, 21 May 1897.
[3]Cases - Supreme Court of MO, 1901, v. 159, pp. 247-248.

"notify the St. Louis and Meramec River Railroad Company to cease within ten days… the running and operating over its road in this city, cars carrying freight, express, baggage or mail." If the Suburban Company did not comply, the aldermen planned to, "take necessary steps… to cause forfeiture of the franchise and right of way…"[4]

During the December 11th town meeting, a response from Thomas Jenkins, the General Manager of the St. Louis and Suburban Railroad Company was read. His response included opinions of Dawson and Garvin, the company attorneys. The company's position was that the city was unfairly trying to restrict its operation which had been approved by its state charter. It refused to comply. In turn, the Board of Aldermen consulted with the town's attorney who disagreed with the company's legal position.[5] The board then approved a new ordinance, #31, which stated that no company could operate a street railroad for any purpose not authorized by the franchise granted by the City of Kirkwood. That same evening the Board read for the first time a bill which became ordinance #32. The new ordinance required street railroad cars to be licensed and for the railroad companies to pay a tax to the city for each car that operated in the city.[6]

A violation of Ordinance 31 was stated to be a misdemeanor. If convicted, an offender would be punished by a fine of not less than $95 nor more than $100 or could be imprisoned in the Kirkwood jail for not less than two months or more than three months. The ordinance also allowed for both the fine and imprisonment to be given at the same time. Any officer of a non-compliant railroad was deemed responsible and liable to arrest and to imposition of punishments outlined by the ordinance.[7]

On December 14, 1899, Kirkwood officially delivered a copy of Ordinance #31 to the St. Louis and Suburban. The management of the company considered the ordinance unconstitutional and chose to disregard it, continuing to operate its mail-express car in Kirkwood.

As a result of that defiance, Town Marshal Secrist of Kirkwood served a warrant for arrest to Thomas Jenkins for violation of streetcar ordinance #31 which specifically prohibited the company from hauling freight, express and mail matter in or through the town.[8] Jenkins appeared in Kirkwood on December 21st, before Police Judge C. O. Bennett and gave bond for his appearance.[9] On the 26th, he returned to Kirkwood for his trial before Judge Bennett and was fined $95 and $100 on two separate counts.[10] Later that same day, company attorneys appealed

---

[4] Kirkwood Board Minutes, 20 November 1899, p. 336.
[5] Ibid., 11 December 1899, p. 339.
[6] Ibid.
[7] Supreme Court, p. 244.
[8] SLCW, 22 December 1899, p. 8.
[9] Ibid.
[10] "The Kirkwood-Suburban Muddle," SLCW, 29 December 1899.

the Kirkwood actions to Judge Hirzel of the St. Louis County Circuit. They claimed that the company rights were being infringed upon and that its employees were not allowed to perform their duties. The company asked that the officers of the town be restrained from any further interference.[11]

The judge granted a temporary restraining order which enjoined Kirkwood authorities from making further arrests under the disputed streetcar ordinance until the matter could be heard in Circuit Court.[12]

County Court Judge Wurdeman was at the same time proceeding against the company for noncompliance with the terms of the county franchise. He was pursuing a legal definition of the, "limit of county authority and the jurisdiction of County Court, as well as the course to pursue to compel railroad companies to live up to their contracts, as set forth in the franchises granted them by the court."[13] Kirkwood's case was watched with interest by Wurdeman and other officials since railroads' compliance with franchises and ordinances had become a problem in numerous places in the county.

Appearing before the Circuit Court, the Kirkwood attorney argued that a street railroad chartered by the state to carry "passengers and property" could not enforce its state charter to carry freight, mail, or express in a city which had given consent solely for carrying passengers. He argued that Kirkwood had the right to dictate terms upon which the street railroad should be operated. State law gave the city the right to reject the whole operation when granting a franchise, so the implication of the law was that the city also had the right to withhold a part of the services the company wished to provide. In addition, he argued the reasonableness of the ordinance. Allowing passenger traffic which would cause little or no inconvenience to the public while denying freight cars which might block the highways and monopolize the streets was believed by Kirkwood authorities to be eminently reasonable.[14]

The Suburban company attorneys argued that its charter required it to move property. The company held that until ordinance #31, there was nothing in the prior ordinances which prevented carrying of freight or mail in and through Kirkwood. Its operation in Kirkwood was consistent with its operation on its entire railroad and was in compliance with its state granted charter. The company further maintained that the original ordinance remained valid. The town government had changed in 1899 to a city of the 4th class. The company attorneys argued that the new governing body had no authority to change the rules of the prior agreement and that the city was illegally interfering with the lawful conduct of its business as a common carrier.[15]

---

[11] Ibid.
[12] Ibid.
[13] SLCW, 22 December 1899, p. 8.
[14] Supreme Court, pp. 239-256.
[15] Ibid.

KING TROLLEY: KIRKWOOD VS. THE SUBURBAN

The Circuit Court found in favor of the Suburban, in effect making the restraining order perpetual. Kirkwood appealed the judgment to the Missouri Supreme Court. Shortly thereafter, the Kirkwood Board of Aldermen approved hiring George L. Edwards as attorney to conduct the litigation on the case which was pending in the Supreme Court. The *St. Louis and Meramec River Railroad Company versus the City of Kirkwood* case was accepted by Edwards. If he was successful bringing in a decision favoring the city, he was to be paid $500 and attorney's fees. If the decision went against the city, he was to receive no compensation above the expenses of the litigation.[16]

In a related incident, both Suburban lines, the St. Louis and Kirkwood and the St. Louis and Meramec River Railroads withheld payment of license fees. The Suburban was pursuing legal relief from the taxes which it considered "excessive" and which they refused to pay. The company held that ordinance #32 assessing the Suburban on every car that ran through Kirkwood was invalid. At the time Jenkins was arrested in December of 1899 for violation of ordinance #31, he was also charged with violation of ordinance #32 and was fined $50 and costs. The company appealed, receiving an injunction which allowed it to continue to operate its cars until the case could be heard. After hearing the case, Judge Hirzel decided in favor of the town. The Suburban asked for a new trial which was granted. In the new trial, concluding on October 30, 1900, Circuit Court Judge Booth affirmed Hirzel's ruling.[17] The Suburban was required to pay the taxes.

On October 8th, 1900, while the case was working its way to a conclusion, the city attorney was instructed to proceed with further litigation against the Suburban for nonpayment of Kirkwood's car license fee .[18] However, the ruling of Judge Booth made it unnecessary to continue the new litigation. In addition, the city aldermen ordered the town clerk to notify the streetcar lines once again to repair street crossings within 15 days.[19]

On December 18, 1900, nearly a year after the legal wrangle began, the judgment of the St. Louis County Circuit Court was ordered reversed by the Missouri Supreme Court. The original petition of the St. Louis and Meramec River Railroad was dismissed. An extensive review of the case is found in Volume 159 of the 1901 <u>Reports of Cases Determined in the Supreme Court of the State of Missouri</u>. Some of the statements of the justices were illuminating in understanding their decision:

If the plaintiff is correct, that it now has the right to haul freight in the streets of

---

[16]Board Minutes, 9 April 1899.
[17]SLCW, 2 November 1900, p. 5.
[18]Board Minutes, 8 October 1900, p. 385.
[19]Ibid.

Kirkwood, without its consent, then there is nothing to prevent its running freight trains of ten or twenty cars and stopping its trains where it pleases. We are clear that its acceptance of the condition imposed in the franchise granted it stops it from now grasping the benefits of the contract with one eager hand while thrusting aside its burdens with another. While plaintiff's charter gives it power to take and convey persons and property, "...and receive compensation therefor," there is no absolute rule of law which compels it to exercise all of its power at all times and all places.

Ordinance No. 31 of Kirkwood is not void by reason of being so unreasonable that this court will declare it void.... The city seeks not to oust the plaintiff of its franchise, but requires it merely to conform to the conditions upon which it is permitted to use the streets.

The violation of the ordinance of said city, was erroneous, and said judgment is reversed and the case is remanded with directions to dismiss the bill at the cost of the plaintiff.. [20]

Despite its victory on one front, the city was not happy with the company's response to repair demands made in October and November, so the city attorney was once again directed on January 21, 1901, to proceed with litigation against the company and their agents for breaches of ordinances.[21]

The City of Kirkwood rehired George Edwards, well-paid and basking in the glory of his Supreme Court victory, to prosecute the St. Louis and Meramec River Railroad Company and to "collect all fines, penalties, debts or chooses in action which have accrued to the city by reason of violation of the said ordinance."[22] Edwards was to be paid 15% of what was recovered with a cap of $3000.[23] He immediately began working with the streetcar company to reach a settlement. At last, the two parties began to talk about compromises. Though the town board records do not explain why the City of Kirkwood agreed to ordinance changes desired by the streetcar lines, one has to assume that Kirkwood was offered a much more lucrative arrangement. Edwards presented a proposal to the aldermen which they passed on May 14, 1901. The bill was labeled, "an ordinance providing for the compromise settlement and amicable adjustment of all existing controversies between the City of Kirkwood and the St. Louis and Meramec River Railroad Company and the St. Louis and Kirkwood Railroad Company and Thomas M. Jenkins and Charles H. Turner."[24] The bill provided for the dismissal of all prosecutions instituted by

---

[20] Reports... Supreme Court, pp. 239-256.
[21] Kirkwood Board Minutes, 21 January 1901, p. 402.
[22] Kirkwood Board Minutes, 11 February 1901, p. 403.
[23] Kirkwood Board Minutes, 18 February 1901, p. 407.
[24] Kirkwood Board Minutes, 14 May 1901, p. 423.

Kirkwood against Suburban's officials Turner and Jenkins. After being signed by the mayor, the bill became Ordinance #104.

On May 17th, 1901, the aldermen passed ordinances 105 through 109. The first two repealed the two previous disputed ordinances regulating streetcars in Kirkwood. The third, #107, authorized the St. Louis and Kirkwood Railroad to "construct, maintain and operate a spur or switch track in the center of Main Street, and connect with its tracks on Clay Avenue, and to run and operate Mail, Express, and Funeral cars into and through the City of Kirkwood."[25] The fourth authorized the St. Louis and Meramec River Railroad Company to operate mail, express, and funeral cars in the city. The fifth authorized the St. Louis and Kirkwood to "construct, maintain and operate a "Y" or loop on or over its streets at or near the southwestern limits of the City of Kirkwood." It also authorized the St. Louis and Meramec River Railroad Company to operate over the "said Y or loop."[26]

A bit of back-patting was also passed, a resolution of thanks to the attorneys, police, judge and marshal for their "energetic, efficient and satisfactory service in the conduct of the litigation between the City and the Railroad Company and its officers."[27]

By 1903, the Suburban with its expanded right to run other types of cars through Kirkwood, allowed the Merchants Express Company to operate express cars not connected with the postal service on all Suburban lines. The *Watchman* on March 20, 1903, noted an accident in which the conductor was killed when a Merchants Express car left the track at Webster Avenue (Kirkwood Road). The car had been delivering packages in Kirkwood and had started its return trip east on Adams toward St. Louis, when the wheels left the track in front of the Presbyterian church. When the car began to jolt along the cross ties, the conductor jumped to save himself but fell in the path of the car. The motorman who held onto the brake was uninjured.[28]

Though the litigation with Kirkwood was settled for a time, the Suburban was still mired in numerous suits from individuals who had been injured in car mishaps or had other grievances against the company. In addition, Webster Groves which had watched Kirkwood's litigation relating to the tax on each car run through the town, initiated their own ordinance on January 4, 1902. Webster Groves Ordinance #161 required the streetcar company to obtain a license for each car that would operate within the city limits. A fee of $25.00 per car was assessed for a period of six months. A violation of the ordinance was deemed a misdemeanor "and upon conviction thereof, fined not less than fifty dollars and not more than one hundred dollars."[29] The ordinance further stipulated that each day a streetcar was run in violation of the provisions of the

---

[25] Kirkwood Board Minutes, 17 May 1901.
[26] Ibid.
[27] Ibid.
[28] SLCW, 20 March 1903.
[29] Franchises of United Railways (1913) pp. 1145-1147.

ordinance was "deemed a separate and distinct offense." The Suburban refused to pay the license fees, causing Webster Groves to prepare litigation against the company.

By 1903, Kirkwood was again at odds with the Suburban over violation of its ordinances, namely depositing passengers before their destination was reached and then turning back the cars. The city clerk was instructed to call attention to the problem and insist on the observance of the ordinances.[30]

Meanwhile, the Webster Groves attorney was negotiating with the Suburban's attorneys. On June 20, 1904, before the case which was pending in Circuit Court could be brought to trial, the Suburban agreed to: maintain in good repair the tracks and streets, widen culverts and bridges to the full width of the street and to keep them in good repair, maintain a light of not less than 20 candle power at each street intersection, to pay the costs of the City of Webster Groves vs. Thomas M. Jenkins suit pending in Circuit Court and to pay $500 in full for all license fees due up to December 31, 1904. Webster Groves agreed to drop the suit and to fix the semiannual license tax at $150 for a period of ten years, after which the amount could be set by ordinance.[31] It is clear that the Suburban's prior losses against Kirkwood worked in the favor of Webster Groves.

On April 17th, 1905, the City of Kirkwood repealed its ordinances 107 and 109. Ordinance 314 took away the rights given to the St. Louis and Kirkwood Railroad to operate a switch track in the center of main Street (Argonne) and to run mail, express, and funeral cars through the city. Ordinance 315 took away the right given to the St. Louis and Kirkwood Railroad to construct a "Y" or loop near the southwestern limits of Kirkwood and to allow the St. Louis and Meramec River Railroad to operate over the loop.[32] The new ordinances primarily cleaned up language deleting stipulations for the no longer existent St. Louis and Kirkwood streetcar company. Though the St. Louis and Suburban retained the right to run mail, express, and funeral cars, the ordinance effectively prevented the company from constructing a "Y" or loop on Main Street and at the southwestern limits of the city. No rights to do so had been given to the St. Louis and Meramec River Railroad. Not until 1914 was the Magnolia Loop built near the southwestern limits of Kirkwood by United Railways.

Though St. Louis County street rail stockholders may not have made much money, the company attorneys were very busy and doing quite well, win or lose.

---

[30]Kirkwood Board Minutes, 28 February 1903, pp. 527-528.

[31]Franchises of United Railways (1913) p. 666.

[32]City of Kirkwood Ordinance #314 and 315, Approved, 17 April 1905. Signed C. G. Ricker, Mayor.

11-1. The mail-express car that was at the center of the controversy between Kirkwood and the St. Louis and Suburban. Photo from the Museum of Transportation.

11-2. 1898 - Regularly appearing front page ad in the *Webster Times* for the Walton-Knost Express Company which obtained a contract from the St. Louis and Meramec River Railroad Company to provide "Cheap, prompt, and reliable delivery of all goods direct to residence or stores."

Chapter 12

SUBURBAN'S RAILWAY POST OFFICE

Though Railway Post Office (RPO) service was established for Webster Groves in January 1897, it almost didn't get underway. In 1896, the president of the St. Louis and Suburban, Charles Turner, was ready to stop operating mail service which had shown continuing losses on the Suburban company lines. The Post Office Department, because of protest by the Suburban and other street rail companies, then increased the amount of compensation for mail service on May 1, 1896. A contract for the rail postal service between downtown St. Louis and Webster Groves was awarded to the St. Louis and Meramec River Railroad which was owned by the St. Louis and Suburban. The service route was a distance of 12.11 miles which included the main post office in St. Louis and ten stops. County substation stops were located in Maplewood, Bartold, Tuxedo, Old Orchard, and Webster Groves. The company was required by the postal service to provide two complete round trips daily as well as shorter trips on a more frequent basis within St. Louis city limits.

Once rail postal service began to Webster Groves, Kirkwood residents were upset not to have the same service, as their rival to the east enjoyed. However, their *St. Louis County Watchman* correspondent shared optimistic tidings with them on May 28, 1896:

> Mr. Hough, our popular postmaster, gives us the gratifying information that probably by August 1st, one or two mails will be received each day from St. Louis over the St. Louis and Meramec River Electric Railroad, which now stops at Webster, but by August 1st will be completed to Kirkwood. This will be hailed with delight, for now much mail is put in St. Louis boxes to hasten delivery.[1]

Construction of the Suburban line through to Kirkwood was delayed by a year, so Hough's optimistic prediction was far earlier than the line arrived. Even after the line arrived, mail service did not immediately begin.

In early 1899, Kirkwood was awarded an extension of the St. Louis and Webster Groves RPO. The route was renamed the St. Louis and Kirkwood RPO. Additional substations were

---

[1]"Kirkwood," SLCW, 29 May 1896.

added in St. Louis, but Kirkwood was the only new county stop. The contract was renewed with the St. Louis and Meramec River Railroad which added new equipment for the longer run. At the same time, the St. Louis and Suburban upgraded its railway postal service to Florissant by replacing the car that began the service on that route with a car almost identical car to the car purchased for the Kirkwood route. The new service and equipment on the Kirkwood route were described in a February, 1899 *Watchman*:

> The St. Louis and Meramec River Railroad has begun operating its new $4000 mail and express car, built by the St. Louis Car Company, from Sixth and Locust streets to Kirkwood. It is a white flyer, vestibuled with open platforms and makes four round trips daily.

> Two of these runs are to Kirkwood, the other two are to Sutton avenue, the city limits.

> The car is divided by a closed wooden partition into two compartments, the front end being the postal section.[2] The only entrances to this side are sliding doors. The express section can be entered by side sliding doors and a rear hinged door with lock. All windows have iron crossbars and the upper ventilating transoms have wire screens.

> Mail carriers meet the car going and coming at Kirkwood, Webster Groves, Benton, Sutton, and other substation points, and box collections are also made at intervals, and the mail is deposited at the general post office on Locust Street. The express department in charge of H. W. Knost is also run on the station system, freight being collected and delivered at regular stopping places… The car leaves Kirkwood at 10:48 and 2:15, Sutton Avenue at 6:55 a.m. and 5:20 p.m. and Sixth and Locust streets at 5:55, 9:15, 1:15, and 4:25.[3]

Postal substations were usually located on a corner in a business operation, most commonly a drug store. When a passenger car was following close behind the mail car clanging for right-of-way or to keep on schedule, one of the two postal clerks on the car had to be fleet of foot. The sporting "local" clerk would jump off the moving car, run at full speed ahead to the mail box to be "robbed," unlock the box, gather the loose mail, lock the box and run to catch the still moving car.[4]

During the streetcar strike of 1900, the RPO cars were protected by federal order and continued to run despite the strike. From the start of St. Louis RPO service in 1893, the Post Office Department required that all streetcar RPOs be painted white to distinguish them from

---

[2]Only postal clerks were permitted in the mail section in accordance with U. S. Post Office strictly enforced regulations. The Suburban RPO cars had the same furnishings as steam railroad RPO cars, including a mail slot on the side of the car. Clerks were kept busy sorting, en route, all of the mail picked up on the way.
[3]SLCW, 10 February 1899.
[4]James Bowers, "When Our Trolleys Carried Mail," PD, Mirror of Public Opinion, 9 May 1953.

passenger trolleys. That was to protect them in case of mob violence during times of labor strife. During the strike in 1900, they were at times delayed by sabotage to the track or by unruly crowds, but police squads were swiftly summoned in those cases to ensure the mail cars were allowed to operate without interference. The crew operating such cars were generally allowed to run the cars close to schedule, but were subject to taunts and catcalls from strike sympathizers at intersections as the cars traveled their routes.

The St. Louis and Webster Groves RPO name resurfaced as the extension to Kirkwood was discontinued for a time, but service was reinstated to Kirkwood as a closed pouch service on July 1, 1903. Closed pouches could be carried by ordinary streetcars, so the Railway Post Office car was no longer required.

At the end of 1906, the United Railways System absorbed the St. Louis and Suburban company and took over both the Kirkwood line and the Florissant line mail contracts on January 1, 1897. United Railways threatened to drop the RPO service unless more money was allocated per mile. In 1907 the rate for independent mail cars was increased from 18 ½ cents per mile to 19 ½ cents. Closed pouch service on ordinary streetcars earned the line only 3 cents per mile. On January 14, 1907, the Post Office Department discontinued the closed mail pouch service to Kirkwood and Webster Groves. When that mail route was discontinued, the Ellendale (Maplewood) Station was added to another RPO line.

1897   ST. LOUIS AND WEBSTER GROVES RPO[5]

Mileage	Station	Trips per Day[6]	Address
0.00	Main Post Office	-	Eighth and Olive
0.65	Substation 9	4-1	331 Franklin Avenue
1.16	Substation 14	4-1	2801 Easton Avenue
1.21	Station C	4-1	3931 Morgan (Delmar)
1.75	Substation 10	4-1	922 Manchester Avenue
3.19	Substation 17	4-1	6802 Manchester Avenue
0.68	Maplewood	2-1	St. Louis County
0.91	Bartold	2-1	St. Louis County
0.65	Tuxedo	2-1	St. Louis County
0.75	Old Orchard	2-1	St. Louis County
1.16	Webster Groves	2-1	St. Louis County

Total 12.11 miles

1899 ST. LOUIS AND KIRKWOOD RPO

Mileage	Station	Trips per Day	Address
0.00	Main Post Office	-	Eighth and Olive
0.65	Carr Park Station	6-4-4	1331 Franklin Avenue

---

[5]Archives of the United States Postal Service, St. Louis, MO.
Various articles on the RPO system in St. Louis used facts provided by the Postal Service.
[6]First number - Weekdays, second number - Sunday, Kirkwood RPO - third number - Holidays.

```
1.16        Leffingwell        6-4-4    2810 Easton Avenue
0.73        Grand Avenue Jct.  6-4-4    (No office)
0.49        Station C          6-4-4    3931 Morgan
0.25        Sarah Street Jct.  6-4-4    (No office)
0.75        Wabash             6-4-4     7 South Vandeventer
2.43        Cheltenham         6-4-4     5833 Manchester Ave.
1.25        Ellendale          6-4-4     6821 Manchester Ave.
0.93        Maplewood          6-4-4    St. Louis County
0.91        Bartold            3-1-1    St. Louis County
0.65        Tuxedo             3-1-1    St. Louis County
0.75        Old Orchard        3-1-1    St. Louis County
1.16        Webster Groves     3-1-1    St. Louis County
3.13        Kirkwood           3-1-1    St. Louis County
Total 15.24 miles
```

RPO cars were not free from accidents. The case of George Deschner versus the St. Louis and Meramec River Railway Company was filed after a boy was run down by a Suburban mail car as he was crossing the tracks with a pail of milk. The white mail car was following a red passenger car on the same tracks, within a block's distance. After the red car passed, the boy checked east, the opposite direction from where the red car had come, then stepped out onto the track without looking back west. Deschner's excuse for not looking to the west was that he did not expect one car to be so quickly following another on the same tracks. After he had checked the tracks for a train going west and finding none, he felt it would be safe to cross.

The motorman of the mail car was not closely watching because his attention was directed to the mail box on a nearby platform. He did not see the child until it was too late to stop. Eyewitnesses reported that the car slowed as if to stop for the mail box; the postal clerk jumped out of the side door of the moving car and ran toward the mail box, nearly reaching it. Testimony indicated that the motorman was watching the running postal clerk. The postal clerk testified that the mail car did not intend to stop for the mail on that trip and that he did not get out of the car until there was a sudden stop and he heard the motorman say that he had, "run over a kid." Despite conflicts in the stories, agreement was reached that neither the postal clerk nor the conductor saw the boy before he was run over by the car. The motorman testified that he had been ringing his gong and had been watching the boy, who turned and darted onto the tracks when the car was only three or four feet away. The use of the gong was disputed by witnesses.

The boy was rolled and smashed under the car for 25 or 30 feet. His injuries included broken bones and serious internal injuries. The circuit court awarded Deschner $5000, finding the railroad was negligent and did not implement reasonable precautions to prevent hitting a pedestrian. The railway appealed the award. The case was heard by the Missouri Supreme Court during the October term, 1906. That court reviewed the case and upheld the $5000 awarded by the circuit court.[7]

---

[7] Reports of Cases Determined in the Supreme Court of the State of Missouri, October Term, (1906) v. 200 Columbia, MO: E. W. Stephens Publisher.

Another death was avoided when a mail car fender did its job and picked up a kneeling woman and carried her twenty or thirty feet. The cool-headed motorman quickly applied his brakes. The car stopped just as the woman was about to be thrown on the tracks. Though badly shaken up, the woman had no broken bones. The *Post-Dispatch* headlines read:

PICKED UP BY THE FENDER, Mrs. William Procter Run Down by a Suburban Road Mail Car. WAS PARALYZED WITH FEAR. KNELT, WITH CLASPED HANDS, WAITING TO BE CRUSHED UNDER THE WHEELS. MOTORMAN NEARLY FAINTED...[8]

St. Louis Rail Post Office service ended in November 1915, a victim of the success of Model T Ford mail trucks. The "motor wagon" service proved to be less expensive and more versatile.

Today cards and envelopes bearing St. Louis RPO postmarks are eagerly sought by collectors. Because of the short duration of the mail car service to Kirkwood, the Kirkwood RPO postmarked documents are rare.

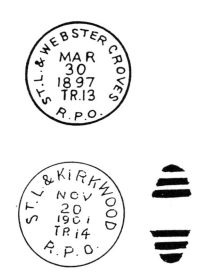

12-1. Postmarks from the St. Louis and Webster Groves RPO and from the St. Louis and Kirkwood RPO. For a time in 1899 when Kirkwood service was started, there may have been an overlap in use of the postmarks.

---

[8]"Picked Up By the Fender," PD, v. 29, no. 22.

12-2. *St. Louis Post-Dispatch* illustration showing Mrs. Procter caught on the tracks by a Suburban mail car.

12-3. Artist's rendition of the Suburban's Kirkwood-Webster RPO car derived from the photograph which appears at the end of the preceding chapter. The illustration was prepared for a 1953 article in *Post Haste*, a publication of the Bureau of Transportation of the Post Office Department. The article was reprinted in the *Mirror of Public Opinion* column in the *Post-Dispatch*.[9]

[9]James Bowers, PD, 9 May 1953.

Chapter 13

ST. LOUIS AND SUBURBAN "ESCAPES" TRANSIT MERGER

The streetcar industry expanded rapidly in St. Louis from 1890 to 1898. Numerous small companies began operation while at the same time larger players in the industry increased their holdings and service. Of the companies that operated in St. Louis County, the St. Louis and Suburban was the largest. Despite its size and apparent strong position in the county, the Suburban was actually loss-plagued. By the time the Suburban reached Kirkwood, company officials were looking for a buyer. Their anticipation that St. Louis streetcar magnate John Scullin was going to expand his lines with the purchase of the St. Louis and Suburban was dashed in July 1897 when Scullin publicly announced that he was prepared to sell his line.[1]

In 1899, powerful streetcar interests lobbied for and were able to push through a bill in the Missouri legislature allowing any street railroad to acquire, lease or purchase the property of any other street railroad. Once the bill was signed by the governor, cutthroat tactics were utilized by rival streetcar interests to "swallow" weaker lines and to come out on top in the no holds barred effort to consolidate the St. Louis streetcar lines into a unified system.[2] Two groups actively pursued consolidation of transit companies in the St. Louis area, the Brown Brothers' Central Traction and their rival, the newly formed St. Louis Transit Company syndicate, financially backed by St. Louis based Mississippi Valley Trust Company.

During the spring of 1899, uncommitted lines including the Lindell and the St. Louis and Suburban were pursued by both. In reality, the backers of the consolidation effort had set up the apparent competition for the purpose of inflating the selling price of the Southern and National lines interests which were represented by the St. Louis Transit Company.

Once the Lindell company was bought by Central Traction, St. Louis Transit's effort appeared to collapse, and the Missouri, Union Depot, Jefferson Avenue, Southern,

---

[1] The Suburban never again had such profitable hopes for a merger. Scullin later rethought his retirement from the field and formed the United Traction Company.

[2] Chapters 13 and 14 in Andrew Young's book, The St. Louis Streetcar Story, discuss the merger period much more in depth. (Glendale, CA, Interurban Press, 1988)

and National Electric Railways entered the fold with their owners being successful in gaining a much inflated price. The St. Louis and Suburban was left as the only major holdout against Central Traction. Suburban president Charles Turner stubbornly rejected all offers that were lower than his stated selling price.

Since the St. Louis and Suburban was the only major holdout, Central Traction officials determined that they did not need the Suburban at that time, figuring that it would eventually fail and have to merge with their combine at a much lower price. Central Traction broke off negotiations with Turner in July of 1899. That left the feisty Suburban as the only major independent streetcar line in St. Louis.

The Suburban management had gambled and lost on their hard line no-compromise stance on their price. They had not yet become profitable and were not likely to realize an increase in revenues and ridership on the far-flung county lines. However, officials of the St. Louis and Suburban took the public stance that they had emerged from the merger battle victorious, escaping the clutches of the monopolistic combine. In reality, company officials knew they were in trouble and began an energetic series of expansions of lines and services which were designed to demonstrate that the company was an effective people-mover and a valuable and desirable property.

The expansion effort was fairly successful. In February of 1900, the *Street Railway Review* reported that an extension of the Suburban's St. Louis and Meramec River Railroad under direction of president Turner and vice-president J. B. Chase, was completed north past the St. Louis Fair Grounds (a race course) to O'Fallon Park where it terminated; construction was nearly completed on the Union line, an addition to the Suburban main line, which connected Forest Park to the Calvary and Bellefontaine cemeteries in the northern part of the city; and most importantly for the county, a new division, the Brentwood, Clayton and St. Louis Railroad under president Hunt Turner was ready to begin construction on a line which would connect the St. Louis and Kirkwood division with Clayton, University City, Wellston, and the Suburban main line. The line which would run north through Normandy Heights, Ramona, and Kinloch to Florissant, would give the Suburban the nearest approximation of a cross-county line as well as an important connection to the county government center.[3]

Turner and general manager Thomas Jenkins had assembled an efficient team which had cut the cost of operations by 25 percent in 1899. They announced that they expected to run even more efficiently in 1900, obviously not expecting a major strike. The Suburban's officers and staff with the exception of Turner, Jenkins and officers listed above with their divisions were: vice-president, Samuel M. Kennard; secretary and treasurer, Thomas C. Kimber; chief of departments, W. C. Jenkins; auditor, L. C. Shipherd; division superintendents, Jas. A. McCabe, D. R. Redden, and Charles J. Crane; master mechanic, G. J. Smith, engineer of maintenance of way, Charles S. Butts;

---

[3]Street Railway Review, 15 February 1900.

superintendent of lines, Nathan Smith; and superintendent of power stations H. W. Tingley.[4]

The *Review* summarized the Suburban assets which did not change substantially before 1900:

> The Suburban system comprises a total of 91.68 miles (measured as single track)... The track is laid with Cambria and Johnson rails, weighing from 40 to 60 lbs. per yd., laid on 6 x 8 in. oak ties, spaced 2 ft. c. to c. The trolley wires are No. 0 and No. 00, and over a considerable portion of the route are carried on iron poles.

> The rolling stock comprises 24 convertible and 130 closed cars, which were made by the St. Louis Car Co.; they are all mounted on maximum traction trucks and equipped with G. E. 1200, G. E. 57, and Westinghouse No. 38 motors. Electric heaters made by the Consolidated Car Heating Co. are used. The company operates two power stations. One is at De Hodiamont Station... The second station is at Brentwood; it is 72 x 60 ft. equipped with three engines..., three Westinghouse generators... and eight 200 h. p. boilers. Current is generated at from 565 to 575 volts.

> Car houses are located at De Hodiamont, Benton, and Brentwood, having capabilities of 85, 85, and 15 cars, respectively; all are brick buildings. The shops are at De Hodiamont.[5]

While the Suburban was fighting for its life, with perhaps a delusion of eventually dominating and taking over the consolidated lines, United Railways, a holding company, was formed on July 10, 1899, to coordinate and operate the finances of the merged St. Louis transit companies. On September 30, 1899, St. Louis Transit Company leased all the lines from United Railways and became the operating company. At that time, United Railways put aside three million dollars in bonds to finance the purchase of the St. Louis and Suburban at a later time. United Railways officials were confident that they would take over the Suburban in time without a fight.

County riders were pleased that the Suburban had escaped the traction merger. Its cars were generally cleaner and warmer in winter with electric heaters as compared to Transit's inefficient coal burning stoves. Its schedules and routes were basically unchanged which allowed many county riders to avoid the confusion prevalent among city riders when changes were made following the consolidation.

A fight was brewing, however, with St. Louis streetcar employees who were making a determined attempt to unionize. Long hours, rigid and sometimes harsh rules of

---

[4]Ibid.
[5]Ibid.

conduct, a barrage of new rules and new schedules which in effect reduced pay, paranoia about unionization by the owners who employed spies to watch the workers, and generally poor management by St. Louis Transit's Jilson Coleman, all gave impetus to the union movement in St. Louis. Both Transit and the Suburban officials were vehement in their resistance to the union movement. Suburban's President Charles Turner and Superintendent Thomas Jenkins ran a more efficient operation than did St. Louis Transit, but they shared the distrust of the union movement, firing workers who were caught trying to organize or participate in union activities. Thus the Suburban was caught in the general maelstrom of streetcar employee discontent and was swirling ever closer to a strike.

The St. Louis and Suburban had "escaped" the St. Louis Transit merger. Could it survive a strike?

13-1. The Suburban was the main holdout in the traction merger of 1899. Car 326 of St. Louis and Suburban poses for its portrait at the St. Louis and Meramec River Railroad's Benton car shed at Kraft Avenue. It served primarily in the city, normally turning back to the city at the Sutton Ave. loop in Maplewood. Photo from the Charles Hamman collection.

Chapter 14

SUBURBAN ON STRIKE

There was unrest and sentiment supporting a walkout in both Transit and Suburban employee unions. However, the most fervid feelings seemed to be centered in the Transit employees. As a result of his escalating difficulties in keeping Transit running without a strike and his perceived ineffectiveness, Transit general manager Jilson Coleman was forced to resign by company owners and officials who needed a scapegoat. He was replaced by company man George Baumhoff, the former Lindell head, who was popular with the workers and who had previously demonstrated the ability to convince his employees not to strike. For a time Baumhoff was able to avert a Transit strike by the force of his personality and hard work. By March, he had worked out agreements to settle the issues raised by Transit employees, except for amount of pay. The Transit employees had asked for union recognition, a 10 hour working day and a pay increase to 25 cents an hour.

With an apparent agreement with St. Louis Transit in place, the national leadership of the Amalgamated Association of Street Railway Employees focused its attention on the St. Louis and Suburban. Starting on April 1, 1900, propositions and counter-propositions between the employees and the company were exchanged. On April 6th, the parties negotiated a short-lived agreement in which the St. Louis and Suburban recognized the union. The points in the agreement were as follows:

> 1. All men who claim to have been discharged on account of connection with the union are to have a fair and impartial hearing with a view to reinstating them if their charge is true.

> 2. Company will arrange straight runs of not more than 10 hours when it is possible.

> 3. Bulletin boards will show when a man is assigned to duty, and he will be immediately notified if his services are not required, and if he is obliged to remain on duty until assigned a run, he shall be paid for that time.

> 4. Men will work in two shifts and will be paid extra when working outside their shifts.

5. Company will treat (meet and confer) with committees from the employees at all times.

6. Union is recognized. But it must be open to all employees of the Suburban, and there must be no restrictions as to membership.[1]

The agreement was soon violated. Each side claimed the other was at fault, so negotiations were opened again. On April 21st, a two man delegation from the Central Trade and Labor Union attempted to resolve the issue by calling on the Suburban's Superintendent Thomas Jenkins. They called for arbitration with the company to pick one man, the employees to select one, and the two Central Trade and Labor Union Council representatives to select a final arbitrator.

Jenkins didn't answer immediately, taking the proposition under advisement. After he consulted with the Suburban's President, Charles Turner, and major stockholders, Jenkins notified the union representatives that he would accept arbitration if the union would give concessions. He provided union representatives with a lengthy document which outlined his requested concessions. The document was signed by Jenkins as the representative for the St. Louis and Suburban (main line), St. Louis and Meramec River Railroad, the St. Louis and Kirkwood Railroad, and the Brentwood, Clayton and St. Louis Railroad. The latter road at that time was still under construction, but nearing completion.

The letter stated that the company would not tolerate any interference from anyone with its acts of hiring or discharging its men, nor would it explain its acts to anyone but the employee hired or discharged. The Suburban stood ready to reinstate any man who was discharged for unionism, guilty of no other infractions of the rules of the company. It had no objection to the men joining an organization or association, but would not tolerate any union interference which might injure the discipline or method of operating its streetcar lines.[2]

Superintendent Jenkins stated that the company had upheld the prior agreement. In his view, the union had not acted in good faith in its failure to permit all employees of the system to join. He said the company had proof that, "by means of armed men," many of the employees had been prevented from becoming members of Division 144, while at the same time union men from other street railroads were allowed to attend and participate.[3] Jenkins did not acknowledge that "company" men had been encouraged to join and act as informants about union activities as was claimed by the union.

---

[1]"Arbiters Make Two Reports," PD, 22 July 1900.
[2]"Strike on the Suburban," GD, 30 April 1900.
[3]Ibid.

KING TROLLEY: SUBURBAN ON STRIKE

Union members did not deny that they had prevented people from joining, but felt justified in preventing "spies" from attending their meetings.[4]

Jenkins' call for concessions was presented to a group of national street railway union officers, local union representatives and to Sam Jolly, President of the Suburban Division 144 of the Amalgamated Association of Street Railways of the United States. They considered his reply in a general session and reported to the rank and file in a mass meeting held late in the evening on Saturday, April 28th. At 1 a.m. on Sunday morning, a committee was selected to notify Jenkins that the union would not agree to his terms.

After the lengthy mass meeting, much of which was spent considering grievances, National President of the union, W. D. Mahon, announced to newspaper reporters that a union committee would offer terms to Superintendent Jenkins on Sunday morning. The terms were essentially the same as those that had been accepted previously by the St. Louis Transit Company in their agreement with the union. He announced that if the union's terms were rejected, the Suburban street railroad would be struck.

At 11:00 o' clock a.m., the committee met with Jenkins who replied that he had no authority to change the company terms. The union men informed him that unless his propositions were withdrawn, the men would leave the streetcars at noon. He refused, causing the union to put its strike plan into action. At noon, Sunday April 29, 1900, the strike began.

As is the case today when there is labor strife, each party in the dispute attempted to put a positive spin on its own actions and opinions when interacting with the press. Widely different accounts of strike-related actions were reported in the papers depending on whom was interviewed, labor or management. To most papers' credit, they usually tried to present both viewpoints. Because the violence connected to the strike was fodder that sold newspapers, the strike immediately became front page news, with numerous side articles.

The newspapers reported the union's position that the strike was declared by the Suburban Branch of the Amalgamated Association of Street Railway Employees because the company had waged "a war of extermination"[5] against their organization, refusing arbitration unless the unionists signed an agreement which annulled previous agreements. Union officials claimed that in violation of the signed agreement, the Suburban discharged 40 men because of union membership.

As the first action of the strike, members of the union grievance committee stationed themselves at the De Hodiamont headquarters, the car barns, the Sarah Street crossing and the down town loop. As cars passed, committee members boarded and notified the crews of the strike. At 12:20 the first crew to abandon a car took it to the De

---

[4]Ibid.
[5]"One Suburban Man Has Died," PD, 30 April 1900, p. 1.

Hodiamont sheds and quietly left the car. Suburban official, James McCabe, stood prepared with a crowd of extra men who had previous experience with cars or had been trained in anticipation of a strike. Without disruption, two replacement workers boarded the abandoned car and returned it to service. Within the hour, eight more crews abandoned their cars and were replaced.

All was very civilized for the first hour, but then one of the first motormen to strike stood in the center of the track near the headquarters blocking an approaching car operated by nonunion men and pleaded with them in an "oratorical way" to quit work:[6]

> For God's sake men, get off the car and join us. For the sake of humanity, for the sake of your fellow workmen, don't run your car any further.[7]

After the man presented a number of impassioned comments, a police sergeant asked him to stop. The two exchanged words, causing a crowd to quickly form around them. Fortunately, the situation cooled when the motorman left to telephone the Chief of Police to complain that his rights as a citizen had been violated by the sergeant.

The first afternoon passed without a major disturbance, but at 11 p.m. violence erupted. A crowd began throwing stones at a Suburban car carrying several passengers near the De Hodiamont station. The conductor drew a revolver and shot twice into the crowd causing it to disperse. The passengers then transferred to another car. Shortly thereafter, at Goodfellow, four men boarded that car. According to the April 30th *Globe-Democrat* report, two of the men remained on the back platform while the other two went inside the car. The two men inside sprang forward with revolvers drawn and put the guns to the head of the motorman forcing him to surrender the car. The two on the back platform pulled the trolley pole down and then subdued the conductor. Both employees were marched at gun point from the car leaving the passengers stranded. Five shots were heard by the frightened passengers. The motorman had been shot in the heel and the conductor in the left hand. The assailants fled after the shootings. The men wore uniforms of the St. Louis Transit Company, though they did not wear their badges.

The next day Suburban President Charles Turner offered a reward for the apprehension of the men who had shot his employees. On May 2nd, two men were arrested in connection with the incident. One was a motorman on the Cass line and was identified by one of the victims as the shooter.

By late Sunday evening, according to the Suburban's McCabe, 48 of the approximately 325 workers had left the cars. The union disputed management figures, stating that the figure was low and that 300 of the 325 workers were expected to be off the job the next morning.

---

[6]Ibid.
[7]Ibid.

KING TROLLEY: SUBURBAN ON STRIKE

In anticipation of trouble on the Suburban's Kirkwood lines and seeing a chance to increase its revenues, on Monday April 30th, the Missouri Pacific Railroad added trains to its daytime schedule, providing hourly departures from Kirkwood and Webster Groves to Union Station and from Union Station back. The Frisco line also increased the number of accommodation trains serving the two towns. Though an inconvenience, the strike posed no major problem for most residents of Webster Groves and Kirkwood because the steam railroads were able to provide transit to the city. Residents were usually able to get to work within a reasonable amount of time. However, many passengers were forced to walk farther than usual to their places of employment.

The day after the strike began, Superintendent Jenkins maintained that only 60 to 65 men went on strike and that all their places had been filled by former employees of the Suburban. Whether the result of strike sympathizers' violence or the result of frightened and rusty employees, there were numerous accidents and incidents during the first couple days of the strike. The union maintained that the incidents were not caused by their members since it had instructed its men and their supporters not to resort to violence. Because of the concern that violence would erupt, policemen were stationed along the Suburban lines in the city and near the car sheds on De Baliver. However, county routes were not heavily guarded.

Early on May 2nd, the engineer and three guards at the Brentwood power house on the St. Louis and Kirkwood Division of the Suburban engaged in a gun battle with strike sympathizers. The walls of the powerhouse showed marks of numerous shots though no-one was injured.[8] Twelve of the striking Suburban employees lived in the Maddenville area near the scene of the attack. Sympathizers for the plight of those strikers were most likely responsible for the action against the power house and for throwing stones at streetcar employees as the cars passed through Maddenville.

As a result of the incidents on the Kirkwood division, Sheriff Peter Kerth and two deputies patrolled the line on May 2nd till the cars quit running at midnight. No further trouble was encountered that evening.

Tensions were high among non-striking Suburban employees who, almost to a man, wore revolvers while on duty. One conductor reported that near Webster Groves he had fired his revolver at a man who had thrown a stone at him as his car passed along Shady Avenue (Kirkham).[9]

Another Suburban conductor began firing his revolver when shortly before 4 a.m., his owl car ran over four cartridges placed on the rails, causing four shots. The frightened conductor pulled his revolver and fired four more shots in the air to attract the attention of the police.[10]

---

[8]"Police Make Four Arrests," GD, 3 May 1900.
[9]Ibid.
[10]Ibid.

KING TROLLEY: SUBURBAN ON STRIKE

Indicative of the rumor and wild hysteria surrounding the strike, the *Post-Dispatch* led its Monday April 30th coverage with headlines: "ONE SUBURBAN MAN HAS DIED, Non Union Employee Killed by a Stone, WILLIAM MC DANIELS, MOTORMAN, THE VICTIM, Was at Work on the Main Line of the Road When a Crowd Stoned Him and the Conductor." Though it made exciting copy, the message that prompted the story was a hoax. The address given to the coroner who sent a wagon to pick up the body was, according to a "snickering" May 1st *Globe-Democrat* report, a vacant lot.[11]

Traffic on the St. Louis and Kirkwood Division was impeded at various points along the line, most notably in the Brentwood neighborhood where several cars were stoned. Though serious for adults, the strike was not without its humor for "naughty" youth. The *Watchman* reported a May 3rd incident:

> Torpedoes on the Suburban tracks at Webster Groves last Thursday badly frightened the train crew, Marshal Secrist of Kirkwood, and one of our deputy sheriffs, who were patrolling the tracks. When the first torpedo exploded the motorman gave his car all the power the wires carried and made a swift run to safety, and when the officers out of breath caught up with the car where it came to a standstill, the frightened operator declared that he had been shot at five times. Mischievous boys had placed the explosives on the tracks.[12]

On May 2nd, only one Suburban Company car was operated on the St. Louis and Kirkwood line, taking an hour to make the round trip.[13] The cars on the Meramec River division ran regularly during the day, but at longer intervals than before the strike.

There were daily reports of numerous incidents. Whether they were caused by replacement workers or as part of the usual hazards of operating a street railway is not clear. A four-year old child was killed by a Suburban car on May 3rd. The child was playing in the street and slipped under the wheels of the car as it passed by.[14] On May 5th, a Suburban motorman was attacked by a passenger who claimed the motorman had made a deliberate attempt to crash into a wagon.[15] The same day another collision occurred when a Suburban mail car collided with a produce wagon driving in the Suburban tracks near 6700 Manchester. The woman driving the wagon was thrown to the ground and was injured, though not seriously.[16]

---

[11]"Couldn't Find the Corpse- A Wild Story Started in Connection With the Strike," GD, 1 May 1900.
[12]SLCW, 11 May 1900.
[13]"Police Make Four Arrests," GD, 3 May 1900.
[14]"Child Killed by Suburban Car," GD, 4 May 1900.
[15]"Attacked the Motorman," GD, 6 May 1900.
[16]"Struck by the Mail Car," GD, 6 May 1900, p. 16.

KING TROLLEY: SUBURBAN ON STRIKE

Part of the union's strike strategy was to pick up support and endorsements from other labor organizations. The Stationary Firemen Local #6 adopted resolutions to the effect, "That any member of the association caught riding the Suburban cars while the strike is pending shall be fined $5.00."[17] Other union locals set their own penalties, such as the Street Car Builders Union #8157 American Federation of Labor which set the fine for patronizing the Suburban at $1.00 per sighting and the Tobacco Workers International Union, which levied a $2.00 fine per Suburban ride. The Carpenters and Joiners Union #173 was but one of many to pledge, "moral and financial assistance."[18]

On May 4th, the *County Watchman* reported that in the first four days of the strike there was little intimidation of the workers. The report ended on an optimistic note:

> In the county, on the line of the Suburban running to Meramec Highlands, sympathizers of the strikers have committed some depredations upon the property of the company, such as cutting trolley wires, obstructing tracks, etc. but no injuries have been reported.

> Sheriff Kerth and a posse of deputies have patrolled the line nightly from the city limits to the southern end of the line, but so far have made no arrests... The cars are running regularly on the county line of the company, by the company's employees, and it is believed that no trouble will occur which cannot be overcome by peaceful and lawful methods.[19]

On May 5th, the first payday since the Suburban strike began, strikers lined up with nonunion men to ask for the pay due them. In each case, a striker was asked to turn in his Suburban badge before back pay would be given. All but two refused. Those two men collected their pay and then divided their pay among the cash-poor strikers who were refused payment. Tensions arose at the Manchester Division pay window when a striker was attacked "without provocation" as he turned to leave the window.[20] Friends started to his aid, but cooler heads restrained the angry men, thus preventing a dangerous brawl, for as the *Globe-Democrat* reported on the 6th, "all the working conductors and motormen still carry revolvers."[21]

The employees' strike placed the St. Louis and Suburban in an untenable situation as an independent fighting for survival against the massive St. Louis Transit Company which was running with no interference by strikers. The difficulties faced by passengers of the day such as overcrowded cars, longer wait times and tighter monitoring of transfer use experienced by the general population after the transit consolidation in 1899 caused public sentiment, especially of the working class that depended on streetcars for travel, to

---

[17]"Indorsed the Strike," GD, 6 May 1900.
[18]"Supported by Carpenters," GD, 1 May 1900.
[19]"Suburban Railway Employees Strike," SLCW, 4 May 1900.
[20]"Streetcar Troubles," GD, 7 May 1900, p. 11.
[21]GD, 6 May 1900.

settle on the side of the strikers. Ridership on the Suburban lines was low due to riders' fears of ridicule and violence, support of a large portion of the population for the strikers, and the longer intervals between cars as a result of the strike.

Businesses along the routes began to suffer. Some businessmen circulated petitions requesting the removal of police squads, stating that the police presence hurt their business and that nothing in the strike warranted so many police squads.

Pressure to prevent the carrying of weapons by Suburban nonunion and replacement workers was placed on St. Louis Chief of Police John Campbell by a committee representing the union interests and separately from prominent citizens concerned with public safety. The common act of motormen or conductors firing into a rock-throwing crowd to disperse it had to that date resulted only in injuries, but saner heads realized that eventually someone would be killed and feared for safety of both the strikers and passengers. The Chief of Police had not responded to either request before the start of the St. Louis Transit strike a few days later.

On May 6th, shaken passengers from Old Orchard, Webster Groves and Kirkwood were sure that strikers had attempted to blow up their car with dynamite. As Suburban car #417 was crossing the Wabash tracks, lightning struck the electric feed wire causing the car to jump and seemingly to leave the tracks. The electric lights had blown, leaving the car in darkness. The motorman cried out that the car had been blown up by strikers, but further investigation showed only that lightning struck the feed wire, traveled to the light circuit of the car and blew it, while at the same time, the car struck and set off a railroad torpedo.[22]

A typical strike incident was reported on May 7th. Strikers boarded a car and verbally abused the conductor and motorman for continuing to work while others were on strike. After the verbal abuse escalated into a fist fight which culminated in an effort to throw the conductor from the car, police were summoned. They broke up the fight, arrested the strikers, and charged them with disturbance of the peace.[23]

On May 7th, as the St. Louis Transit strike became imminent, Suburban car #154 was wrecked in the early morning hours by a bomb. The May 8th *Globe-Democrat* reported:

> Halfway between Gambleton and Etzel avenues, Motorman William Whitaker saw a man standing not far from the track. As the car approached him, the motorman claims, the stranger raised his arm and hurled a bright round object at the car. The missile struck the front of the car and a loud explosion followed.... Examination showed that 6 inches of the flange of one wheel had

---

[22]"Street Car Troubles," GD, 7 May 1900.
[23]Ibid.

been torn away by the explosion and several windows broken. A wrecking car sent to the scene replaced the car on the tracks after considerable effort.[24]

Though the car left the track, it did not overturn, and no one was injured in the blast.

On the afternoon of May 7th, Division 144 held a mass meeting with 232 Suburban employees reported to be in attendance. Strikers cheered an announcement of solidarity; union leadership announced that no one had defected from their ranks. Rank and file members were encouraged by an announcement that strike benefits would be paid at the end of the week to all striking union members.[25]

For almost two weeks the Suburban had been alone in the fray, trying to keep its lines running while Transit was unaffected. Charles Turner was frustrated because he felt the police were not providing enough protection in order for his lines to run safely, even though he had enough men to keep the cars running on a regular schedule throughout the system.

Meanwhile, frustrations among the St. Louis Transit Company employees were mounting because they believed the company was not abiding by the terms of the negotiated agreement. Within a few weeks after the settlement between Baumhoff and the Transit employees, the union demanded a closed shop. In response, Transit took the stance that the union had reneged on its deal. The company then refused to honor the agreement and continued what union employees called its "pattern of victimization" of union sympathizers. As a result, increasingly angry Transit union members anxious to start their own action, were fervent supporters of the strike against the Suburban, gathering along the Suburban lines' street crossings to jeer and harass non-striking workers and replacements.

Union officials of both the Suburban and Transit divisions insisted that their men had been instructed not to engage in acts of violence, citing as perpetrators misguided friends of the strikers and toughs who enjoyed the opportunity to fight and vandalize. Despite the union's stated position, it is clear from arrest records that angry union men were involved in violence against the Suburban and its strike-breaking workers.

The cash poor St. Louis and Suburban was in trouble. How long could it hold out against the strike?

---

[24]"Car Wrecked by a Bomb," GD, 8 May 1900.
[25]"Suburban Union Meets," GD, 8 May 1900.

THOMAS M. JENKINS,
who will be a congressional candidate from Missouri.

CHAS. H. TURNER,
CHAS. H. TURNER & CO., GEN'L R. E. & FIN. AGTS.,
PRES. ST. LOUIS & SUBURBAN R. R.

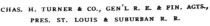

NOTABLE ST. LOUISANS IN 1900.

14-1. Suburban President Charles Turner and General Manager Thomas Jenkins defied the strikers and spared no effort to keep the Suburban lines running during the strike against their street railway company. Jenkins later tried unsuccessfully to ride his "fame" from the streetcar strike into a political office. Drawing from the *St. Louis Post-Dispatch*. Photograph from *Notable St. Louisans in 1900*.

Chapter 15

HOLD 'EM OR FOLD 'EM?

The only thing that may have saved the St. Louis and Suburban from financial ruin as a result of the strike was St. Louis Transit Company's entry into the fray. On May 8th, the St. Louis Transit strike began. Union efforts to keep the strikers from resorting to violence quickly failed, causing the Transit strike to become a bloody battle over the employees' right to participate in union activities without fear of consequences from the street railroad companies. The Transit strike initially made matters even worse for the Suburban.

On May 8th, *Post-Dispatch* headlines shouted: "STRIKE BRINGS RIOTING… NEARLY ALL CREWS ATTACKED."[1]   By that afternoon, Suburban cars were running only as far as 14th street because of the concentration of rioters in the downtown areas. The paper reported:

> Several hundred persons in sympathy with the strike gathered Tuesday morning at Thirteenth street and Washington avenue, where the Suburban and St. Louis Transit Co.'s lines cross, and for several hours wild disorder prevailed. More than 30 cars were stoned and in several instances passengers were injured. Ten motormen and as many conductors of the Suburban line, terrified by the crowd, deserted their cars… A Webster car, No. 301 of the Suburban line, passed Washington avenue and someone hurled a large stone against one of the rear windows. The crash of glass created a panic among the passengers and there was a desperate scramble to escape from the car. As the passengers were filing out, three or four pieces of iron struck the car windows and demolished them.[2]

That incident was representative of many as Suburban cars were stoned or stopped by threatening crowds. In some cases, the motormen tried to increase the current and car speed to break through the crowds, in others the streetcar crew fired revolvers into the crowd in an attempt to free their cars. When the crowds were successful at running off a crew, they vandalized the car, breaking out the windows and ventilators. A squad of 25 St. Louis policemen were woefully inadequate to restore order in the area,

---

[1]"Strike Brings Rioting," PD, 8 May 1900, p. 1.
[2]Ibid.

and were, in fact, in danger themselves. The violence that occurred on the first day of the Transit strike precipitated the Suburban's decision to discontinue operation of their cars east of 14th street. Suburban crews with police escorts were sent out to retrieve the abandoned cars. The *Globe-Democrat* reported:

> The crews were accompanied by a squad of police as well as a dozen mounted men. This cordon had some effect on the crowd for a time, but when the cars began to move, a yell brought hundreds more to the place and the police had much difficulty in making an opening.[3]

The cars were finally moved only to encounter a curve where the rails had been coated with soft-soap. The crowd, nearly two blocks deep in every direction, gathered around the stuck cars and enjoyed the sight of the streetcar wheels spinning uselessly and reveled in the obvious discomfort of the crew and police. Catcalls and taunts were all that occurred until a small boy threw a brick at the motorman. That unleashed a barrage of rocks and bricks. The motorman ducked, and as he knelt behind a shield was believed to have fired a shot which hit a man in the leg. After the presumed shooting, the crowd surged toward the car in an attempt to reach the motorman, but the police drove them back until the car was able to move with the help of liberal amounts of sand on the rails. In the incident, one spectator was hit over his right eye by a brick, fracturing his skull.[4]

In some cases strikers were successful in converting streetcar crews to their cause.. The *Post-Dispatch* reported that Suburban motorman John Hawkins and conductor John O'Brien in Webster car 318 had enough of the strike when they reached 13th street. As they left the car, strike supporters grabbed them and shook their hands. O'Brien was quoted:

> I'll tell you boys that I didn't realize the kind of proposition that I was up against. I can't afford to lose my life for a few dollars. The best thing I can do I guess is to join the union.[5]

Car 351 of the Webster line was behind O'Brien's car. Its conductor and motorman called out to the crowd not to throw at them because they were giving up. The motorman later said, "It was a case of leaving the cars or running the risk of being killed."[6]

At one point in the mob scene, a man who identified himself as a union member unsuccessfully asked the crowd to stop stoning the cars. He stated to reporters, "We are

---

[3]GD, 8 May 1900, p. 1.
[4]Ibid.
[5]"Strike Brings Rioting," PD, 8 May 1900, p. 1.
[6]Ibid.

not responsible for this. The crowds pelting those cars with stones have no connection whatever with the street railway men's union."[7]

Riot calls were turned in and additional squads of police were sent to the area. The large crowds were finally dispersed by noon.

Conditions in the county were better since the concentrated effort of the Transit men was directed toward shutting down the city streetcar operations. The main effect noticed in Kirkwood and Webster Groves was a dramatic increase in ridership on the steam railroads.

The Suburban made a great effort to keep its cars running on the first day of the Transit strike. It did so fairly well till the early afternoon, despite crowds that jeered and hooted at the streetcar crews, called them names and acted in a threatening manner. At two p.m. that day, the Suburban management gave up and suspended running of the cars.

Though the Suburban strike had been a lesser irritant to St. Louis, the magnitude of the St. Louis Transit strike in connection with the existing Suburban strike and the accompanying violence, galvanized politicians and newspapers. The *Post-Dispatch* publicized its proposal to appoint seven Circuit Court judges as arbitrators, while St. Louis Mayor Ziegenheim wrote to Transit officials and the union suggesting arbitration, offering to serve in any capacity for that purpose.

On May 9th, Transit suspended all operations except for mail-cars until assured better police protection. George Baumhoff stated Transit's rationale, "No further attempt will be made to move cars until we are assured of better police protection than we had yesterday… it would be folly for the company to attempt to run cars under these conditions."[8]

Post-Dispatch headlines on the 9th announced in large type, "SUBURBAN ROAD IS RUNNING. The Line Resumes Service Under Police Guard Wednesday Afternoon, but No Attempt to Move Transit Company Cars Will Be Made Before Thursday… SUBURBAN CAN HAVE ENTIRE POLICE FORCE." The article continued:

> President Hawes of the police board says the protection promised the Suburban shall be given if the entire force of policemen is necessary to secure it. A large squad of police will be stationed at De Hodiamont to see that the crews of the cars are allowed to discharge their duties, and several officers will escort the cars on their runs.[9]

---

[7] Ibid.

[8] "Suburban Line is Running - The Line Resumes Service Under Police Guard Wednesday Afternoon, but no Attempt to Move Transit Company Cars Will be Made Before Thursday," PD, 9 May 1900, p. 1.

[9] Ibid.

KING TROLLEY: HOLD 'EM OR FOLD 'EM

Charles Turner angrily proclaimed that the Suburban had three hundred men ready to return to work if their lives could be protected. He submitted a statement to all the major newspapers:

> To the Public: If the police will prevent the congregating of strikers and their sympathizers at points along the lines for the purpose of stoning, assaulting or intimidating our motormen and conductors, and will see that our men are protected in the discharge of their duties, we will put our cars in operation from the instant we receive this assurance and run them every one and a half minutes during business hours… we will guarantee that the public will no longer be inconvenienced as far as the Suburban and its branch lines are concerned.[10]

Hawes testily replied that he would see that Turner had all the police protection he needed and that, if the Suburban failed to run, it would not be the fault of the police department.[11]

After the violence of the day before, the second day of the Transit strike began much quieter with only Suburban cars running and even those cars not starting operations until three in the afternoon. Tensions soon rose as the cars began running their schedule, leading to the strike's first fatality which occurred in a riot about 8:30 p.m. at the intersection of Taylor Avenue and the Suburban tracks. Frank Liebrecht, a 21 year old veteran of the Spanish-American War, was part of a crowd of several hundred persons protesting the streetcar operations. He was on the lawn in front of the Baptist Sanitarium watching as a westbound Suburban car was stoned by the crowd. When it stopped at Taylor to discharge passengers, shots were fired from inside the car, one of which fatally wounded Liebrecht. Six men on the car were arrested in the shooting incident, but Chief of Police Campbell did not hold Liebrecht blameless. He stated in the *Post-Dispatch* on the 10th, "I do not know whether Liebrecht was stoning the car or not, but he was in the crowd and therefore equally guilty."[12]

On the second day of the mass strike, the Suburban concentrated its efforts on its city lines. The only car that ran on the Manchester line was the white mail car carrying mail to Maplewood, Webster Groves and Kirkwood. The Brentwood powerhouse was heavily guarded. Even when no cars were running because of the strike, its dynamos were kept running to send a small flow of current through the lines in order to tell if trolley feed wires were cut.

On the 10th, Chief Campbell imparted a no-nonsense message to the public via a statement that he gave to the *Post-Dispatch* for publication:

---

[10]"President Turner's Position," PD, 9 May 1900, p. 2.

[11]"Suburban Road is Running," PD, 9 May 1900, p. 1.

[12]"To Settle the Strike.. Frank Liebrecht, The Strike's First Victim," PD, 10 May 1900, p. 1.

We have the situation well in hand. We are going to show the people that we can run the cars. We have shown that we can run the Suburban line and later on we will show that we can operate the Transit Company's lines. When the public finally finds out that we are determined, there will be no more foolishness… [13]

Early the next morning an incident occurred at Webster Groves in which a car was wrecked by dynamite. The *Globe-Democrat* reported:

An explosion occurred under a car on the Houseman line at Webster Groves at 2 o'clock yesterday morning, tearing out a foot or so of the rails and a section of one of the car wheels… It is supposed that a stick of dynamite was placed on the rail and the weight of the car exploded it… Deputy Sheriff Will Barron reported that he and a posse had been patrolling the tracks but were nearly a mile east of Webster when they heard the report.[14]

The Suburban management expected obstructions or vandalism on the Houseman line and ordered the car out to inspect for damage. After the car filled with employees rounded a curve near Rock Hill Road and was running down an incline to Shady Avenue, an explosion occurred on a small bridge spanning a branch of the River Des Peres. The car's speed carried it over the break in the rail, but the damaged front wheel caused the car to leave the tracks. The frightened employees loosed a couple dozen shots into the darkness to scare off any men in hiding. The car was then abandoned for the rest of the night.[15]

"Suburban Cars Ran All Day Regularly," stated a *Globe-Democrat* headline on May 11th. On the previous day, the "Meramec River Division" to Kirkwood was opened for regular traffic for the first time since the Transit strike was declared. Protected by police, both on the cars and stationed at crossings, cars were able to run every 13 minutes without violence, though the car crews were subjected to derisive yells. Service was discontinued at nightfall on all Suburban lines.

On the 11th, the only Suburban line not running a full complement of cars was the Houseman-Kirkwood line which had not run since the start of the Transit strike because its Lindell connection with the city was blocked by strikers. Even though there had been no interruption of service throughout the day, Jenkins was not yet willing to risk running Suburban cars in the evening.[16]

---

[13]Ibid.
[14]"Suburban System Cars Run," GD, 10 May 1900, p. 1.
[15]Ibid.
[16]"Suburban Places Its Full Complement of Cars on All Urban Divisions," GD, 12 May 1900, p. 1.

KING TROLLEY: HOLD 'EM OR FOLD 'EM

Despite the strike, construction work continued on the Brentwood, Clayton and St. Louis line. In fact, the Transit strike in a small way speeded up the construction, as the stoppage of the Clayton and Forest Park cars allowed Suburban crews to complete construction of a crossover at the corner of St. Ferdinand (Forsyth) and Central Avenue in Clayton without interference of Transit's Clayton and Forest Park cars.

Service resumed on the Houseman line on May 12th. The *Globe-Democrat* reported that the roadbed damaged by dynamite at Webster Groves had been repaired. However, few passengers patronized the line because it was still blocked at the city connection. Only one car was operated on the line with no attempt at a regular schedule. The cars of the Meramec (Manchester) division, with police support, operated without interruption as they had the day before.[17]

Sunday the 13th of May provided an opportunity for the lines to take a day off and allow their employees, who had been working long stressful hours, a chance to rest. The police were exhausted. The Chief of Police notified both lines affected by the strike that there would be no police protection on Sunday, so that his men could recover. Representatives of the Suburban and Transit companies met and agreed that they would not run cars.[18]

On the 14th, 50 shots were fired in a mini-battle between guards and wire cutters about 1 a. m. near Brentwood.

> The fight took place near the long bridge a quarter mile from the power house at Brentwood. Four men guarding the property of the Suburban saw two men on foot and one on horseback moving along the car tracks. The three men held a conference, and one began climbing a trolley-pole while carrying wire cutters in his hand.
> The guards opened fire at the climber, who slid to the ground. The three armed men returned the shots and fled, with more bullets following them.[19]

Suburban officials claimed that they were running at full force on the 14th, operating as many cars as were run before the strike. However, delays still occurred. Spikes in the rail joints at Sarah and Channing avenue delayed the Suburban mail cars by an hour while the spikes were removed. The incident was reported to Federal authorities who then forcefully stated to the unions that mail cars were not to be impeded by the strike.

An oddity of the strike was reported in the *Post-Dispatch*. A large number of people had attempted to get to work via bicycle. Many were stymied by flat tires

---

[17]"No Cars Today...," GD, 13 May 1900, p.1.
[18]Ibid.
[19]"Arbitrators Work on Both Systems...," PD, 14 May 1900.

punctured by the glass shards from streetcar windows left in the downtown streets after the riots of previous days.[20]

For the first time, a glimmer of hope for settlement of the Suburban strike was reported on May 13th. The day before, five men formed a committee representing Suburban crews still operating cars. They met with Superintendent Jenkins and asked his permission to negotiate a settlement. They were given permission and a clear signal that he was ready to compromise in order to settle the strike. The committee then met with the union president and the members of the grievance committee. Union president Jolly gave them a draft of an agreement which the union considered acceptable. Jenkins, who did not accept the agreement as proposed, stated that he was willing to take the union men back and was willing to receive a representative committee from the striking men in order to settle their differences.

Though willing to negotiate, Jenkins was not contrite, stating his position regarding the work action in the May 14th *Globe-Democrat*:

> The fact is, but 121 men left the company employ. Of those some thirty men had been discharged before the trouble. Sixteen men left their work of remodeling cars in the shops.... On the Tuesday following the strike thirty-four came back in a body and went to work. They are working now. Of the 121 men who went out, that left but forty-one men who are now holding out against coming back to work. Does that look like a strike?[21]

Though Jenkins' math didn't add up, his message was clear. Since only about one-fifth of the Suburban men remained on strike, Jenkins believed that he could operate without them. However, because of the Transit strike, the situation had become more violent and complicated than he had expected and was having a detrimental effect on the Suburban's financial well-being.

Eager to be out of the strike, after consulting with Suburban president Charles Turner, Jenkins agreed to submit the issues to arbitration. He realized the Transit strike could be long and that his company stood to make more by operating during the strike than it would lose, even if the arbitrator found in favor of the workers. As a result, he swallowed his angry feelings and agreed to negotiate.

On May 14th, the *Post-Dispatch* headlines reported, "Situation on the Suburban Lines is Hopeful, BOTH SIDES TALK FAIR. They Agree to Abide by the Results of the Conference No Matter What It May Be."[22] Three men met to select an arbitration board to settle the Suburban railway strike. President of the Police Board, Harry B. Hawes represented Jenkins and the men working for the company. The strikers were represented

---

[20]Ibid.

[21]"Suburban Trouble Again Becomes Subject of Negotiation," GD, 14 May 1900, p. 1.

[22]"Arbitrators Work on Both Systems...," PD, 14 May 1900, p. 1.

by Chairman Woodworth of the grievance committee and by the national union President Mahon. After the meeting, Hawes was hopeful that the strike would be settled that afternoon, as a result of an arbitration plan that he had offered earlier in the day to union president Jolly on behalf of Manager Jenkins:

> The striking employees to select one arbitrator, the employees, not striking to select another, and the two to select a third man, all of whom shall constitute a board of arbitration. This board shall decide whether he (Jenkins) or the men violated the agreement entered into April 6 by himself and his employees. If the decision is in his favor all employees are to return to work; if against him, then he agrees to submit all questions of differences between himself and his employees to arbitration.[23]

Following the afternoon meeting, Woodworth sounded skeptical but affirmed the union's commitment to abide by the arbitration decisions:

> …We want a fair and square deal all around, and you can say for me that if this matter is arbitrated by mutual agreement, the union will stand by the decision. Even if it goes against us, we will swallow our medicine, and expect the Suburban company to do the same if it goes in our favor.[24]

After Jenkins and Woodworth signed the agreement to arbitrate, Woodworth notified all union men not discharged before April 29th to report for work.

On the 15th, the *Post-Dispatch* headlines signaled the end of the strike: "SUBURBAN CARS RUN AS OF OLD: Strike Practically Ended by an Agreement. ENTIRE SYSTEM IS OPERATING. OLD SCHEDULE FOR DAY AND NIGHT IS IN FORCE..." Police guards were withdrawn from the Suburban properties for the first time since the strike had begun. Owl cars ran for the first time since May 7th.[25]

Despite the agreement, hard feelings and accusations abounded. A committee of union men claimed that a great many of them who had reported for duty at the general offices of the Suburban had not been put to work, but were told that the company would not return them to work until all of the men, as stipulated in the agreement, had made application for reinstatement. National union President Mahon urged restraint, citing a clause in the agreement that the signers of the agreement could not promise the return of all men to work by the next day since some were unavailable. He assured them that he thought the company would keep its agreement and was only waiting until all of the men had made their formal application. Had Mahon not taken such a conciliatory stance, the strike would most likely have been resumed.[26]

---

[23] Ibid.
[24] Ibid.
[25] "Suburban Cars Run as of Old..," PD, 15 May 1900, p. 1.
[26] Ibid.

Two arbitrators were quickly selected; representing Suburban non-strikers was Scott H. Blewett, a sales agent of the American Car and Foundry Company; the union representative was H. W. Steinbiss, a well-known local labor leader and editor of the *Labor Compendium*. By the close of their meeting at the St. Nicholas Hotel on the 18th, they believed that most issues were resolved, and that a third arbitrator, W. T. Anderson, a St. Louis grain dealer, had been selected. Before action could be taken on the agreement, Steinbiss learned that Anderson had signed an anti-strike document circulated among businessmen of the city. Steinbiss then requested that a different man be named. Eventually, after much debate and a long delay, Steinbiss agreed to Anderson's selection if the union men were willing to accept him.

Tensions still ran high. The grievance committee representative stated that the men who reported back for work "have been received with indignity, and even insult..." He further charged that a number of the men who were working on April 29th were refused return to their runs.[27] Mahon urged the union grievance committee to investigate the claims of the three men to see if they were eligible for assistance of the union, and encouraged the union to allow the arbitration process to proceed.

Even though the county lines were running, their feed lines were popular targets for vandals and thieves. The *Post-Dispatch* reported on the 21st of May that 300 feet of feed wire strung for the use of the new Brentwood, Clayton and St. Louis line had been stolen during the past few nights. The thick copper cables were valuable for their copper content, so it was likely that the action was not that of strikers but that of thieves.[28]

In the early morning hours of May 25th, the Suburban union men voted to walk out again over the issue of reinstatement of all its men. At issue was the rehiring of one man against whom Jenkins planned to bring criminal charges for his actions during the strike. Jenkins had already agreed to take back 10 of 11 men who were in question. Ben Clark, the workers' attorney addressed the men urging them not to be hasty in their actions. The *Globe-Democrat* reported, "While he was speaking, both the strike and anti-strike elements hissed the speaker, as his advice was for or against them."[29] As a result of his exhortations, the union then voted to give Jenkins another 24 hours to reinstate all the men, but they also agreed to an amendment that Mr. Jenkins be given opportunity to substantiate his charges against the one man to whom he especially objected. Clark then arranged a meeting with Jenkins at his office that afternoon. Jenkins conferred with grievance committee head George Woodworth over their differences. After the two finally reached agreement, Jenkins gave orders which were agreeable to the union officers who then returned to union headquarters to report to their men.

---

[27] PD, 19 May 1900.

[28] Not until December 21 was the wire thief apprehended. A former linesman of the Suburban was arrested at Eager Avenue south of Clayton. At the time of his arrest, he was equipped with a full set of linesman's tools and a revolver, not to mention about 200 feet of cut copper feed wire. SLCW, 21 December 1900.

[29] "All Men Back or Walk Out... ," GD, 25 May 1900.

Once the Suburban strike was over, there was humor to be found in the Transit strike at Suburban Gardens which was served by the non-striking Suburban lines. The park opened on Sunday, May 20th to the "largest crowd in the history of that popular West End Resort."[30] The *Watchman* reported, "The Suburban cars ran without molestation or accident and thousands of people from all parts of the city reached by the line went out in the afternoon and evening and enjoyed a cool ride and a good show."[31] The vaudeville show featured a spoof of the rail strike problems.

The three arbitrators met together for the first time in the director's room of the Merchant's Exchange on July 9th. They required several meetings to hear all the evidence from both sides of the dispute. On Saturday, July 21, 1900, they completed a final review of the evidence documented by a court stenographer prior to making their decision.

"ARBITERS MAKE TWO REPORTS. Two Aver That Suburban Employees Were Wrong… Both Sides Have Agreed to Abide by The Board's Decision, Which Was Made After Several Meetings," read the headlines of the July 22nd *Post-Dispatch*. Blewett and Anderson, as the majority found that the employees had violated their agreement with Superintendent Jenkins. The result of arbitrators' decision was that the agreement of April 6th was still in effect. Anderson and Blewett wrote a brief statement which stated:

> Gentlemen: We have carefully read and considered the agreement made and signed by you on April 6, and have taken evidence from each party to the agreement, and from the evidence submitted to us we decide that the employees of said Suburban Railroad Co. have failed to keep said agreement with T. H. Jenkins, superintendent of the Suburban Railway Co. Respectfully yours, W. T. Anderson, Chairman (and) Scott H. Blewett[32]

Steinbiss, who acknowledged some irregularity by the union, issued a dissenting statement that all who had difficulty joining the union were now members of the division and therefore the union was not at fault.

Suburban lines ran without major incident during the remainder of the five month long Transit strike. Many passengers boycotted St. Louis Transit's cars in favor of the Suburban's. During the strike, the Suburban operated well above capacity loads, especially in the morning and afternoon rush hour periods. A cartoon appeared in the May 20th *Post-Dispatch* showing an overloaded St. Louis and Suburban car with commuters packed on the roof and hanging from the ends of the car. The caption read,

---

[30]SLCW, 25 May 1900.
[31]Ibid.
[32]"Arbitrators Make Two Reports…," PD, 22 July 1900, p. 11.

"YOU MIGHT HAVE THOUGHT THAT THIS A JOKE A MONTH AGO BUT IT IS REALITY NOW."

On June 10, the *Republic* featured a half page illustration of an overloaded Suburban car #327 with a Webster Groves as its destination. The headline read, "How the Only Unembarrassed Street Car Line in St. Louis Handles Its Patronage."[33] To give credence to its drawing, the caption proclaimed that it was made from a photograph taken earlier in the week for the *Sunday Republic*. The timing of the article was an irony since later that day, the worst violence of the Transit strike emphasized the advantage of riding the Suburban. A battle erupted between the strikers and an appointed posse of citizens established to protect Transit operations. Three were left dead and fourteen were injured.

The *Republic* article written without knowledge of the impending violence, illuminated the extent of the patronage enjoyed by the Suburban as a result of the Transit strike:

> The sardine simile has become a fact, and the sight of men huddled in close order on top of street cars, as well as hanging over the platforms and from the windows, can be seen any morning or afternoon along the route of the Suburban street railroad.[34]

At first the passengers who climbed up on the roof had a free ride, but the company decided to remove the ladders at the front ends of the cars, leaving only the rear ladders. Before a customer would be allowed to climb to the top he was required to see the conductor and pay his fare. One Suburban conductor reported to the paper that he had carried 178 passengers on one trip and rang up that many fares. Not every conductor was so diligent:

> On an eastbound car the other night, the seats, aisles, front and back platforms and roof were filled until a forty day's faster could not have found standing room anywhere. The register at the end of the trip showed forty-three fares collected. It is possible that the conductor went on the theory of, "no seat, no fare," for there were seats for forty in the car.[35]

Amazingly, the paper reported that with all the crowding there had been only a few accidents. Since the Suburban had begun carrying such heavy traffic, only one man had been badly injured as a result of a fall from the roof of a car. Usually as a car ran further west the top riders exited. However, a policeman had reported to the paper that one evening he saw at least twenty men still riding a car, "as far west as King's highway,

---

[33] "How the Only unembarrassed Street Car Line...," Republic, 10 June 1900.

[34] Ibid.

[35] Ibid.

and they were still going."[36]   By the time Suburban cars neared the county ends of their runs at Webster Grove and Kirkwood, virtually all passengers were able to enter the cars.

Not until September did the hungry and weary Transit strikers give up. Though unsuccessful in meeting the streetcar union's goals, the strike brought to public awareness the poor state of municipal services provided in St. Louis, the corporate arrogance of the power elite, the rampant corruption of local and state politicians and the need for fair taxation of utilities, including the streetcar companies.

Once the strike was settled, Jenkins had approval of Suburban head man Charles Turner to push expansion. He stated to newspapers that his purpose was to build up the Suburban's property physically. Instead of paying dividends from the big profits made during the strike, he extended the road, made improvements on equipment and upgraded routes with heavier rail. He vowed not to stop until the Suburban was a model street railroad property. Though not stated to the papers, Turner's purpose was to force United Railways to purchase the Suburban in order to stop its competition. To do that, he would need to hit closer to Transit's pocketbook with competition from new routes such as a three mile extension to Union Station. Establishing those new routes was his next order of business by any means necessary, legal or not.

15-1. "Frank Liebrecht, 21 years old, who lived at 4872 Easton avenue, and was a private in the Sixteenth Infantry at San Juan, was the first victim of the (Suburban) strike." Front page of the *St. Louis Post-Dispatch*, May 10, 1900.

---

[36] Ibid.

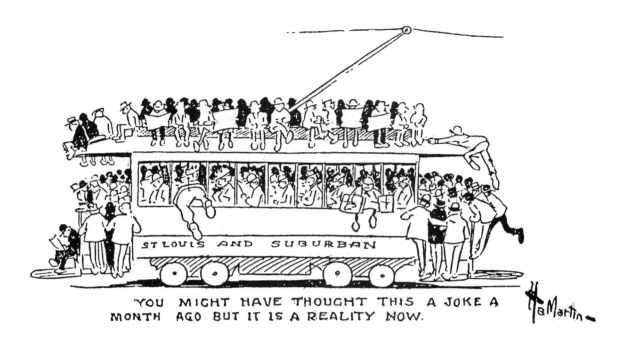

15-2. Cartoon from the May 20th *Post-Dispatch*, which showed a Suburban car overloaded as a result of the St. Louis Transit strike.

15-3. The St. Louis Transit strike made the operation of the Suburban very difficult in the first days. This illustration from the May 9th *Globe-Democrat* shows a Suburban car being stoned by a pro-strike crowd at Thirteenth Street. On May 8th, at various city locations, many of the cars on the Suburban lines suffered the same fate.

"FOUR MEN STANDING ON THE 'BUFFER'."

15-4. **After the Suburban settled the strike, its cars were often overloaded. This illustration from Charles Delbridge's attack on St. Louis transit lines, Move it Forward!** shows the practice of riding the buffer, a fender only four inches in width. During the Transit strike, after the Suburban had settled, it was not unusual to see riders standing on Suburban car buffers, especially as cars neared the downtown terminus.

15-5. **Photo of a Suburban car overloaded during the Transit strike. From the Charles Hamman collection.**

Chapter 16

THE SUBURBAN'S CLAYTON CONNECTION

Though St. Louis newspapers were filled with news of the Transit strike in the Spring of 1900, the *County Watchman* was much more interested in the progress of the Suburban's new Brentwood, Clayton and St. Louis line. Promoters had been pursuing street rail franchises to connect Clayton with St. Louis county since 1889. The first to be granted approval by County Court was the effort by the Clayton and Forest Park Railroad Company, organized on August 23, 1891, with Thomas Skinker as president. The *Watchman* reported on Skinker's effort, "The latest project is to run a narrow gauge railway from Union Avenue in St. Louis through the northern end of Forest Park to the North and South Road (Meramec Avenue) at Clayton."[1] After a delay, in July 1892, approval for a city connection with the St. Louis and Suburban at Union Boulevard in Forest Park was given by the St. Louis House of Delegates. The passage was assured only after obligatory bribes had been distributed. The route passed through the Catlin tract to Skinker Road and then west on what has since become Wydown Avenue.

Skinker optimistically announced that the Clayton and Forest Park cars would be in operation by December. However, the line quickly ran into financial difficulties resulting in numerous delays. Track was laid by 1894, but money ran out before the trolley poles and electric lines could be installed. In April 1895, the company was declared bankrupt and sold by the sheriff on the courthouse steps. Clayton residents were becoming skeptical that the line would ever operate. They were pleased that the Lindell Railway, one of the strongest city lines at the time, purchased the bankrupt line. The Lindell Company immediately set to work on their new acquisition erecting trolley poles and stringing electric lines. The work was finally completed on December 9, 1895.

Though long awaited, the Clayton and Forest Park line opened with minimal ceremonial fanfare. Despite the presence of flags hung on the courthouse and some stores and homes, "the only unusual things were the cars themselves."[2] Once the line opened for business, cars operated every 20 minutes during the day and every 40 minutes from six p.m. to midnight. The fare was a nickel from Clayton to Forsyth Junction. There most

---

[1] "A New Railroad," SLCW, 28 June 1899. The St. Louis Cable and Western Railroad switched to electricity and by 1892 was known as the St. Louis and Suburban. The connection would allow passengers to ride all the way to Florissant or to the city after a transfer at Union Avenue.
[2] SLCW, 13 December 1895.

passengers boarded a Lindell car for the trip to Third and Washington in downtown St. Louis. The trip from Clayton to downtown St. Louis took one hour and four minutes.

Without competition, the Lindell saw no need to double track its line on Central Avenue, but in 1898 when the Brentwood, Clayton and St. Louis Railroad Company was granted a franchise to serve Clayton, Lindell Railway's head George Baumhauff decided to strike before the competition was ready. He defended the Lindell position on Central Avenue by sending out a crew early in the morning of September 24, 1898 to lay a second track along that street in front of the county courthouse. By the time the Suburban realized what had happened, it was too late for the company to get an injunction to stop the construction. As a result, the second track granted to the Suburban could not be built due to lack of space on the street. The Suburban was forced to lay a single track on the west side of Central Avenue.

Despite the St. Louis connection and the round about county connections offered via transfers to other lines, the county seat needed the direct connections with other parts of the county provided by the Suburban. Clayton and county residents watched the progress with interest. Ties had been delivered by the Brentwood, Clayton and St. Louis Company to Clayton's Central Avenue in October 1899 for the "third track on that thoroughfare."[3] Construction of the line continued despite the Suburban strike. Work was nearing completion and in fact was aided by the Transit Company strike with the stoppage of the Clayton and Forest Park cars. Crews did not have to interrupt their work to allow the cars to pass as they constructed a crossover of the Clayton and Forest Park tracks at the corner of Central and St. Ferdinand. [4]

On May 18, 1900, after eight months of waiting, the rails were "down" on Central Avenue.[5] The *Watchman* noted wistfully on June 1st, "The work of ballasting the new railway on Central is progressing slowly, but is progressing. What we want to see is the line in operation from end to end."[6]

A last ditch effort by one property owner to prevent the line from going down 66th Street required the electric line to obtain a restraining order from the Circuit Court. William L. Mayers stood with a shotgun in front of his property and defied the street railroad employees to lay tracks over his property. Another owner on 66th Street asked for an injunction against the railroad because he claimed that County Court did not have the right to award right-of-way down 66th Street since it was a private thoroughfare. When he failed to file $15,000 bond, the issue was dropped and construction proceeded.[7]

A construction car and its crew were busy stringing trolley wire through Clayton on May 29th in preparation for the line to begin operation from end to end. The next day,

---

[3] SLCW, 20 October 1899, p. 8.
[4] SLCW, 11 May 1900, p. 8.   St. Ferdinand Avenue is now Forsyth Boulevard.
[5] SLCW, 18 May 1900.
[6] SLCW, 1 June 1900.
[7] Though northeast of Clayton the 66th street right of way was needed to complete the connection between Clayton and De Hodiamont.

streetcars began running on a half hour schedule between Clayton and De Hodiamont, the connection with the main Suburban line. As the first car arrived in Clayton over the Brentwood, Clayton and St. Louis line, it was greeted with fanfare. The *Watchman* reported that car #404, manned by conductor W. D. Smith and motorman W. S. Whittaker, was given a "rousing reception."[8] All day long that first day, the line was well patronized, right up until the late car turned in at 12 o'clock that night.[9]

In keeping with the practice of making influential people happy, the officials of the Brentwood, Clayton and St. Louis line sponsored a "Grand Opening" trolley ride and a show at Suburban Gardens on the evening of May 30th for several hundred Clayton residents. The reviews were good:

> ...although the two cars were somewhat crowded, the crowd was as pleasant and agreeable as was the evening. About 8 o'clock... the start was made from Clayton, amid cheers and shouts from those who had come to see the party off, and within fifteen minutes all were landed in the Suburban Garden... The new road, although as yet unballasted in its entirety, is remarkably smooth and free from the jarring and jolting so often noticed in roads of older construction, and the time made was almost equivalent to that of the other lines of the Suburban system.... all who enjoyed the outing were loud in their praises of the gentlemen of the Brentwood, Clayton and St. Louis line, who had given them such a pleasant evening.[10]

Suburban superintendent of construction, C. S. Butts, reported to the newspapers that cars had begun running from Clayton to Kirkwood on May 31st and that he hoped to have the wires up and track laid through the St. Louis Country Club grounds by Saturday, June 2nd, in order to haul the United Workmen of the county to the Grand Union Picnic at Bartold's Grove.[11]

Despite the pleasure in having the second line in operation, Clayton residents were upset that Central Avenue was overcrowded by the presence of three tracks. As the latest arrival, with much to gain by capturing loyalty of the Clayton residents while the St. Louis Transit Company was still on strike, the Suburban announced plans to increase driveway space on Central Avenue. It set its poles back to the line of the granitoid (concrete) walk and converted the strip between its tracks and the pavement into part of the street. However, even that action was not satisfactory to the editor of the *County Watchman*:

> This will necessarily do away with the row of shade trees set out by Sheriff Kerth a couple of years ago, which will be a great loss indeed. It has seemed to us all along that both companies should have been compelled to use the

---

[8]SLCW, 1 June 1900.
[9]Ibid.
[10]"A Pleasant Outing," SLCW, 1 June 1900, p. 4.
[11]SLCW, 1 June 1900.

same tracks from Bonhomme to St. Ferdinand avenue, which would have kept the third track off Central avenue.[12]

By September, the "substantial granitoid curb and gutter" along the section with three tracks was completed by the Suburban. Telford paving was laid by the company, prompting the *Watchman* to query, "Will the Transit Company do likewise?"[13] The work on the Brentwood, Clayton and St. Louis Railroad was finally considered completed and was given a stamp of approval by St. Louis County officials in December 1900.

Until January 1906, the two competing lines operated the three sets of track on Central Avenue. Despite an act passed in 1903 which allowed the County Court to remove one set of tracks on a public thoroughfare and require both competing lines to share the tracks, no further action was taken until January 1906. As a compromise, the St. Louis and Suburban agreed to remove its single track on the west side of Central Avenue. United Railways agreed to allow the Suburban to join its tracks at Bonhomme and Central and at St. Ferdinand and Central. The Suburban was given the responsibility to maintain the southbound track and the connection at Bonhomme, while United Railways was responsible for the northbound track and the connection at St. Ferdinand. The use of the track by the Suburban was provided rent free, but the Suburban had to provide the electrical power for both lines on the section that they shared.[14]

Clayton, by the end of 19th century, was well connected by street rail to both city and county. The 'Suburban Queens" and their county cousins were at last able to travel on King Trolley in a direct route to the county's "Queen Mother."

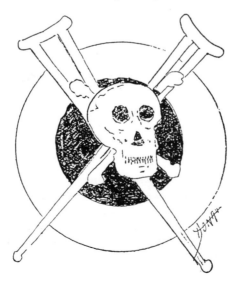

16-1. Despite Charles Delbridge's pessimistic proposal for a coat-of-arms for the street railways, Clayton residents were happy to be connected by the new electric railway to Kirkwood, Webster Groves, Ferguson and other county towns.

[12]SLCW, 27 July 1900, p. 5.
[13]SLCW, 28 September 1900, p. 8.
[14]Franchises of United Railways ..., (1913).

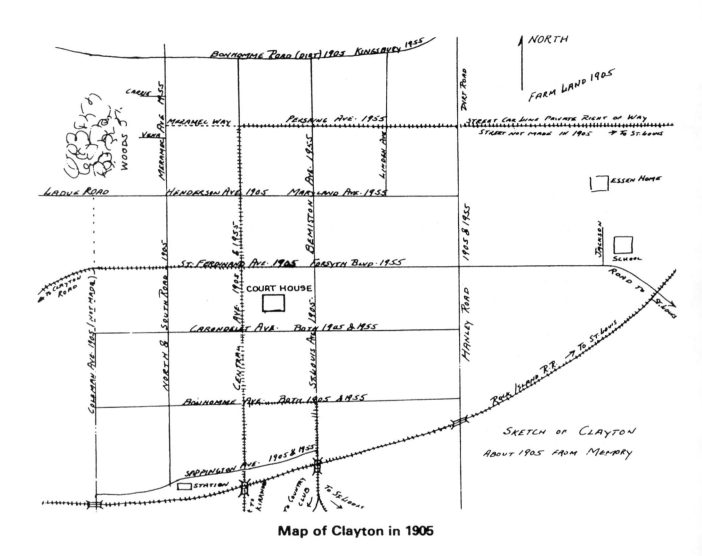

Map of Clayton in 1905

16-2. Map of Clayton, drawn from memory by Henri Chomeau, indicates street changes in Clayton between 1905 and 1955. Chomeau was the surveyor that laid out the town of Clayton in 1877. He later headed a team of engineers that surveyed the proposed route of the Clayton and Forest Park Electric Railroad. The map was published by students of Wydown Jr. High in 1976 accompanying an article entitled, "The Clayton Dinky."[15]

---

[15]Members of the Wydown Eighth Grade of 1976, <u>Images of Our Community - Clayton</u>, (Clayton, MO)

Chapter 17

LOOP ANCHORS MAPLEWOOD'S DEVELOPMENT

Maplewood was the name given to a new subdivision platted circa 1896 near the St. Louis city limits on the south side of Manchester Road and east of Sutton Avenue. The subdivision developers were banking heavily on the presence of the Manchester streetcar line to bring new residents. Since Manchester was a main east-west highway, the corner of Manchester and Sutton already had some businesses. However, the addition of the streetcar line and the greatly increased number of people traveling through the town was expected to generate the development of a more robust business district. As hoped, the advent of the Manchester streetcar line made Maplewood the spout in a funnel through which the population of Webster Groves, Kirkwood and surrounding towns flowed into the city. The flow through the funnel reversed daily as commuters headed home from work. The reverse occurred on summer days and weekends when city residents traveled west for recreation in the rural areas served by the line.

The presence of the Manchester line was a major selling point for the Maplewood subdivision promoters. Advertisement fliers of the subdivision plots were illustrated with streetcars operating on Manchester and on Sutton Avenue. The ad's copy stated, "A BEAUTIFUL SUBDIVISION ON THE MANCHESTER ELECTRIC R'Y, to Sixth and Locust Streets for a FIVE CENT FARE."[1] The ad also pointed out the advantage of Maplewood's location bordering the city, only "2,000 feet outside city limits... ."[2] From Maplewood, a streetcar trip could be made for five cents without a transfer between Sixth and Locust in St. Louis and Sutton Avenue. Most county residents had to pay an additional five cent fare at Maplewood, making streetcar transportation for Maplewood residents a real bargain.

As a result of the Suburban's loop constructed at Sutton Avenue, Maplewood's business district grew rapidly to serve the business generated by the streetcar riders. The loop which was a block south of Manchester was the turn around point for city cars and a transfer point for many county riders. The formerly quiet little hamlet had changed

---

[1]Papin and Tontrup Realtors, "Maplewood Subdivision," advertisement circa 1896.
[2]Ibid.

significantly by 1899. The *County Watchman* correspondent noted, "Maplewood is the sight of busy times by constant crowds at the loop."[3] On June 2, 1899, the *Watchman* noted, "Maplewood residences are more sought for than any other suburb. The one fare to the city makes it popular."[4] In the August, the *Watchman* correspondent further noted, "Maplewood has a building boom at a great rate."[5] As a result of good access to the city, by the end of the century, many more residents had settled in the area, which gave further impetus to the development of the bustling business district as well as to the development of public institutions such as schools, parks, and a library.

The main reason for a wait at the passenger facility at Maplewood's loop was to make the right connection with another car. Certain cars such as the Benton cars ran only as far west as Maplewood before turning back to the city. Riders could catch a Benton car to Maplewood and then transfer to a Webster or a Kirkwood car. The time spent at the transfer point was a perfect opportunity to pick up a few things, i.e. medications, sundries, food or clothing. Riders could take a few minutes shopping at the Maplewood transfer point to avoid having to make a special shopping trip at a later time. In those days before the automobile, shopping trips were a planned event, not like today's spontaneous decision to hop in the car and go shopping.

Streetcar passengers really appreciated the opportunity to shop en route. Merchants and other business owners quickly realized that with a location near the loop, they had access to virtually all the populace served by the Manchester lines, residents from the county as well as from the city who were just passing through. Once the business district near the loop became well developed, Maplewood became known as a good shopping district and thus became a destination for shopping, movies, restaurants, and other business such as banks and real estate offices.

In July of 1899, the *Watchman* reported that a new grocery store, a new pharmacy in the Baker building, and other businesses had opened near the loop. Postal officials, recognizing that the loop was a center of activity, moved the Maplewood post-office to the loop in 1899. In less than a month, it had doubled its money order department, rented all of its lock boxes, and had to add more. The news of the sold out lock boxes prompted the Maplewood correspondent to state, "(It was) an incident never before known in the history of the Maplewood post-office."[6] However, Maplewood citizens were bitterly divided over the politics of the removal of a young local lady who had been post mistress and the relocation of the office to the waiting room of the Suburban Railroad Company. Petition drives, suits and counter-suits over the location and management of the post office occupied much of the attention of the small town in 1899. Though many were not

---

[3]"Old Orchard, Tuxedo and Maplewood," SLCW, 1 December 1899.
[4]"Old Orchard, Tuxedo and Maplewood," SLCW, 2 June 1899.
[5]"Old Orchard, Tuxedo and Maplewood," SLCW, 11 August 1899.
[6]"Old Orchard, Tuxedo and Maplewood," SLCW, July 1899.

pleased, the move to the loop was a good business decision. Mail arrived and departed Maplewood via mail cars run on the Manchester line.

One immediately popular addition to the loop was an ice cream parlor. The June 23, 1899 *Watchman* stated:

> The new ice cream parlor and newsboys' quarters has been doing a rushing business. A convenient spot to patrons of the railroads taking an evening's ride to the loop. W. E. Pyle has become quite popular."[7]

However, Pyle's business failed once the winter set in.[8]

In 1899, a public telephone made its appearance at the loop. The *Watchman* correspondent commented, "The Bell telephone at the loop is doing lightning business."[9]

In 1900, during the course of the streetcar strike, the *Watchman* noted that residents of Maplewood were overjoyed by the installation of a town "timepiece" in the station house of the Suburban Railway Company.

> It is not a clock but an electrometer, which does not run down and does not have to be wound up, and tells of the time as long as the batteries which operate it do their duty. As it is a felt "want," the citizens of that hamlet are much pleased with it.[10]

The clock news item underscored how important the loop and its station house had already become to the Maplewood residents.

Despite the rapid development of Maplewood, much of the area was still rural and found the streetcar line to cause its own set of problems. A Maplewood man, E. W. Lee, sued the Suburban for damages after his cow was killed by a streetcar. In October 1899, the *Watchman* reported that he and his cow had become famous in the county.[11] He won his case, gaining $65 and costs. The paper noted that the Suburban would appeal.

Nearly a month later, the paper reported that Maplewood was jolted by a human death:

> The community was shocked and saddened by the sad accident which befell old man Hall. While driving Grocer Carmody's wagon, the wagon and a

---

[7]"Old Orchard, Tuxedo and Maplewood," SLCW, 23 June 1899.

[8]"Old Orchard, Tuxedo and Maplewood," SLCW, 1 December 1899.

[9]"Old Orchard, Tuxedo and Maplewood," SLCW, 28 July 1899.

[10]SLCW, 11 May 1900.

[11]SLCW, 6 October 1899.

Suburban car collided, throwing him from his seat and killing him instantly. A coroner's jury found the motorman guilty of criminal carelessness.[12]

Accidents occasionally led to fist fights. In April 1899, the newspaper noted that in Maplewood a farmer's wagon and a Suburban car, "came together as well as the driver and the moterneer. The affair was short and very bitter. The wagon was not damaged outside a few bolts or nuts knocked out. The two men had a one round conflict which resulted in a draw, giving satisfaction to both parties."[13]

Cold streetcars and long waits were identified by the *Watchman* as a causative factor of misery for many Maplewood residents:

> Dr. C. F. Pool is having a bustling time. The condition of our street car service, the colds and pneumonia effects are causing very many medical calls.[14]

The waiting station at the Maplewood Loop was the most substantial on the county portion of the Manchester line. It featured large exterior overhangs to shelter waiting passengers from sun and rain as well as a large interior area of seats and benches. It also provided restroom facilities for public use. The north end of the station was a restaurant well known to most passengers on the Manchester line. The station provided a separate rest area and bathroom facilities for streetcar crews. A storage area in the station was provided for coke, pellet sized chunks of clean burning coal-like fuel, used in the streetcar stoves. Sand for the cars' sandboxes was also stored at the loop. The loop provided a pleasant park-like setting in the spring and summer. At those times many passengers preferred to wait outside on the wooden benches installed there.

The loop at Maplewood was not always genteel. At least one gentleman from Webster Groves who was inebriated from a night of drinking in the city, was robbed of his belongings and most of his clothes, while he lay passed out on a bench awaiting a Webster car. Pockets of the area around the town of Maplewood and in St. Louis were populated by a tough breed of individuals who frequented the saloons and bars near the streetcar lines, resulting in reports in the *Watchman* of barroom brawls, at times including streetcar employees. Law enforcement officials were frequently requested at the loop to run off vagrants, drunks, panhandlers, pickpockets, petty thieves and con artists. The *Watchman* correspondent noted on June 16, 1899:

---

[12]"Maplewood," SLCW, 3 November 1899.
[13]"Maplewood," SLCW, 7 April 1899.
[14]"Maplewood," SLCW, 10 February 1899.

The loungers who come to watch the cars at Sutton avenue and Manchester road, after imbibing too freely, are a great annoyance and the residents look to Clayton for (law enforcement) assistance.[15]

Residents began to realize that the town must incorporate in order to cope with both the benefits of the growth brought by the streetcar line as well as the negative aspects. Police protection provided by the county would be insufficient for their increased needs as Maplewood moved into the 20th century. However, police protection was but one of many needs that resulted in a drive for Maplewood's incorporation.

An intelligent appreciation of the need for community provision of modern sanitary requisites, water for domestic use and fire protection, light, good streets and sidewalks, police protection and the desiderata that can only be obtained through equitable taxation, was a symptom of "growing pains"...The question of incorporation became one of the moment.[16]

The battle for incorporation was bitter, but after a fire in January 1908 which destroyed a great deal of property in Maplewood, backers of the initiative gained enough momentum to garner the needed votes for passage. Maplewood no longer looked to Clayton for governance. As a result, the streetcar company gained one more governmental entity to satisfy.

S. V. WISE,
CONTRACTOR AND BUILDER,

Plans Furnished. Maplewood, Mo.

17-1. Ad from the *1896 St. Louis County Directory* which visually couples the idea of building in Maplewood with the presence of the Manchester streetcar line.

[15]"Maplewood," SLCW, 16 June 1899.
[16]Thomas, History of St. Louis County, (1911)

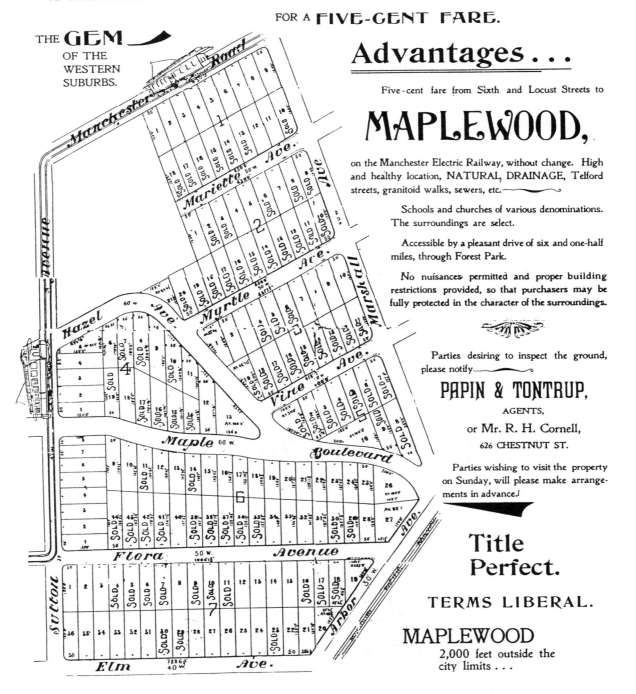

A BEAUTIFUL SUBDIVISION ON THE MANCHESTER ELECTRIC R'Y, To Sixth and Locust Streets

FOR A FIVE-CENT FARE.

THE GEM OF THE WESTERN SUBURBS.

Advantages...

Five-cent fare from Sixth and Locust Streets to

MAPLEWOOD,

on the Manchester Electric Railway, without change. High and healthy location, NATURAL, DRAINAGE, Telford streets, granitoid walks, sewers, etc.

Schools and churches of various denominations. The surroundings are select.

Accessible by a pleasant drive of six and one-half miles, through Forest Park.

No nuisances permitted and proper building restrictions provided, so that purchasers may be fully protected in the character of the surroundings.

Parties desiring to inspect the ground, please notify

PAPIN & TONTRUP,

AGENTS,

or Mr. R. H. Cornell,

626 CHESTNUT ST.

Parties wishing to visit the property on Sunday, will please make arrangements in advance.

Title Perfect.

TERMS LIBERAL.

MAPLEWOOD

2,000 feet outside the city limits . . .

17-2. **Maplewood Subdivision map (reduced in size) published by Papin and Tontrup shows the Manchester line in its early days, presumably about 1897, running along the edge of Maplewood instead of through the heart of the town. It does not show the loop which was constructed later at Sutton Avenue between Hazel and Flora. Courtesy of the Maplewood Public Library.**

17-3. View of the Maplewood loop at Sutton Avenue featuring a Manchester car bearing the Maplewood destination sign. Note the park-like setting with benches placed under shade trees and the shelters. The Suburban Electric sign does not refer to the St. Louis and Suburban, but rather to a power company based in Webster Groves that served the Maplewood area. From the Charles Hamman collection.

17-4. Breggstone real photo postcard from the early 1900s showing the Maplewood business district and a moving Manchester car. Note the streetcar's open vestibule with crew and passengers present. Courtesy of the Maplewood Public Library.

Chapter 18

THE FERGUSON CONNECTION

In 1900, Ferguson, incorporated in 1894, was a residential suburb of 1015 residents which was largely dependent on Wabash Railroad commuter trains for travel into St. Louis. However, street rail became feasible in late 1891, when electrification of the former Wells Narrow Gauge Railroad[1] was completed by the St. Louis and Suburban Railroad Company. It had recently acquired the struggling St. Louis Central and Western Company which operated a narrow gauge railroad from St. Louis to Florissant, its route taking it through Wellston and near Ferguson. Residents of the suburb were tantalized by the newly electrified line. The all important streetcar link with the city and county was so near but bypassed the town. Negotiations by the town officials for construction of a streetcar connection were begun with the St. Louis and Suburban and other street rail companies.

Initially, the Suburban was lukewarm to the prospect of connecting Ferguson to its line, but when the move toward street rail consolidation became apparent, it began a concentrated expansion effort in order to establish itself as a prime takeover target, a profitable electric railroad with a lucrative county business. It needed a connection with Ferguson in order to serve more county passengers on what was the longest electric railroad route in the St. Louis metropolitan area. The company seriously negotiated with Ferguson city fathers for the right to operate a franchise on the streets of Ferguson. Despite years of waiting for an offer from the Suburban, the town politicos remained committed to their efforts to obtain streetcar service from the Suburban as well as from other street railroad companies. They wanted an agreement that would benefit the residents while maintaining the appearance and the quality of life in Ferguson, not just a slapdash connection by a street rail company.

In December, 1900, an editorial which appeared in the *County Watchman* titled "We Are Ready For It" stated that Ferguson was, "straining every nerve to obtain rapid

---

[1]Completed by Erastus Wells in 1875 to serve his interests in Wellston and those of wealthy landowners living between the city and Florissant, the line was also known as the as the West End narrow gauge. In 1883 the line became the St. Louis, Creve Coeur Lake, and St. Charles Railway which was purchased in 1884 by the St. Louis Cable and Western Railway. It went bankrupt in late 1889, was operated briefly by the St. Louis Central and Western, which was then purchased by the St. Louis and Suburban Railroad.

transit by means of electric railroads to that city." In addition to reporting the progress of the new Suburban franchise, the editorial reported that rights of way were given through the town to the St. Louis, St. Charles and Western electric railroad, adding, "the people of Ferguson will soon be happy."[2]

The franchise for the St. Louis and Suburban to operate in Ferguson was approved by the Ferguson Board of Alderman on October 31, 1900. It granted permission to build a loop over several streets about a mile and a quarter in length. The line's compensation to the city was to be in the form of street improvements; grade all streets over which tracks were to be built, macadamize Florissant Rock Road and Chambers Avenue, extend culverts and bridges on the line to street width and complete all road improvements in six months.

Construction of a spur line connecting Ferguson to the Florissant line near Ramona Park was started immediately and proceeded smoothly until the crews began laying track in Ferguson. In early January 1901, Ferguson's Mayor Cunningham stopped the Suburban's work on the right of way because the company was preparing the road bed on the side of Florissant avenue instead of down the middle as the terms of the franchise stipulated.[3] After a few weeks of bickering, the two sides adjusted their differences. Construction renewed with the tracks being "laid in the center of the thoroughfare instead of the sides of the same."[4] Ferguson won round one against the Suburban. More battles were to follow.

The Ferguson connection was part of a larger Suburban plan to extend the line to Jennings, according to the *Watchman*. It speculated that the line "will no doubt be built to Baden, from where it will be constructed to a connection with the O Fallon Park division."[5]

While trying to impress potential buyers, the Suburban was, in fact, strapped for cash and had become anxious to shed all expensive capital projects that would bring in little additional income. Since the Ferguson loop was not needed to gain income from the town, once it was reached by street rail, the Suburban scrapped its plans to build the loop. The company reneged on its agreement with the city, constructing its tracks only two blocks into the city along Florissant Rock Road,[6] and ending its tracks in the middle of the road about 300 feet south of the Wabash Railroad bridge. There it constructed a "large ugly bumper." No loop was constructed, nor was much of the agreed upon grading work completed.

---

[2]"We Are Ready For It," SLCW, 21 December 1900, p. 4. The reported link with James Houseman's "All Saints Line" - the St. Louis, St. Charles and Western was never built.
[3]SLCW, 18 January 1901, p. 4, col. 7.
[4]SLCW, 1 February 1901, p. 8, col. 3.
[5]Ibid.
[6]Now named South Florissant Road.

KING TROLLEY: THE FERGUSON CONNECTION

The Suburban grew tired of what they considered harassment by Ferguson's Mayor Cunningham and his successor Mayor Reid who diligently sought to have the loop and street improvements completed. The Suburban refused to build beyond the Wabash Railroad bridge until the city compelled the Wabash to raise the bridge in order to give a clearance of 15 feet. In January 1902, the Wabash Railroad raised the bridge to the specified clearance, but the Suburban refused to begin construction under the bridge as it had promised. In an effort to buy out the terms of the franchise agreement, the Suburban sent representatives to a Ferguson Board of Aldermen meeting where they offered a cash settlement of a few thousand dollars. That offer was viewed as an insulting figure substantially below Ferguson's estimation of the cash value of the work. The offer was flatly refused. The Suburban officials then dug in their heels and stubbornly refused to consider any further payment or work in Ferguson. In a letter to the mayor, the company stated that it "doesn't intend to spend another cent in Ferguson."[7]

Though Ferguson's Mayor Reid protested mightily and sued the Suburban in 1903 for completion of the work, the Ferguson loop was never completed by the Suburban. Ferguson's 1903 suit asked for $32,000 in compensation for non-fulfillment of the franchise, for undone street work and loss of tax revenue in the area not served by the agreed upon loop. In the complaint, the city attorney stated that tracks were six inches higher than was allowed by ordinance and were "unsightly and dangerous, depreciating the value of property."[8] In addition, the city also asked for $10,000, due from a surety bond signed by former president Charles Turner for fulfillment of the contract.

The Suburban considered the action a nuisance suit with no merit. Ferguson considered the Suburban to be arrogant and remiss in its legal responsibilities. Litigation round two eventually was settled in March 1903. The suit was dropped by Ferguson attorney Paul Janis after the two parties reached a compromise settlement of a payment of $6000 given to Ferguson with the company also agreeing to make the improvements on Florissant Road which were specified in the franchise agreement. In return, the Suburban received an agreement from Ferguson to drop the suit and to allow the company to retain the rights to make extensions through the town. The company's bond of $10,000 was allowed to continue in force.[9] As a result of the settlement, the terminus of the line remained in the same location.

Not until a major change in streetcar models occurred was there a need for a loop as far as the Suburban and later United Railways were concerned. For 13 years Ferguson was served by streetcars with no loop.

Despite the disagreement with Ferguson, as far as the Suburban was concerned, the line was open for business from Ferguson to Suburban Gardens from which one could transfer and travel to St. Louis, Clayton, Webster Groves, and Kirkwood. The lack

---

[7]PD, 16 January 1903, p. 1.
[8]PD, 16 January 1903, p. 1.
[9]"Ferguson Case Settled," SLCW, 20 March 1903, p. 1 col. 3.

of a loop was not considered a problem for the double ended Suburban cars of the day. When a Ferguson car stopped at the Florissant Rock Road bumper, the crew simply changed the controls to the opposite end of the car, switched trolley poles, changed the direction of the seats, and returned in the opposite direction.

Service on the Suburban's Florissant and Ferguson Division was described by the *St. Louis Post Dispatch* in June 1901:

> The Florissant and Ferguson division is really a continuation of the Suburban division (which ran all the way to 4th and Elm in the city). The cars of this division start at Suburban Park and run to Carsonville, Ramona Park, and Ferguson Junction. At Ferguson Junction, the division divides. The cars carrying a sign "Ferguson" turn, and those carrying the "Florissant" sign, go on to Florissant. The Florissant cars go on to Kinloch Park. Cars leave the Suburban Park for Ferguson every 30 minutes, from 5 a.m. till 11 p.m. Returning cars leave Ferguson every 30 minutes from 5:45 a.m. till 12:15 a.m. ...After 7:45 p.m. (Florissant) cars go only as far as Ferguson Junction where they connect with the Ferguson cars. A single fare will carry a passenger from Suburban Park to Ferguson or Kinloch Park. At Kinloch Park, another fare, this time of 10 cents, is collected, which takes the passenger to the end of the division, which is Florissant.[10]

In 1905 the Suburban contructed a double track with heavier rail from Suburban Gardens to Ferguson and Florissant. Forgiving the earlier dispute with the Suburban over building a loop, Ferguson residents enjoyed and patronized their Suburban streetcar connection. A Ferguson loop was finally constructed in 1914.

18-1. Photo showing part of the Ferguson business district centered around the loop. Courtesy of the Ferguson Historical Society.

[10]PD, 18 June 1901.

18-2. United Railways car 643, a former Suburban palace car built in 1903, poses with its crew at the Ferguson loop which was constructed in 1914. Note the evidence of prior collisions in the car's metal end panel, the *Pay As You Enter* vestibule, and the typical United Railways wooden passenger shelter on the right. The Ferguson Methodist Church is in the background. Courtesy of Ferguson Historical Society.

18-3. End of the Kirkwood-Ferguson line, Note the Wabash train depot at the top of the steps. The photo was taken at the line's terminus on Florissant Rock Road southeast of the depot. Today the depot remains, but signs of the streetcar line have almost vanished. Courtesy of the Ferguson Historical Society.

Chapter 19

FROM A SCANDAL LOW TO A WORLD'S FAIR HIGH

Once the St. Louis Transit strike was settled, the United Railways conglomerate began to focus its efforts on putting down the upstart St. Louis and Suburban Company that had profited so much from the prolonged strike. Meanwhile, the Suburban continued its aggressive efforts to expand. Charles Turner intended to invade some of Transit's most profitable areas in order to force the company to buy out the Suburban. To do that, he sought approval from the City of St. Louis for 12 additional lines.

The Suburban also added power capacity, installing new generators in the main power house and updating equipment in substations at an estimated cost of $270,000. Initially, the company planned to add direct current machinery and copper feed lines but found the cost to maintain voltage in the downtown end of the line would be enormous. To solve the problem, the company installed two 1200 kw., three-phase generators which could supply the downtown end of the line as well as more distant points if desired. The Brentwood power house then became a substation, except on Sundays during the heaviest traffic periods. At those times, the Brentwood steam plant was started up. In 1901, another substation was being considered for installation at Ramona near Ferguson on the Florissant and Ferguson Division.[1]

In the month of June 1901, the *St. Louis Post-Dispatch* ran a series of updates of all street rail lines complete with route maps. Number one in the series of "STREET CAR LINES OF ST. LOUIS", appearing on June 18th, was the Suburban System. The Suburban consisted of eight divisions: the *Suburban* division which ran from Fourth and Elm to Suburban Park; *O'Fallon* division which ran from Fourth and Elm to O'Fallon Park; *Union Avenue* Division which ran from Forest Park to Walnut Park along Union; *Florissant and Ferguson* division which ran from Suburban Park to Ferguson and Florissant; *Benton* division which ran from Fourth and Elm to Benton and Maplewood; *Kirkwood* division which ran from Fourth and Elm to Kirkwood; *Brentwood, Clayton and St. Louis* division which ran from De Hodiamont to Clayton, Brentwood, Webster,

---

[1] Street Railway Journal, 1 July 1901.

Kirkwood, and Meramec Highlands; and the *St. Louis and Kirkwood* division which ran from Brentwood to the southwest corner of Forest Park.

The article, accompanied by a map of the entire Suburban system, detailed division running times, signs carried, distances, transfers, and in some cases the color of the cars:

> The Brentwood, Clayton and St. Louis… Cars are marked "Meramec" or "Clayton." Cars leave De Hodiamont beginning at 5 a. m. at intervals of 30 minutes until 11 p.m. Running time between Meramec Highlands and De Hodiamont is one hour. Cars over this division for Clayton leave De Hodiamont at 30-minute intervals beginning at 5:15 a.m. and running until 6:45 p.m. These cars run as far as the (St. Louis) Country Club. The running time between De Hodiamont and Clayton is 15 minutes. The running time over this division to Kirkwood is 50 minutes and to Webster is 35 minutes.[2]

The Brentwood-Clayton division also served the Delmar Garden Race Track and Washingon University. A junction was located at the university where a new fare zone began. Distances: De Hodiamont to Washington University - one mile, Washington University to Clayton - two miles, Clayton to Brentwood - three and a half miles, Washington University to Kirkwood - eleven miles, and from Kirkwood to Meramec Highlands - two miles.

The Benton area was a section of the city which bordered Maplewood. Cars on the Benton division left Fourth and Elm at 15 minute intervals, beginning at 5:38 a.m. and running until 12:02 a.m. Returning cars left Maplewood at intervals of 16 minutes beginning at 4:42 a.m. and running until 11:06 p.m. From Fourth and Elm to Sarah was three and a half miles, to Benton - seven miles, and to Maplewood - eight miles. The running time from downtown St. Louis to Maplewood was 56 minutes. Owl cars returned to the city from Maplewood at 11:22 p.m., 12:10 a.m., 12:58 a.m., 2:34 a.m., 3:22 a.m., 4:10 a.m. and 4:58 a.m.

The Kirkwood division ran from Fourth and Elm through Benton, Maplewood, and Webster Groves to Kirkwood. A second fare was collected at Maplewood.

> Cars on the Kirkwood division leave Fourth and Elm streets beginning at 5:22 a.m. at 16-minute intervals till 10:26 p.m. After 10:26 p.m. cars connect at Maplewood with owl cars that connect with other points in the system. From Sarah street to Kirkwood is 12¾ miles. At Kirkwood the Kirkwood division cars connect with the cars of the Brentwood division which run to Meramec

---

[2]"Street Car Lines of St. Louis. No. 1. - The Suburban System," PD, 18 June 1900.

Highlands. From Fourth and Elm streets to Webster is 45 minutes and to Kirkwood is 88 minutes.[3]

The St. Louis and Kirkwood division connected at Forest Park with the cars of the St. Louis Transit Company. Passengers had to leave the Suburban line and walk to Transit's waiting shelter at that point. The line was short, only three miles from Forest Park to Brentwood. Cars left Brentwood at intervals of thirty minutes beginning at 5:30 a.m. and ran till 11:30 p.m. Cars left Forest Park at 6 a.m. and ran till 12, midnight. The running time on the St. Louis and Kirkwood division was 15 minutes.[4]

Some physical altercations ensued when the Suburban's work crews ran into Transit's crews, but most of the battles between the two companies were legal battles over trackage rights. Transit did not want the Suburban competing with its major city routes. In October 1901, Suburban backers filed bills for twelve new lines, most of which were in direct competition with existing Transit routes. Intense lobbying against the Suburban proposals was carried out by United Railways officials and their influential supporters. Only one of the 12 bills ultimately passed the Railroad Committee of the House of Delegates, but it was later killed by action of the Missouri Supreme Court.

In an unwise attempt to get the bills passed, Suburban's President Turner resorted to bribery which was a common St. Louis business practice of the day. Attorney Joseph Folk, who was attempting to put the St. Louis "Boodle Gang" out of business, caught wind of Turner's bribes and began to aggressively pursue the matter. He had a dual motivation; during the strike he had represented strikers and had little love for street railway management; he also had political ambitions and sensed an opportunity to make a big name for himself with another splashy scandal spread across the front pages of the St. Louis newspapers. When the bribery issue was brought before the Grand Jury, Folk convinced Turner and the Suburban officials to voluntarily testify under a provision which allowed them immunity from prosecution.

Turner's attorney testified that Charles Turner had told him to pay up to $135,000 to secure passage of the bill. The *Street Railway Review* quoted the attorney, "I believe that every large corporation in the city has been compelled to act in a similar manner whenever it has wanted legislation."[5] In the corrupt St. Louis political climate of the day, his belief was not too far from the truth.

The resulting trials brought national exposure to Folk including support from the "Trust-Buster" himself, President Theodore Roosevelt. As a result of the scandal, Charles Turner was forced out of the presidency of the St. Louis and Suburban and was replaced

---

[3] Ibid.
[4] Ibid.
[5] Street Railway Review, 16 February 1902.

by Samuel Kennard in 1902.[6] The change in head man made little difference to residents of Kirkwood. They had concerns about the service of the two Suburban divisions which they expressed to their aldermen. One example of a delay in service which resulted in numerous complaints was reported by the *Kirkwood Argus* in 1902:

> Tuesday was a bad day for all those traveling on the streetcar — especially bad for all those wishing to go anyplace in any reasonable time. Car No. 329 for the fourth time jumped the tracks on Woodbine Avenue, near Clay… and buried the front wheels and fender deep in mud. This blocked the passage of cars for about four hours. Several other cars jumped the tracks at different places, this was chiefly due to the condition that the heavy rains left the tracks in.[7]

In July, 1902, still more complaints were engendered when a streetcar carrying 45 passengers was derailed a block west of Kirkwood city limits when heat expanded the rails. The tracks were obstructed until the next day. Such typical interruptions in service were a major frustration for Meramec Highlands, Kirkwood, and Webster Groves residents who depended on the streetcars for daily transportation. At least in one instance, according to an article in a 1902 *Watchman* bearing the subtitle, "Romantic Sequel to Street Car Accident at Brentwood," a streetcar accident precipitated a marriage. George Marvin and Eulalia Sappington, both of Kirkwood, scrapped plans for an extended engagement and a big society wedding and eloped to Clayton to be married. A week earlier, the groom had been slightly injured in a collision between a Suburban car and a Missouri Pacific passenger train at Brentwood.[8] Most accidents, however, did not have such happy outcomes.

Kennard, isolated from the day to day concerns of riders, inherited a company that was in desperate need of cash flow. The negative publicity given the bribery case had dried up the usually available credit lines which left Suburban unable to complete several partially constructed capital projects. Kennard was ineffective and resigned after only one year. Though the company didn't prosper during his tenure, it wasn't for a lack of effort. Kennard poured 1.5 million dollars into capital projects in 1903, reconstructing track with T-rails of the heaviest pattern, constructing new loops, and reconstructing the De Hodiamont power station in order to increase the capacity of the steam plant by 75%, as well as completing other smaller projects.[9] The Suburban was positioning itself for a

---

[6]The Post-Dispatch's muckraking reporters thoroughly covered the Suburban bribery scandal story. A good synopsis is found in James Neill Primm's Lion of the Valley and in Andrew D. Young's The St. Louis Streetcar Story.
[7]Kirkwood Argus, 1902.
[8]"Romantic Sequel… ," SLCW, 13 June 1902.
[9]"Extensions at St. Louis," Street Railway Journal, 14 February 1903. Described expansion plans of the Suburban for 1903 and 1904.

large share of the World's Fair ridership in 1904 and needed to upgrade its lines to handle the heavy traffic.

Local editors were not impressed with the Suburban's efforts. An editorial castigating streetcar service was printed in the February 21, 1903 *Kirkwood Weekly Courier*:

> We are indeed in a sad plight in regard to electric car service with... the danger of being put off and compelled to walk to one's destination whenever a conductor on the Suburban takes a notion to turn back. The people should be protected by law from these outrages, and if not, the day will come when they protect themselves.[10]

In 1903 St. Louis city officials were determined to gain more revenue from St. Louis Transit and the Suburban streetcar lines. A law passed by the St. Louis Municipal Assembly enabled the city to collect license taxes of about $145,000 based on the number of passengers carried in 1902. Under the previous law, the streetcar companies paid a $25 tax per car operated in the city. The new law required a tax of one mill for each passenger carried. As a result, each car was required to have a register which allowed city authorities to determine how many passengers had been carried. The Suburban complied though not happy with the law. Transit refused to pay and embarked on a long legal battle with the city over the mill tax issue.

At the same time, the city's regulations regarding operation of streetcars were updated. Many of them were similar to those in effect in Webster and Kirkwood at the time. After describing the new mill tax, the April 18, 1903 *Street Railway Journal* listed some of the provisions of the new St. Louis law:

> Cars shall be stopped so as to leave the rear platform partly over the crossing or cross-walk.

> The motorman, etc., shall keep a vigilant watch for all vehicles and persons on foot, especially children, either on the track or moving toward it, and on the first appearance of danger to such persons or vehicles, the car shall be stopped in the shortest time and space possible.

> Conductors shall announce to passengers the names of streets about to be crossed.

> All cars shall be kept comfortably heated whenever the temperature without is below 40 degrees. Fahrenheit.

---

[10]Editorial, Kirkwood Weekly Courier, 21 February 1903.

All cars shall be kept in cleanly condition and free from filth and rubbish.

No car shall be propelled at a speed greater than 10 miles an hour in the central district of the city, nor more than 15 miles an hour in the outer district.

All cars carrying one or more passengers shall be required to run to the end of their routes, and passengers shall not be required to change or transfer to take a preceding or succeeding car traveling over the same route…[11]

The city was allowed by the law to levy a fine not less than $5 nor more than $500 against every person or corporation that acted in violation of the provisions, an act considered a misdemeanor.

A car repainting program was instituted to bring the livery of all Suburban cars to a standard olive green, though apparently some of the Suburban cars serving Kirkwood remained red. Kirkwood resident Guy Trulock recalled that red Kirkwood-Ferguson cars still operated in the town circa 1907.[12] The Suburban's efforts to standardize the olive green car color on all of its cars was evidently incomplete.

The Suburban had plans to retrofit all of its cars with St. Louis Car Company 47 MCB trucks, air brakes, and four new motors per car. Orders were placed for 50 new cars with updated specifications including enclosed vestibules and a Smith arc electric headlight. The new cars were to be 9 feet longer than the cars in service at the time.

The company also planned to rebuild and improve existing car houses by installing pits to facilitate repairs to the cars. Other plans were drawn for construction of buildings and grounds for a new car house, general market stores, rental flats, and a large hall and employee club house.[13]

All of the Suburban's plans suffered a massive setback when the De Hodiamont car house was destroyed by fire on February 24, 1903. The fire broke out at 5 o'clock in the morning when the sheds were occupied almost to full capacity. Employees tried to run the cars out of the sheds, but after only a few were saved, a car derailed and blocked the entrance, thus sealing the doom of sixty-three passenger cars and four other cars.[14] Though the downtown service was crippled by the fire, the regular schedule was

---

[11]"St. Louis Transportation Regulations," Street Railway Journal, 18 April 1903, p. 599.
[12]Guy E. Trulock, "Local Transportation in Kirkwood Circa 1907," Kirkwood Historical Review, December 1978. Though the Kirkwood-Ferguson operated in 1907 as a United Railways line, it is probable that the red car was a Suburban car running in 1906, prior to the United Railways acquisition.
[13]"Extensions at St. Louis," Street Railway Journal, 14 February 1903.
[14]The Suburban ordered 20 Robertson Semi-Convertible Cars from St. Louis Car Company on 8/16/02. When the cars arrived they were numbered 100-119. Only numbers 100, 102, 103, 105, and 111 survived. No. 102 was rebuilt as the private car "Meramec." In 1907, United Railways gave the cars numbers 620-623, excluding former 102.

followed on the Meramec division. Its cars, stored in a different car barn, were spared from the fire. That afternoon, the *Post-Dispatch* covered the Suburban car shed fire:

> The conflagration was a fierce one and the flames threw out a glow easily seen as far as Clayton. Many persons believed the World's Fair buildings were burning... Only a few weeks ago the Suburban placed in operation 16 new coaches, green colored, of the most modern finish and equipment. They were marvels of luxury in street service. Of these 14 were consumed.[15]

The Suburban's official report to the insurance company indicated $145,000 was lost in rolling stock with an additional loss of $25,000 on the building and $5,000 on other property. The greatest part of the rolling stock loss was from the brand new cars valued at $4500 to $5500 each. The other cars ranged in cost from $800 to $3000.

The Suburban immediately borrowed cars from all possible sources. It even pressed its parlor cars, the "Suburban" and the "Kinloch" into passenger service. Arch-rival St. Louis Transit Company loaned twenty cars. Twenty newly constructed Robertson Sill semi-convertible cars built by the St. Louis Car Company for Chicago City Railway, which was headed by former St. Louis streetcar man Robert McCullough, were delivered to the Suburban at his direction.[16] The St. Charles line, headed by James Houseman, began running some of its cars on the Suburban lines, and the St. Louis Car Company immediately delivered 10 reconstructed cars to the Suburban. The acquired cars were sheltered in the Manchester shed and stored on nearby switches until the new shed was completed. With all the measures taken to obtain cars, the service was quickly brought back to 5 minute intervals on most city lines. Intervals on affected county lines returned to 15 to 20 minutes. One positive outcome of the disaster was that the Suburban was able to operate more new cars than it had prior to the fire. Another was addition of new car sheds, 350 ft. by 125 ft., which were built with fireproof materials.

Serious work on the city and county infrastructure such as sewer systems, roads, water systems and rail beds could not be completed in time to handle the requirements for the 1903 celebration of the Louisiana Purchase, so the exposition was postponed to 1904. The delay gave the St. Louis and Suburban time to get its rolling stock operational and to complete improvements before the Fair started.

Financial restructuring of the Suburban was completed on April 1, 1903, at which time the company formally acquired the deeds for two of the county lines which it had operated for several years, the Brentwood, Clayton and St. Louis and the St. Louis and Kirkwood railroads. At the same time, the St. Louis and Suburban refinanced its mortgage for $7,500,000 for the purpose of refunding the indebtedness of the company

---

[15]"Carshed Fire Destroys Sixty-seven Suburban Cars," PD, 24 February 1903, p. 1.
[16]The cars received from Chicago City Railway Co. were numbered 101, 104, 106-110, and 112-124. United Railways later renumbered them 600-619.

and to make improvements. $3,700,000 was dedicated to pay for immediate improvements such as track upgrades and new terminals at the Worlds Fair grounds, $500,000 was reserved for future improvements, and $3,300,000 was used to pay off outstanding bonds. The Suburban subsidiary, the St. Louis and Meramec River Railway, filed a mortgage for $3,000,000 , classified as a "technical detail" of the larger Suburban financial package. Of that mortgage, $1,000,000 was used to take up the 6% bonds which were issued for 20 years in 1896. The remaining sum of two million dollars was used as partial collateral for the Suburban's $7,500,000 issue. Though the company had gained access to more money for improvements, its debt load was greatly increased. However, the improvements were appreciated by the riders who were unconcerned about the Suburban's debt load. The *Watchman* stated, "… the (Suburban) company has installed equipment and other improvements which places it among the best electric street railways in the United States."[17]

With the postponement of the World's Fair, the Suburban had time to upgrade its two Forest Park loops; the Lindell loop just east of the Fair's main entrance at De Baliviere Avenue and Lindell Boulevard was made capable of handling 7000 passengers an hour while the Skinker loop located at the northwest corner of the Pike near the Colorado steam railway tracks was made capable of handling 2500 passengers per hour.

The *Street Railway Journal*, in April 1903, reviewed the ability of the St. Louis lines to handle traffic for the Fair. At that time, it was stated that the Suburban could carry 8000 passengers an hour. The main concern of the streetcar lines was getting the crowd home when all wanted to leave at the same time in the evening after the grand fireworks. The *Journal* reporter estimated at 1903 capacities, after the fireworks ended around nine o'clock, the streetcar lines would take till 7 a.m. before the half million people were all returned home. St. Louis Transit and the Suburban were determined to prove that the *Journal*'s estimate was wrong.[18]

A World's Fair dedication ceremony in May 1903, which concluded with grand fireworks, provided a test run for the streetcar lines. Happily, the dispersing of the crowd was fairly efficient and took only a few hours.

The *Street Railway Journal* of May 16, 1903, reviewed the Suburban's World's Fair preparation:

> The Suburban Company has two lines touching the grounds, and it is contemplated to make both of them popular with sightseers by equipping them with an abundance of palace cars. The main line of the Suburban, with a large

---

[17]"Suburban Filed Two Big Mortgages. County Lines Also Formally Transferred to Old Company. Reorganization is Now Complete and the Company is in Shape to Add Valuable Improvements," SLCW, 3 April 1903, p. 1.
[18]Street Railway Journal, April 1903.

entrance at the Administration Building, penetrating as it does the business district of the city, will become one of the principal Worlds Fair feeders.[19]

In the August 8th, 1903 *Street Railway Journal*, the Suburban's plans to spend $1,125,000 on improvements were detailed. The Hodiamont power house was to be given new storage batteries, a larger capacity boiler room and new engines in order to increase its output to 8000 hp and a rotary converter was to be installed at the remodeled Brentwood powerhouse.[20] The *Journal* reported on the relaying of Suburban track, a common occurrence based on the demands of larger and heavier cars wearing out the rails and of obsolete track layouts which could not accommodate the new larger cars:

> The Meramec Highlands line[21] is being improved from Sarah Street to King's Highway, on Manchester Avenue, with 9 in. rails, but as it is necessary to grade the streets from the building line to building line, the work is progressing slowly. None of the new steel has been laid. The south side of the street has already been cut down and the old south track replaced. Another improvement will be made in the Meramec Highlands line by eliminating the double curve on Sarah Street, a short distance north of the Wabash tracks. This curve is dangerous, and it is so sharp that two large cars cannot pass there. For this reason the company has not been able to operate the large cars on the Meramec Highlands line. With the improvements on this line, the company will be able to run cars on schedule time, which cannot always be done at present. The schedule time for making the run from Meramec Highlands to the intersection of Fourth Street and Elm Street is 96 minutes. Larger cars will also be run on this line.[22]

Fifty new 52 passenger capacity Robertson "palace" cars, so named because of their luxurious touches like the beveled mirrors mounted on the frames between the windows, etched window glass in the transom and fine painting details, were ordered from the St. Louis Car Company.[23] The car houses at De Hodiamont and Manchester Avenue were rebuilt to create space for them. Both gained a steam heating plant and an air plant for the purpose of cleaning cars.

The *Electrical Handbook*[24] prepared for electrical engineers attending a convention in St. Louis during the World's Fair year, detailed the history and operations

---

[19] Street Railway Journal, 16 May 1903.

[20] "Improvements of St. Louis and Suburban Railway," Street Railway Journal, 8 August 1903, p. 212.

[21] The Suburban's Kirkwood Division, in later years was called the Manchester 53-56.

[22] "Improvements of St. Louis and Suburban Railway," Street Railway Journal, 8 August 1903, p. 212.

[23] The Suburban numbered the new cars 200-249. They were later renumbered 624-673 by United Railways. "Palace" cars are not to be confused with private party cars, though they were much more "palatial" than many cars of the period.

[24] American Institute of Electrical Engineers. (1904). The St. Louis Electrical Handbook Being a Guide for Visitors Abroad Attending the International Electrical Congress,, St. Louis: pp. 151-154.

of the St. Louis and Suburban. Its trackage was reported to consist of a single line to the city's business district with all other Suburban Divisions either intersecting or branching from it at points west of Vandeventer Avenue. Track was reported to be new, having been replaced in 1903 with standard 80-lb. T-rail within city limits while county lines were given 60-lb. standard T-rail, except for a stretch of 10 miles on the Florissant line where the original 35-lb. rail was still in use.[25]

Large cars, (46 ft. 8 in. long, weight 48,000 lb., 52 passenger capacity) advertised as "Palace" cars and small cars, (38 ft. long, 34,000 lb., 40 passenger capacity) were reported in use, both being equipped with St. Louis Car Company's No. 47 trucks and air brakes.

The Suburban's statistics for the year ending December 31, 1903 were reported:[26]

Gross earnings from operation....................963,806.96
Total number of passengers carried............19,931,178
Total car-miles run.......................................5,515,536
Total miles of track......................................95
Miles of public highway occupied...............46.5
Miles of private right of way occupied.........48.5
Percentage of transfers..................................12.1%

The Suburban loop at the main entrance to the fairgrounds on Lindell served traffic direct from downtown St. Louis, while the loop on Skinker was more often used to serve passengers who headed for the World's Fair from Kirkwood, Webster Groves, and other county locations. By 1904, the Suburban had increased its carrying capacity to 16,000 passengers per hour. The company placed over 100 of its 195 cars, at one point exceeding 130 cars, in World's Fair service. On the opening day of the World's Fair, the St. Louis and Suburban reported carrying 94,000 passengers. The Fair was obviously lucrative for the Suburban.

The Suburban's loops were more attractive and efficient than were the Transit loops. Its loops were nicely landscaped with shrubs and grass as opposed to Transit's mud and rock. At the Suburban's Lindell loop, no passenger was allowed inside the loop except on a car. Passengers waited to leave the Fair in a roofed over area in one corner of the loop. Cars discharged arriving passengers at a separate gate then moved forward so that front and back platforms were level with the loading gates.

In a bid for patronage of visitors to the St. Louis World's Fair, the Meramec Highlands Company, primarily owned by Jacob Bernheimer, produced a booklet illustrated with photographs which described the advantages that the Meramec Highlands

[25]Ibid.
[26]Ibid.

Resort had to offer over other hostelries in St. Louis. One advantage that the booklet highlighted was the ease of using the inexpensive and convenient streetcar transportation provided by the St. Louis and Suburban. From Meramec Highlands, one could avoid city crowds and travel directly to the Fair:

> For the benefit of World's Fair Visitors, the Electric Roads will run Cars through from the Meramec Highlands to the WORLD'S FAIR GROUNDS in 40 minutes, which is less time than it takes from heart of the city to Fair Grounds; cars from Highlands but six minutes apart. Fare, 5c [cents][27]

Local poor and middle class people often could not afford to spend much time at the Fair or stay at the Highlands Inn, even though its prices had been dropped to compete with hotels closer to the Fair. However, large numbers rode out to the Highlands on the Suburban's streetcar lines to enjoy the swimming, boating, horse rides, picnic groves, and the healthful baths. At night, before the last train or streetcar returned to the city from the resort, patrons enjoyed music and dancing in the Sunset Pagoda, the spacious dance hall adjacent to the Highlands Inn and near the streetcar loop. Passengers returning from the Fair or heading home from a day of fun at the resort were entertained at the loop by a concert band and other musical groups.

Riders were at risk from falling from the moving streetcars. Newspapers of the day reported both passengers and conductors falling off backward from platforms as streetcars lurched. In some cases the injured person was not even missed or helped until the next streetcar came along and discovered the person lying on the rails. The *Watchman-Advocate* reported such an incident:

> Edgar Woods, a son of the man in charge of Almont Dairy, was knocked from a Suburban car in Kirkwood by another going in an opposite direction and seriously injured. He lay in the road until another car came along and found him....[28]

In July, 1904, the *Watchman-Advocate* described the exploits of conductor W. C. Murphey who arrested three men for picking pockets on his streetcar near Kirkwood. To make the arrest, Murphey drew his revolver but had to call on the motorman for help before the three would surrender. He stated that he had caught them in the act of picking pockets of several passengers on the car. As he headed toward Clayton from Kirkwood, he saw the men working in a bunch and covered them with his revolver. At Clayton, he stopped the car and turned them over to the sheriff. Two passengers on the car stated that a wallet and a purse had been taken.[29]

---

[27]Meramec Highlands Company, Highlands Inn and Cottages, St. Louis Co. Mo. Opens for World's Fair Season Sunday April 30, 1904, advertisement booklet, MHS.
[28]"Kirkwood," SLCWA, 20 May 1904.
[29]"Con" Arrests Pickpockets," SLCWA, 29 July 1904.

The presence of streetcars connecting with Forest Park made Kirkwood and Webster Groves bedroom communities for the Fair. It seemed that nearly every home became a boarding house, some entertaining a stream of friends and relatives and some taking in strangers for profit. A new Kirkwood hotel - the Lexington Hotel,[30] which later was renamed the Woodlawn Hotel, nicknamed by residents "Old Woolie" - opened in 1903 at the southeast corner of Adams and Woodlawn. Its location was ideal. The hotel with its large verandah, spacious lawn ornamented with flowers and shaded by cooling trees, drew admiring glances from streetcar passengers, many of whom disembarked from the streetcar at that very corner to stay in the hotel. It had 25 rooms, a dining room that could seat seventy-five, and a verandah for visiting, offering a combination of commercial boarding house with "home town warmth." [31]

Though 1904 had been a record breaking year for the Suburban, it was blighted by a fatal streetcar-train accident. Marring the success of the World's Fair year was a spectacularly horrible accident on September 3, 1904, a nice sunny Saturday afternoon. Readers of the *St. Louis Globe-Democrat* awoke to Sunday's front page headlines, "WABASH SHUTTLE TRAIN STRIKES CROWDED CAR, KILLING SEVEN PERSONS. Deadly Sarah Street Crossing is Scene of Another Fatality — World's Fair train Dashes Into Suburban Car Filled with Passengers-- Several Ground to Pieces — Nineteen Injured."[32]

Not to be outdone, the *Post-Dispatch* front page featured lurid headlines accompanied by a photograph of the wreckage and an illustration showing the layout of the site and the relative positions of the train and the streetcar.

The doomed Suburban car was southbound on its way to Meramec Highlands when it came to the Sarah Street crossing where two flag men were employed by the Wabash Railroad to signal streetcars if it was safe to cross the tracks. Miscommunication between a flag man and the conductor resulted in the motorman on the car going ahead with the crossing of the double tracks. When the motorman saw the speed with which the train was approaching, he tried to reverse the power. At that point a power surge blew the circuits and stranded the streetcar square in the path of the oncoming train. According to some accounts, the trolley pole jumped the wire, and the conductor was unable to replace it soon enough to restart the car and clear the Wabash track. Had the motorman been able to keep going forward, it would most likely have been just a close miss.

---

[30]Mary Williams, "The Woodlawn Hotel," Kirkwood Historical Review, September 1979, p. 7.

[31]Shirley and Adele Seifert, (1959) Grace Church Kirkwood, Missouri Its Story, Kirkwood: Messenger Printing Co. p. 42. After years of a bitter fight over the use of the former Woodlawn Hotel property for a parking lot, the courts ruled in favor of the Kirkwood Baptist Church which had purchased the property and demolished the former hotel with the intention of constructing a parking lot. The City of Kirkwood ruled that it could not use the property for a parking lot. Despite neighbors' protest, in late 1997, the church finally prevailed in its plan to cut down trees, and to complete its landscaped parking lot.

[32]"Wabash Shuttle Train Strikes Crowded Car, Killing Seven Persons," GD, 4 September 1904, p. 1.

KING TROLLEY: A SCANDAL LOW TO WORLD'S FAIR HIGH

A coroner's jury was convened to determine fault. Testimony pointed out a lack of proper caution on the part of the streetcar crew and a poor flag signaling system on the part of the Wabash.[33] For days after the fatal crash, the papers were filled with details of the coroner's investigation, scathing editorials,[34] suggestions for making the grade crossing safe, and funeral arrangements and biographies of the deceased - including victims from Maplewood, Webster Groves and Kirkwood.[35] The injured included residents of those towns as well as city residents on their way to work.

That accident provided a topic of heated discussion and finger pointing. Kirkwood resident, F. Travers Burgess, as a child in a family with close railroad ties, heard relatives talking about the people that they knew who were killed in the wreck. Some eyewitnesses had stated that the trolley wheel jumped the wire while the car was crossing the Wabash tracks, causing the car to stall. Burgess stated that as a result of the outcry over the incident, the state of Missouri required installation of continuous safety mesh above trolley wires at all railroad crossings. The metal mesh was slightly arched which allowed the trolley wheel to remain in contact with the wire until the car was past the intersection.

By September 13th, a suit stemming from the crash had been filed in St. Louis Circuit Court against the St. Louis and Meramec River Railroad. William Ryan asked for $5000 for the death of his adopted son, Andrew Mc Kinley of Maplewood. Mary Bristol, a resident of Webster Groves, filed on the 14th against the Suburban and the Wabash asking $5000 damages for the death of her husband. Numerous other suits resulting from the crash were filed in the following months, adding to already heavy load of lawsuits against the company.

Despite the accident, ridership to the Fair remained high, especially on September 15, 1904, St. Louis Day. Most major employers in St. Louis released their employees for the day, resulting in over 400,000 passengers carried by the streetcar lines. The Suburban reported 125,000 two way fares to the fair that day. Streetcar companies' failure to close during St. Louis Day at the Fair, caused one unhappy conductor to write a letter to the editor of the *Post-Dispatch* chastising the money-hungry companies for making their crews work the regular long shift without any release time, keeping them from the only opportunity that many of them would have to see the Fair.

The World's Fair was a "cash cow" for the St. Louis and Suburban while it lasted. However, business plummeted the following year.

---

[33]"Flag at Grade Crossing Meant Either "Come on" or "Stay Back," PD, 6 September 1904.
[34]"Sarah Street Catastrophe," editorial, PD, 6 September 1904. The *Post-Dispatch* launched into a grade crossing safety campaign.
[35]"Suburban Wreck, Seven Killed and Nineteen Injured, Most of Whom Lived in the County, Car Crew Negligent," SLCW, 9 September 1904.

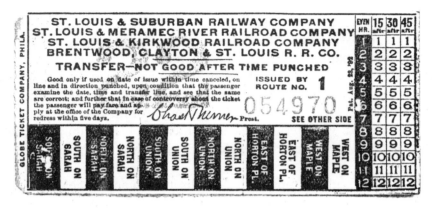

19-1. St. Louis and Suburban transfer showing signature of President Charles Turner can be roughly dated as being issued between June 1, 1900, when the Brentwood, Clayton and St. Louis Railroad began operation, and Spring of 1902, when Turner was forced out of the presidency due to his guilt in a bribery scandal. The transfer was issued by route no. 1, the main line which ran from Fourth and Elm to Suburban Park. "West on Maple" was the connection with the Brentwood, Clayton and St. Louis, which ran all the way to Meramec Highlands. "South on Sarah" was the connection with the St. Louis and Meramec River Railway, the Manchester line, which served Maplewood, Webster Groves and Kirkwood. Charles Hamman collection.

19-2. Political cartoon from the front page of the January 30, 1902 *St. Louis Post-Dispatch*, which pictured the Suburban bribery scandal as the latest in a number of issues investigated by a grand jury at the direction of city attorney Folk.

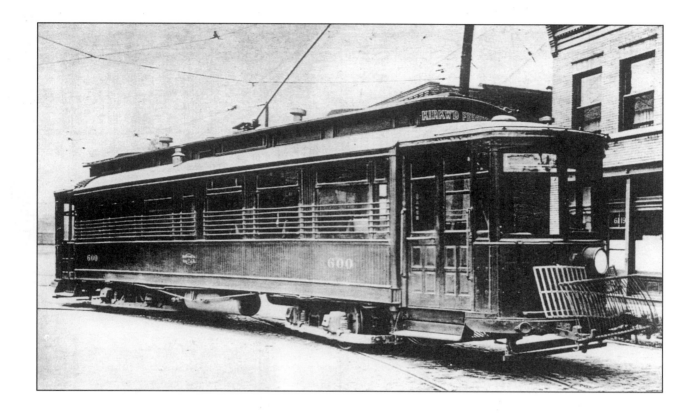

19-3. The Robertson semi-convertible streetcars, first introduced in 1899, were built by the St. Louis Car Company as a way of inexpensively coping with climate extremes. The cars could be completely closed in the winter and almost completely opened in the summer, featuring unusually large windows which could be lowered to create a semi-open car. As a result, companies did not have to maintain a separate fleet of open cars for summer use. The car featured the Robertson side sill, a pair of steel channels running the length of the car body and spaced transversely to form a downward extension of the window sash pocket which allowed the entire main window sash to disappear into the side pocket. A hinged wooden flap was pulled up over the gap so a customer could rest his arm comfortably on the window frame. The conversion was simple and could be completed by customers very quickly, as was often required when summer rains occurred. This Robertson style car was operating on the Kirkwood-Ferguson line in 1918. It had been built for the Chicago City Railway, but was instead sold to the St. Louis and Suburban to replace cars lost in the 1903 car barn fire. It was renumbered as #600 in 1911. Its original St. Louis Car Company #47 trucks had been replaced by DuPont style trucks. It had been converted to a single-end Detroit-platform car.

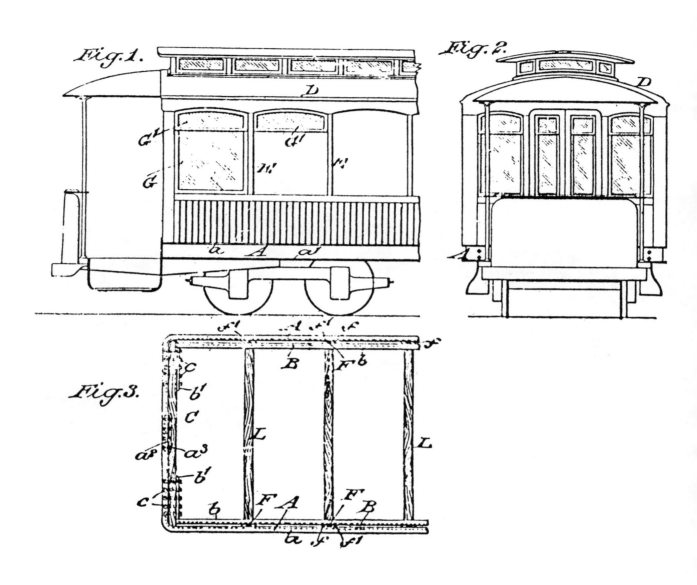

No. 621,142.

J. H. ROBERTSON,
RAILWAY CAR.
(Application filed Nov. 25, 1898.)

(No Model.)

Patented Mar. 14, 1899.

2 Sheets—Sheet 1.

19-4. Robertson's patent application drawings for the
Semi-Convertible car. Drawings courtesy of Travers Burgess.

19-5. One of the St. Louis and Suburban's five new Robertson palace cars to survive the 1903 De Hodiamont car shed fire. Note the car's easily identifiable characteristic - seven windows on the side of the car, three windows with a narrow window separating them from a second set of three windows. Charles Hamman collection.

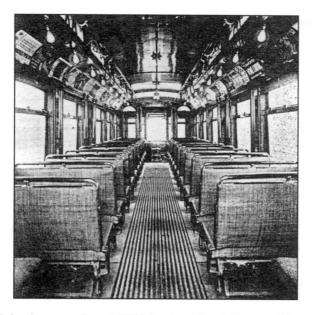

19-6. The Suburban purchased 75 Robertson Semi-Convertible cars to augment its rolling stock for the World's Fair. Photograph shows the interior of a Robertson Semi-Convertible car. From *The St. Louis Electrical Handbook - Being a Guide for Visitors Abroad Attending the International Electrical Congress* (1904).

Standard Car

19-7. Illustration from *Electrical Handbook* (1904) showing a "Standard" Suburban car. It actually depicts a new Robertson style palace car.

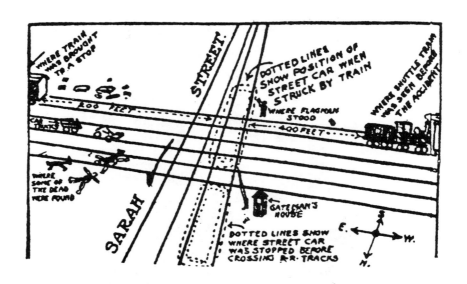

19-8. Diagram of the scene of the fatal Suburban-Wabash crash printed on the front page of the September 4, 1904, *St. Louis Post-Dispatch*.

19-9. *St. Louis Republic*'s, May 4, 1900, front page illustration of the Wabash-Suburban wreck.

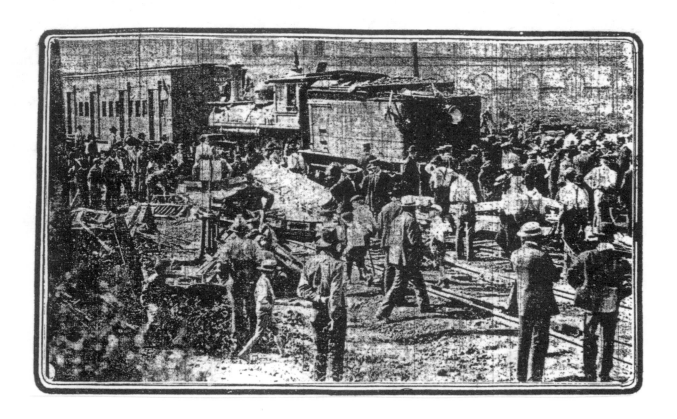

19-10. Photograph from page 1 of the September 4, 1904, *Post-Dispatch*, showing the wreckage of the Suburban car and the Wabash train that hit it.

19-11. September 15, St. Louis Day at the World's Fair saw streetcar lines "taxed to the limit" to carry the over 400 thousand passengers desiring to be part of the spectacle. The Globe-Democrat stated, "Every car bore its capacity of human freight." Editorial cartoon from the September 15, 1904 *Post-Dispatch*.

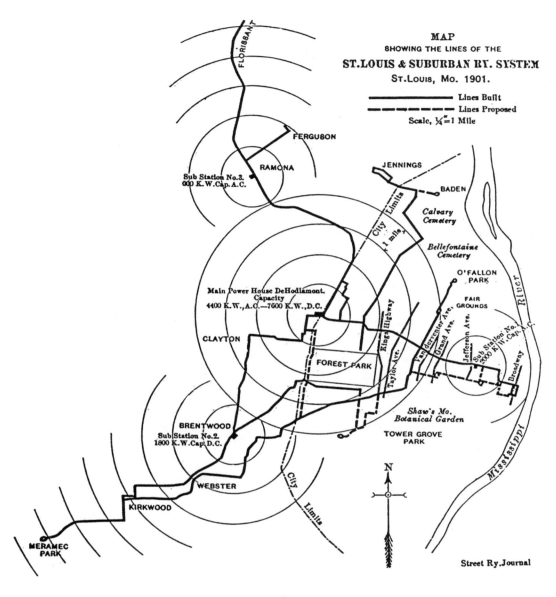

19-12. Map from the July 6, 1901, *Street Railway Journal* **showing the location of the power stations and the tracks of the St. Louis and Suburban Railway Company.**

Chapter 20

UNITED RAILWAYS SERVICE 1907-1919

During the first decade of the 20th century, political scandals in St. Louis often centered around the streetcar lines. Too often, the only people who made money were the promoters who set up the lines. Small stockholders were typically the ones who lost money when lines went into receivership or were absorbed by other larger lines. The St. Louis and Suburban was no exception. However, excellent patronage and unusually high profits during the World's Fair delayed the almost inevitable United Railways takeover of the St. Louis and Suburban.

After the Worlds Fair closed, patronage slipped abruptly, so the Suburban immediately began to make improvements to its service in an attempt to regain passengers. In 1905, despite financial difficulties, the Brentwood-Kirkwood portion of the line was double tracked. Though the company's passenger totals were much lower, all available income not used for salaries was dedicated to maintenance and physical upgrading of the Suburban property.

Meanwhile, a new line proposed by the St. Louis, Webster and Valley Park Railway Company was projected to run from University City through Richmond Heights, Webster Groves, Brentwood, Glendale, Kirkwood and on to Valley Park. Right-of-ways were secured and grading was started. Grading on the right of way was completed all the way to Woodlawn in Kirkwood and then started up again near Kirkwood's Geyer Road. The only other portions of the line to be completed were the steel railroad bridges in the Brentwood to University City section of the route. Speculators plotted subdivisions in farm and wooded areas through which the line was to pass. The project was abandoned for lack of capital before the start of World War I.

Other county towns such as Manchester needed a streetcar connection with the city and county. In 1905, Manchester was still served by stage coach and express wagons. Though lines were proposed to run west to serve the town, none were built due to lack of financing. By 1905, investors were beginning to see the risk in street railroad investments and were leery of them.

The major streetcar news story of interest to county residents in 1906 was the demise of the St. Louis and Suburban. . Despite a good year in 1904, the bribery scandal and the lack of profit in most prior years made investors wary of loaning money to the Suburban. By the end of 1905, the Suburban had a short term debt of $158,000 and ongoing expenses were greater than the income. In August 1906, the company carried a long term debt of seven and a half million dollars. While unsuccessful in obtaining the line earlier, United Railways had only to wait long enough because no other company had any interest in buying the Suburban. Both sides were frustrated after a long drawn-out negotiation session on June 29th at the Mississippi Valley Trust Company. United Railways' leader John Beggs provided a statement to St. Louis newspapers designed to force the reluctant Suburban to bring its asking price down. The *Post-Dispatch* covered the merger discussions, including Beggs' statement:

> (The) Suburban… has never paid a cent in dividends and has no surplus in its treasury. In taking it over, UR is assuming a financial burden of $353,000 which represents the dividend on the Suburban stock and the deficit…[1]

Beggs shared numerous thoughts about the proposed merger including an odd discourse on the Suburban's dark olive green color scheme:

> The Suburban will lose its identity completely just the moment the merger takes place. The color of the cars will be changed… I don't like to see streetcars in funeral colors.   I like to see something bright and dressy and surely there is a somber appearance to the present Suburban cars.[2]

On August 8, 1906, an agreement was signed transferring the St. Louis and Suburban's lines and assets to United Railways effective December 31, 1906. United Railways agreed to assume the Suburban's seven and a half million dollar debt. It paid for the Suburban with 40,000 shares of preferred UR stock after stockholders of both companies voted to approve the agreement. On January 1, 1907, all former Suburban streetcars, including those operating in towns served by the former St. Louis and Kirkwood and the former St. Louis and Meramec River electric lines, ran under the banner of United Railways. With the acquisition of the Suburban, United Railways had nearly become a street railroad monopoly in the St. Louis area, lacking only a few lines such as the city-owned St. Louis and Chain of Rocks, the Illinois Traction (Mc Kinley) System and the East St. Louis and Suburban.

United Railways absorbed the entire Suburban fleet, even the oldest cars dating back to 1895, many of which were then rebuilt and operated on St. Louis routes up to World War II. The only immediate changes in the routes were within St. Louis city limits and did not significantly alter riding patterns of county residents. United Railways continued the improvement program started by the Suburban because the right-of-way, though improved in previous years, was in unsafe condition in some spots, especially over old wooden bridges, trestles and viaducts.

An immediate change to the former Suburban division was the appearance of the "new" Kirkwood-Ferguson route. United Railways connected the already existing pieces to form one of the longest routes in the area. One could then ride from Kirkwood to Ferguson without a transfer or paying an extra fare. Guy E. Trulock, a longtime county resident, recalled for readers of the *Kirkwood Historical Review* the streetcar service in Kirkwood circa 1907:

---

[1]PD, 8 July 1906.
[2]Ibid.

UNITED RAILWAYS SERVICE 1907-1919

As the big red Kirkwood-Ferguson cars stopped, the conductor hopped out to change the trolley around. The motorman put his controller and air brake handle in his pocket - a rule of the road - got out to lift the big headlight from front to back, then went back to pick up his stool and fit his controls in the front end. Meanwhile the conductor lifted the two tally registers, one for cash fares and one for transfers, from their perch and set them up on the other end of the car. The motorman used a long thin wedge to throw the switch and the car moved over to the other track. As the Manchester car came over the bridge from its run to Meramec Highlands, the Kirkwood-Ferguson moved out.[3]

The route of the Kirkwood-Ferguson changed very little once it was established. In 1907, the first year of operation by United Railways, the new line carried three-million passengers. The northern half of the Kirkwood-Ferguson route was described in *The History of St. Louis County*:

As you travel towards Ferguson on the electrical line of the United Railways, you are prepared to expect a town of exceptional attractiveness by the sights along the way. Your car passes through De Hodiamont, Wellston, Hollywood, Suburban Gardens, Pine Lawn, Kenwood Springs, where is a famous mineral spring, Westover, Davis Station, Nelson Station, Glen Echo Park and golf links, Normandy Grove, Florissant Golf Club, Normandy Hills, Carsonville, Rosemont, and Ramona Park, until Florissant Junction is reached. Here the car turns to the right and takes you into the heart of the business section, right to the Wabash Railroad Station.[4]

Streetcar service had helped bring an influx of city weary residents to Ferguson. Though the town was primarily residential, the county history indicated that there was a "business air" about it "down in the valley - up which come the street cars - and in the vicinity of the Wabash depot." By 1911, the town had the Bank of Ferguson as well as 20 other business establishments. At the time, only 4 automobiles were licensed to drive on Ferguson streets - the beginning of the end of streetcar service to the town, though no-one anticipated such changes at the time.[5]

On December 20, 1907, the *St. Louis County Watchman-Advocate* reported that United Railways Company was double tracking the former Houseman line from St. Louis to Kirkwood. However, that did not come to pass. United Railways extended the double track of the Market Street line along the former Houseman line to the Dale Avenue loop in Richmond Heights. From there to Maddenville, where the Kirkwood-Ferguson turned north from the Houseman line, the line remained single track, though consideration obviously was given to double tracking the line. When Big Bend Road was paved, a double track Brentwood crossing, paved with rails, was built there. When Manchester Road was widened to four lanes, the Brentwood crossing was built as a double track crossing paved with brick. In addition, just west of Hanley Road, the three span single track steel bridge carrying the Brentwood line across Deer Creek was built with a design

---

[3]Guy E. Trulock, "Local Transportation in Kirkwood Circa 1907," Kirkwood Historical Review, December 1978, pp. 9-10.
[4]Thomas, (1911) History of St. Louis County, p. 290.
[5]Ibid.

designated for a double track bridge. Despite the preparations for double track on the Brentwood line, the second track was never built.

The portion of the former Houseman Air Line from Brentwood to West End Heights was commonly known as the Brentwood line. It featured a shuttle affectionately called the "Brentwood Dinky" which connected the St. Louis Market Street line to the Kirkwood-Ferguson.

One of the more memorable types of cars used as the Brentwood Dinky was a World's Fair class car featuring controls on both ends. Rather than turning the car around, the motorman got off the car at the end of the line, unhooked the trolley at the other end of the car and let it rise until it rode on the wire. At the opposite end, the motorman pulled the trolley down and secured it under a hook on top of the car. Before the car was ready to roll, the motorman carried the control crank and the brake handle from the "back" of the car and put them in place on the "front." Friendly motormen often let children enamored with the streetcar help with the ritual of changing the car to go the opposite direction. The seat backs moved so the passenger could face forward no matter which way the trolley headed.

The Dinky operated with a motor at each end along with two control boxes, two sandboxes and two trolleys. The car featured manually controlled doors at each end, a "cannon ball" stove set in the middle of the car, advertisements all along the top sides of the car and a wooden floor. In later years the wooden floor had become quite splintered, causing some concern for people who were afraid of falling from their seat when the streetcar suddenly lurched or quickly stopped.

A ritual was followed by the crew of the Kirkwood-Ferguson near its connection with the Dinky:

> In those days of little traffic and fewer trains, the streetcar motormen were bound by a rule that upon approaching a railroad track they must stop the car, physically get out of it (usually the conductor), look both ways up and down the track, and then get back in before proceeding. They had to follow the routine in snow and ice and in heavy rain, where the Kirkwood tracks crossed the train tracks at Brentwood and Russell.[6]

On Halloween, a bad night for streetcar crews, it was common for older boys to soap the tracks at the switch where the Brentwood tracks joined the Kirkwood-Ferguson line. More than once, according to Brentwood historian, Mary Hilke, the Brentwood car slid into a loading Kirkwood car well filled with passengers. Like other youth along the Kirkwood-Ferguson and Manchester lines, under the cover of darkness, Brentwood teens enjoyed darting out from the underbrush along the line, grabbing the trolley rope, pulling it down and letting it snap up causing a flurry of sparks and then darkness. When the trolley wheel left the power line, the motorman or the conductor had to go to the rear end of the car, find the trolley rope, and reposition the trolley on the wire. Passengers did not like being in the dark on a deserted stretch

---

[6]Mary Hilke, "Musings From Memory," Brentwood Public Library files.

of the line late at night, but fortunately the delay was usually brief. Kids in Brentwood preferred to target the Dinky because its trolley pole spring was not as stiff as the springs on the larger cars that operated on the Kirkwood-Ferguson. The Dinky's trolley was much easier to dislodge.

As the year 1907 unfolded, United Railways began implementation of a construction plan to replace all the wooden trestles, viaducts and bridges on the cheaply built county lines with concrete and steel structures. As a result of one of the first replacement projects, the company received loud complaints from Kirkwood residents when it stopped service on the St. Louis side of a county bridge that needed immediate rebuilding. Kirkwood residents were not denied access to the city, but they were forced to endure a more roundabout route with several transfers. For a period in 1907, Kirkwood residents south and west of the Clay Avenue bridge received no streetcar service while the bridge was replaced. United Railways and the Missouri Pacific Railroad shared in the cost of constructing the new bridge. Not until 1914 were the last of the county replacements completed. Another major project undertaken by United Railways soon after the merger with the Suburban was the renovation of the ex-Suburban De Hodiamont power plant which was in poor electrical condition. It was enlarged and made more reliable.

Meanwhile changes were taking place in the towns along the routes. Maplewood incorporated as a town in 1908. Thomas, in the *History of St. Louis County*, reported on the growth of the business enterprises. Many of these businesses were spawned by the presence of the loop operating in Maplewood:

> The commercial and manufacturing enterprises of Maplewood number 74, consisting of six dry goods, four hardware, two lumber yards, twelve groceries, five drug stores, nine meat shops, three shoe stores, three florists, two laundries, nine saloons, and two get-any-little-thing-you-want stores… The city has one bank and a large number of dealers in real estate; also a newspaper called the *News*, and a commercial printery.[7]

A Maplewood city directory published by the Business Men's Association[8] featured numerous ads which referred to locations at or near the loop. Pat Usher's "Loop Lunch Counter" at 2815 Sutton Avenue advertised:

> Go to PAT USHER at Maplewood Loop for Cigars, Tobacco, Candies, Hot Coffee, and Sandwiches At All Hours of the Day or Night.[9]

Harper's Pharmacy simply advertised, "Opposite the Loop." Strassner's Buffet at 7407 Manchester Avenue pitched its ad to streetcar riders:

> End of the nickel fare either way… Stop and think, Your last Drink, Going South or West.[10]

---

[7]Thomas, 1911.

[8]Business Men's Association, (1912) <u>Directory of the City of Maplewood</u>. in historical archives of Maplewood Public Library.

[9]Ibid.

[10]Ibid.

UNITED RAILWAYS SERVICE 1907-1919

Despite United Railways' dominant position in the St. Louis street railroad business, it encountered financial difficulties throughout its reign. Required increases in salary for employees were reluctantly given. The April 23, 1910, *Street Railway Journal* reported terms of a notice of a pay increase that was posted in all United Railways car houses.

> Beginning May 1, 1910, the rate of wages of conductors and motormen of United Railways will be as follows; 20 and 21 cent men will be advanced to 22 cents an hour; 22 cent men to 23 cents; 23 cent men to 24 cents; 24 cent men to 25 cents; and 25 cent men to 26 cents. And in the future employment will begin at 22 cents per hour, advancing 1 cent each year until the 26 cent rate is reached.[11]

Though the employees were happy to get a raise, they felt that it was too little for the difficult jobs they held. An editorial comment in the *Street Railway Journal* reflected management's view; the men were well paid for a secure job that was one that any unskilled person could quickly learn. They should not complain about their lot.

A major complaint by many streetcar passengers was the discourteous behavior of the conductor and motorman. Streetcar lines had been hit by numerous lawsuits and were eager to project a better image with the public. As a result, a bulletin addressed to the United Railways employees was posted at all car houses in an attempt to change the crews' behavior:

> 1. All passengers are entitled to civil, polite treatment. Do not lecture, nor scold, nor make sharp retort. Keep silent if you can not make a courteous reply. All this, notwithstanding there may be provocation.
>
> 2. Be patient and courteous, especially to women; do not offend a woman by word or act; do not lay your hands on a woman or child, except to save them from injury; do not have a woman arrested or in any way offer her an indignity.
>
> 3. Stop for passengers; do not run by anyone. Take them on in safety and land them safely. It is not humane to injure anyone, nor is the responsibility for having done so pleasant. All the passengers place their comfort and safety and the pleasure of the ride in your hands; do not disappoint them.
>
> 4. Be prompt, industrious and persistent in the collection of fare. Disputes as to payment of fare or the validity of transfers are unfortunate, but when the conductor has made every civil and respectful endeavor to set the matter right, he has performed his duty — there being a possibility of error on both sides — and he will not go to the extreme of a quarrel, fight or an ejection from the car.
>
> 5. In making change, take pains to be accurate, and if the change given is unsatisfactory, give other change, and do not dispute over it; a very important part of your duty is to please every passenger.[12]

---

[11] Street Railway Journal, 23 April 1910, p. 760.
[12] "Bulletin to St. Louis Employees on Courtesy," Electric Railway Journal, 18 June 1910, p1078.

UNITED RAILWAYS SERVICE 1907-1919

Despite cash crisis followed by cash crisis as a result of the millions of watered stock from previous administrations of the system, the number of riders increased rapidly from 1907 to 1913. No automobile or motor bus competition was yet in place, leaving the streetcar company, "King of the Road." Where its lines ran, it had become a speedy efficient crowd-mover. However, increases in revenue from ridership growth were never enough to make progress on the bonded indebtedness and the inflated expenses of United Railways.

As is currently the case with Bi-State busses in off-peak periods, the streetcars ran virtually empty for long portions of the day. Kirkwoodian Grace Taussig shared with readers of the *Kirkwood Historical Review* a story about one of those empty streetcars and her brother Warren Taussig, who graduated from Kirkwood High School in 1911:

> One Halloween, Warren and some of his companions watched the conductor (crew) of a Manchester street car leave the passenger-less vehicle at Heinzelmann's Drug Store while they had a cup of coffee before continuing the journey to Meramec Highlands. When the pair came out, Warren, naturally adept with machinery, had the situation well in hand and was on his way with the other boys to the Highlands.[13]

Though it is unknown if the boys were caught, it is almost a certainty the crew were in hot water for leaving the car unattended. Despite the trouble the crew faced, they would be loath to exchange places with a crew whose streetcar killed a pedestrian. An October, 1911, *Watchman-Advocate* reported details of a man being struck and killed by an eastbound United Railways Meramec Highlands streetcar which was empty except for crew and "was running fast":

> Newton Cook of Meacham Park was instantly killed by a streetcar Saturday night about 10:30. He was walking from Frank Repetto's Saloon to Bach's crossing intending to take a car home, but failed to get off the track in time. He was dragged about fifty yards and badly mangled. The car was thrown off the track and the wrecker came before they could get the body from under the car.[14].

As the primary transit system in the teens, United Railways lines served not only business commuters, but also youth and young adults interested in social events and dating. Miller Donovan reminisced in the March 1978 *Kirkwood Historical Review* about breakfast picnics at Meramec Highlands made possible by the availability of Manchester line. Circa 1912, she and some girls from Webster and Kirkwood arranged early morning picnics with newspapermen from the *St. Louis Republic* and the *Globe-Democrat*. The men had experienced difficulty meeting girls because of their work hours.

---

[13]Grace Taussig to Mary Chomeau, " Vignettes of the Taussig Family," Kirkwood Historical Review, March 1972, p. 291. Heinzelmann's store was located at the corner of Main (Argonne) and Clay.
[14]"Newton Cook Killed by Car," SLCWA, 27 October 1911. The former Bach's crossing is located where Ballas Road dead ends at Old Big Bend Road.

Very few people owned automobiles in 1912, certainly not young reporters. But there were streetcars that ran to Meramec Highlands on the Manchester run. They had "Manchester" in big letters across the top… The last 56 car left St. Louis at midnight unless the theater had a late show and the car waited for the theater crowd.[15] It began again, leaving St. Louis car barns at 3:45 a.m. The reporters caught that car.

The men got on the first car in the morning and began picking up girls in Webster. The men would always pay the fare for the girls as they got on - only a nickel in those days clear to the Highlands.[16]

The car picked up Miller at Dickson Street in Kirkwood at 4:20 a.m. The twelve or thirteen reporters, laden with food, and about eight to ten still sleepy girls all piled out of the car near Marshall Road and walked down the hill to the Meramec River where they picnicked at Moser's Landing. They rarely had more than two picnics per summer, waiting till July and August when it got light early in the morning, though some couples dated at other times.

For one visitor to the Meramec Highlands, the streetcar bell was a lifesaver. Kirkwood storyteller Francis Scheidegger recalled:

> There was a bell underneath the streetcar and the plunger was on a spring on the floor underneath the motorman's foot, and he would press that down and it would go, ding, ding, ding. That reminds me of a story… They had quite a few big picnics there (Meramec Highlands). It so happened a male individual, the story goes that it was a person of minority race, was caught in the women's toilet, "peeking." They caught the person. The crowd gathered around, and the deputy sheriffs couldn't control the crowd. Finally they pushed this guy down into the toilet, and then somebody got a rope and threw it over the limb of a tree. They were going to hang this person. That went on until 12 o' clock. The last streetcar to leave Meramec Highlands loop was called the owl car. The motorman would warn everyone that it was ready to take off by ringing his bell ding, ding, ding. That broke up the crowd and saved this guy's neck… [17]

Glendale's subdivisions had grown strong by 1910. A further subdivision of note was Highland Place, filed by Craig Realty Company in 1911. It was designated as a private place, the first in Glendale. It was bordered by Venemann on the west and Collins on the east. By 1912, most of the streets near the Manchester line were virtually sold out and were filled with well-built homes of a substantial nature, many of which were rather pretentious for the time. Due in large part to the presence of two streetcar lines, the Glendale area was rapidly changing from rural to suburban. In fact, the real estate developments were so attractive that the city of

---

[15]Manchester cars were not numbered in 1912, though Kirkwood residents later routinely referred to the Manchester car as the 56.

[16]Miller Donovan, "Long Ago Breakfast Picnics," Kirkwood Historical Review, March 1978, pp. 6-8. From the city to Maplewood loop was 5 cents. From the Maplewood loop to Meramec Highlands was 5 cents. Fare for a Webster Groves or a Kirkwood girl going out to the Highlands was 5 cents, but the fare for the man from the city totaled 10 cents.

[17]Francis Scheidegger, Cassette tape of streetcar memories for the author, January 1997.

Kirkwood decided to attempt to annex the area consisting of present day Glendale and Oakland. In 1912, as a result of the annexation threat, Glendale area residents petitioned the County Court for incorporation as a village. In December of 1912, Glendale was recognized as a village by the court, just days before the annexation vote was held. Following the court ruling, the populace of the area unanimously rejected annexation as did most Kirkwood residents.

Seasonal conditions had definite impact on the streetcar services. Mrs. Rhey Mc Cord, who lived in one of the Meramec Highlands cottages, was able to observe the streetcar track near the Highlands loop from the rear windows of her cottage. Years later she related to her daughter, Margaret Logie, an account of so much snow falling in one winter circa 1913 or 1914 that it didn't melt all winter. The sweeper brushes on the snow removal work cars kept throwing the snow in banks higher and higher till all she could see of the streetcar when it passed was the trolley pole.

The July 26, 1912 *Watchman-Advocate* reported the advent of the "pay as you enter" (PAYE) car on the Kirkwood-Ferguson line. On the former cars, it was difficult for conductors to keep track of which customers had paid during rush hours when new arrivals and existing passengers mingled together. United Railways officials believed that large numbers of fares were being missed. Since the PAYE system required payment before passengers could enter the car, no longer could pay dodgers mingle in with the crowd in order to avoid paying the fare. The PAYE system was especially attractive because receipts could be increased without increasing labor costs or adding service. It helped keep the conductors honest [18] and decreased the number of accidents by having one of the crew always on station at each end of the car. The system also reduced the passenger irritation resulting from being asked to pay more than once. Cars had to be specially designed for the PAYE operation. The rear platform area was enlarged so it could hold a large number of boarders. It allowed the conductor to signal the car forward as soon as all boarders were on the platform. While the car was in motion, the conductor then finished collecting the fares. According to the *Watchman-Advocate*, regular passengers on the Kirkwood-Ferguson line were creatures of habit: "The passengers insisted on handing fares to the conductor, and he had a busy time telling them to drop it in the little box."[19] Because the PAYE cars with their extra large rear platforms were not suitable for double end operation, turn around tracks such as loops or wyes[20] were required. United Railways planned an almost universal use of big cars with the large Detroit rear platforms which required single end working. No longer could the motorman change ends at a terminus and operate the car from the other end. Some small shuttle routes or connector runs such as the Brentwood line, known as the "Crawfish Special" by city folks who rode out to fish in Deer Creek[21] or from Kirkwood to the Meramec Highlands, still maintained the "dinky" with its controls at either end and its reversible seats. Major county lines such as the Kirkwood-Ferguson and the Manchester lines were given the

---

[18]Travers Burgess was told by his grandmother that the PAYE system was implemented because United Railways believed that its conductors were pocketing much of the fare money, and ringing up much less on the fare registers than they were actually collecting.

[19]SLCWA, 12 July 1912.

[20]A wye, shaped like the letter Y, is a stub track into which a car can be moved and then headed back out in the opposite direction.

[21]Celeste Wagner Blann, (1976) A History of Rock Hill, self published, p.12.

bigger cars. Wye lay outs which were fine for double end operation posed safety hazards when cars had to be backed out, especially at night and in heavy traffic. As a result, short extensions were added to many wye lay outs to make them into loops where streetcars could safely turn around.

A wye was used by Manchester cars on the north side of Lockwood Avenue in Webster Groves a short distance east of the intersection of Gray Avenue and Lockwood. Webster cars turned back there prior to the completion of a loop at the beginning of the private right of way west of Rock Hill Road. Since it was necessary for the conductor to handle the trolley pole when backing into the wye and to flag automobile traffic on Lockwood Avenue, it required two men to work the wye. Around 1930, the Rock Hill loop was built and use of the wye was discontinued in anticipation of one-man car operation.

The Ferguson loop was completed in 1914 as a result of the switch to larger cars. United Railways also purchased land at Woodbine and Magnolia in Kirkwood for use as a streetcar loop. The *Watchman-Advocate* stated:

> It is reported here that both the Market Street and Ferguson Line will have that as their terminus. The end of the Ferguson line at present being Main Street, Kirkwood, and the Market Street Line, West End Heights with a dinky run between there and Brentwood to connect with the Ferguson line.[22]

Any Manchester cars that had not turned back at Clay and Adams passed the Magnolia loop, commonly known as the Kirkwood-Ferguson loop until 1931, on the way to the Meramec Highlands. According to the late Kirkwood historian Harlan Gould, debris from the Missouri Athletic Club fire in the city was hauled out to the Magnolia site to fill in a ravine, making the area level enough for construction of the loop, not to mention later construction of the Loop Lounge.

At times the secluded Meramec Highlands loop proved to be hazardous. Disturbing to Highlands residents was a typical accident on board a streetcar which was reported in a September, 1914 *Watchman-Advocate*. Mrs. Sarah Rowe, a Highlands resident, got up to exit a stopped car at the Meramec Highlands loop. When the car suddenly started, she was thrown down, striking her back on one of the car seats. She spent several weeks at St. Luke's Hospital before she was able to get up for short periods of time.[23]

The loop was also hazardous to the crew. It proved to be an ideal staging point for nefarious deeds. "STREET CAR ROBBERS AT MERAMEC HIGHLANDS - HIGHWAY MEN SHOT MOTORMAN AND ROBBED CONDUCTOR OF $13.50 SUNDAY NIGHT" read a *Watchman-Advocate* headline. The report continued:

---

[22]"Meramec Highlands," SLCWA, 20 March 1914. To reach the Magnolia loop from the Market Street line, one had to transfer to the Brentwood line and then transfer again to the Kirkwood-Ferguson. To call the Magnolia loop a terminus for the Market Street line seems a stretch.

[23]"Meramec Highlands," SLCWA, 11 September 1911.

Two highwaymen held up a Manchester car at the loop at Meramec Highlands Sunday night and robbed the conductor of $13.50 at the point of a revolver, and shot the motorman in the leg when he failed to comply with a request to hold up his hands… "As we drew up to the loop," said Koehler (the conductor), "I was standing in the front of the car and Enochs (the motorman) told me that two young men wanted to board the car… The car was one of those of a new design that opens from within, and I pulled the lever, opening the door… One passed on up to the front of the car while the other stopped, as I supposed, to pay his fare… As I glanced up to the front of the car, I noticed the man who had gone up had drawn a revolver and pointed it at Enochs. Then I saw a revolver thrust in my face, and I was commanded to hold up my hands… The man who had me covered began tugging at my money belt, and I took it off and handed it to him. The other fellow then brushed by me and snatched some envelopes from my pocket. They were empty. I had $15.00 in my pocket but was not searched, and I saved that."[24]

After taking the money belt, the men jumped off the car and ran into the darkness. The conductor said it was so dark at the loop that he could see only a few feet. The Kirkwood deputy sheriff was called and arrived on the next car. He made a search of the premises but found no trace of the robbers. A special car took Enochs to St. Joseph's Hospital where his wound was treated and proclaimed "not very serious."[25]

Beginning in 1913, the United Railways Company purchased much of its electricity from the Keokuk, Iowa hydroelectric plant of Union Electric. Since all the streetcars, in conformity with general street railroad practice, used direct current, the alternating current purchased from Union Electric had to be converted to lower voltage direct current. A series of substations with rotary converters was installed on many lines of the United Railways. A new substation was built at the corner of Fillmore and Washington in Kirkwood for the Kirkwood-Ferguson while the Brentwood power station was retained as a converter substation. The Kirkwood substation still stands and today is used as a residence. Where the driveway for the residence exists today, there was a paved siding next to the building on which a portable substation, two permanently coupled cars with a rotary converter and transformer, was parked. It was used when the substation was shut down. The two car portable substation was frequently seen at the Kinloch, Brentwood and the Kirkwood substation facilities.

In 1914, the fleet was repainted, refreshing the yellow-orange paint-scheme of the United Railways cars. All wood cars took about three weeks to repaint. From 12 to 18 separate coats of paint were applied. After each coat dried, it was sanded smooth by hand before another coat was applied. To protect the finish, several coats of varnish were added. For a minimal cost, the life span of a wooden car was extended by many years with no loss of attractiveness. The Suburban had previously used gold and silver leaf to letter their cars, but United Railways, mindful of cost, did not continue that practice. Even so, the cars emerged from their makeover looking fresh and attractive. While repainting of the fleet was in progress, the company also began enclosing the rear platforms.

---

[24]SLCWA, December 1914.
[25]Ibid.

UNITED RAILWAYS SERVICE 1907-1919

Streetcar accidents were still prevalent, sometimes as the result of a poor roadbed. The July 31, 1914 *Watchman-Advocate* reported:

> Five persons were injured Sunday night about 8 o'clock when a Kirkwood-Ferguson car left the track at Newport and Shady avenues, Webster Groves... The place at which the wreck occurred has been the scene of numerous accidents. A Kirkwood-Ferguson car was wrecked at that point Sunday night several weeks ago.[26]

In response to citizen complaints about streetcar service, the Missouri Public Service Commission was created in 1914. One of its first major projects was to review the standards of car line service in the United Railways' operation. In 1915 the PSC ordered specific minimum service requirements. It found winter heating of cars inadequate and ordered that stoves in all the cars be fitted with forced air blowers to better distribute the heat and provide ventilation.

On September 30, 1915, United Railways helped Kirkwood celebrate its 50th anniversary. Streetcar traffic was heavy, bringing thousands to Kirkwood for the various events such as a ball game between the Kirkwood All-stars and the County All-stars, a barbecue lunch which served over three thousand people, a parade of over 125 units, dignitaries giving speeches (which included St. Louis Mayor Henry Kiel who in later years was to be the receiver in charge of the Public Service Company while it was in receivership), and a grand finale pageant featuring important aspects of the city's history. United Railways provided a streetcar, a dinky of the type first used in Kirkwood, for use in the pageant. At the last minute before the trolley was scheduled to arrive at the Adams and Kirkwood Road site of the pageant, a fuse blew. While the crew quickly worked to replace the fuse, the pageant orchestra filled in with an unscheduled rendition of a popular song of the day, "My Bird of Paradise." By the time the song was completed, the trolley was on the roll again and arrived with its load of distinguished guests amidst the good natured cheers of the throng.[27]

Until 1915, children in Glendale had to attend school in Kirkwood since there were no public or parochial schools in Glendale. Once the town was incorporated as a fourth class village, residents hoped that Kirkwood would build a school in Glendale. Kirkwood school district did not disappoint them. Henry Hough School opened in 1915 at the corner of Lockwood and Collins (Sappington) to serve area students up to fourth grade. Since the streetcar lines ran east and west through Glendale and there were no busses, the only way for children who did not live near the Manchester line to get to and from Hough School was to walk. So walk they did, often through fields and woods, hills and valleys, by ponds and streams. Morton Lange recalled:

> Maude Snider was the only teacher at the time and acted as principal, disciplinarian, general manager and teacher of all four grades in the same classroom. She lived somewhere in west St. Louis, rode the Kirkwood-Ferguson streetcar to and from her

[26]"Car Wrecked at Webster Scene of Many Accidents," SLCWA, 31 July 1914.

[27]GD, 1 October, 1915. St. Louis Republic, 1 October 1915, Kirkwood Courier, 2 October, 1915.

house, and walked - often with her students - on Collins Road to and from the street car tracks to the Henry Hough School.[28]

Despite the opening of Hough School, most Glendale students rode the streetcars to Kirkwood to school. Hilbert Heisker recalled traveling to school in Kirkwood from his home on what is now Edwin Avenue in Glendale:

> I remember being taken by Mother to a kindergarten at the public school in Kirkwood. In good weather most of us walked to and from school. In bad weather, we took the Manchester trolley if we had a nickel. Time and time again, one conductor we all called "Good Guy" would stop his car in bad weather and tell us to get in whether or not we had the fare.[29]

In the winter, when the rain froze and the trolley wires were covered with ice and the tracks were slick, a display of lights and sparks flashed as the trolleys cut through the ice on the wires. There were times when the ice was so thick on the wires that no cars could run, giving the area children a holiday from school.

By year's end of 1916, all United Railways passenger cars were fitted with Peter Smith coke-fired furnaces with electric forced air blowers. They were mandated with the intent of making winter more bearable in the cars. The Public Service Commission's new requirement for enclosing all rear platforms was already being implemented by the company prior to the order. The heaters and enclosed platforms helped to battle the cold, but cold wasn't the only natural element to be battled by streetcars. In June 1916, a very bad storm hit Kirkwood about 5 p.m. The *Watchman-Advocate* reported:

> It was so dark that lamps were lit, and the wind blew so strong that a street car was stalled for about half an hour, as it could make no headway against the wind.[30]

The last county streetcar line construction, the "City Limits" line, was completed in 1917, when the Hamilton line was lengthened via Delmar, Skinker, Wydown, DeMun. New track was laid on Yale Avenue, to Manchester Road in Maplewood. The City Limits Line, later numbered #16, ended in the Yale Avenue loop adjacent to Manchester Road, thus giving Maplewood two streetcar loops. It gave Maplewood a good north city and north county connection.

Though it was possible with a good deal of effort to move a car from the Manchester line via a spur onto the Yale Avenue loop so it could operate on the City Limits line, it was rarely done and then usually for work cars. On occasion it was done for a special excursion car. Other

---

[28]Morton Lange, "Morton Lange Remembers Old Glendale: Part II," Glendale Historical Society Bulletin, September 1992, vol. VIII, no. 3.
[29]Hilbert Heisker, "Edwin Avenue: Originally Elsa Place," Glendale Historical Society Bulletin, September 1987, vol. II, no. 3.
[30]"Meramec Highlands," SLCWA, 30 June 1916.

city and county extensions and routes were proposed after 1917, but funding was never secured to do the work.

The most difficult issue dealt with by United Railways was appropriate scheduling of routes. Scheduling cars to satisfy reasonable demand and at the same time to arrange departure times for all cars so that an approximately equal number of passengers was carried on each car remained a constant headache. The company frequently counted passengers on its cars in an effort to develop a better schedule. In 1917, the Kirkwood-Ferguson ran 18 cars per rush hour each ten minutes apart. Non peak times featured fewer cars with 20 minute intervals. For passengers who were used to the idea that a streetcar should be in sight at all times, the 20 minute intervals seemed entirely too long. As a result, complaints about the schedule from county residents were frequent.

Accidents and injuries were still all too common. The *Watchman-Advocate* reported in a December 1917 edition, an accident in which the Frank DeSuza family from Meramec Highlands was riding on a Manchester car which collided with a Hodiamont car (a Kirkwood-Ferguson car which operated out of the De Hodiamont car barn) at Kirkwood. Though the collision was not serious, little Frankie DeSuza was thrown against the hot stove. He was not burned but was badly bruised in the incident.[31]

In April 1918, Manchester line Owl Car stops in Webster Groves were listed in the local paper along with stops at Fourth and Walnut. "Webster 11'25, 12'10, 12'50, 1'30, 2'10, 2'50, 3'30, 4'10, 4'45, 5'10 .Fourth and Walnut 12'00, 12'15, 12'30..." Earlier practice of ending service by 1:00 a.m. had changed perhaps because of the wartime need for workers to get to and from night shifts. Before automobiles became numerous, the majority of the Glendale men commuted to work via streetcar, though the Missouri Pacific and the Frisco railroads were more convenient for residents of Oakland. Service on the streetcar lines was frequent with time lapses between cars generally lasting no more than 15 minutes. The work commute became an integral part of the daily routine according to Glendale resident Bruce Tanner:

> The trolley played a big part in all of our lives. The motormen would get to know you. If you fell asleep on the way home after the late shift, he would awaken you. You came to know all their names and the times of their usual trips.[32]

Florence Delling lived a few houses from the Manchester line at 115 Elm Avenue during the World War I years. Elm was the second street east of current day Sappington Road. She remembers that both streetcar lines had heavy cables strung overhead from pole to pole along the sides of the right-of-ways. At the time the village of Glendale still consisted of woods and fields from a few blocks north of Lockwood to the right-of-way of the Kirkwood-Ferguson line. Florence often walked through the fields to ride the Kirkwood-Ferguson. The path was not convenient as she had to climb over or crawl under barbed-wire fence on one piece of property

---

[31] "Meramec Highlands," SLCWA, 21 December 1917.
[32] Bruce Tanner as told to Donna Lykens, "Memories of Glendale," Glendale Historical Society Bulletin, March 1988, vol. III, no. 1.

in an area known as Moreland Place. When the ground was frozen or the weather was wet, she walked through a lane to Collins Road and then walked north on it to the streetcar stop.[33]

In 1918, United Railways and the city of Maplewood became embroiled in a controversy over taxes. In order to detour traffic around Maplewood, the company obtained right-of-way through private property to construct a bypass, the Bartold cutoff. The cutoff connected with the Manchester line at the east end of the Edgebrook bridge and at the Brentwood line near where it crossed Manchester Road. United Railways had completed much of the grading for the cutoff by January 1919, but had not laid track or erected poles. Shortly thereafter, Maplewood and United Railways came to an agreement which resulted in the abandonment of the cutoff as a passenger carrying line before it was completed. A wye was located at the north end of the Edgebrook bridge, which was on private right-of-way and did not require flagging of auto traffic. That wye was never converted to a loop and remained in use until the abandonment of the Manchester line in 1949. It was the stub of the Bartold Valley cutoff that connected the Brentwood 57 (original Houseman line) with the Manchester line.[34]

World War I created a shortage of males to operate the system and caused increases in prices for the materials needed by the company. Those situations exacerbated the United Railway's money shortage. A successful employee strike in 1918 resulted in a wage increase to 45 cents an hour and also achieved union recognition which had not been fully gained in the strike of 1900. In order to raise more revenue, fares in the city were increased for the first time since streetcar service began. City residents were charged 6 cents while 5 cents remained the rate for county passengers. However, the fare increase did not generate enough revenue to pay the salary increases, other increased costs and the service on the debt. Since 1906, no dividends on common stock had been paid. The company secured a short term War Finance Corporation loan, averting bankruptcy for a time, but when that loan came due, United Railways was unable to pay the 2 ½ million dollars owed.

Fares fixed at 5 cents since the start of streetcar service, gradual loss of ridership, the costs of all the improvements, plus the staggering debt that United Railways had inherited in acquiring other lines resulted in insolvency and receivership.

United Railways faced the receivership with determination to resolve its financial problems and to emerge as a viable company.

---

[33]Florence Delling, "Glendale As I Remember It," Glendale Historical Society Bulletin, March 1989, vol. IV, no. 1.
[34]Though a 1928 map shows the cutoff connecting the two lines, there is disagreement whether the cutoff was ever used. There is consensus that it was not used for passenger traffic. However, a few venerable streetcar enthusiasts state that they personally witnessed operation of maintenance cars on the cutoff. Others believe it was never used nor electrified.

20-1. A winter hazard for streetcar motormen and passengers was snow fall. The first of two Manchester cars appears to have derailed in the snow. Note the skewed angle of the car while the electric wires overhead continued straight ahead. Despite the derailment, the car's trolley pole and wheel remained in contact with the power source. Typical of problems which later led to automobile supremacy, one broken down car prevented others from reaching their destination. Despite the streetcar's troubles, area children were happily at play. Photograph from the National Museum of Transportation.

20-2. United Railways Transfer. On January 1, 1907, the St. Louis and Suburban's Manchester lines became part of the United Railways Company. In that year, United Railways immediately began to replace wooden bridges, trestles, and viaducts on the Manchester and other county lines.

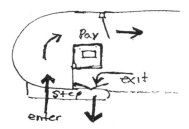

20-3. 1903 ex-Suburban Robertson Sill car 237 converted to a PAYE car 661 by United Railways. The enlarged platform was added to allow the car to use the Pay As You Enter system. The diagram shows the entry and exit flow on the enlarged PAYE platform. The large platform allowed a number of passengers to board while waiting to pay. Charles Hamman collection.

Chapter 21

RECEIVERSHIP YEARS 1919-1927

On April 12, 1919, former St. Louis Mayor Rolla Wells was appointed receiver for the bankrupt United Railways company by U. S. District Court Judge Dyer. Ironically, Wells was the St. Louis mayor who had initiated the mil tax ordinance which the streetcar company had vigorously fought in court for many years. In Episodes of My Life, Wells described his resistance to the "trial balloons" about becoming the receiver. He resisted the appointment until pressured in a private meeting with by Judge Dyer, but once he accepted the position, he was a very "hands on" administrator.

> I gave the receivership my undivided attention, proceeded cautiously, and not until July 7, 1919, did I make any changes in personnel of the management; at that time… I then appointed Colonel Albert Perkins as Manager for the Receiver, and Mr. H. O. Butler as General Superintendent.[1]

Despite changes in management and operation, one of the first resolutions passed by the newly formed Kirkwood League of Women Voters in 1919 was the request that the speed of streetcar service between Kirkwood and St. Louis be improved.

Perkins, came decorated with the Distinguished Service medal received during World War I for his work as the Director of Light Railways for the American Expeditionary Force in France. He was immediately hit with a barrage of suggested route extensions which he turned down to focus on the business of upgrading the car stock and running a more efficient operation. In 1919, the United Railways shops contained a number of 1895 vintage ex-Suburban cars being remodeled. Deck roofs were replaced with arched roofs on some cars. Inside well steps replaced outside folding steps. New motors and trucks were added. The cars ended up being practically new, ready for double ended service on county lines such as the Clayton, the Brentwood, and the Berkely lines. In part because of the glut of remodeling work, Perkins changed the long standing policy of having all new cars constructed in UR shops and began ordering from outside car builders.

He contracted for research and work on a new prototype car, which made its appearance in St. Louis in 1920. The "Peter Witt" car was named after a Cleveland street-railway commissioner who developed the design concept where the conductor was stationed in the

---

[1]Rolla Wells. (1933) Episodes of My Life, p. 393 St. Louis.

center of the car to supervise two side doors. The "Pay as You Pass" car utilized the entire front half as an internal platform or payment area featuring a front entrance and a center exit.. Passengers could pay as they passed the conductor and the fare box as they walked to the rear of the car to find a seat, later leaving by the rear center door, or they could remain standing in the front section and pay the conductor as they departed through the front center door. United Railway's car 777 was put into service for a year and was determined to be effective for heavy city service. It became the new standard. Orders were placed with the St. Louis Car Company for more Peter Witt cars and for fifty trailers with a similar design. By 1927, 250 Peter Witt cars had been ordered and were in operation or were soon to be completed. Though not advertised at the time, an advantage of the new cars for the company was that they could be changed over to one man operation. What the public saw was a larger steel bodied car that operated with smaller lightweight high speed motors which allowed for a moderately low floor.

United Railways used posters placed on the cars during the receivership period to remind riders of safety rules and to encourage increased patronage. Examples were displayed at the 1922 Chicago Convention of the Electric Railway Association. One warned drivers, "Hundreds of automobile accidents would be averted if automobiles would not try to dash across the streets in front of moving streetcars." Others warned parents, "Stealing Rides! Annually many boys are injured "stealing" rides on sides and backs of street cars. Warn YOUR boy of this danger." And, "'Children First' is all right when leaving a sinking ship - BUT NOT WHEN GETTING OFF A STREET CAR. Help the little ones off and avoid possible accidents - with subsequent sorrow."

The transit company also used the car front posters as a political forum. Posters showed the "Thinker" contemplating this message, "The street railway system is to the city what the veins and arteries are to your body - VITAL. The healthy development and growth of street railway is vital to you. It is an integral part of every citizen's life. Don't strangle it with excessive taxation, burden it with unjust claims, or weaken it by thoughtless criticism. They all lead to higher fares." Another poster attempted to disperse traffic throughout the day, "If the water that flows down the Mississippi River in twenty-four hour had to be carried in two hours, it would submerge St. Louis. The same principle applies to street cars. Spread out the traffic over the day by going home from your shopping before the rush." One poster which urged the public not to block the tracks showed a line of streetcars behind a wagon. "The greatest good for the greatest number is a fundamental principle - yet street cars are blocked, traffic held up, thousands of passengers delayed, with great loss to the public... by drivers blocking the tracks." In a thinly veiled cut at automobile drivers, a safety message reminded passengers, "The law requires automobiles to stop when a car is discharging passengers - nevertheless, LOOK when alighting from street cars as some drivers take chances and ignore the law." Other frequently used posters shown in the display advertised special recreational destinations such as the St. Louis Zoo, Jefferson Barracks, and Creve Coeur Lake. The photographs featured in the Chicago Convention displayed the lower front portion of various working streetcars which sported United Railways' posters.[2]

---

[2]"How the United Railways of St. Louis Keeps Its Public Informed," Electric Railway Journal, 2 December 1922.

KING TROLLEY: RECEIVERSHIP YEARS 1919-1927

One of the patrons for whom the posters were targeted, Glendale resident Florence Delling was a regular rider on the Kirkwood-Ferguson after she obtained a job in the city. One day while riding to work, she met Dr. Hillel Unterberg, a neurologist and one of Glendale's most interesting residents, who later opened a residential facility for mental patients on his Glendale property. He was en route to his office in St. Louis. Unterberg regularly entertained young Florence during their streetcar commutes with tales of his travels and war experiences as a medic during the First World War. The shared rides stopped in 1923 when Florence moved away.[3]

In 1922, United Railways made plans to run buses as feeders and as extensions of the streetcar system, but a ruling from the court controlling the receivership would not allow the United Railways to implement its plans. The court ruling opened the bus transit field to others. In 1922, Peoples' Motorbus Company was given permission to run along United Railways routes, thus skimming off much of the streetcar traffic. On May 29, 1923, Peoples' Motorbus Company began operation in St. Louis. The first line on Delmar was in direct competition with the Delmar streetcar line. Because the bus company had none of the tax burden and none of the responsibility for paving streets, the company became immediately successful. United Railways felt an immediate ridership decline. After a year of operation, the bus lines had siphoned off nearly 13 ½ million passengers. In 1924, after an unsuccessful attempt to merge interests with Peoples' Motor Bus, United Railways was allowed to start its own motor-bus lines. Its bus lines soon began to show profitability, thus helping the company's bottom line. The loss of passengers to bus service had become obvious, though United Railways was determined to maintain and increase ridership on the streetcars. In 1925, the Kirkwood-Ferguson carried 4 and a half million passengers, but the exodus to the automobile and the movement of the population to areas in the county not served by streetcars had begun in earnest.

Despite the decline in total passenger numbers, the streetcar lines were still heavily utilized by many Kirkwood and Webster residents each with their own experiences.. Somewhat typical was fifteen year old Verne Twelker lived near the Meramec Highlands loop. In 1923, she rode the streetcar daily to Yeatman High School in St. Louis. At the time, Meramec Highlands had no high school. Even though Kirkwood High School accepted students from Meramec Highlands on a tuition basis, some students like Verne were able to earn scholarships to other schools, making them cheaper to attend. For entertainment, Verne and her boyfriend rode the streetcar into Kirkwood, Maplewood or St. Louis to view movies. At Maplewood, Verne recalled, her boyfriend had to pay another fare to go on into St. Louis. She remembered that the conductor who took their fares was always in the back of the streetcar, and the motorman was in the front.[4]

Elizabeth Schillk Dorr, a student who attended school in the Meramec Highlands School District #51, remembers Osage Hills youth in the 1920s jumping on the back of United Railways

---

[3]Florence Delling, "Glendale As I Remember It," Glendale Historical Society Bulletin, March 1989, vol. IV, no. 1.

[4]Verne Twelker Browne, telephone interview with author, 1993.

streetcars to dislodge the trolley poles and smashing Osage Oranges on the rails to make them so slippery that the cars could not climb the grades. Other youth soaped rails so that a motorman who was trying to gain time after a delay would find the car almost out of control, slipping backward on an uphill grade or sliding downhill on the soapy rails. For that reason and for natural causes such as ice storms, the cars always carried a well stocked sand box, designed to spread sand on the rails. The motorman released the sand when he hit a slippery set of rails. Even though they bedeviled the motorman, the same youth patronized the streetcars- hoping not to be recognized.

A description of the dependence of Meramec Highlands residents on their streetcar connection to the world was provided by Florence Delling, who lived near the Highlands loop in 1923. She described a winter in which rain and sleet froze on the trolley wires and rails so thickly that no streetcars could come through to the Highlands:

> .… so for days we were isolated. Then finally we heard the first car coming up the line. It crackled and snapped, throwing out flashes of red, yellow and green as the trolley broke through the ice. It was a glorious sight and we were overjoyed to know the cars were running again.
>
> Living at the Meramec Highlands was like living at the end of the world.… There was no way to get anywhere but to walk when the streetcars did not run.[5]

Some former patrons connect vivid food memories to the riding United Railways streetcars and the food establishments at the loops. Like children elsewhere, Maplewood children learned that you could save a nickel by walking instead of riding and then use the saved money to buy candy or sodas. Travers Burgess, who grew up near Maplewood, recalled an incident in which he as a young boy had purchased a pound of heavenly hash, a confection of chocolate, nuts and marshmallow, prior to his trip on the streetcar with his family to Meramec Highlands. While on the streetcar traveling from the Sutton Avenue loop to Meramec Highlands, he ate a half pound of the candy. At the resort, he ate a large sausage (hot dog). On the return to Maplewood, he ate the rest of the heavenly hash. After arriving back at the Sutton Avenue loop, he begged his parents to buy him an ice cream soda. He finished off a two scoop ice cream soda, then walked home with his parents. The next day he became very ill with scarlet fever. In his mind, the hot dog was the cause of his woes. As a result, he avoided hot dogs and sausages for many years.[6]

Prior to 1927 when Brentwood High School opened, many of the town's students rode the Kirkwood-Ferguson to Clayton High School which had opened in 1916. Miss Gladys Barlow in an interview with Robert Eastin, revealed that even after Brentwood High School opened, her father allowed her to continue to ride the streetcars to school in Clayton so she could graduate

---

[5]Florence Delling, "The Streetcars and Meramec Highlands," Kirkwood Historical Review, Vol. XXVII, no. 1, p. 7.
[6] F. Travers Burgess, conversation with the author, Kirkwood, 1997.

with her classmates.[7]   Riding the opposite direction to school were Catholic school children from Clayton's St. Joseph's parish. They were regular commuters to and from Kirkwood's St. Peter's School until 1928 when St. Joseph's school was opened. Older students used the cars to reach classes at Washington University.

In an unusual incident in 1926, a Kirkwood-Ferguson car contributed to the destruction of an old Kirkwood landmark when it ran over and severed a fire hose which was stretched across the tracks to the nearest fire hydrant. The venerable house burned to the ground for lack of water.[8] The owner's complaints were but one of many that year. Kirkwood residents were still complaining that streetcars moved too slowly between Kirkwood and St. Louis. For some residents, dust and dirt from unpaved sections of streets between the tracks were an irritant; while for others the amount of space required in the street for tracks was a problem because it caused traffic tie-ups as automobiles became more numerous.

Rolla Wells had performed well despite his belief that the only real solution to mass transit in St. Louis was a subway system which he discussed in *Episodes of My Life*:

> Rapid transit in mass transportation is not practicable on the street surface… The conveyances used in mass transit are large and ponderous, and they carry heavy living loads. To attempt mass transit on the street surface with such vehicles, in the combination of weight bulk and speed, is a hazard which would not be justified by any other consideration.[9]

Though Wells was a strong advocate for a subway system which included a change of the Suburban Railway System private right-of-way from Vandeventer Avenue to Florissant into an open or shallow covered subway, his vision of a subway system was never accepted by conservative St. Louis.

Wells' receivership remained in place until 1927. Under his stewardship and program of investing in services, equipment, and facilities, United Railways became strong in its operation despite its week fiscal structure. Of the 55 million debt owed by the company in 1919, only 2 ½ million had been retired by 1927.

When St. Louis Moves was published by United Railways in 1927 to give a positive outlook to the public and to its investors with an eye toward assuring creditors about a fiscal reorganization that was being promoted. It was designed to instill confidence that United Railways was ready to come out of receivership and described the entire operation from maintenance to car building to leadership:

---

[7]Gladys Barlow to Robert Eastin, (1969) <u>Brentwood Anniversary - 50 Years</u>.
[8]"Old Kirkwood Landmark Burns When Streetcar Severs Fire Department Hose," SLCWA, 12 January 1926.
[9]Rolla Wells, (1933) <u>Episodes of My Life</u>, p. 197.

United Railways today has 482 miles of track, exclusive of the yard tracks and tracks in sheds around the city. It employs some 6,000 persons. It has in operation more than 1,600 passenger cars. It has one general shop at Park Avenue and Thirty-ninth Street in which there are 300,000 square feet of floor space. And there are thirteen division sheds, yards and shops.[10]

The publication went on to give the best picture possible relative to receivership, not mentioning the staggering debt that still remained.

Since April 1919, the United Railways property has been operated by Rolla Wells, who was appointed Receiver. He sought an expert transportation man familiar with local conditions, Col. A. T. Perkins General Manager. At that time street railway receiverships were general throughout the United States. The World War had brought about tremendous increases in prices of materials, supplies and everything necessary to railway operation. It was impossible to increase revenues because of existing franchises and regulations laid down by the city and state public service commissions. The receivership here was precipitated when the Company found itself unable to pay or refinance a loan from the "War Finance Corporation."[11]

The uncontrolled bus lines, increased use of the automobile, movement of population away from high density city areas, and the zooming popularity of radio (which decreased night traffic to entertainment locations in the city and county), were all factors in the decrease of ridership on streetcars. However, the revenue from increased ridership on United Railways bus lines helped mask the bleak financial picture of the streetcar operation. As a result, the streetcar lines and bus lines were allowed to reorganize with the St. Louis Public Service Company taking over the United Railways assets through foreclosure. St. Louis Public Service Company assumed operation of the former United Railways system on December 1, 1927.

The Public Service Company would find itself hard pressed to succeed financially against the odds with an aging system, societal changes, and a large debt stacked up against it.

---

[10]United Railways, (1927) <u>When St. Louis Moves</u>.

[11]Ibid.

UNITED RAILWAYS COMPANY OF ST. LOUIS
ROLLA WELLS, Receiver
This transfer issued pursuant to decree of the Circuit Court, which provides that it shall be good only at first intersection within the time limit, and in the direction as punched.
IT IS UNLAWFUL to sell, give away or exchange this transfer or to alter it in any way, and its use by any person other than the one to whom issued is also unlawful.
A complete record of every transfer is kept. In case of dispute, passenger is requested to pay fare and notify this office. Any just claim will be promptly adjusted.

BARNEY W. FRAUENTHAL,
General Traffic Agent.

21-1. By 1919, the once proud United Railways Company was bankrupt. As the back of the transfer from that era indicates, Rolla Wells was appointed as receiver. City fares had been raised to 6 cents, but county residents were still paying 5 cents per ride at the time of the bankruptcy.

21-2. United Railways token illustrated in the 1927 publication, *When St. Louis Moves*. The caption next to the illustration stated, "The token you drop in the box is what makes the wheels go round." The actual token size at 5/8ths of an inch in diameter was smaller than a dime.

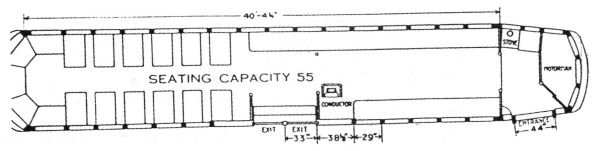

SEATING CAPACITY 55

21-3. Layout of a Peter Witt "Pay as You Pass" car. By 1927 250 of the Peter Witt cars had been ordered for St. Louis operation.

21-3. Cover (reduced in size) of United Railway's 1927 publication showing an efficient, modern - not to mention stylish - operation, ready to leave receivership and to become the St. Louis Public Service Company.

Chapter 22

PUBLIC SERVICE COMPANY   1927-1939

The St. Louis Public Service Company, a public utility company, was created to take over the aging United Railway's street railway system which served the St. Louis and its older suburbs as well as United Railways' rapidly expanding network of buses which served new suburbs that were springing up in St. Louis County. The Public Service Company not only took over assets and functions of United Railways. It also took over the financial woes and the difficulties inherent in the public transit industry at a time when an explosion of new hard surface roads, new suburbs and a dramatic increase in the use of the automobile was occurring. Though the portents were not good, stockholders were optimistic. The reorganization appeared to have resolved many of United Railways' financial issues.

During the reorganization effort, St. Louis and Suburban bondholders had been given several good offers for their securities. The Suburban could have once again become an independent company if the offers had been accepted, but they were rejected by cautious bondholders. Operators of the Illinois Traction System wanted the Suburban to serve as a feeder line for Illinois Traction's St. Louis terminal and approached bondholders about buying the St. Louis and Suburban bonds. The interest of an outside party in taking over the Suburban forced United Railways to give Suburban bondholders special consideration in the reorganization. They were given new (overvalued) City and Suburban Public Service Company bonds 5% for par with a maturity date of July 1, 1934.

St. Louis and the streetcar companies had battled for a several decades over the city's right to collect a usage tax. Though litigation and numerous mediation efforts to settle the dispute had failed, the reorganization plan settled the problem by giving the city 16,212 shares of preferred stock to pay the outstanding claims for unpaid mill tax. That solution weakened the fiscal status of the new company, but without the compromise, the reorganization would not have been agreeable to St. Louis officials. Despite the reorganization, fixed costs such as property tax on the wire, track, poles and land holdings was passed on the new company. Bus companies did not own the roads they used and were required to pay no tax to use the roads which were built and maintained at public expense. They escaped the substantial fixed costs of streetcar operators: maintenance and repair of lines, roadbed, track, power stations and passenger facilities. Buses had an obvious advantage for transit operators over streetcars.

KING TROLLEY: PUBLIC SERVICE COMPANY 1927-1939

Though a great deal of the debt had been resolved by the reorganization, cash shortages continually occurred as notes came due. The cash shortfalls were due primarily to a ridership decline, a result of an increasing availability of affordable and dependable automobiles and smooth hard surfaced roads which allowed people to become independent of streetcar routes. Not only did the Public Service Company streetcar operation suffer, businesses dependent on the lines were also hurt. The county's "streetcar resorts" such as the Meramec Highlands Resort, Suburban Gardens, and Ramona Park withered and died.

After the Meramec Highlands resort declined in the 1920s, the property was purchased in 1925 by developers and was renamed the Osage Hills Country Club and subdivision. Reflecting that change, on December 1, 1927, the main Manchester line from 4th street to the Meramec Highlands loop was renamed the "Manchester-Osage Hills" line. After the resort closed, the line to Osage Hills served primarily daily commuters. Osage Hills Country Club generated enough traffic to merit its own stop complete with a shelter.

A numbering system for all Public Service Company routes was introduced on June 28, 1928. The company manager explained that placing route numbers on all streetcars and buses would facilitate the efficiency of streetcar traffic, reducing the number of people who missed streetcars because they were unable to read the signs. The addition of large illuminated number screens was touted as a way to aid visibility in dark and foggy weather.

In the first assignment of route numbers, the Kirkwood-Ferguson became the 01, pronounced "Oh one." The Manchester Division routes were numbered consecutively, 53 - Maplewood, 54 - Webster Groves, 55 - Manchester-Osage Hills, and 56 - Brentwood. Later in 1928, the numbers were changed on some routes when a short run of the Manchester line to Kirkwood was inaugurated. It ran from 4th street in St. Louis to Kirkwood, looping via Fillmore, Washington, Clay, and Adams and was designated as the "55 - Manchester-Clay and Adams" line. The previous #55 line to Osage Hills was renumbered "56 - Manchester-Osage Hills," and the "56 - Brentwood" was changed to "57 - Brentwood," which it retained until the line closed. The numbering system grew to be well accepted with riders often referring to the routes by number rather than by name. When recalling the streetcar service of their younger days, many older residents talk about riding the 01, the 04 (Clayton), the 05 (Creve Coeur), the 53, 54, 55, 56, and the 57. Perhaps some of the most nostalgic memories were of the Brentwood 57.

For Brentwood resident Regina Gahr, the 57 - the Brentwood Dinky, is fondly remembered because it was the magic carpet that took her and her young friends to West End Heights for days of fun at the Forest Park Highlands amusement park. Less exciting were her regular rides to piano lessons in Richmond Heights.[1]

The old 57 Dinky was also memorable for Jim Kalb. In a September 1977 *"As I Remember Brentwood"* column contained in the *Pulse Special 75th Anniversary Edition*, he recalled a once in a lifetime thrill on the Brentwood Dinky.

---

[1]Regina Gahr, conversation with author, 1997.

One night we left Richmond Heights, crossed Dale and Big Bend and all of a sudden Mr. O'Shaughnessy slowly stopped the car, turned to me and said, "Son, you drive a while, I'm getting tired." Scared out of my wits, I crawled into the big seat sitting between his legs, with both hands on the tiller. "OK, kick her up a notch at a time up to four." It took both hands to advance the big brass tiller. When I hit the fourth stop, he said, "Let her roll." Boy! Looking out the big windows and watching the Dinky's powerful yellow headlights shine on the glistening tracks ahead was a thrill I would never forget. All at once the buzzer sounded and the old motorman told me to cut it down to the first notch and get my hand on the air brake. Of course his fingers were in control all the while, but I didn't notice. Our passengers smiled, thanked me for the ride and gave me a nickel. When we reached Brentwood, Mom and Dad had to wait while I helped Mr. O'Shaughnessy change ends of the car. Then with a grin and a wave he hit the tiller and took off.[2]

In later years, the age and condition of the cars on the Brentwood - 57 became a concern to passengers who would watch the roof sections of the car move in a different directions as the car was running. Brentwood historian Robert Eastin shared a story told to him by Dan Donnerman, that one night on an owl car run, the center section of the roof crashed down onto the seats. No one was hurt because there were no passengers and because the motorman was standing in the vestibule. For years passengers had been warning, "One of these days...," worried that the car would fall apart. That night it happened.[3]

Though the numbering and renumbering of routes and the uncertain financial stability of the streetcar companies were topics of conversation, passengers on the Manchester lines 54, 55, and 56 had more mundane matters to ponder, one of which was the smoke streaming from the ground near the Edgebrook bridge approach. A 40 foot deep ravine bordering the tracks had been filled by dumping cinders from the Central Power Station. Other materials such as old pine paving blocks from streets were also dumped in the fill. It is believed that cinders which were still hot caused the wood covered by them to ignite and smolder underground. The fire was allowed to burn itself out, taking about four years.[4]

In an effort to stem the decay of revenue caused by Sunday pleasure riders switching to automobiles, on January 29, 1929, a 25 cent Sunday-holiday pass was introduced. It allowed unlimited travel on city lines and some county routes. Other ways to lure customers, such as speedier express services were tried. A new "X1 - Kirkwood-Webster Express" route was inaugurated on April 15, 1929. In early May 1929, it was made even speedier, "18 MINUTES FASTER DOWNTOWN."[5] The new time table advertised an additional six minutes cut from the time of the express, "through a change in schedules and a general speeding up." The fare for the express was 16 cents or two tokens. The route generally followed the old St. Louis and

[2]Jim Kalb, "As I Remember Brentwood," Pulse Special 75th Anniversary Edition, 20 September 1994, originally printed in the September 1977 Pulse.

[3]Dan Donnerman as told to Robert Eastin, Eastin to author, 1997.

[4]L. H. Doolittle, letter from Wayne Leeman files, Webster Groves, 23 February 1949. and "Manchester Car Notes, " Arthur Wilson to Wayne Leeman, undated.

[5]18 minutes faster than the regular line. The new express was only 6 minutes faster than the previous one.

Kirkwood Railroad right of way to the city: From Woodbine/Magnolia loop via trackage of the
01 - Kirkwood-Ferguson line to the juncture with the 57 - Brentwood line at Maddenville: thence
via trackage of the Brentwood line to the juncture with the 51 - Market line. At that point it
proceeded via trackage of the 51 - Market line on Oakland, Kingshighway, Chouteau,
Vandeventer, Clark and Market to Broadway. The time table closed with the usual caveat,
"Subject to change without notice." Thirty-one stops including "Magnolia" and "Broadway and
Market" took 57 minutes to run as scheduled. Despite initial optimism about its success, on
October 1, 1929, after less than six months of operation, the Express was discontinued due to
insufficient revenue.

In 1929, the St. Louis Transportation Survey Commission report suggested the
abandonment of streetcar lines and the replacement by bus lines as an appropriate solution to the
Public Service Company's financial woes. No funding was provided to implement the suggested
changes, so nothing was immediately done. However, all car lines recommended in the report for
abandonment were closed within six years. One of those recommended for abandonment was the
portion of the "56 - Manchester-Osage Hills" line from the Woodbine and Magnolia loop to
Osage Hills.

With the loss of resort traffic to Meramec Highlands, and with ridership limited primarily
to commuters, the service to Osage Hills was perceived as a financial liability by the Public
Service Company. During November 1929, the Public Service Company asked the Missouri
Public Service Commission to allow it to abandon the portion of route 56 from the
Woodbine/Magnolia loop to Osage Hills and to substitute bus service. The company reported to
the commission that the revenue from that portion of the line did not justify the continuation of
street car service, especially since the company accountants estimated and reported to the
commission that the replacement of the deteriorated tracks and the company's share of Big Bend
Road repaving would cost $100,000. In June 1930, the Public Service Commission agreed to
allow the company to abandon that section of the line if Kirkwood paved Woodbine Avenue and
the company substituted bus service. Legal wrangling ensued. In order to keep streetcar service
to Osage Hills, Kirkwood refused to grant a permit to operate a bus on the route. Its officials
vowed to take the matter to the Supreme Court if necessary.

The Missouri Public Service Commission reversed its decision in January 1930 allowing
service to continue to Osage Hills. St. Joseph College had produced for the commission a record
showing payments of $500 to the streetcar line's predecessors between 1896 and 1898. In return,
the St. Louis and Meramec River Railroad Company agreed to continue service to the college as
long as it was in operation at the Geyer and Big Bend Road location. The commission honored
the old arrangement, so the Public Service Company was required to continue to operate the line.

The Public Service Company officials did not easily give up. On August 4, 1930, the
west terminus of the "56 - Manchester-Osage Hills" line was cut back to the
Woodbine/Magnolia loop and was designated as the "56 - Manchester-Kirkwood" line. To
comply with the Public Service Commission ruling, shuttle service was inaugurated on the "58 -
Osage Hills" line from the Woodbine/Magnolia loop to Bach (Ballas) Road. At the time, St.
Louis County was paving Quinette Road, (now Big Bend Road) so the run was not extended all

the way to the loop at Osage Hills until the paving work was completed. An assumption had apparently been made by St. Louis County road commissioners that the Osage Hills portion of the line would be abandoned.

Opportunistically, some believe, the Public Service Company used the new road work as an excuse to state that it was forced to use a small older model streetcar with less overhang as a result of the new higher pavement. The company announced to the public that regular streetcars in the fleet could not be used on the Osage Hills line because they would not adequately clear the pavement and would scrape on the concrete. As a result, the president of the Public Service Company expressed "grave fear" for his passengers on the Osage Hills line and continued to actively pursue legal authority to abandon the line.

Kirkwood and Osage Hills residents believed that the Public Service Company was overstating the safety risk and was manipulating the situation to justify abandoning the run. The late George Dobson Sr., a long time Osage Hills area resident, remembered Big Bend Road in the early thirties, when the dinky was still operating, as being two concrete strips with the streetcar tracks running down the middle between them. While Kirkwood officials and the Public Service Company were arguing about reinstating regular service, Osage Hills and Kirkwood residents complained about the poor shuttle service provided by the single streetcar. It operated on a random schedule. Some residents believed that the company wanted the connections with the "56" cars at the Magnolia loop to be so poor that residents would give up and request "more efficient" bus service.

Meanwhile, in an effort to become profitable, the Public Service Company requested an increase in fares and asked the union for a wage reduction of 10%. The wage reduction was grudgingly accepted by the union because jobs were scarce during the Depression. However, the Public Service Commission turned down the request for higher fares.

The company was looking for other ways to reduce costs. It introduced a new fare box which allowed one-manning on some lines in the late twenties. In September 1930, the Public Service Company introduced one-manning on the Kirkwood-Ferguson route. In response to complaints about the one-manning, officials of the Public Service Company stated that the revenues of the line were insufficient to justify two-man operation. The *Watchman-Advocate* discussed the advent of the move and the union reaction:

> One man cars have been running on the Clayton line for the past few years and on the Creve Coeur line for several weeks. The carman's union is objecting to this type of service.[6]

Cars of the 1000/1100 series were rebuilt for one man operation, remotored and regeared for higher speed service on long county routes such as the Kirkwood-Ferguson and the Manchester lines. Many cars were given automotive-type foot pedal brake controls and two window fronts.

---

[6]SLCWA, 5 September 1930.

Meanwhile, the dispute between Kirkwood and the Public Service Company lasted another year. In May 1931, Kirkwood won its case in Circuit Court in Clayton. Judge Nolte ruled that the company had engaged in a form of "legal intimidation or coercion" because it tried to force the city to pave Woodbine Avenue. For a brief time, starting April 18, 1932, the Osage Hills shuttle was extended to Clay and Adams. However, the company had appealed Nolte's ruling to the Missouri Supreme Court. On May 27, 1932, the high court found that the order ending streetcar service on the Osage Hills line was reasonable.

On Sunday, July 24, 1932, the "58 - Osage Hills" line ceased operation. It was replaced on the 25th by bus route "114 - Osage Hills," which operated on a thirty minute schedule to and from Osage Hills loop and downtown Kirkwood. The bus service that replaced the Osage Hills shuttle did not last long, being discontinued on May 14, 1933.

Following the Osage Hills line abandonment, former passengers either took the bus (until it was discontinued) or walked from the Magnolia terminus to Osage Hills. The streetcar right-of-way was used for years as the most direct route to the area. Scouting and other youth groups from the city would often hike to the Meramec Highlands quarry from the Magnolia loop for a day of fun. Residents of Osage Hills had to depend primarily on the automobile for transit after 1933 as a result of the streetcar and bus line abandonments.

Separate county fare zones were eliminated in April 1932 when free transfer privileges to and from the city system were granted. That move, which decreased the amount a rider had to pay to ride from county towns to the city, was anticipated to make the streetcars more desirable, thus attracting a greater ridership and bringing an increase in revenue. *Transit News*, a publication of the Public Service Company which was distributed free to its riders, discussed the extra fare elimination in the April 19, 1932 issue:

> Extra Fare On County Lines Eliminated for Experiment. Single-Fare Riding Between County and City Now in Effect, Sending Fare as Low as One-Half Cent Per Mile.
>
> …Under the new plan, free transfers will be interchanged between county and city lines, the only exceptions being the Osage Hills shuttle line[7] and the Creve Coeur line west of Crows Nest, on which the extra fare will continue. Trips which prior to the change required four fares can now be made on a single fare, the cost in some cases being less than one-half cent a mile… Since the experiment practically cuts the fares in half, riding must roughly double to make the experiment "break even" financially. The continuation of the plan will depend on the increase in riding… With the experiment in progress it is possible to end the difference in fare collection on the county lines, and now all fares in the county as well as in the city, are pay-as-you-enter.[8]

The same *Transit News* issue discussed procedures for use of the Sunday passes:

---

[7]Full fares continued on segments of the lines that the company wished to discontinue.

[8]"Extra Fare Eliminated as Experiment… ," Transit News, Public Service Company, 19 April 1932.

Sunday and Holiday passes, which provide unlimited daily transportation within the city fare-zone for 25 cents, automatically become good for transportation on all county lines on which the extra fare was discontinued. Regular transfer rules applying to the city fare-zone will be followed, the most important of which is the provision requiring that the most direct and practicable route without unnecessary transferring must be taken.[9]

The previous day's *Transit News* had already promoted the new Sunday fares.

Here is a hint for your next nice Sunday. Take your family, and your lunch if you wish, buy enough Sunday passes for the crowd and ride around the county all day. If you see a place that looks nice for walking, drop off the car and walk for a while. Board the next car — your pass is good all day long. You will be surprised how pleasant riding in the county in street cars is. No fighting traffic or "Sunday drivers," no hot motor in front of you, and — consider the saving.[10]

The fare zone experiment wasn't as successful in increasing ridership as the company had hoped, so in some areas, old fare zones were reinstated.

A November 1, 1932, dispatch in the *Kirkwood Monitor* announced the beginning of one-man service on the Manchester line. The Public Service Company announced that it would increase its number of cars by 23% in the morning rush hour and 17% during the evening rush hour. Time between the cars during rush hours was promoted as being approximately two minutes with the space between cars being brought down to five minutes during the day. Clarification of which cars were one-manned was provided:

Cars to be operated are of the type recently placed in service on the Eighteenth street line, with both entrance and exit being at the front. The fronts of the one-man cars have been altered so they are easily distinguished by passengers from the two-man cars of the same type to be used during rush hours.[11]

Unrest was building in Webster Groves and Kirkwood regarding the Public Service Company's routes, car conditions and services. In an article titled, "STREET CAR SERVICE IS STILL VERY POOR," the *Kirkwood Monitor* was scathing in its criticism, especially of the effects of the recent one-manning of the Manchester lines:

It looks as though the Public Service company has it in for Kirkwood, Glendale and Webster, and doesn't seem to care whether it gives these cities any decent street car service at all. In the first place the car service is the poorest in the history and the one-man cars are a failure in every respect as one man cannot handle the job as he has too many jobs to do at one time - operate the car, watch for boulevard signs, and traffic at cross streets, collect fares, make change, issue transfers and answer

---

[9]Ibid.

[10]"How to Spend the Next Nice Sunday," Transit News, Public Service Company, 18 April 1932.

[11]Kirkwood Monitor, 1 November 1932.

questions. Therefore, if there is a stove in the car, he has no time to attend to it, and in most cases there is no stove and the street car rider has to freeze to death almost before he gets to his destination. The cars are the poorest heated, besides being the dirtiest we have ever seen.[12]

The fare structure also came under fire in the *Monitor* article.

If you are downtown and want to come to Kirkwood or Webster you are compelled to wait for 56 for the one fare. If you get on 54 or 53, you will be dumped off at Webster or Maplewood and then have to pay another fare to Kirkwood, or wait in the cold and rain as was experienced by this writer Friday of last week.

If the company can give you a transfer from the Delmar or University Olive line to the Kirkwood-Ferguson line, making it one fare from downtown to Kirkwood, why can't they do the same thing on the Manchester line — transfer a passenger from Nos. 53 or 54 to 56 from Maplewood and make it all one *fair*? This we believe is an outrage on the public and until the public arises in protest the company will continue to heap hardships upon the public. The company has been allowed to raise its fare and at the same time to cut the men's pay, but never have improved the service. Where is the Public Service Commission?[13]

The *Globe-Democrat* reported on the Public Service Company's emerging competition from both bus lines and service car companies in an article entitled, "KIRKWOOD - MAPLEWOOD BUS LINE AUTHORIZED."[14] Providing additional competition for the Manchester streetcar line was the new Kirkwood-Maplewood bus line. Prior to November, it had been operated by the Baird Bus Company but was then taken over by Red Line Service Company. The new line was controlled by the Bangert Brothers who also operated a bus line between Wellston and Kirkwood. The company was authorized by the Kirkwood City Council, in December 1932, to operate between Kirkwood and Maplewood, one bus over Manchester Road and one bus over Big Bend Road. The bus service was scheduled with thirty minute intervals. The article also described another company which desired the Kirkwood market.

Application has been made to the (Kirkwood) Council by the St. Louis County Service Car Company to operate a service car line from Maplewood to Argonne Drive and Kirkwood. During rush hours the company promises ten and fifteen minute schedules and during the day a regular 20 minute schedule. This petition asserts this service has been widely requested by Kirkwood residents.[15]

By January 1933, the Red Line Bus Service Company had extended its route from Kirkwood and Webster Groves to downtown St. Louis. After 8:30 a.m., North and South

---

[12]"Street Car Service Is Still Very Poor," Kirkwood Monitor, 16 December 1932.

[13]Ibid.

[14]"Kirkwood-Maplewood Bus Line Authorized," GD, 6 December 1932.

[15]Ibid.

KING TROLLEY: PUBLIC SERVICE COMPANY 1927-1939

Webster residents had to ride a shuttle to get to the main line at Big Bend Road. Prior to that time, they could catch busses routed directly to downtown St. Louis.

In 1932, the Public Service Company was reorganized with a dissolution of various wholly owned or subsidiary companies. The dummy company, City and Suburban Public Service, remained as a Public Service Company subsidiary. Despite reorganization, by the end of 1932, none of the efforts of the Public Service Company had solved its financial problems. Liabilities exceeded assets by nearly a million dollars, causing bankruptcy to loom once again on the horizon. Even though it was sliding toward insolvency, the organization appeared to be relatively well run. Track reconstruction and replacement and rebuilding of cars was continued. A new policy of realigning county tracks into central median strips of roads in new subdivisions was implemented, sharp curves in the system were eased and the old De Baliviere car house was completely remodeled as was the Wellston loop. As a cost saving measure, the Manchester division carhouse across Manchester Road from the Scullin Steel Plant was closed on February 3, 1933.

The Public Service Company was placed in receivership after it was unable to pay a bill for Westinghouse pneumatic foot pedal brakes which had been installed on most cars. In April of 1933, former St. Louis mayor Henry Kiel was appointed Receiver. His lack of expertise was viewed by many as a real disaster for the streetcar system. He used all the money available to reduce a ten million dollar loan, which left the company with no money except daily revenue to meet current obligations. As a result, City and Suburban Public Service 5% bonds could not be paid when they were due.

Despite receivership, the company's maintenance standards were consistently high. Thirty-five year old Robertson Sill semi-convertible palace cars were still immaculately turned out and continued to ride smoothly due to regular upkeep. Kiel was hoping to restore financial health while at the same time demonstrating that the management could take good care of its fixed assets.

In 1937, street improvements were made on East Adams Avenue in Kirkwood, the former private right-of-way between Sappington and Dickson. The electrical poles were moved from the center of the street to the side, and the streetcar tracks were then made level with the street so that motorists no longer had to worry about dropping from the street into the streetcar right of way. The preeminence of the automobile had become obvious. Streetcar companies could no longer brush aside concerns of the automobile drivers.

Trends toward suburban living and use of private transportation intensified while at the same time sections of old inner residential suburbs lost housing through dereliction or replacement by manufacturing plants. Construction of major highways to the suburbs signaled further difficult times for streetcar transit. Despite the effort to reorganize, it became obvious that the Public Service Company was losing ground as the major carrier of people, perhaps, as some believe, due to the incompetence of the Kiel management. Ridership on bus lines proved more profitable to the Public Service Company than did marginal streetcar lines.

Financial reorganization of the debt in November 1939 removed the Public Service Company from receivership. In the reorganization, City and Suburban Public Service Company bond holders were given $80 cash, $350 first mortgage 5% bonds, $550 25 year convertible income bonds and two shares of class A stock for each $1000 City and Suburban 5% first mortgage bond.

The reorganization was of little concern to riders from Kirkwood, Webster Groves and Maplewood. As long as streetcars and buses provided good service, its patrons were not particularly concerned with the company's profitability. However, Public Service Company as a result of reorganization was at last in a position where it could finally operate at a profit. To increase patronage, the marketing department tried a new approach in 1939, a weekly pass allowing unlimited riding for $1.25. The new pass was well received by many on the Kirkwood-Ferguson and Manchester lines. As the economy rebounded, sparked by the European war, ridership increased. Things were looking up for the transit company.

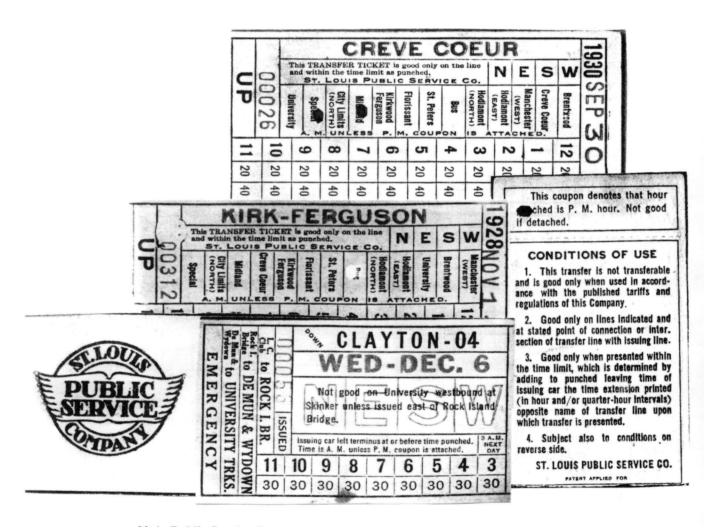

22-1. Public Service Company transfers from the collection of Ralph Von Doersten. His father, an avid streetcar fan, collected the transfers. His father met his wife-to-be while she was on the job as one of the United Railways' women conductors hired during World War I.

KIRKWOOD-FERGUSON
Subject to Change Without Notice
FEBRUARY 15, 1937
SOUTHBOUND

DAILY		SATURDAY		SUNDAY	
Leave Ferguson AM	Leave Big Bend AM	Leave Ferguson AM	Leave Big B'd AM	Leave Ferguson AM	Leave Big B'd AM
5:00	4:47	5:00	4:47	5:30	4:57
5:20	5:07	5:20	5:07	5:50	5:17
5:35	5:27	5:40	5:27	6:10	5:37
5:50	(10 min.)	6:00	5:47	6:30	5:57
6:00	6:17	6:15	5:57	6:50	6:17
6:10	6:22	6:30	6:07	7:10	6:37
6:13	6:37	6:45H	6:27	7:30	6:57
6:25	6:47	7:00	6:47	7:50	7:17
6:31C&A	6:57	7:10H	7:02	8:10	7:37
6:36	7:05	7:20	7:17	8:30	7:57
6:41H	7:12	7:30	7:32	8:50	8:17
6:46C&A	7:18C&A	7:45	7:47	9:10	8:37
6:52	7:23	8:00	7:57	9:30	8:57
6:59	7:28	8:15	8:07	9:50	9:17
7:06H	7:33C&A	8:30	8:17	10:10	9:37
7:14	7:39	8:45	8:32	10:30	9:57
7:22	7:46	9:00	8:47	10:50	10:17
7:30	7:53	9:15	9:02	11:10	10:37
(10 min.)	8:01	9:30	9:17	11:30	10:57
8:10	8:09	9:45	9:32	11:50	11:17
(20 min.)	8:17	10:00	9:47	PM	11:37
PM	8:27	10:15	10:02	12:10	11:57
4:10	8:37	10:30	10:17	12:30	PM
(10 min.)	(20 min.)	10:50	10:32	12:50	12:17
5:40	PM	11:10	11:47	1:10	12:37
5:43W	2:37	11:30	11:02	1:30	12:57
5:50	2:47	11:45	11:17	1:50	1:17
5:55W	2:57	PM	11:37	2:10	1:37
6:00W	3:07	12:00	11:57	2:30	1:57
6:10	3:12	(15 min.)	PM	2:50	2:17
6:20W	3:17	6:30	12:17	3:10	2:37
6:25W	3:27	6:50	12:32	3:30	2:57
6:30	3:37	7:10	12:47	3:50	3:17
6:40W	3:42C&A	7:20W	1:02	4:10	3:37
6:50	3:47	7:30	1:17	4:30	3:57
7:00W	3:52	(20 min.)	1:32	4:50	4:17
7:10	3:55C&A	10:10	1:47	5:10	4:37
7:20W	3:57	10:30W	2:02	(20 min.)	4:57
7:30	4:07	10:50	(15 min.)	10:10	5:17
(20 min.)	(10 min.)	11:10W	7:17	10:30W	5:37
10:10	6:37	11:30	(20 min.)	10:50	5:57
10:30W	(20 min.)	11:50W	10:57	11:10W	6:17
10:50	10:57	AM	11:37	11:30	(20 min.)
11:10W	11:37	12:10	AM	11:50W	10:57
11:30	AM	12:30W	12:17	AM	11:37
11:50W	12:17	1:10W	12:57	12:10	AM
AM	12:57	1:50W		12:30W	12:17
12:10				1:10W	12:57
12:30W					
1:10W					
1:50W					

W—To Wellston only.
C&A—To Clay and Adams only.
H—To 4th Street via Hodiamont line.
Approximate running time from Ferguson: 31 min. to Wellston; 42 min. to Delmar.

KIRKWOOD-FERGUSON
Subject to Change Without Notice
FEBRUARY 15, 1937
NORTHBOUND

DAILY		SATURDAY		SUNDAY	
Leave Kirkwood AM	Leave Easton AM	Leave Kirkwood AM	Leave Easton AM	Leave Kirkwood AM	Leave Easton AM
5:30	4:31	5:30	4:31	5:40	5:01
5:50	4:51	5:50	4:51	6:00	5:21
6:10	5:06	6:10	5:11	6:20	5:35
6:20	5:21	6:30	5:31	6:40	5:55
6:30W	5:31	6:45	5:46	7:00	6:15
6:40	5:41	7:00	6:01	7:20	6:35
6:50W	5:49	7:15	6:15	7:40	6:55
7:00	5:56	7:30	6:25	8:00	7:15
7:10W	6:02	7:45	6:40	8:20	7:35
7:20	6:06	8:00	6:45	8:40	7:55
7:30W	6:12	8:15	7:00	9:00	8:15
7:40	6:16	8:30	7:05	9:20	8:35
7:50W	6:21	8:40	7:25	9:40	8:55
7:58	6:25	9:00	7:40	10:00	9:15
8:06W	6:33	9:10D	7:55	10:20	9:35
8:22D	6:40	9:20	8:10	10:40	9:55
8:30W	6:45	9:40	8:25	11:00	10:15
8:38	(10 min.)	9:50D	(10 min.)	11:20	10:35
8:46D	7:15	10:00	8:55	11:40	10:55
8:54W	(20 min.)	10:15	9:10	PM	11:15
9:02	8:35	10:30	9:25	12:00	11:35
9:10D	8:53	10:45	9:35	12:20	11:55
9:20	9:09	11:00	9:55	12:40	PM
(20 min.)	9:33	11:15	10:15	1:00	12:15
PM	9:57	11:30	10:35	1:20	12:35
3:20	11:30	11:45	10:55	1:40	12:55
(10 min.)	(20 min.)	PM	11:10	2:00	1:15
3:50	PM	12:00	11:25	2:20	1:35
(8 min.)	3:35	12:20	11:40	2:40	1:55
5:10	(10 min.)	12:40	11:55	3:00	2:15
5:20	4:45	1:00	PM	3:20	2:35
5:30	4:53	(15 min.)	12:10	3:40	2:55
(10 min.)	5:00	6:00	12:25	4:00	3:15
6:00	5:07	6:20	12:40	4:20	3:35
6:10D	5:10	6:40	12:55	4:40	3:55
6:20	5:15	6:50D	1:05	5:00	4:15
6:30D	5:22	7:00	1:15	5:20	4:35
6:40	5:26	7:20	1:35	5:40	4:55
6:50D	5:33	7:40	1:55	6:00	5:15
7:00	5:41	7:50D	2:10	6:20	5:35
7:10D	5:49	8:00	(15 min.)	6:40	5:55
7:20	5:57	(20 min.)	6:55	7:00	6:15
(20 min.)	6:05	11:00	(20 min.)	(20 min.)	6:35
11:00	(10 min.)	11:20D	11:55	11:00	6:55
11:20D	6:55	11:40	AM	11:20D	7:15
11:40	7:15	AM	12:35	11:40	(20 min.)
AM	(20 min.)	12:20	1:15	AM	11:55
12:20	11:55	1:00D		12:20	AM
1:00D	AM	1:40D		1:00D	12:35
1:40D	12:35			1:40D	1:15
	1:15				

W—To Wellston only.
D—To Delmar only.
Approximate running time from Kirkwood: 14 min. to Rock Hill Rd.; 30 min. to Clayton; 45 min. to Delmar.

22-2. February 15, 1937 Kirkwood-Ferguson schedule. Note approximate running time of 45 minutes from Kirkwood to Delmar and 42 minutes from Ferguson to Delmar.
Museum of Transportation collection.

22-3. Motormen pose in front of one of the converted one-man cars at the Ferguson loop circa 1930. The Kirkwood-Ferguson car pictured was of the 1000/1100 series which was rebuilt, given a two window front, given a larger motor and was re-geared for higher speed service on the long county lines. This car was later used as a "Tiger Stripe" one man car on the Manchester line after the 1903 vintage 600 series cars were removed from service on that line. The Kirkwood-Ferguson cars were converted to one man operation in September 1930. Charles Hamman collection.

22-4. Manchester car of the same vintage at Kirkwood's Woodbine and Magnolia loop in the mid to late 1930s. The distinctive Tiger Stripe pattern was introduced to make identification of one-man cars easy for the public.

To Our Patrons

Which Do You Prefer?

Front Entrance on this car
or
Rear Entrance, as we used to have.

A vote will be taken February 27th.
Ballots and boxes will be in this car.

ST. LOUIS PUBLIC SERVICE COMPANY

If

you prefer Rear Entrance, the (Just tear off this Corner
old method of boarding this car)

Drop this Card in
box at Rear Door.

If

you prefer Front Entrance, as (Just tear off this Corner
now in effect on this car)

(See other side for explanation)

22-5. Public Service Company polled riders on February 27, 1928 to determine whether the rear entrance pay-as-you-enter system or the front entrance pay-as-you-leave system was preferred. 63% of the 303,000 votes cast favored the rear entrance system which was then put back into use. The ballot and poster were shown in the May 26, 1928 *Electric Railway Journal*.

18 MINUTES FASTER DOWNTOWN

6 MINUTES MORE CUT FROM TIME OF KIRKWOOD-WEBSTER EXPRESS

Through a change in schedules and general speeding up, the Kirkwood-Webster Express will make the run in six minutes less time than at present.

The trip now leaving Broadway on Saturday afternoons at 1:29 will be discontinued and a trip leaving at 12:33 P. M. substituted. This will make two convenient Saturday afternoon trips, 12:33 and 12:53, from Broadway, which will arrive at Magnolia Avenue, Kirkwood, at 1:30 and 1:50 P. M., less than an hour from one end of the line to the other. The present evening trips will leave Broadway at 4:51 and 5:09 P. M., arriving in Webster at 5:37 and 5:57 and in Kirkwood (Clay and Adams) at 5:47 and 6:07 P. M. The leaving time of the morning trips will be unchanged, but the arrival in St. Louis will be 6 and 4 minutes earlier, respectively. These trips will reach Broadway at 8:19 and 8:39 A. M.

STOPS

Car stops are shown on reverse side.

FARES

All fares are 16 cents, or two tokens, except that certain transfers are accepted.

TRANSFERS

Free transfers are issued to city lines on eastbound trips, and a city transfer with 8 cents is accepted for fare on westbound trips.

A transfer from the Osage Hills line and 8 cents is good for fare on eastbound trips at Magnolia, and transfers are issued to westbound Osage Hills cars on westbound trips.

A transfer from a southbound Kirkwood-Ferguson car and 8 cents is accepted at Brentwood for fare on eastbound trips, and transfers are issued to northbound Kirkwood-Ferguson cars at Brentwood westbound.

Subject to change without notice.

ST. LOUIS PUBLIC SERVICE COMPANY.

(OVER)

NEW KIRKWOOD EXPRESS TIME TABLE

EFFECTIVE MAY 10, 1929

STOP	EASTBOUND Read Down Daily Except Sun. A.M.		Daily Except Sat. and Sun. P.M.	WESTBOUND Read Up P.M.	Saturday Only P.M.	
MAGNOLIA AVE.	7:20	7:40	5:50	6:10	1:30	1:50
Geyer Road	7:20	7:40	5:50	6:10	1:30	1:50
CLAY AND WOODBINE	7:22	7:42	5:49	6:08	1:29	1:48
Moorec	7:23	7:43	5:48	6:08	1:28	1:48
Argonne	7:23	7:43	5:47	6:07	1:27	1:47
CLAY AND ADAMS	7:24	7:44	6:47	6:07	1:27	1:47
Clay and Washington			5:45	6:06	1:26	1:46
Kirkwood Road	7:24	7:44	5:46	6:06	1:26	1:46
Fillmore and Adams	7:25	7:45				
Fillmore and Washington	7:26	7:46	5:45	6:05	1:25	1:45
Woodlawn	7:27	7:47	5:44	6:04	1:24	1:44
Yenneman Ave.	7:28	7:48	5:43	6:03	1:23	1:43
Sappington Road	7:28	7:48	5:42	6:02	1:22	1:42
Moreland	7:29	7:49	5:41	6:01	1:21	1:41
Berry Road	7:30	7:50	5:40	6:00	1:20	1:40
Harper	7:31	7:51	5:39	5:59	1:19	1:39
Rock Hill Road	7:32	7:52	5:38	5:58	1:18	1:38
GORE AVE.	7:33	7:53	5:37	5:57	1:17	1:37
Newport	7:34	7:54	5:36	5:56	1:16	1:36
Marshall Ave.	7:36	7:56	5:34	5:54	1:14	1:34
Maddenville	7:37	7:57	5:33	5:53	1:13	1:33
BRENTWOOD	7:37	7:57	5:33	5:53	1:13	1:33
Pendleton	7:38	7:58	5:32	5:52	1:12	1:32
Manchester Road	7:40	8:00	5:31	5:51	1:11	1:31
Weaver	7:42	8:02	5:29	5:49	1:09	1:29
Bruno	7:43	8:03	5:28	5:48	1:08	1:28
Big Bend	7:44	8:04	5:27	5:47	1:07	1:27
Dale Ave.	7:45	8:05	5:27	5:47	1:07	1:27
Vandeventer & Chouteau	8:00	8:20	5:16	5:28	12:51	1:11
18th and Market	8:13	8:33	4:57	5:15	12:39	12:59
BROADWAY AND MARKET	8:19	8:39	4:51	5:09	12:33	12:53

From Dale Ave. eastward all eastbound cars make regular city stops to permit passengers to alight, and westbound cars make all Market line stops to load through passengers.

SUBJECT TO CHANGE WITHOUT NOTICE

22-6. In 1929, as part of an effort to lure more riders the Public Service Company implemented the Kirkwood Express. The time table for the run was distributed widely to passengers on Kirkwood-Ferguson and the Brentwood line.

THIS NEW TRANSFER TICKET IS DESIGNED TO PROMOTE YOUR CONVENIENCE AND

SAFETY, ECONOMY, FREQUENCY—

These Three Are Yours To The Highest Degree In

SAINT LOUIS TRANSPORTATION
via PUBLIC SERVICE

CONDITIONS OF USE

This transfer is—

1. Not transferable and is good only when used in accordance with the published tariffs and regulations of this company.

2. Good in each case only when presented on first car or bus of transfer line passing transfer point, on which passenger is able to obtain passage.

3. Good only when passenger boards car or bus of transfer line at regular transfer point.

4. Good only via the most direct route without unnecessary transferring from starting point to destination.

5. Not good for second or subsequent transfer on car or bus going in direction opposite, or practically so, to that of issuing car or bus or of previous transfer car or bus, unless strip showing locality in which transfer was issued indicates that the first intersecting or connecting line was used as the intermediate line in each case.

6. Not good on car or bus going via a direct route toward locality in which issued or toward a point previously passed by passenger on his trip.

7. Subject also to any limitations on reverse side. HENRY W. KIEL RECEIVER
PATENT APPLIED FOR ST. LOUIS PUBLIC SERVICE CO.

22-7. Back sides of Public Service Company transfers both promoted the company and explained the conditions of use. Many transfers were simply blank on the back side. The transfer to the right was given during the period of Public Service Company's bankruptcy, beginning in 1933, when former St. Louis mayor Kiel was appointed Receiver. Courtesy of Ralph Von Doersten.

22-8. Photograph illustrates the rural nature of the Brentwood line. Note that the line always remained single track. Museum of Transport collection.

Chapter 23

THE END OF THE LINE

Streetcar route changes and cutbacks began to be implemented by the newly reorganized Public Service Company. Of interest to Kirkwood, Glendale, Webster, Brentwood and Clayton passengers was a grade separation project at Maple Avenue and the Wabash tracks that led to the severing of the Kirkwood-Ferguson line on September 1, 1940. The western portion, the "01 - Kirkwood," was cut back to run between the Kirkwood loop at Magnolia and the Big Bend loop near Washington University, while the "16 - City Limits" running north from Maplewood was extended from Suburban Gardens to Ferguson.

Gasoline was rationed in the 1940s because of World War II, so the reduced use of automobiles combined with the large number of women joining the work force, caused the streetcars to become indispensable in getting workers to their jobs. The cars were frequently so full that there was standing room only for the workers heading to their shifts.

For children traveling to school the cars were less crowded. If one was fortunate to live near the Manchester line, no transfer was required to reach Webster Groves High School, Kirkwod High School or Nipher Junior High. Rosann Reisenleiter Kemper lived in north Glendale and recalled the experiences of those in her neighborhood:

> To get to school we would walk to the Kirkwood-Ferguson (or 01) streetcar, ride it to Clay and Adams, transfer to the Webster streetcar and get off at Woodbine and Clay, then walk down Kirkwood road to the school. If it was decent weather, we would always walk the three miles home... Most of the kids from north Glendale went to Nipher Junior High and Kirkwood Senior High School. The Old Folks Home was across the street. We would always joke that by the time we finished high school, we would be ready for the Old Folks Home.[1]

Junior high student Bruce Tanner was given 50 cents a week to ride the streetcar from his home in Glendale to Nipher School. He soon realized that if he walked, the five cent fare was spending money. One of the ways he enjoyed spending his saved fares was to take a Sunday afternoon three hour round trip on the Kirkwood-Ferguson, costing him a grand total of ten cents. A number of other Glendale children, instead of riding the streetcar as their parents intended, walked home from school in Kirkwood and saved up their nickels. JoAnne Lyons recalled:

---

[1]Rosann Reisenleiter Kemper as told to Donna Lykens, "Growing Up In Glendale," Glendale Historical Society Bulletin, June 1987, vol. II, no. 2.

When we were older, we all dated in groups. We rode the streetcar to school and walked home, saving our money for ice cream at Carpenter's Ice Cream shop in Kirkwood.[2]

For "real excitement" they saved up their fares and walked to Kirkwood or Webster Groves on Saturday to buy a cherry Coke at the drugstore soda fountain.

Streetcar riders and crew were, on occasion, subjected to loud groups of children. Donald Alter, a former member of the Grace Church Boys Choir, recalled for readers of the June 1971 *Kirkwood Historical Review* an occasion when the boys choirs from all over the area were riding to St. Louis for a Sunday School event.

I remember Mike (Page) in connection with the "Missionary Host," which met in St. Louis and to which the boys of the choir rode as a group on the street cars. Mike made up cheers to let the rest of the passengers know just who we were:

Ice cream, soda water
Ginger Ale, pop.
Grace Church Choir Boys
Always on top![3]

Alter reported that he was much embarrassed at first, but soon found himself joining in with full voice. He didn't say what reaction the cheers elicited from other passengers or crew.

Starting in 1940 the Public Service Company began to replace cars in its fleet with modern PCC cars. In 1929, the streetcar industry formed a group called the Electric Railway President's Conference Committee (PCC). The PCC pooled its ideas on what an ideal streetcar should be, collected more than a million dollars from the industry and hired a Belgian chief engineer with no preconceptions from prior experience in trolley design. After five years of work, the "dream streetcar," the PCC car was unveiled.

In April 1940, the Public Service Company burned 100 obsolete streetcars and 29 work cars. The cars were taken to Crows Nest, a spot on the Creve Coeur line west of Ashby road, where the frames were pulled off, stripped and burned. Junk dealers bought the metal scrap and hauled it from the site, except for the streetcar trucks, which were taken to the main yards at Park Avenue where they were broken up and then sold as scrap. The destroyed passenger cars were part of a group that were built in 1903 and used for World's Fair service. The April 17th

---

[2]Joanne Lyons, Seventy years of Friendship," Glendale Historical Society Bulletin, December 1992, vol. II, no. 4.

[3]Donald Alter, "Grace Church Boys Choir," Kirkwood Historical Review, June 1971. Grace Church was located at the corner of Taylor and Main (Argonne) in Kirkwood. That designated Landmark structure is the Eliot Unitarian Universalist Chapel.

Post-Dispatch stated the destruction was to make way for 100 "Modern Carriers."[4] Cars were also scrapped at the Brentwood car yard and at Suburban Gardens.

The new PCC cars were delivered beginning June 1, 1940. To the surprise of the public, the PCC cars with their rubber on steel sandwich wheels with "cushion impact between wheel rim and axle"[5] and rubber springs were strangely silent on good track, having none of the familiar growling and grinding noises of the previous fifty years of streetcars. A St. Louis Public Service Company's brochure advertised the new PCC car model as the St. Louis Streamliner, "Made in St. Louis for St. Louisans."[6] Though overstated, the brochure's claims were found to be fairly accurate in the early days of PCC car use. "The generous use of rubber throughout, 860 pounds per car, eliminates road shocks, jars, vibration and noise. Sixteen massive rubber springs and eight rubber sandwich wheels float the car over the rails."[7] The new cars featured smooth but brisk acceleration with, "Get Away ... equal to that of the finest automobile with a good driver,"[8] and four motors, one to each axle. Smooth powerful braking by motor, spring and magnetic rail brakes, a quiet ride, and automobile-like features such as pedal controls, sealed-beam headlights and a pair of bright red stoplights on each new car's back end were featured. The exterior of mountain ash scarlet complemented by natural ivory and 400 feet of stainless steel moldings was pleasing to the eye of most riders.

An article in the July 1940 *Transit Journal*, a public relations piece provided by Public Service Company, hailed "Super Modern Cars for St. Louis."[9] The piece, illustrated with photographs of attractive and affluent appearing St. Louis "riders" demonstrating the improved features on the new "Streamliner," listed the improvements and general specifications of the new cars.

> ...distinctive features of improvement in appearance, security, and ease of operation, and features for improved servicing have been incorporated. These include non-glare windshield and side window, simplification in braking, electric operation of doors and auxiliary equipment from the storage battery, improvements in motor and car ventilation, simplification in operator's equipment, and the novel use of "piped" light for "pattern" route designation.[10]

The beams of piped light showed color patterns for route designations. The light was piped from a projecting lantern through bent Lucite rods and color film. The color pattern was designed to be seen and recognized long before the name or route number was legible. At the

[4]"World's Fair Streetcars Among 100 Junked by P.S.C.," PD, 17 April 1940.

[5]"The St. Louis Streamliner," brochure of the St. Louis Public Service Company, 1940.

[6]Ibid.

[7]Ibid. Regular streetcar rider, Travers Burgess, noted that the PCC cars rode well on good track, but not so on bad track with low joints.

[8]Ibid.

[9]"Super - Modern Cars for St. Louis," Transit Journal, July 1940, pp. 240-241.

[10]Ibid.

time, Lucite, the "latest synthetic product from research laboratories," had never been used before for "piping" light.[11]

The general specifications of the "Streamliner" were listed: "Length overall - 46 ft. Length between truck centers - 22 ft. 9 in. Width overall - 8 ft. 4 in. Height, rail to top of roof - 10 ft. 1/8 in. Seat spacing - 28½ in. Seating capacity - 59. Wheelbase - 6 ft. Wheel diameter - 25 in. Track gage - 4 ft. 10 in. Weight, complete car - 34,620 lb. Weight - each truck with motors - 7,400 lb."[12]

The Public Service article proceeded to extol the features of the car with the verbal descriptions and images of a fashion layout. The seating was described:

> Graceful contour of seats combines with spring and rubber cushions upholstered in mohair to make a restful ride. The luxurious appointments and graceful lines, with the green and silver tones, provides a pleasing and modern interior...[13]

The public was pleased with the new cars. However, for some die-hard trolley enthusiasts, the modern PCC cars lacked character and looked too much like the despised bus.

Most of the innovations lived up to their billing, with the exception of the "Faretaker," a self-service turnstile situated in the aisle behind the driver. It was found to slow entry of boarding passengers, so the turnstile was quickly removed and replaced with a more traditional fare box.

Webster News-Times readers' responses to a Webster Groves Chamber of Commerce survey about the town's transportation needs were reported in April 1941. The shiny new PCC cars had not yet been introduced to the Manchester lines, causing some unrest among the Webster Groves residents who considered their service to be sub-par. The paper printed the complete text of one letter from a resident of Tuxedo Avenue. Though the letter was, perhaps, overstated, portions of it give today's readers a feel for the writer's frustration, which the paper indicated reflected that of many residents:

> ...The street car transportation to Webster is beyond description. Dirty cars, everybody smoking, no ventilation, spitting permitted, and with one man control disorderly and unsatisfactory.... The equipment has been in bad shape for years, cars starting with a tremendous jerk. If we can get new cars same as now being operated in the city, I say O.K. street cars, but not what they are giving us now... In plain

---

[11]Ibid. Travers Burgess stated that he saw no PCC car signs with piping light on the Manchester line. Manchester PCCs continued to use conventional roll signs.

[12]Ibid.

[13]Ibid.

words it (streetcar service) is rotten and stinks. I honestly believe express bus service to and from St. Louis would be advisable.[14]

Due to satisfactory performance of the first 100 PCC cars in St. Louis, an additional order for 100 cars of the 1600-1699 series was awarded to the St. Louis Car Company. Following delivery of the new cars on New Year's Day, 1942, the 15 mile long Manchester trunk, which included the 53 - Maplewood, the 54 - Webster Groves, the 55 - Clay and Adams, and 56 - Kirkwood ran the new PCC cars for the first time.

Controversy immediately reared its head in Kirkwood. The Public Service Company terminated the Manchester line at Clay and Adams, because, as the company stated, it believed the heavier PCC cars could not safely cross the Clay Avenue bridge over the Missouri-Pacific Railroad. City of Kirkwood officials insisted the bridge was sound and did not need to be replaced. Local residents believed that the company's real but unstated reason was that it did not believe there was enough revenue to be gained by running to the Magnolia loop. Because the rails south of the Clay bridge had sunk over time into the pavement, the company was required to chip a beveled edge in the concrete along the rails in order to run the PCC cars, an expense that it did not wish to incur. Kirkwood prevailed. The concrete chipping work was done; the bridge was used without any problems in bearing the weight of the PCC cars; and the streetcars ran to the line's terminus at the Magnolia loop.

Despite changes in the streetcars on the Manchester line, youth along the line continued to play pranks. Adding "fun" to the streetcar routine was not unusual for Glendale youth. They enjoyed soaping the rails on upgrades and watching the motormen fume and fuss. One such upgrade on the Manchester line was located east of Berry Road near the current Mary Queen of Peace School and church. The Manchester, though not as hilly and curving as the Kirkwood-Ferguson line, had its share of pranks. Glendale resident John Hagar related a memorable prank in "Tram-atic Experiences." He told how two Glendale youth, Fletcher Walther and his cousin Julian Payne, deployed a life-size dummy which they had made and carried from Walther's house on Edwin Avenue to Lockwood Avenue.

> They laid the dummy flat between the tracks on the downhill grade heading west from Sappington to Park Avenue and threw the attached rope over the trolley wire. As the street car approached, they pulled the rope, raising the dummy right in front of the oncoming tram. As they disappeared into the night, the boys heard a distraught motorman screaming, "My God, I've killed a man."[15]

Other stories of streetcars driven away by passengers or bystanders abound, often taking on the proportions of an urban myth. Francis Scheidegger, renowned Kirkwood story teller, recalled that a local character also took off in empty streetcars:

---

[14]"Riders Have Opinions on Car Service," Webster News-Times, 25 April 1941.

[15]John N. Hager Jr., "Tram-atic Experiences," Glendale Historical Society Bulletin, September 1987, vol. II, no. 3.

… he loved streetcars so much that he would take a streetcar (from the Magnolia loop) when the motorman was out in the rest room. He would get in the (Kirkwood-Ferguson) streetcar and take off and take it out to the Manchester loop and then come back and get out. Then the motorman would take it over again. That would make the motorman's schedule late because it was an 01 car that was out longer than it should have been.[16]

In 1942 ridership exceeded all previous records. The leaders of the Public Service Company optimistically believed that riders would catch and keep the streetcar use habit, leading to a long-term resurgence of streetcar transit. However, the end of the war found an even greater migration to the suburbs where the automobile had become a standard possession for each family. As a result, streetcar ridership again returned to the doldrums.

In his 1985 Oxford Press book, *Crabgrass Frontiers: The Suburbanization of the United States*, Kenneth Jackson cited factors which tipped the transit balance in favor of automobiles. (1) The number of cars registered jumped from one to ten million from 1913 to 1923. (2) Real estate interests, construction companies and bankers lobbied for policies which favored construction of roads with taxpayer money in order to open up the landscape to single family homes, not to mention the accompanying loans and construction contracts. (3) Local governments ruled that privately owned streetcar lines must be self-funded while roads, a "public good," were given taxpayer subsidies. (4) General Motors attempted to monopolize transit through the operation of a front company, National City Lines, which purchased major city transit systems and systematically replaced streetcars with G. M. busses.[17]

In 1936, National City Lines was formed and soon began to take over major markets. It rarely just canceled streetcar service. Instead, its critics charge, it routinely cut route times back 20 to 30 minutes. Every time the service was reduced, it was less attractive, thus garnering fewer riders. Then the company would cite the fact that they couldn't make money on the line and abandon it. Others maintain that the company was merely making good business decisions and efficiently operated the transit services.

Edwin Quimby in 1946 attempted to warn cities of General Motor's plan, but he was quickly branded as a crackpot and mostly ignored by city officials. However, his efforts alerted the Justice Department of the United States. After lengthy investigation and litigation, General Motors, the major holder of National City Lines, was found guilty of conspiracy to monopolize the local transportation field. However, minimal fines were levied, and General Motors, according to its critics, was never effectively controlled until the arrival of foreign competition.

Not all agree that the streetcar demise was a result of General Motors and oil company duplicity. On January 18, 1997, George Price in a letter to the editor of the *Chicago Tribune*

---

[16]Francis Scheidegger, Cassette tape recording of memories for the author, Kirkwood, January 1997.
[17]Kenneth Jackson, (1985) Crabgrass Frontiers: The Suburbanization of the United States, Oxford Press.

web-posted his take on the demise of the streetcar, "Now I would rather ride a streetcar than a bus, but I must admit that streetcars have serious drawbacks that force their replacement by buses."[18]

Price cited (1) heavy construction and maintenance costs of tracks and overhead trolley wires, (2) limitations of being tied to where the rails go, unable to detour, and (3) difficulty in operating in mixed traffic, needing a limited right of way. He concluded that, "the above factors explain the disappearance of streetcars without having to blame auto and oil companies."[19]

A May 29, 1996 article in the *Pictures* section of the *Post-Dispatch* marked the close of streetcar service to St. Louis. It pointed at National City Lines but also supported Price's points.

> St. Louis's streetcars first went on the skids after World War II, when a holding company, National City Lines Inc., controlled the Public Service Co. here and 41 other transit systems in 16 states. National City Lines' big investors were five major gasoline, tire and bus interests. A federal antitrust suit broke up the powerful combine in 1949, but St. Louis's urban rail system — 494 miles of it in 1924 — was already down to 190 miles.

> By 1949, too, the postwar growth of the city had given new reasons for "phasing out" the streetcars. Their fuel was cheaper but their overhead lines, their roadbed and pavement between the tracks and for a foot on each side of them had to be maintained at company expense; busses can run on publicly-maintained streets, vary routes at will to avoid an obstruction or reach a more populous zone. Above all they can dodge.[20]

In 1947, St. Louis County published a modernization plan which envisioned the provision of modern transport services (buses) and the elimination of traffic clogging county streetcar lines. Public Service was very willing to be rid of the perennial loss-makers, so a three year program which dovetailed with the county's plans was developed. In an effort to illustrate the viability of the Manchester line, Photographer Francis Scheidegger used his camera. He recalled:

> I also made and have a picture which I took of a streetcar at Dickson and Adams Avenue. At the time they were claiming that there wasn't enough patronage of the streetcars. I had a young man that took a speed-light, that was electronically fired, activated by slave light. I was out at the corner. I gave this guy a dime, and I says, "Get on the streetcar and hold the light toward the people after you put your money in the box." He did, and I flashed a picture and showed the streetcar full of people, but

---

[18]George Price, "Sick Transit...," web-posted Voice of the People - Letters to the Editor, Chicago Tribune, 18 January 1997.
[19]Ibid.
[20]Pictures - PD, 29 May 1996, pp. 22-27.

that still didn't stop them from giving up the streetcars. I think today if we had left those tracks alone and kept them there and used the modern streetcars that we have now, it would have been great transportation.[21]

A group of streetcar supporters secured the pro bono services of a lawyer from Alton to fight the streetcar line closings. The National City management was quite disturbed by the public opposition to their modernization plans and, according to critics, used their corporate muscle via "good old boy network" connections and via veiled threats to withhold business from companies where the vocal National City opponents worked. National City Lines wanted to silence its critics who were "standing in the way of progress."

In Maplewood, as elsewhere, motor vehicles became predominant. Independent transit companies began running buses between Maplewood and the city as well as to other county locations such as Webster Groves and Kirkwood. As a result of declining patronage and income from Maplewood, the Public Service Company cited the cost of maintaining the streetcar lines as a reason to abandon the lines and to change over to bus service.

The first section of track to be discontinued in Maplewood was the City-Limits route along Yale Avenue. Though bus service was instituted on the City Limits line, February 21, 1948, was the sad date for streetcar supporters that marked the beginning of the end of streetcar service to Maplewood.

In the Southwest county area, the next line to close was the Brentwood -57. The Dinky was so revered by some regular riders that on its last run, they arranged a party with toasts being drunk in coffee and wine. Even the motorman on that run, Charles Kratky, joined in the toasts and singing of sentimental songs. Bus service started the next day, January 30, 1949. The Dinky, gone but not forgotten and steeped in nostalgia for Brentwood residents, was selected as the symbol of the city for its 50th anniversary history publication.

The Public Service Company announced additional closure dates. A more substantial county streetcar line abandonment was scheduled for April 3, 1949, when the entire Manchester group of lines, the former Meramec Division of the Suburban was to be abandoned. The division's 58 streetcars were to be replaced by 71 buses. A group calling itself the Citizen's Transit Committee, in a last ditch effort to stop the Manchester abandonment, asked patent attorney F. Travers Burgess to present its position to a special session of the Maplewood City Council. The committee maintained that Maplewood's temporary permit allowing the change to buses should be revoked because fewer seats and less service would be provided than by the Manchester streetcar line. A *Post-Dispatch* headline told the results: "Manchester Line Shifts to Busses after 11th-Hour Effort to Bar Them. Maplewood City Council Refuses Plea of Citizens' Transit Committee to Revoke Permit for Change."[22]

---

[21]Francis Scheidegger, cassette tape recorded for the author, January 1997.
[22]"Manchester Line Shifts to Busses After 11th Hour Effort to Ban Them," PD, 3 April 1949.

KING TROLLEY: THE END OF THE LINE

When the Maplewood, Webster Groves and Kirkwood routes were closed, the Manchester route became the first modernized set of lines served by PCC cars to be abandoned. Traffic hazards caused by the contra-flow car tracks on the south side of the busy Manchester highway made the line a headache for the city and county. Though the county government and the Public Service Company were happy to see the lines closed, many residents of Maplewood, Webster Groves, Glendale and Kirkwood were not at all happy to be switched to bus lines. The mayors of some of the towns along the Manchester line stated their opposition to the move - without success. However, the Webster Groves mayor, who was annoyed by the noise made by streetcars passing Webster's city hall, favored bus service.

The passing of the Manchester line did not go without parties and tears. Francis Scheidegger recalled:

> I also recall taking a photograph in front of the Loop Cafe which was across the street from the (Magnolia) loop. When they took the streetcars off the tracks, which I think was a big mistake, there was a crowd there. I took a picture of it... There was an enthusiastic streetcar person named Buck Edward Carter. He lived where the Depot Park is right now at Madison (and Clay)... This guy Buck Carter... rode the last streetcar downtown. I don't know how he got home - hitchhiked or something, but he actually cried tears that night. I laughed at him then, and I've regretted laughing at him every since because we still should have those cars there.[23]

The new bus service followed the Manchester streetcar route with only one deviation in the route at the Edgebrook bridge. A detour was put in place until the streetcar tracks on the bridge were replaced with special channelized bridge flooring which allowed bus operation. The conversion to allow bus traffic used 106,000 board feet of timber.

In an effort to appease its critics, the Public Service Company stated that the new Manchester service would be "faster and more frequent," with 71 buses used on the line for morning rush hours whereas only 58 streetcars were used. The buses were scheduled to follow the previous owl car schedule and to make the run from the Kirkwood loop to the downtown terminal in 71½ minutes, 2½ minutes faster than streetcars had done. The number of runs was increased from 17 to 20. In the evening, 64 busses were dispatched, compared to the 56 streetcars.[24]

Once the Edgebrook bridge was resurfaced, the route remained virtually unchanged from August 26, 1949, when the first buses crossed the bridge, until March 12, 1968 when the bridge was taken out of service - never to be used again. Earlier that year, a routine annual inspection revealed weaknesses in the bridge's structural supports. In order to be on the safe side, the bridge was retired. Buses were detoured around it on Marshall Avenue and Laclede Station Road. The

---

[23]Ibid.
[24]Ibid.

route continued unchanged, except for the necessary detour, until March 25, 1985. On that date, Bi-State dropped local service on Marshall and Summit, leaving only three express runs in each direction. On September 3, 1985, the express runs were dropped, leaving much of Northeast Webster Groves without a direct link to downtown St. Louis. The finality of the loss of transit in the area was punctuated when the last Bi-State shelter was removed from the corner of Marshall and Summit on September 11, 1985, ending the nearly 100 years of transit presence at that corner.

Due in part to Brentwood's insistence that the 01 Kirkwood line was vital to the economy of the city, and the vigorous opposition of the Brentwood mayor and the city council, the 01 remained operating longer than the Manchester lines. Though delayed over a year, the abandonment date was eventually posted. The Kirkwood Chamber of Commerce then made a last ditch effort to head off the closing of the Kirkwood -01, the last remnant of streetcar transit from Kirkwood to St. Louis. Their transportation committee consisted of Samuel Murphey, Hale Brown, F. Travers Burgess and A. H. Pauli. The Chamber of Commerce arranged for the summary of the work and recommendations of the committee written by Burgess to be published in the *Kirkwood View* with an admonition to readers to submit their approval of the recommendations in writing to the Chamber's Transportation Committee. A negative that would have been better addressed a couple of years earlier was the dismantling of the Brentwood line. Burgess stated:

> Although the Brentwood right-of-way is still physically intact, upon abandonment it probably ceased to be the property of the Public Service Company, consequently, in order to build a new railway line on it, it would be necessary either to purchase it outright, lease it, or obtain easements on it from the present owners.

> By rebuilding the Brentwood line and by bringing the remainder of the track structure up to standards required for high speed operation, it should be possible to operate at speeds in excess of 50 miles per hour much of the distance between Filmore and Kingshighway. With the installation of grade crossing protection where necessary and elimination of unimportant stops, it should be possible to average 25 miles an hour between these two points with a running time of 23 minutes...

The Chamber of Commerce proposal was unsuccessful. On August 2, 1950, the last cars on the Kirkwood 01 line were run, leaving Kirkwood, Glendale, Webster Groves and Brentwood with no streetcars in operation. Commuter trains still connected with the city, providing one round trip daily Monday through Friday, but the bus had become the dominant mass transit conveyance.

Streetcars still operated in other places in the county and in St. Louis, but the "Streetcar Era" was ended for Kirkwood, Webster Groves, and neighboring towns. For one woman who returned from living in Europe in 1952, the change to buses was unsettling. Previously when she lived in Glendale, she took the Kirkwood-Ferguson to go to Clayton to do errands. Service was not good on the 01 in later years, so she was prepared for a long wait. One day when she had to go to the county courthouse, she walked to the stop and settled in and waited - and waited - and waited some more. At last, after an hour and a half wait, she went over to the firehouse and asked how often the street cars ran. She was embarrassed to find that she had not noticed that the streetcar tracks had been removed during her absence from Glendale.[25]

Though the overhead trolley wires were immediately removed, some the streetcar lines literally left behind their tracks under paved streets. On the corner of Woodbine and Clay avenues one recent winter, a vast pothole exposed the rails of the old streetcar route used by the St. Louis and Kirkwood Electric Railroad Company and all of its successors. Today, those rails are still there, covered with asphalt, mute testimony to the faded glories of the streetcar age. Since much of the trackage in the county was on private right-of-way, in many areas, all vestiges of the tracks were removed. The incentives to pull up the rails were high. The sooner the tracks were removed, the less chance that opponents of bus service could mount an effort to return to streetcar service. At the same time there was financial incentive. Full page ads in the 1949 issues of the *Mass Transportation* magazine stated, "Turn Your Old Rail Into Cash! Scrap Is Urgently Needed! Scrap Prices Are High! Now Is the Time To Remove Abandoned Rails." The Gorbett Brothers Welding Company's ad indicated a net profit of $25.00 per ton.[26]

After streetcar service was discontinued, the Maddenville Power House property at Brentwood was one site used to burn "obsolete" Peter Witt cars. The Public Service Company then sold the remaining metal body frames and trucks to scrappers. The power house on the former St. Louis and Kirkwood line was soon converted to industrial use. Today, though the Maddenville streetcar barns are long gone, the nearby Brentwood Bi-State bus garage continues the tradition started by Houseman's St. Louis and Kirkwood Railroad, of Brentwood being a county site for storage and service for mass transit vehicles. The legacy of the Kirkwood-Ferguson also remains today in Brentwood in the form of a delightful strip park between Mary and Dorothy streets east of Brentwood Boulevard and north of Manchester Road. The long narrow park was created from the streetcar right-of-way and has a walking path, playgrounds and benches complete with residents enjoying the park.

Because of its original role as the headquarters for the St. Louis and Kirkwood Electric Railroad, its long term love affair with the Kirkwood-Ferguson and the Brentwood Dinky, its role in providing rock for streetcar roadbeds and because of the residents' fond memories of streetcar travel, many of its residents consider Brentwood to be St. Louis County's "Streetcar City."

Throughout the Fifties and into the Sixties streetcar ridership was down. Additional streetcar lines closed as road widening, new bridges and highways caused disruption in streetcar routes. Without state or federal subsidies for the streetcar lines, the choice was frequently made to abandon lines rather than rebuild them. Despite public outrage at the closings, the transit

---

[25]John N. Hager Jr., "Tram-atic Experiences," Glendale Historical Society Bulletin, September 1987, vol. II, no. 3.
[26]"Turn Your Old Rails Into Cash!", Mass Transportation, January 1949, p. 65.

company stated that it had little choice but to discontinue unprofitable lines. During that time, the Public Service Company was but one of fifteen transit companies operating in the St. Louis metropolitan area. Most provided bus service.

In 1960, the city of St. Louis proposed a municipal solution to the transit woes rather than an area wide one. In response, St. Louis County Supervisor James H. J. Mc Nary suggested that the Missouri-Illinois Bi-State Development agency acquire and operate public transit in the metropolitan area. That agency, which was established in 1949, coordinated port and harbor facilities. Public Service Company's position was that given acceptance by transit companies to be bought and given relief from local taxes in the individual municipalities as well as the four counties to be served, it could do the job better than the Bi-State people who were inexperienced in bus and streetcar transit.

The Bi-State public plan won out, and Public Service assets were sold for over $20,000,000 to the new operator. By 1963, only three streetcar lines remained in operation. A proposal was on the table from St. Louis Mayor Tucker to eliminate the remaining three in order to ease traffic flow between Sixth and Eighth streets on Pine. Replacement bus routes were announced in February 1964. Petitions protesting the Bi-State plan were circulated and presented because the new bus routes eliminated service on many of the streets formerly served by streetcars. In April 1964, the Delmar and University lines were closed, leaving the De Hodiamont line as the sole survivor. A little over two years later, De Hodiamont's run ended. May 21, 1966 marked St. Louis' last streetcar run. Within weeks, most of the trolley wires, tracks, and poles were taken down, torn out or covered over.

The recognition of the advantages of streetcar service over automobile gridlock began a long slow metamorphosis, which eventually led to the construction of the light rail MetroLink. Due to the success of the first MetroLink route, Bi-State has planned and constructed an additional route and is in the development stages for other routes. One transit route that was proposed, investigated and rejected proposed returning commuter rail service on the Burlington-Northern route through Webster Groves and Kirkwood.

Had the private right of ways for the county lines been retained, the expansion of MetroLink would have had ready made high speed corridors. Kirkwood residents can only dream of a route that would have been ideal for high speed electric rail service - the majority of which was private right-of-way; from Barnes Hospital through the private right-of-way of the Forest Park line along Oakland Avenue to the connection with the original Houseman line all the way to Kirkwood. Unfortunately for MetroLink, most private right-of-ways reverted to prior owners or were sold after the streetcar lines ceased operation.

As of 1996, one hundred years after the beginning of streetcar service to the "Suburban Queens," no final solution to the light rail puzzle was yet in place. Many wanted new MetroLink lines to serve their area and were working to influence the planning process for determining routes. The "Suburban Queens" preferred MetroLink light rail but were open to commuter rail, though details such as FUNDING, locations for parking facilities, stops and schedules provided numerous potential stumbling blocks. Even with the possible addition of new routes, the fact remains, "King Trolley" has given way to the ubiquitous automobile. Decades of the automobile habit will have to be reversed before light rail can again become the major transit force.

Light rail developers have a long history from which they can learn some valuable lessons. One fact is clear, history shows that in order for the new lines to succeed, residents of the county must have high levels of ridership combined with sound fiscal management by the transit company. With good planning, governmental subsidies, and public demand, perhaps in some future day light rail may again be known as the "King" of mass transit.

23-1. The Public Service Company is gone but not forgotten at the Rock Hill Road Loop. Photo by author.

23-2. End of the line: United Railways work car 136 was part of a batch of obsolete passenger and work cars burned in order to make room in the car barns for 100 new PCC cars and to realize profit from the salvageable metal in the cars. Scrap metal brought a premium price in the early days of World War II before the United States entered the war. On April 16, 1940, *Post-Dispatch* staffer Wayne Leeman photographed the scene, showing the destruction process. The cars were moved to the "Crows Nest" salvage area under their own power, tipped off their trucks, and then were doused with an inflammable substance such as gasoline or kerosene.

23-3. After the wood burned away, only salvageable metal remained for the scrap metal dealers to purchase and haul away.   Photographs courtesy of Wayne Leeman.

23-4. Trouble wagon and repair crew work to repair damage at Marshall and Summit in Webster Groves after an ice storm caused downed power lines. While the repairs took place, streetcars lined up on the south approach to the Edgebrook bridge. The first car was built prior to 1940. The other Manchester cars lined up behind it were modern PCC cars that began operation January 1, 1942. Photograph by Wayne Leeman.

23-5. Manchester 54 PCC car southbound entering Webster Groves after exiting the Edgebrook bridge. The photograph was taken by Webster Groves resident Wayne Leeman prior to 1949 when streetcars were dropped in favor of buses.

23-6. Manchester PCC car #1683 heads west on Lockwood Avenue to Kirkwood from Webster's Rock Hill Road loop. Note the location of the utility/trolley poles between the two sets of streetcar tracks, the 40's vintage automobiles and the two lane highway. After the closure of the Manchester line, the rail bed was converted to a westbound paved street, while the existing pavement was change to an eastbound street. Museum of Transportation collection.

23-7. Transfers for the Kirkwood 01 indicated that riders went DOWN from the Big Bend loop to Brentwood, Webster Groves and Kirkwood. The 01 UP transfer ran from Kirkwood to the Big Bend loop. Since the p.m. coupon is attached to the Brentwood -57 transfer, we know by the punch mark that the car left the terminus at 2 p.m. Brentwood transfer courtesy of Ralph Von Doersten.

23-8. The bustling Maplewood business district at the corner of Sutton and Manchester, featured a traffic mix of PCC streetcars, automobiles and pedestrians. The photograph illustrates how vibrant the area was in the Forties. Courtesy of Museum of Transportation.

23-9. One of the last runs of the Brentwood 57. Car 820, which was also used on the Clayton 04 line, bears the 57 designation for the Brentwood line, but the operator neglected to change its sign which still reads "Clayton." Note the poster signaling the demise of the Brentwood Dinky. The text of the posted sign reads, "Effective January 30 buses will replace streetcars on the Brentwood line and will operate from the Forest Park streetcar loop on Dale, west on Dale to Big Bend, to Folk, to Laclede Station, to Manchester, to High School Drive, to Litzsinger to Brentwood, to Manchester, thence east on Manchester returning over same route." Photograph from Museum of Transportation.

23-10. Passengers of a variety of ages take advantage of the Manchester 56 as it heads west toward Kirkwood on Adams. This Peter Witt car stopped for passengers in Kirkwood at Dickson and Adams. Photograph by Francis Scheidegger.

23-11. Patrons of the Loop Lounge and Cafe, situated on the south side of the Magnolia loop and Woodbine Avenue, hold a high-spirited wake as the last Manchester streetcar prepares to leave Kirkwood forever. Buck Carter, who shed tears that night, did not join in the revelry, staying instead inside his beloved streetcar. He is looking through the front windshield at its lower edge. Photograph by Francis Scheidegger.

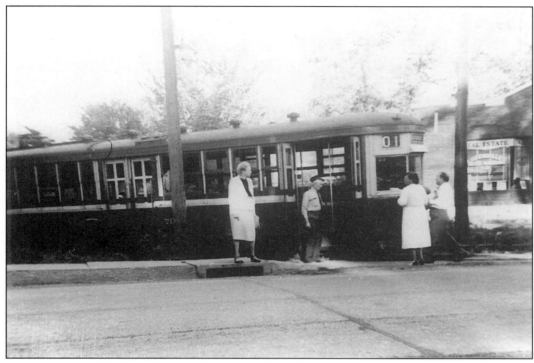

23-12. August 2, 1950, the day of the last run of the 01, the Kirkwood-University. The motorman of the Peter Witt style streetcar stopped to chat with friends and nostalgic passengers at Glendale's Sappington Road crossing. Photo courtesy of the Glendale Historical Society.

23-13. Demolition - the historic Edgebrook bridge falls. Dismantling was nearly completed when this photograph by Wayne Leeman was taken on December 14, 1974. The view is to the northeast with the Missouri Pacific tracks under the span still in operation despite the demolition.

Chapter 24

MEMORIES OF THE
KIRKWOOD-FERGUSON AND MANCHESTER LINES

Many area residents retain fond memories of streetcar service on the Kirkwood-Ferguson 01, the Manchester 54, 55, and 56 and the Brentwood 57. Their memories range from the early 1900s to the end of streetcar service. The degree of satisfaction varied, but all agreed that the streetcar service was unforgettable.

Mary Ann Vuylstehe Carter wrote to the author of her relatives' use of the streetcar line to Meramec Highlands. Their use of the streetcars spanned a time period from 1907 to about 1925. She didn't indicate if all the little passengers were charged.

> The Mount Pleasant Homing Pigeon Club would take the streetcar from St. Louis to Meramec Highlands to let their pigeons loose. Sometimes the pigeons would get home before the owners… My grandfather Mauriets Odin Vuylstehe was instrumental in starting the club (circa 1907-1908)… They trained the young pigeons from this distance (about 12 miles) and then further until they shipped them 500 to 1000 miles away… After Morris got older, my dad, Raymond, helped transport them to Meramec Heights by streetcar.[1]

As a young girl in the early 1900s, Florence Delling lived in Webster Groves on Oak street. It ran west from Rock Hill Road between the Kirkwood-Ferguson tracks, the "lower line," on the north and the Manchester tracks, the "upper line," on the south. The upper and lower names were used because of elevation; the Manchester followed the top of a ridge, while the Kirkwood-Ferguson followed a stream valley. Florence recalled sitting on a dirt bank at the edge of her parent's property during spring and summer days writing down the numbers of the Manchester streetcars as they passed going west and then crossing them off as they returned going east.[2]

Lester McKelvey, who grew up in Webster Groves, recalled for the 1975 edition of *In Retrospect*, a publication of Webster Groves Senior High School, a harrowing winter experience: Children with bobsleds gathered to coast down Prehn's Hill at Gore

---

[1]Mary Ann Carter, letter to author, 1996.

[2]Florence Delling, "The Streetcars and Meramec Highlands," Kirkwood Historical Review, Vol. XXVII, No. 1, pp. 5-7, and interview with author, 1996.

Avenue, starting at the Missouri-Pacific tracks and riding down to Kirkham road where the lower streetcar line ran. The bobsledders had to be careful to watch for the Kirkwood-Ferguson cars. On one occasion, some children didn't pay attention, and the bobsled and the streetcar arrived at the same point at the same time. Fortunately, the streetcar motorman stopped the car; the bobsled went right underneath. The children on the sled were unhurt though they got brushed off by the bottom of the car.[3]

Paul Johnson, a resident of Kirkwood, recalled an adventure in which he rode both the Kirkwood-Ferguson and the Manchester lines. His story goes back to 1917 when he was 5 years old. At the time his family lived on Bismark Avenue near the North Webster line, west of Rock Hill Road.

> My Sainted mother thought it was time for me to enroll in Sunday-School, so we walked over a half mile and boarded a Kirkwood-Ferguson street car just west of Rock Hill and just south of Kirkham. We took the street car to Clay and Clinton in Kirkwood, walked a couple of long blocks, and I joined the Sunday School at the Concordia Lutheran Church at Clinton and Taylor.

> The church picnic was a few weeks later. Mother took my four-week-old brother, Walter (Ted) and me to the picnic. After a couple of hours, I missed my mother, not knowing that she was feeding Ted in the parsonage. I had no money, but a fine young man gave me a nickel for the fare to Webster. I went to Clay and Clinton, but couldn't read very well and got on a Manchester instead of a K-F street car. I asked the motorman if he knew where Rock Hill Road was, and he said that he didn't. He was kidding a little fellow, but I didn't trust him. I stood at the front of the car (and was) just tall enough to see fairly well out the front window to the right of the motorman. I watched all the way and then told the motorman that Rock Hill was coming up and that's where I wanted to get off. He gave me a cheerful, "Good-bye." I got off and walked north on Rock Hill to my home. My mother learned that I had gone home, so all was well. Some 73 years later returning to Kirkwood, my wife and I met the kind "nickel" man, and I offered him a quarter which included "interest" on the nickel. He said (joking) that I had received a 1917 nickel that was what he wanted returned.[4]

Johnson continued with a memory of St. Louis that we today tend to forget:

> ...When we took the Kirkwood-Ferguson car, by the time we reached Skinker or Washington University, the smoke was so thick that visibility was cut to less than a mile. Scullin Steel and other factories were emitting all kinds of soft coal smoke. When one returned home, the clothes and the nose needed a

---

[3]R. Lester McKelvey, (Spring 1975) <u>In Retrospect</u>,Webster Groves: Webster Groves High School, , p.5.
[4]Paul Johnson, letter to author, 1996.

thorough cleaning.… But just think! One could get transfers to Shaw's Garden, the old Sportsmen's Park, Creve Coeur Lake and other important stops, and cheap too. One didn't have to worry about stop lights, other drivers, flat tires or other trouble of that kind. Now Metro-Link is a shining example of that type of transportation.[5]

Edith Witteborn Hauk's family moved to Glendale at Berry and Kirkham Roads in 1919 when she was five years old. Her father was a florist working for a wholesale grower. Since the family had no car, the streetcar line was their means of transportation. Near where she lived, the Kirkwood-Ferguson ran east and west at the bottom of a hill, through the Algonquin Golf Club grounds, past a creek and through "many, many trees." She wrote to the author that she and her husband after 57 years of marriage returned to the area to live on the corner of Woodbine and Clay at the same location where she and her sisters got on and off the streetcar while attending Kirkwood High school. The school was about two blocks away located where Nipher Middle School is today. Edith recalled the motorman frequently having to get out of the streetcar to put the trolley back on the line when it was disconnected. "Also it was his duty to keep the fire going in the little stove at the front of the streetcar to keep us warm in cold and snowy weather," she stated. But of all her streetcar experiences, one incident remained etched in her mind forever - the day she was struck by a Kirkwood-Ferguson streetcar:

I remember many interesting things happening during the years that I rode the Kirkwood-Ferguson streetcar, but the most memorable was the day I was struck by that streetcar just west of Berry Road. I was seven years old and on my way to Alice Atchison's birthday party. She lived between Berry Road and Sappington Road, very close to the tracks. I was walking on the tracks (which I was told NEVER to do) instead of crossing through the fields, because I had on new shoes and my best clothes. This was in the 1920s, and there were no sidewalks. (I was)… anticipating the party, a big event in my limited social life and did not hear the streetcar coming around the bend, nor the clang of the bell. The motorman could not stop in time. I was hit and caught on the "cowcatcher" underneath. Fortunately one of the passengers knew who I was. I was unconscious. The motorman picked me up, leaving all the passengers on the streetcar, and carried me home! I do not remember any of this part, but when I regained consciousness, Mr. Atchison had brought me a book, cake and candy, and a blue box with marshmallows. I was later checked out by Doctor North, only had a few bruises and a slight concussion, and my father would not even accept the streetcar company's offer to pay the bills. I never again walked on the tracks.[6]

---

[5]Ibid.
[6]Edith Witteborn Hauk, letter to author, 1996.

KING TROLLEY: STREETCAR MEMORIES

Another child of a florist, later to become a Kirkwood institution, professional photographer, recycler, bee keeper, city councilman and a walking repository of local history, the late Francis Scheidegger shared many memories of streetcar service with the author. The following excerpts have been transcribed from a tape he recorded in January 1997, his 78th year, for use in this historical record. He began: "I am Francis Scheidegger. I was born and raised in Kirkwood at 645 Florist Avenue. My memories of streetcars are..."

There were some boys who lived in a stucco house two doors south of the (Kirkwood-Ferguson and Sappington Road) intersection. Their names were Allen and Clifford Brady. They took the streetcar to St. Peter's School and they always rode on the sandbox... The oldest one, Clifford Brady, ended up as a streetcar motorman in later years after he grew up.

(West of Sappington) There was a stop called Armstrong stop that is now Hill Avenue... (At) Dickson Street, the crossing was about a block north of Essex Avenue. That is where we caught the streetcar to go to the business district of Kirkwood, or church, or school. My father used that streetcar to take his flowers to the wholesale market. He was a florist on Florist Avenue off of Dickson Street. He had some great big baskets, and that's the way he took the flowers into the wholesale district at LaSalle Avenue near Rutger Street and California Avenue...

As kids we used to walk the streetcar tracks on our way into school... There was a big drainage ditch about a hundred feet east of Woodlawn Avenue. We had to be real careful in walking over that because there was no path. We had to walk on the tracks and keep our balance... The tracks cut through the Woodlawn Country Club, a golf course, and went all the way to about a line even with Fillmore Avenue, and then it made a left turn. There was a dead part of the line there. At night when they hit that certain spot, the lights would go out in the streetcar; all the power was off. It would coast close to the turn to warn the motorman that there was a turn there. Then he'd make the turn at a reasonable speed. If they didn't (have the dead spot), at night and in bad weather, it would be difficult to tell that the turn was there.

Then the line proceeded south along the edge of the golf course - tee #1 and also green #1... on the east side of Fillmore Avenue. The streetcar would then turn right on Washington Avenue. The Old Folks Home was on the northwest corner of Taylor and Washington. That building is still there and is used as an apartment house. To the left was the parish house (now the YMCA).

At the Clay Avenue bridge, (on) Halloween night the kids used to soap the tracks as a prank and give the motorman a bad time... The wheels would spin and make sparks. The sand box... that the Brady boys sat on, was used by the motorman on... slippery tracks like that. There is a little bit of history connected to that bridge. There was a boy named Max Myerover who went to the Katherine Tracy kindergarten which was where St. Peter's School now is. He lived on the 500 block of South Harrison Avenue and was walking (home) on the ledge between the sidewalk and the streetcar tracks. (He) fell some way or another and the streetcar cut off one of his legs. Elmer Quarnheim, a policeman who was the crossing guard at Argonne and Clay Avenue, went out and picked the boy up and carried him down to Hummert's confectionery which was in the building at the southwest corner of Clay and Argonne. And then Bopp's ambulance took him to St. Mary's Hospital which was the closest hospital. He recovered and grew up to be an accomplished musician...

(At Van Buren) there was a grocery store on the corner... That was Portner's Grocery... At the Kirkwood-Ferguson loop, the 01 loop, there was a refreshment stand near the Woodbine side. A George Fuzner ran it and lived there... That's (the loop) where some of the motormen and conductors had a little time off or a little rest. There was a restroom there...

(On the Manchester line) at Maplewood near the city limits was another streetcar... It came from the north ....At that loop (Yale Avenue)... by asking the conductor for a transfer, you could get that car and transfer and go to St. Mary's Hospital and Clayton Road... At Manchester and Sutton Avenue, the streetcar tracks turned left and went south on Sutton. Bettendorf's Supermarket was on the left side; that was the originator of the Schnucks Market years ago. There was also a loop (Sutton Avenue Loop) on the right side... some of the cars looped there and went back where they came from because they weren't needed. The further west (one went) on the line, there were fewer passengers...

At Rock Hill Road, there was another loop... for streetcars that said "Webster" only.... If you got on one of those cars and wanted to go to Kirkwood, you could get off and get a transfer, and the motorman would let you on the Manchester 56 car.. At Berry Road... it turned right onto Lockwood. On the left side was what now is Westborough Country Club and the Webster Christian Church. Prior to (becoming) Westborough Country Club, that was a Jewish club which was called Westwood...

It passed the 01 loop (Magnolia) and continued west. It was just streetcar tracks on what is now called Craig Drive... (At) the Manchester 56 loop (Meramec Highlands)... There was a big dance hall on the north side of the loop. Also, on the other side of the tunnel, there was an amusement area, and people used to go out there and hike. The streetcars were full of people that wanted to come out there on Saturdays and Sundays — and boy scouts for hiking.... Some of the people that came out on the streetcar, had cabins down on Marshall Road... When they didn't have any other transportation, they would walk (from the loop) through the woods down to Marshall Road to spend the weekend down there...

In the summer time, a person would get a little bit cooled off by taking a streetcar ride, especially when there weren't a lot of stops between. You got a little breeze from that....

There was a switch that guided the streetcar to the right or to the left. The motorman had to go out and would "throw the switch" with the switch bar. It was like a big crowbar... The section of the track was moved to the right or left. There was (switching) at Washington and Fillmore, two switches there, one for northbound and one for southbound, at Adams and Fillmore, and ... at Clay and Adams... [7]

The streetcar was the method of transportation used by a young golf caddie to get the jump on the other caddies. Cliff Krienkamp was 10 years old in 1926. He lived on Van Buren and recalls getting up in time to catch the first streetcar out to Osage Hills at 4 a.m. for a 5 cent fare. He would get off at the Osage Hills Country Club where Jim Fogerty was the golf pro and sign in. The caddies were on a rotation, so the first one there was the first to go out on the course. Usually he was paid 50 cents for 9 holes and went around twice. On one of the first days the course was open, he earned $1.50 when he was caught in a rain shower and was given a 50 cent tip. That was big money for a 10 year old in 1926. For a day's work, minus his round-trip streetcar car fare, he usually made 90 cents if he got to the course early enough.[8]

Carol Miner, who lived in Glendale 2½ blocks north of the Kirkwood-Ferguson crossing of Sappington Road, recalls that when she was a high school student she rode the streetcar to the Osage Hills Country Club to play golf and to Meramec Highlands for parties. Many of the members of the country club used the streetcar line to travel there. The Kirkwood-Ferguson also provided Carol with access to the Wabash Club in Ferguson, which was at the far end of the line. The club for Wabash employees featured a lake which was used by members for swimming and the grounds were popular for picnics. Another memorable destination for Carol was Creve Coeur Lake. She would transfer from the Kirkwood-Ferguson where it crossed the Creve Coeur line and ride to the lake on the open streetcars serving that line.

Young men dating Carol and girls in the area listened for the sound of the last car at 2:00 a.m. and then made a mad dash to catch it where it crossed Sappington Road.

---

[7]Francis Scheidegger, cassette tape recorded for the author, January 1997.
[8]Cliff Krienkamp, phone conversation with author, 1996.

KING TROLLEY: STREETCAR MEMORIES

During rush hours, a car came by every ten minutes, but late at night, they came every hour. If the boy missed the last car, he had a long walk home.

At the time, Carol didn't wasn't aware of segregation on the streetcars. During her commutes to Washington University as a student, she often sat with a group of African-American high school students on their way to school. They boarded every school day at Brentwood. "I always sat in the back. I enjoyed it because they always had a good time."[9]

Because it was easier than carrying 7 cents in change for each ride, Carol purchased multiple tokens at a time. Each token cost 7 cents. With a token she could ride and transfer to "go anywhere" with a transfer, which was a slip of paper that the motorman punched when a transfer was made. She recalled that once cars changed to one man operation, the motorman operated the token box and made change. Passengers had to get off on the front end by the motorman.

(Prior to the advent of PCC cars) Carol believed that nicer newer cars were on the 01 than on the 56. She described the interior of the cars. They featured seats of tight wicker on a metal frame. Secured to the back of each seat was a "metal u" six inches wide which looked like a mail drop. The streetcar company sold the right to put advertising circulars in them. Brochures were about 3 inches wide and six inches long and featured ads for coal companies, new medicines and other goods. Double windows on the cars could be raised but one could not get out the windows because of three metal bars across them. In the front, near the motorman, was a straight bench seat against the side of the car where four people could sit. In the back, where the conductor used to be in earlier years was a rounded wooden seat running from the exit around the back wall. It seated about ten people.

The motorman could release sand from inside the streetcar. The sand would cause the wheels to spark as they slid and tried to gain traction on the sanded rails. Carol was very aware of that because of a slight curve and hill near Sappington and Moreland where ice on the tracks was a problem in winter. The same spot was tricky in the summer due to youthful pranks such as soaping the rails. The motorman rang the bell when he came to main cross streets or if people were on the tracks. It was popular (and cheaper than riding) for Glendale youth to walk the ties of the Kirkwood Ferguson tracks to Kirkwood.[10]

In Glendale, the Upper Line, the Manchester, and the Lower Line, the Kirkwood-Ferguson, were within easy walking distance of each other via Sappington Road. Carol and her parents attended the Congregational church in Webster Groves. After church when the weather was beautiful, they would sometimes return to Glendale

---

[9]Carol Miner, phone conversation with author, 19 July 1996.
[10]Ibid.

on the Upper Line and walk the half mile home rather than take the Lower Line which ran near their residence.

Though most of her travel was on the Kirkwood-Ferguson, Carol remembered the Edgebrook bridge on the Manchester line. "The viaduct was very high. It was thrill to ride on it."[11]

Margaret McCord Logie recalled saving pennies during the Depression to get money to pay her fare out to Osage Hills and ride horses. She had to change streetcars three times to get there from her home in the city.

School picnics were often taken via streetcar. The specially chartered picnic cars were bedecked with flags to add to the festive nature of the occasion. Elisabeth Dorr, who in 1931 was in the last class to graduate from Meramec Highlands Elementary School, wrote to the author of one such streetcar picnic.

> I remember my mother, Mrs. Schillck, making arrangements for our school picnic at Forest Park. We always had Picnic Lot 1 reserved sometime around the 15th of May. The reserved streetcar came out to the Highlands circle (circled the loop) and came back to Highland Avenue, then the street straight up from the Frisco Station. We all marched up from the school there where we boarded the streetcar. It took us over the Manchester Line to City Limits, went over the City Limits Line to Oakland Avenue and went over the Forest Park tracks to the main entrance to Forest Park where we all got off and marched to the reserved picnic ground. We also had the streetcar reserved to go back. It was a lot of fun. We always had 5 gallons of ice cream at the picnic, but sometimes it was so cold we didn't want any. Everybody brought their own picnic basket and after lunch had races (and other games) with prizes.[12]

Elisabeth stated that the boys would put hedge apples on the rails between Couch and Bach (Ballas) so that the frustrated motorman had difficulty getting his streetcar up the hill. That formerly slippery stretch is now Craig Road.

From 1931 to 1935, Dorothy Etavard traveled over an hour each school day from Kirkwood to Loretto Academy in the city. She rode the Manchester line. When she got to Maplewood, she signalled another classmate to get on the right streetcar by hanging a hankie out the streetcar window. Her school passes for the streetcar were 75 cents for ten rides. Dorothy had to transfer at Grand and take that line south to school. One day a horse and wagon were stuck in the tracks at Chouteau which caused the girls to be late. After

---

[11]Ibid.
[12]Elisabeth Dorr, letter to author, 1996.

When Dorothy told the principal why they were late, the nun rode out to Kirkwood to see how long it took. After her investigation, she didn't count them as tardy.[13]

Leo Merz, a longtime Kirkwood resident recalled the Meramec Highlands/Osage Hills loop:

> In good times the streetcar pulled a trailer. There was a big bullpen in the loop. They would leave 3 or 4 cars there. You just had to get on. They wouldn't let you off until the intersection of the other line… Children could ride for 3 cents, later it went up to 10 cents.[14]

Leo was the longtime operator of the Loop Lounge situated across Woodbine Avenue from the Magnolia Loop. He recalled the sadness on the last day the streetcars operated in Kirkwood. It was a photo event, but so was the arrival of the first bus. Leo had a picture hanging in the lounge of the first bus to take over the line and use the Magnolia Loop.

The late Fred Stewart, who lived in the old Meramec Highlands section of Kirkwood, remembered the Manchester line. Fred was born in and grew up in the middle of St. Louis, and recalled trips from there to Meramec Highlands on the streetcar.

> Around 1930, we would take the Sarah streetcar south past Chouteau and transfer to the Manchester-Kirkwood 56. The tracks turned south in Maplewood, eventually passing over a trestle, through the back yards of Old Orchard and down Lockwood in Webster Groves. The 54 cars looped at Rock Hill (Road). Going down the tracks from Berry to Sappington, the 56 motorman would spin the rheostat "wide open." The tracks turned south again at Clay and west on Woodbine to the loop, a block west of Geyer. From the loop, we would take a "dinky" to Meramec (Highlands) Quarry for scout outings. At the end of the line, the motorman would walk the trolley around with a cable to reverse the direction of the dinky. After the dinky stopped operating, we would hike over Craig (which follows the path of the former streetcar line) from the Woodbine loop to the quarry.[15]

Like many other Webster, Glendale and Kirkwood students in the early 1940s, Fred, as a Glendale resident, rode the Kirkwood-Ferguson back and forth to school at Washington University. He boarded the car at Sappington Road.

Vangy Weidler Eifert who lived in Kirkwood from 1954 to 1970 and returned in 1990 to live in the Concordia House Apartments, first saw Kirkwood aboard a

---

[13]Dorothy Etavard, phone conversation with author, 1996.
[14]Leo Merz, phone conversation with the author, 1993.
[15]Fred Stewart, letter to author, 1996.

KING TROLLEY: STREETCAR MEMORIES

Manchester car in 1946. She was with a group riding out from St. Louis to the Concordia Lutheran Church to attend a Walther League meeting. She emphatically states her opinion of the bus system which replaced the streetcars:

> One of the most foolish decisions... ever made was to get rid of our extraordinary streetcars. The clang-clang-clang of the trolley cars has never been fully replaced by the exhaust-belching buses. Except for bad foresight, we might still be enjoying this unique transportation![16]

Frank Rouse grew up in Kirkwood in the 30s. As a child, he sold *Globe-Democrat* newspapers to streetcar riders. He bought the papers for 90 cents a hundred from Max Keller who serviced the streetcar route in Kirkwood covering all main corners with his "boys." Frank sold the papers for three cents a piece. Riders would open the windows and stick their hands out with money. The motorman gave him time to give them papers. One day a man took a paper and didn't pay. The next day the conductor who had been on the back of the car and saw the incident, asked Frank if a guy had "got" him for a paper. The conductor pulled the cord and stopped the car. Frank identified the window where the man sat. The conductor went up to the guy who was reading his paper and told the man to give "this kid his money." The man was so embarrassed that he paid 15 cents, which more than paid for the back issue.[17]

Frank later became a Kirkwood policeman and had some crime-related streetcar memories. One such memorable event was the arrest of a killer. The man killed his stepmother's sister. Witnesses saw him throw a gun in a manhole. He then boarded a car at Adams and Taylor. Police were alerted and boarded the car to arrest him.

Another incident occurred when a motorman fell asleep at Adams and Fillmore. The streetcar, which happened to have a police car right behind it with Bill Cavender driving, jumped the track and turned over. Four passengers were in the streetcar. Three of them got out and then fell down on the ground in pain. The police were right there to assist.

A third incident involved a woman who worked at a factory during World War II. She had been accosted by a man on a late night car as she returned from her job. His intent was to rape her, but she talked him out of it by saying that she was on the car every night, that he could meet her "tomorrow night." She then reported to the Kirkwood police who asked her if she would go on the car the next night with a plain clothes policeman on board. She agreed. Her signal was to comb her hair if the man was on board. She signaled; the police officer then arrested the man. He got 20 years in prison.[18]

---

[16]Vangy Weidler Eifert, letter to author, 1996.

[17]Frank Rouse, phone conversation with author, 1996.

[18]Ibid.

KING TROLLEY: STREETCAR MEMORIES

Kirkwood police didn't have radios in their cars in those days. If the dispatcher needed to talk to a man on patrol in the evenings, he would blink the streetlights. The policeman would go to a call box, frequently using the United Railways call box at the corner of Washington and Fillmore, to check in at the station.

In the streetcar days of the thirties and forties, parents didn't think twice about letting children ride to their destinations on their own. Betty Beck recalls her commute to grade school at a young age:

> At age six, my parents sent me alone on the street car from Bartold Avenue in Maplewood to St. Peter School in Kirkwood. It seems strange today, but apparently was safe then as I didn't have any problem until I lost my nickel fare! This happened in front of Kinkhorst Drug Store on the corner of Clay and Argonne Avenues as I waited for the Manchester 56 across from St. Peter School. In those days there was a metal grate in the sidewalk. My nickel dropped down the grate, and (I as) a tearful six-year-old told the druggist what had happened. When he gave me a nickel from the cash register, I protested that *that* was not *my* nickel.[19]

Betty's family moved a lot, living in four different suburban towns in the 30s and 40s, but was always within walking distance of the Manchester line during her school years. She recalls those days:

> Most families we knew had one car at best, and most everyone used the streetcar to go to work, school, church, movies, or just about anywhere you wanted to go in St. Louis or St. Louis County. It was possible to transfer to many other street car or bus lines. The fare for children was a nickel, and a dime for adults, or adults could buy four tokens for thirty-five cents.

> If someone would have told me that some day I would get nostalgic over those swaying orange-yellow street cars that sometimes gave me motion sickness, I wouldn't have believed them. I remember the metal signs on the back of the wicker seats which read "Read as you ride."[20]

An experience made possible only by the location of a drugstore next to the Kirkwood-Ferguson stop at Collins Road was related by Glendale resident Bruce Tanner:

> One time the musical South Pacific was playing in St. Louis. I was working in the drug store and heard a voice. I had to walk around from behind the counter and cash register to see a small man standing there. There was no doubt in my

---

[19]Betty Beck, letter to author, 1995.
[20]Ibid.

mind that there before me stood Ezio Pinza. He had come out to Glendale on the streetcar all by himself.[21]

Pinza stopped at the store to ask directions to the house of a prominent Glendale resident and patron of the arts, Madame De Mette.

Other stars also appeared, though on screen. Al Winkler, reminisced in the June 1993 *Kirkwood Historical Review*, "Watching the Stars at the Kirkwood Theater." When it was dark enough, films would be shown outside under the stars at the Airdome near the corner of Jefferson and Clay Avenues. Sometimes interruptions occurred when a streetcar passed and then groaned loudly going up the Clay Avenue bridge over the railroad tracks or when a Mo-Pac train chugged by "drowning out the romantic sighs from the screen."[22] After the show, the streetcar line was conveniently available for a ride home.

Al lived near the intersection of the Kirkwood-Ferguson and the Manchester line at Adams and Fillmore. He detailed many of his memories of growing up with a streetcar passing his front door in the March 1976 *Kirkwood Historical Review*.

When a switch was not in the correct position and the streetcar missed the turn, the motorman was required to back up the streetcar, throw the switch, and try again to make the turn. Of course at times, accidents occurred at the location because the motorman was driving too fast to make the turn or because of ice coated rails combined with a sandbox that was either clogged with moisture or was empty. Then the cars slid out of control through the switch. Area residents were used to hearing the crash of a derailed streetcar. The crashes at night were more spectacular because the trolley bounced on the live wire causing flashes of light. When a live wire snapped and hit the ground, a tongue of flame flared each time the wire hit the ground until the wire burned off and no longer hit the roadway. After the derailment, curious spectators would wait for the repair crew to arrive, knowing that they would come soon, since the streetcar line was off schedule and not generating new revenue. Al recalled the repair truck:

> Then we waited for the trouble wagon as it was called. This venerable old truck had solid rubber tires, a chain drive to the rear wheels and a scissors type platform that could be cranked up to allow the men to work on the wires. The weight of a streetcar is considerable, and the truck always wound up with

---

[21] Bruce Tanner as told to Donna Lykens, "Memories of Glendale," Glendale Historical Society Bulletin, March 1988, vol. III, no. 1. Pinza was a famous Italian American singer/actor who performed in the New York City Metropolitan Opera and on Broadway in *South Pacific* in 1949.

[22] Al Winkler, "Watching the Stars at the Kirkwood Theater," Kirkwood Historical Review, June 1993, p. 19.

the rubber tires smoking before it could coax the iron-wheeled monster back on the track.[23]

Distinct personalities emerged from crew and passengers of the streetcars. Al recalled a motorman who would stop the streetcar in front of the house and clang the bell until Al's sister would come out to see him. Other motormen took the time to stop to remove animals from the track, such as a neighbor's deaf dog that enjoyed sleeping between the rails.[24]

Streetcars also provided entertainment for children and youth who put nails and pennies on the tracks to be flattened or stretched. Some were intrigued by the whir and hum of the transformers at the booster station at Fillmore and Washington. Older more daring kids would ride on the bar that stuck out from the back of the car or pull the trolley off the wire. Sometimes inside a car, a group of rambunctious kids rocked it back and forth till it seemed that the car would surely tip over. However, the heavy base of the streetcar prevented the car from tipping. Nearby, where the tracks ran through the Kirkwood Country Club, boys searched for the golf balls lost among the white limestone rocks of the Kirkwood-Ferguson roadbed. They used the balls as a medium of exchange. Motormen routinely pushed the streetcars to full speed through the golf course, perhaps to reduce the chance of errant golf balls hitting the car.[25]

Taking the streetcar into the city to shop at Famous-Barr or Vandevoort's was an event which called for a girl to wear her best dress. If she was fortunate, her parents would take a break from shopping and dine with her at the Famous-Barr Tea Room. As a child growing up in Glendale, Dottie Maselter remembered riding the trolley to such shopping excursions: "It was like gliding or flying along." However, she also remembered that erratic service caused some people to grumble.[26]

Robert Eastin remembered fondly the Peter Witt cars on the 01 in the 1940s - car 902, 908, 909, 910... For him, the ride was especially memorable late at night when the streetcar with its headlight beam leading the way raced straight into the darkness of the woods between Kirkwood and Brentwood.[27]

All manner of riders were found on the streetcars: men in suits and ties dressed for work, ladies dressed for shopping, workmen with their tools, salesmen with suitcases full of product samples or items for sale, children on their way to school, baseball fans (both adults and members of the "Knot Hole Gang") on their way to the transfer point at

---

[23]Al Winkler, "Riding the Rails in Kirkwood," Kirkwood Historical Review, March 1976, pp. 9-12.
[24]Ibid.
[25]Ibid.
[26]Dottie Maselter LeRoi as told to Jackie Blumer, "Seventy Happy Years in Glendale," Glendale Historical Society Bulletin, September 1995, vol. X, no. 3.
[27]Robert Eastin, phone interview with author, 1997.

KING TROLLEY: STREETCAR MEMORIES

Grand Avenue where they boarded a car to Sportsman's Park, the blind broom salesman with his brooms and even an occasional organ grinder with his monkey on his way to a new location. The streetcar was a "melting pot" for many ages, races, and classes of people.

Most St. Louisans over the age of 50 have memories of riding streetcars. To remember riding the Kirkwood 01 or the Manchester 53, 54, 55, or 56, one would have had to been born by 1946. To remember the Manchester-Osage Hills 58, one had to be born prior to 1930. Fortunately, many area residents were born before those dates and can still share their streetcar memories. Several of the persons who contributed memories for this chapter have since died, but their reminiscences live on.

24-1. The last run of the Manchester line on April 3, 1949. The operator poses with his PCC car in front of the Katz drug store located in Maplewood. Courtesy of the Museum of Transportation.

24-2. Photograph circa 1908, of Mauriets Vuylstehe holding one of his prized pigeons, his son Morris (age 8 or 9) and Louis Mertens, members of the Mount Pleasant Homing Pigeon Club, preparing to take their pigeons on the streetcar to Meramec Highlands for a training flight. The pigeons often returned home before their owners returned on the streetcar. Photograph courtesy of Mary Ann Carter.

24-3. Some of the Peter Witt cars on the Kirkwood 01 were in poor condition near the end of their service. In some of the older cars, passengers could look through holes in the car floor and see the ground rushing along beneath them. The Peter Witt car in the photograph stopped at Glendale's Sappington Road crossing where the motorman said good-bye to his regular riders on the last day of service on the Kirkwood 01 line. Presumably the car used for the last run was in better condition than some of the other cars used on the line.

24-4. April 3, 1949. The red and white PCC car 1684 makes its last run on the Manchester 56 line carrying a load of somber passengers west into Kirkwood. Photograph by Francis Scheidegger.

24-5. The Rock Hill Road loop on the Manchester line is still used as a loop by Bi-State/Metro buses. The original small brick building built in 1914, contains a rest room for drivers. As a reminder of its early streetcar days, the building displays a vintage St. Louis Public Service Company logo on the wall facing Lockwood Avenue. Photo by author.

Chapter 25

MAPS AND MORE

Maps of county towns served by the Kirkwood-Ferguson or the Manchester lines (up to 1950) illustrated the location of streetcar lines in relation to the street layouts, while maps of streetcar lines serving St. Louis County tended to show the location of the lines in relation to the location of towns, rivers and railroads. In comparing maps made between 1907 and 1945, usually little change in a streetcar route is noted, but in a later map, one frequently notes additional streets and subdivisions built around a streetcar line. Once in a while, as in the case of the 1920 map of Maplewood when compared to the 1915 map, a new streetcar line (the City Limits line - culminating in the Yale Avenue loop) makes an appearance on a map. Though not perfect, maps of towns usually give a reliable location of the streetcar lines. An even better result is achieved, adding life to the map, by comparing the accounts of former streetcar riders to the graphics of the maps.

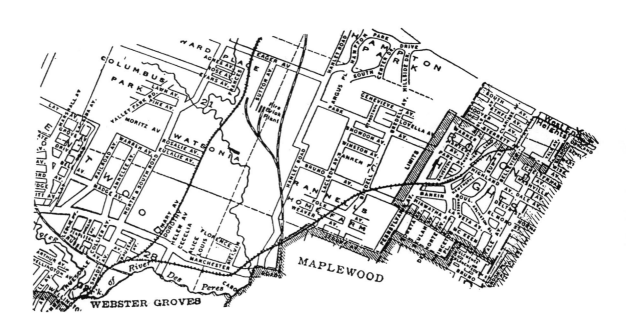

25-1. 1915 *Directory of St. Louis County* **map showing Brentwood and Richmond Heights. Where the #28 is located at the bottom of the map, the Kirkwood- Ferguson continues north while the Brentwood "Dinky" heads east toward West End Heights.**

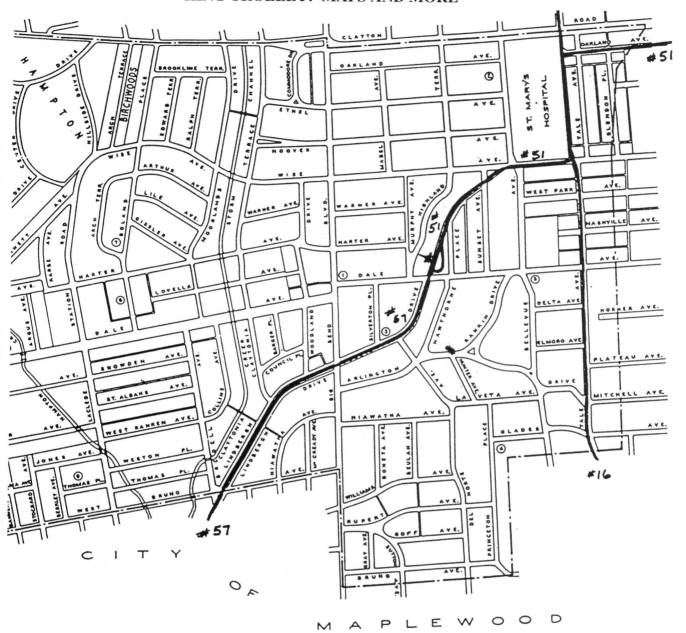

25-2. Detail of the eastern portion of Richmond Heights which shows the alignment of streetcar lines in the 1940s. The Brentwood 57 terminated at the Dale avenue loop. There the Forest Park 51 picked up passengers from the Brentwood Dinky and carried them past St. Mary's Hospital, then turned east on Oakland and ran next to the park. The City Limits 16 ran straight north from Maplewood through Richmond Heights on Yale avenue except for a portion bordering the hospital. The 16 - City Limits-Ferguson streetcar was replaced on February 22, 1948 by the 16 - City Limits bus line. On August 13, 1950, 51 - Forest Park streetcar service west of Euclid and Laclede was replaced by the 52 - Forest Park bus. The 57 - Brentwood streetcar was replaced by the 57 - Brentwood and the 58 - Dale-Hanley bus lines on January 30, 1949.

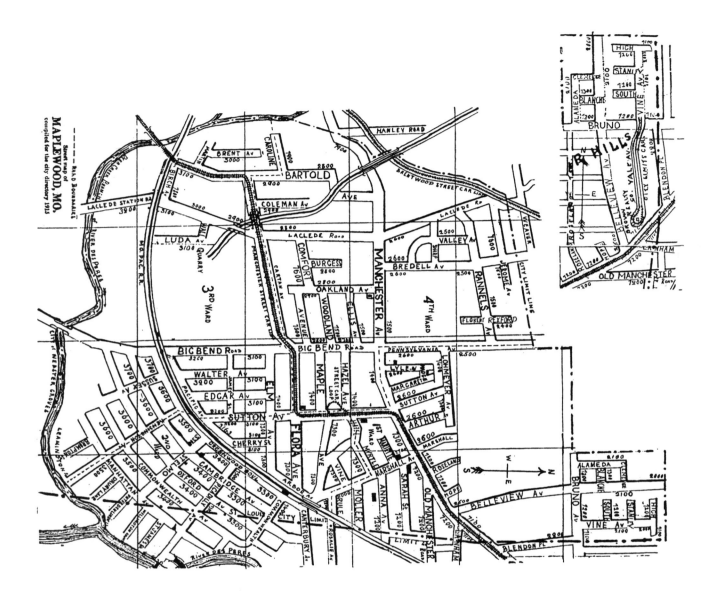

25-3. 1915 *Directory of St. Louis County* map of Maplewood shows the Brentwood line, the old Houseman Air Line, in the upper left corner, barely within Maplewood city limits. The Manchester line traverses Maplewood with a central loop at Sutton Avenue and departing via the Edgebrook bridge in the lower left corner. In 1915, the City Limits line with its loop on Yale Avenue had not yet been constructed. The insert at top right from the 1920 *Directory of St. Louis County* shows the new loop.

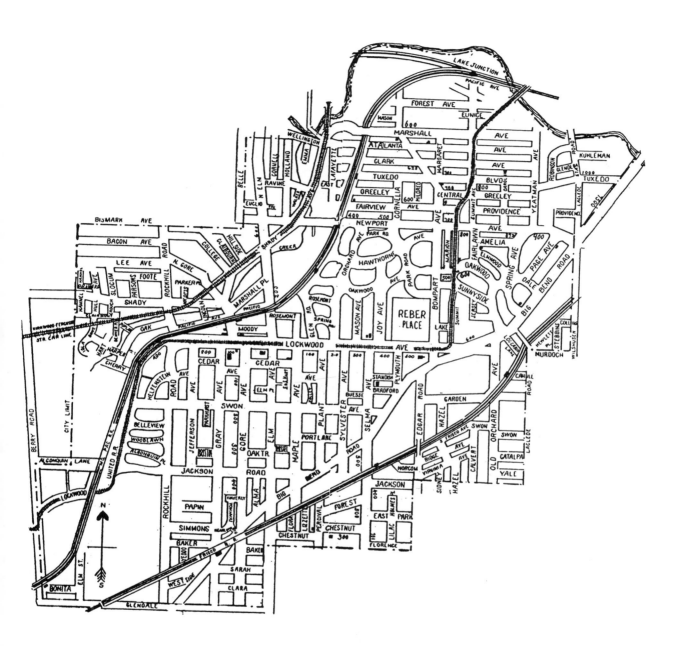

25-4. 1915 *Directory of St. Louis County* **map of Webster Groves shows the route of the Kirkwood-Ferguson south and west from the Brentwood line on Shady Avenue. The Kirkwood-Ferguson followed the route of the former St. Louis and Kirkwood electric railroad. The Manchester (St. Louis and Meramec River) line entered Webster Groves in the northeast part of town via the bridge at Edgebrook and ran through the heart of Webster on Summit and Lockwood before exiting in the southwest corner. Note the proximity of the lines at Rock Hill Road where the Upper (Manchester) and Lower (Kirkwood-Ferguson) lines come within two blocks of each other.**

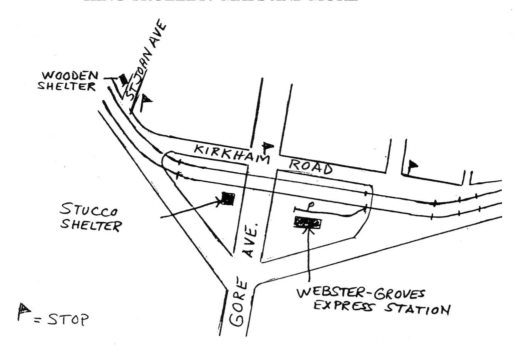

25-5. **Detail of the Kirkwood-Ferguson route and associated structures located in Webster Groves near the intersection of Gore Avenue and Kirkham Road. Stops in Webster Groves from east to west were: Marshall Avenue, East Avenue, Newport Avenue, Elm Avenue, Hillside Avenue, Gore Avenue, current site of St. John Avenue, Rock Hill Road, Murphy car stop, site of Denver Place and at a private road for Algonquin Country Club. Note the name change from Shady to Kirkham.**

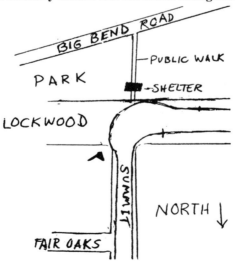

25-6. **Detail of the Manchester line where it turned from Summit Avenue onto Lockwood. After the turn, it proceeded straight west through the Webster Groves business district. Note the passenger shelter on the public walk between Big Bend and Lockwood. For many years, from Summit to Rock Hill, Lockwood was concrete paved with brick between the tracks. The wide Devil's Strip formerly contained center poles.**

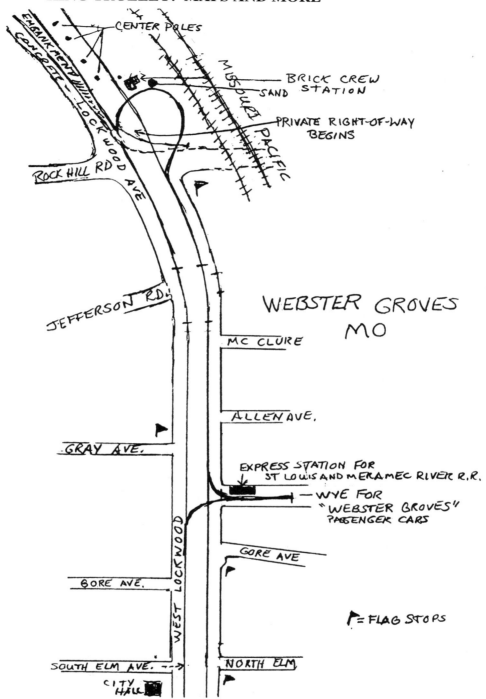

25-7. **West Lockwood section of the Manchester line. Of special interest is the Wye used by express cars for the St. Louis and Meramec River Railroad and as a turn around point for the Webster Groves passenger cars prior to the construction of the loop shown at Rock Hill Road. The loop at Rock Hill is still used by Bi-State as is the brick crew station at the loop. Flag stops on East Lockwood (not shown on the map section) from Summit Avenue west: NE corner of Summit, NE corner of Bompart, opposite Plymouth by Eden Seminary, SW corner of Selma, corner of Orchard Avenue, opposite Plant Avenue east of Glenn Road, and the NE corner of Elm opposite Webster Groves City Hall.**

271

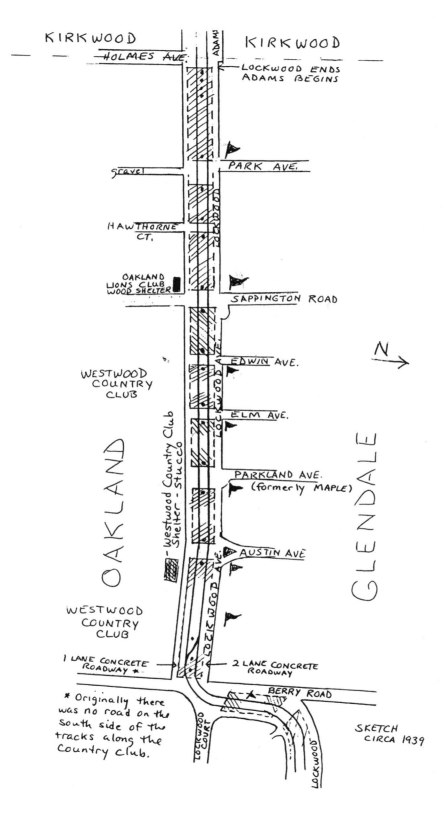

25-8. Sketched map of the route of the Manchester route through Glendale - circa 1939. Note Oakland is no longer part of Glendale on this map. Glendale was the next town west of Webster on both the Kirkwood-Ferguson and the Manchester lines. Manchester stops in Glendale from east to west were: west side of Berry Road north of Lockwood, north side of Lockwood midway between Berry and Austin, NE corner of Austin, the Westwood Country Club stop on the south side of Lockwood across from Austin, NE corner of Parkland (formerly Maple), NE corner of Elm, NE corner of Edwin, NW corner of Sappington, a wooden shelter on the SW corner of Sappington and the NW corner of Park Avenue. Kirkwood-Ferguson stops in Glendale (not shown) were from east to west: a wooden shelter at Berry Road, a flag stop at Elmwood located by a trailing switchback, a wooden shelter at Chelsea (now Idlewood), Moreland, a wooden shelter at Collins Road (now Sappington), Venneman and a wooden shelter at the Armstrong stop at Hill Road.

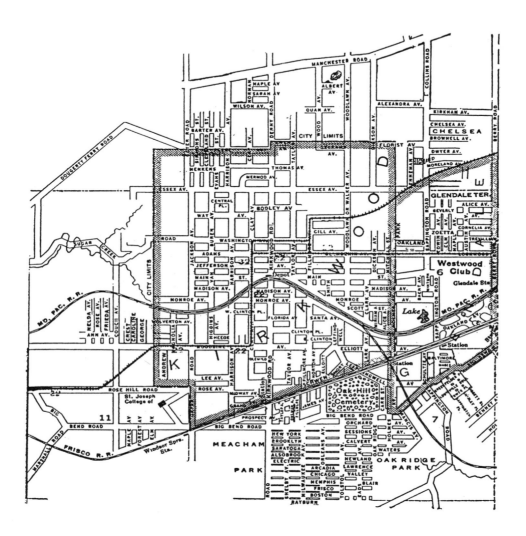

25-9. 1915 *Directory of St. Louis County* map of Kirkwood. Note the connection of the two streetcar lines at Washington and Fillmore. Meramec Highlands does not show on the map since it was not part of Kirkwood until 1925. The Woodbine and Magnolia loop had not been completed when the map was rendered, though it was in operation in 1915.

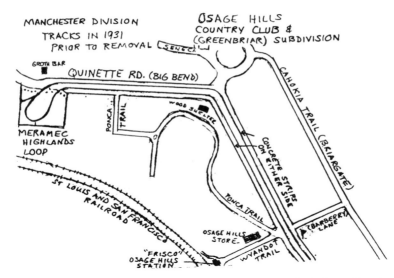

25-10. Sketched map of Meramec Highlands area of Kirkwood as it existed in the early 1930s. Distances are not to scale, but the general lay out of the loop and the Manchester tracks used by the Osage Hills Dinky is correct. Note the presence of a wood shelter for streetcar passengers across from the entrance to the Osage Hills Country Club.

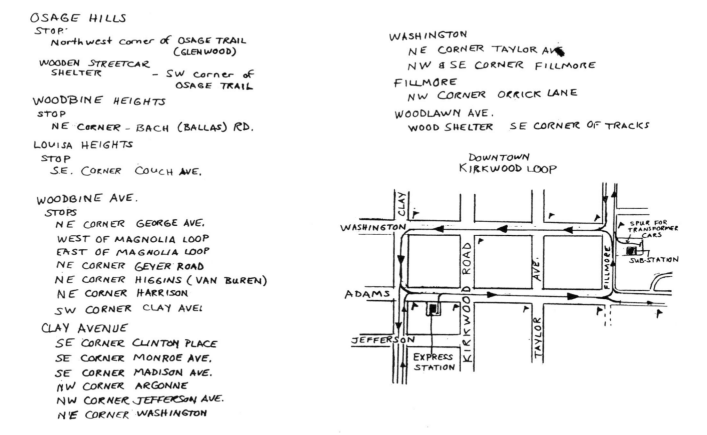

OSAGE HILLS
STOP:
Northwest corner of OSAGE TRAIL
(GLENWOOD)
WOODEN STREETCAR
SHELTER   — SW corner of
OSAGE TRAIL

WOODBINE HEIGHTS
STOP
NE CORNER — BACH (BALLAS) RD.

LOUISA HEIGHTS
STOP
S.E. CORNER COUCH AVE.

WOODBINE AVE.
STOPS
NE CORNER GEORGE AVE.
WEST OF MAGNOLIA LOOP
EAST OF MAGNOLIA LOOP
NE CORNER GEYER ROAD
NE CORNER HIGGINS (VAN BUREN)
NE CORNER HARRISON
SW CORNER CLAY AVE.

CLAY AVENUE
SE CORNER CLINTON PLACE
SE CORNER MONROE AVE.
SE CORNER MADISON AVE.
NW CORNER ARGONNE
NW CORNER JEFFERSON AVE.
NE CORNER WASHINGTON

WASHINGTON
NE CORNER TAYLOR AVE
NW & SE CORNER FILLMORE

FILLMORE
NW CORNER ORRICK LANE

WOODLAWN AVE.
WOOD SHELTER   SE CORNER OF TRACKS

25-11. Listing of stops in Kirkwood and a sketch of the Clay and Adams loop. Note the substation on Fillmore and the express station off Adams.

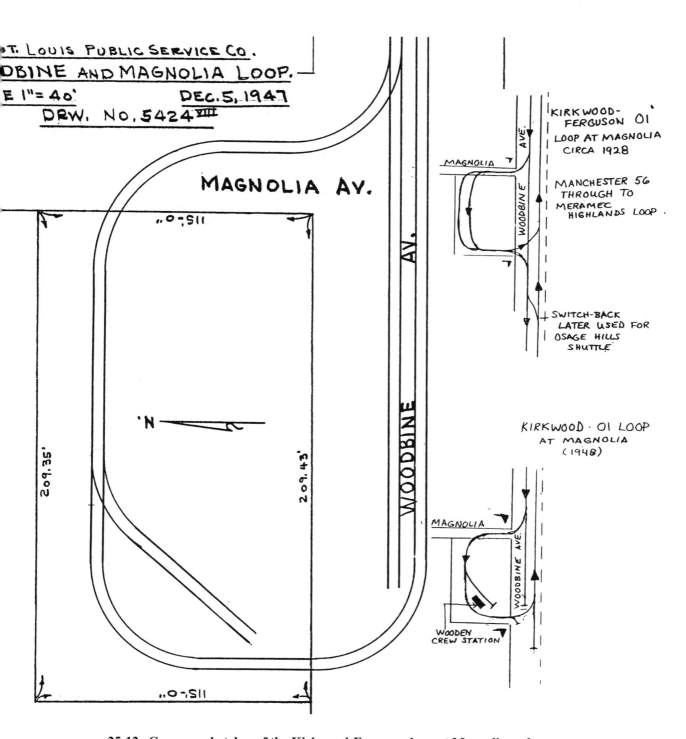

ST. LOUIS PUBLIC SERVICE CO.
ODBINE AND MAGNOLIA LOOP.
E 1"= 40'   DEC. 5, 1947
    DRW. NO. 5424 VIII

MAGNOLIA AV.

115'-0"

209.35'   209.43'

'N

WOODBINE AV.

115'-0"

KIRKWOOD-
FERGUSON 01
LOOP AT MAGNOLIA
CIRCA 1928

MANCHESTER 56
THROUGH TO
MERAMEC
HIGHLANDS LOOP.

MAGNOLIA

WOODBINE AVE.

SWITCH-BACK
LATER USED FOR
OSAGE HILLS
SHUTTLE

KIRKWOOD - 01 LOOP
AT MAGNOLIA
(1948)

MAGNOLIA

WOODBINE AVE.

WOODEN
CREW STATION

25-12. Compare sketches of the Kirkwood-Ferguson loop at Magnolia and Woodbine circa 1928 and 1948. In the 1948 version, note the change in name to the Kirkwood 01, the deletion of the second track on the north side of the loop with the addition of a spur within the loop, the addition of a wooden crew station and the removal of track beyond the loop. By 1948, Manchester cars no longer ran to the Magnolia loop. Public Service Company rendering is from the Museum of Transport.

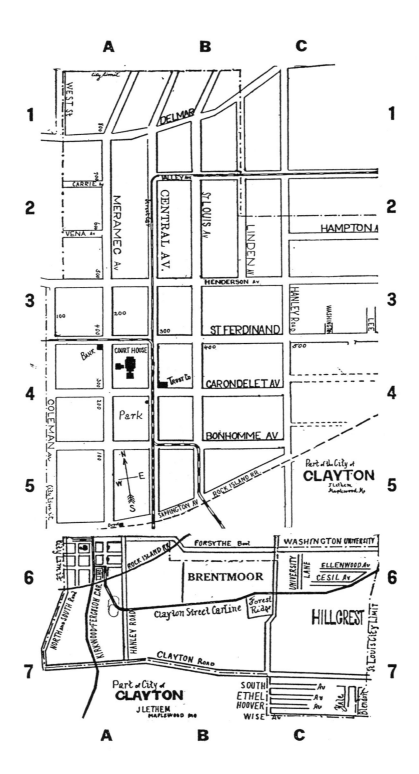

25-13. 1915 *Directory of St. Louis County* **map of Clayton shows both the Kirkwood-Ferguson (01) and the Clayton (04) streetcar lines.**

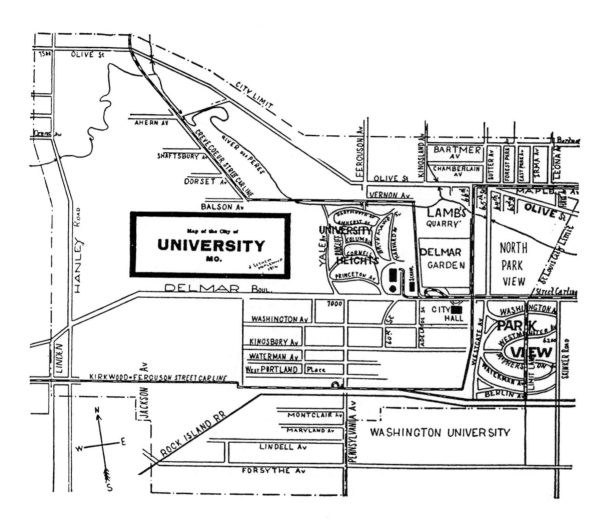

25-14. Map of University City drawn in 1914, shows the Kirkwood-Ferguson serving Washington University before turning north to intersect with other lines at Delmar Boulevard. From University City on Maple, the line then entered the city of St. Louis and turned on Hodiamont, running near the city limits to the Wellston loop. From the 1915 *Directory of St. Louis County.*

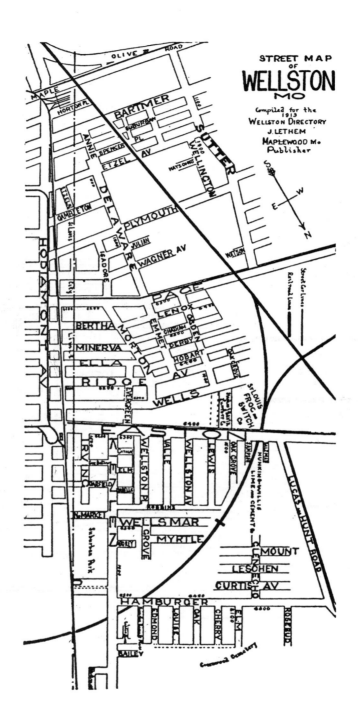

25-15. 1913 map of Wellston from the 1915 *Directory of St. Louis County* shows the Kirkwood-Ferguson streetcar line as a thin black unbroken line veering away from Hodiamont toward the Wellston city limits. It connected with the Wellston loop and a loop at Suburban Park, then proceeded on private-right-of way through Jennings toward Normandy.

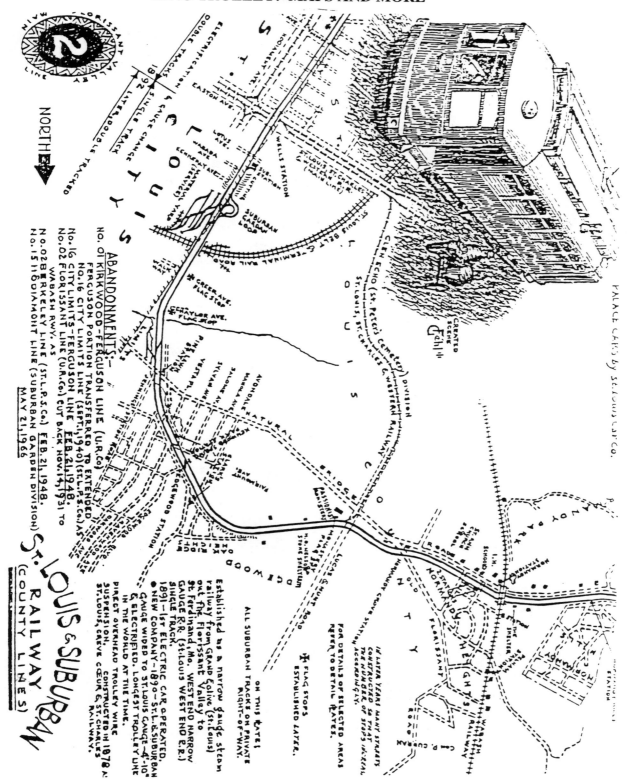

25-16. One plate from a series of drawings self-published by Sarno and Gehl shows the route of the Kirkwood-Ferguson and the Florissant Valley main line through private right of way.

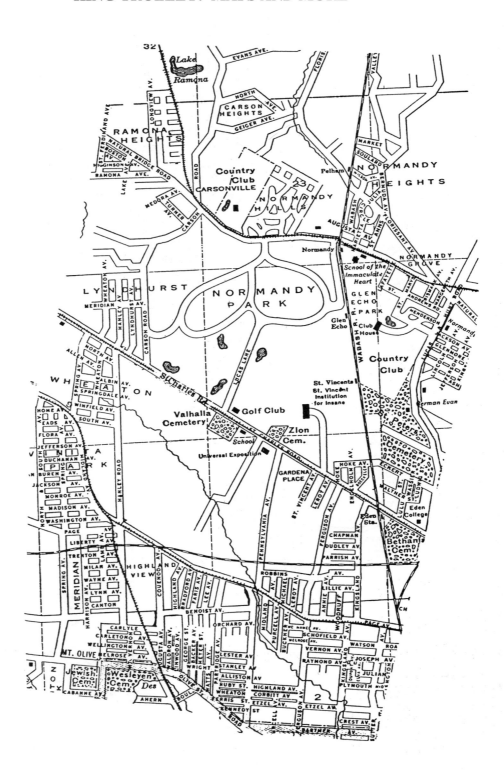

25-17. 1915 map of Normandy and surrounding areas shows the
Kirkwood-Ferguson following Natural Bridge Road from Florissant Avenue to
Carson Road where it veered into private right-of-way heading toward Lake
Ramona and Ferguson. From 1915 *Directory of St. Louis County*.

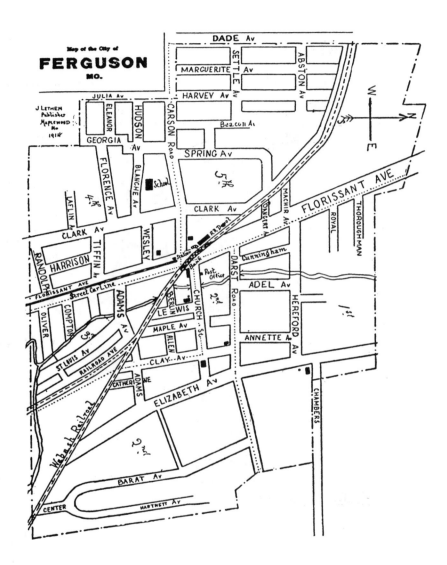

25-18. After passing Ramona Park, traveling away from the city, the Kirkwood-Ferguson came to the Ferguson junction and turned on a spur line that ran to the Ferguson terminus. The loop built in 1914 was situated near the Wabash Railroad depot and the Ferguson business district. Upon reaching the terminus, intrepid pleasure riders often turned around and traveled the line all the way back to the other end. Map from 1915 *Directory of St. Louis County*.

281

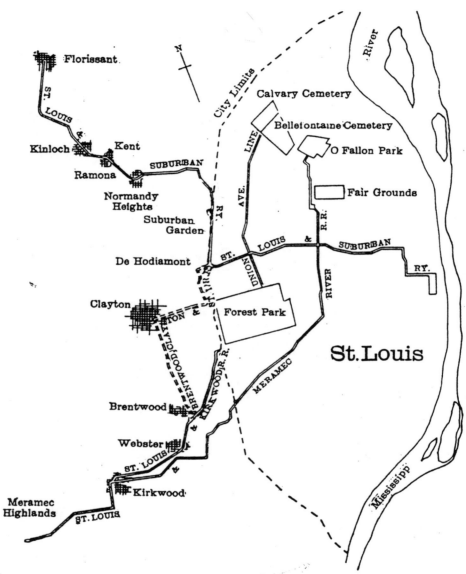

MAP OF ST. LOUIS & SUBURBAN SYSTEM.

25-19. Map of the Suburban system (enlarged) printed in the February 15, 1900 *Street Railway Review*. **The Brentwood, Clayton and St. Louis branch shown as dashed lines was not completed until June 1900.**

STREET CAR LINES OF ST. LOUIS.
NO. 1.—THE SUBURBAN SYSTEM.

25-20. 1901 map (reduced) of the Suburban System from the June 18, 1901, *St. Louis Post-Dispatch.* **Transfer points are noted with a star.**

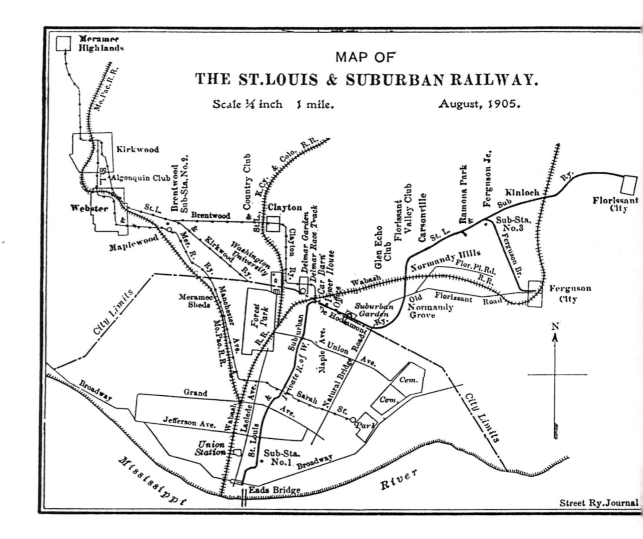

25-21. 1905 map of the St. Louis and Suburban Railway from the *Street Railway Journal***. The scale is incorrect as stated For ease of viewing the map has been enlarged. Note that the pieces to the Kirkwood-Ferguson line are all in place but would not be connected until United Railways took over the Suburban.**

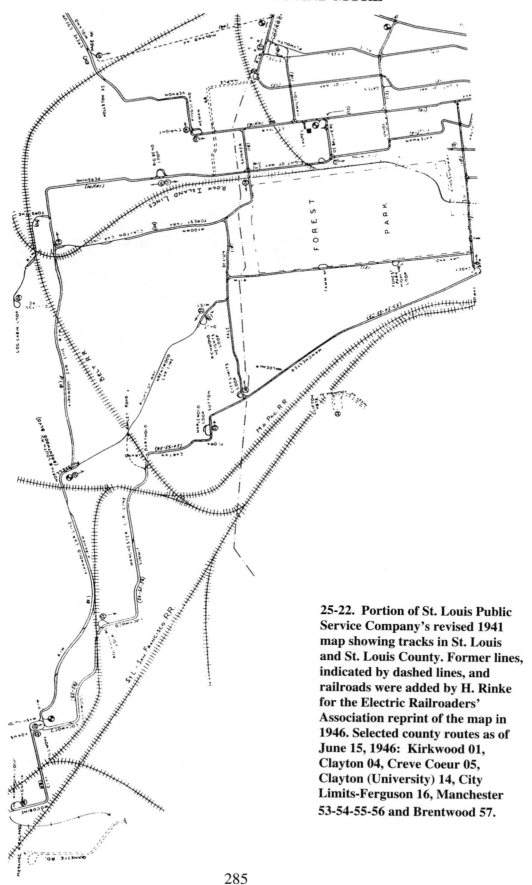

25-22. Portion of St. Louis Public Service Company's revised 1941 map showing tracks in St. Louis and St. Louis County. Former lines, indicated by dashed lines, and railroads were added by H. Rinke for the Electric Railroaders' Association reprint of the map in 1946. Selected county routes as of June 15, 1946: Kirkwood 01, Clayton 04, Creve Coeur 05, Clayton (University) 14, City Limits-Ferguson 16, Manchester 53-54-55-56 and Brentwood 57.

285

25-23. Featured illustration in St. Louis Public Service Company brochure introducing the PCC car circa 1940. Brochure courtesy of the Museum of Transport.

25-24. Interior of the PCC car as shown in the St. Louis Streamliner brochure. The turnstile was never effective and was rapidly discontinued. Courtesy of the Museum of Transport.

25-25. Maintenance on a Manchester PCC car 1696 in 1942. This Public Service Company publicity photograph was used in an article about the company in a trade publication. Photograph from the St. Louis Car Company archives at Washington University.

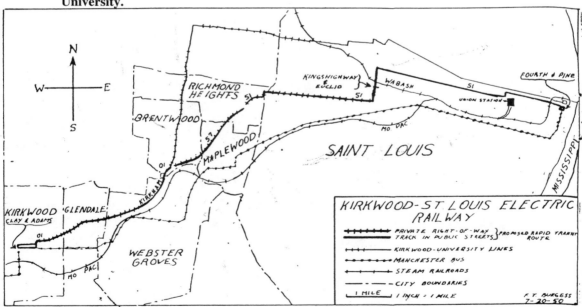

25-26. A Kirkwood-St. Louis electric railway rapid transit route proposed by the Kirkwood Chamber of Commerce Transportation Committee. The map is by F. Travers Burgess, a member of that committee. It was presented to the Kirkwood public by the Chamber of Commerce in *The Kirkwood View* in the July 31, 1950 issue with an appeal for residents to express their support for the plan in writing. The plan was not accepted by the Public Service Company.

287

25-27. One can still ride an operable PCC car in St. Louis. A restored PCC car from the Philadelphia System runs on special days at the Museum of Transportation. The work of a dedicated group of St. Louis area volunteers keeps the PCC car running at the St. Louis County park. Work is underway on restoration of other cars. Photo by author.

25-28. Tourists and streetcar enthusiasts enjoy a ride on the PCC car at the Museum of Transportation. Photo by author.

25-29. A last look at the Brentwood Dinky as it nears the end of its service. Photo from the Museum of Transportion.

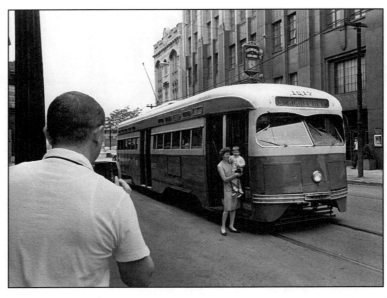

25-30 On May 21,1966, home movies were taken to record the passing of streetcar service in St. Louis. This family was preparing to board the Hodiamont car 1617 going east on Olive Street at Grand Avenue. Photo courtesy of Wayne Leeman.

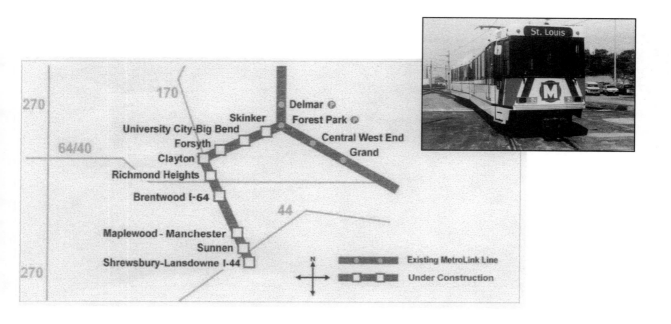

25-31. MetroLink car and the MetroLink Cross County route - Segment 1 (still unfinished as of summer 1995) that will end in Shrewsbury. It will serve University City, Clayton, Brentwood, Richmond Heights, and Maplewood. It comes close to Webster Groves. Sadly, the "Suburban Queens" will have no light rail transit stations in the near future.

KING TROLLEY: BIBLIOGRAPHY

American Street Railway Association, edited by Robert Mc Collough, *Official Souvenir of the Local Committee of Arrangements of the American Street Railway Association*, St. Louis: 1896.

Baker, James F., *Glimpses of Meramec Highlands, St. Louis' Only Exclusive Health and Pleasure Resort*, Kirkwood: Meramec Highlands Books, 1995.

Blann, Celeste Wagner, *A History of Rock Hill*, St. Louis: self published, 1976.

Brentwood 50 Yr. Anniversary 1919-1969, Brentwood: in Brentwood Public Library.

Business Men's Association, Directory of the City of Maplewood, 1912, Maplewood: in historical archives of Maplewood Public Library.

Byerly, Barbara, and Lester, J.B. *Kirkwood, Missouri - The Greentree City - A Pictorial History*, St. Louis: Webster-Kirkwood Times, Inc.,1994.

City of Kirkwood, *Board of Aldermen Minutes*, 1895-1903, Kirkwood: City Hall.

Dahl, June Wilkinson, *A History of Kirkwood*, Kirkwood: Kirkwood Historical Society, 1965.

Delbridge, Charles, *Move Forward Please*, St. Louis: 1901, in Missouri Historical Society Archives.

Directory of St. Louis County, 1915, St. Louis: telephone directory, in St. Louis County Library.

Electric Railway Journal, industry journal, located in Washington University Library and at Museum of Transport.

Essex, William, letter to William Vincent Byars, Kirkwood: August 1896, in Missouri Historical Society Archives.

Electric Railroaders' Association, *E.R.A. Headlights*, in Museum of Transport.

Glendale, *The City of Glendale - 75*: 1987.

Glendale Historical Society Bulletin, Glendale: 1986-1998.

Hemphill, Carol A. *Webster Groves Centennial 1896-1996 1st One Hundred Years*, Webster Groves: Webster-Kirkwood Times, 1995.

Highlands Inn and Cottages, St. Louis County, Mo., Opens for World's Fair Season, advertisement booklet, St. Louis: Meramec Highlands Company, 1904.

Hyde, *Encyclopedia of the History of St. Louis,* vol. 4, "Street Railways," St. Louis: 1899.

KING TROLLEY: BIBLIOGRAPHY

Jackson, Kenneth *Crabgrass Frontiers: The Suburbanization of the United States,* New York: Oxford Press, 1985.

Kirkwood Historical Review, Kirkwood Historical Society quarterly publication.

Kirkwood Historical Society, Pictorial Glimpses of Early Kirkwood, Kirkwood: 1974.

Kirkwood Monitor, local newspaper.

Kirkwood View, Volume 2, #25, July 31, 1950.

Kirkwood Weekly Courier, local newspaper.

Klersch, Lillian and Sadlier, Mary Maddden, *A History of Brentwood , Missouri,* Brentwood: Brentwood Public Library, 1951.

Linscott, Mrs. Herbert B., *Bright Ideas for Entertaining*, 9th ed., Philadelphia, 1905.

Middleton. William O. *The Time of the Trolley*, Milwaukee: Kalmbach Publishing Co., 1967.

Nicholls-Ritter Realty, *Meramec Highlands*, foldout advertisement, April 1895 .

Papin and Tontrup Realty Company, *Maplewood Subdivision*, circa 1896.

Primm, James N. *Lion of the Valley - St. Louis, Missouri*, Boulder: Pruett Publishing Company, 1981.

Pulse, Brentwood 75th Anniversary Special Edition, Brentwood, local newspaper, 1994, located in Brentwood Public Library.

Reports of Cases Determined in the Supreme Court of the State of Missouri, Columbia: E. W. Stevens Publisher, 1900-1935.

Rowsome, Frank Jr. *Trolley Car Treasury*, New York: Mc Graw Hill, 1956.

Seifert, Shirley and Adele , *Grace Church Kirkwood, Missouri Its Story,* Kirkwood: Messenger Printing Co., 1959 .

Thomas, William, *A History of St. Louis County*, St. Louis: J. Clarke Publishing Company, 1911.

St. Louis County Watchman, Clayton: (SLCW), *St. Louis County Watchman-Advocate,* Clayton: (SLCWA), *St. Louis Globe-Democrat*: (GD) , *St. Louis Post-Dispatch*, (PD), and the *St. Louis Republic*, St. Louis: microfilm in St. Louis County Library.

St. Louis Public Service Company, *Transit News*, St. Louis: in Museum of Transport archives.

St. Louis Public Service Company, *The St. Louis Streamliner*, St. Louis: brochure, 1940.

KING TROLLEY: BIBLIOGRAPHY

Street Railway Review, industry journal, published from 1890-1908.

Street Railway Journal, trade publication, published between 1884-1942.

Suburban Leader, Kirkwood: newspaper, 1895, in Kirkwood Public Library.

Swyers, F. A. *Street Railways of St. Louis*, St. Louis: self published, 1956.

The St. Louis Electrical Handbook - Being a Guide for Visitors Abroad Attending the International Electrical Congress, St. Louis: 1904, at Missouri Historical Society archives.

Transit Journal, industry journal in Washington University library.

United Railways, *United Railways Bulletin*, St. Louis: archived at Museum of Transportation.

United Railways, *Franchises of United Railways and Constituent Companies*, St. Louis: 1913.

United Railways, *When St. Louis Moves*, St. Louis: 1926.

Wells, Rolla, *Episodes of My Life*, St. Louis: self published, 1933.

Wydown Eighth Grade, *Images of Our Community - Clayton,* Clayton: Clayton Public Schools, 1976.

York, Howard, *I Can't Forget*, St. Louis: independently published, 1991.

Young, Andrew D. *St. Louis and Its Streetcars*, St. Louis: Archway Publishing, 1996.

Young, Andrew D. *St. Louis Streetcar Story*, Glendale, CA: Interurban Press, 1988.

Young, Andrew D. and Provenzo, Eugene, *Quality Shops: The History of the St. Louis Car Company*, Berkeley: Howell-North Books, 1978.

Webster Groves - Queen of the Suburbs - A Pictorial History, St. Louis: Webster-Kirkwood Times, 1991.

Webster - Queen of the Suburbs, Webster Groves - Webster Park, St. Louis: President Buxton and Skinner Stationery Company, 1890.

Webster Groves High School, *In Retrospect III*, Webster Groves: Webster Groves Public Schools, 1978.

Webster Groves Times, local newspaper on microfilm at the Webster Groves Public Library.

Webster-Kirkwood Times, Webster Groves: local weekly newspaper.

Footnote abbreviations: **GD** - St. Louis Globe-Democrat, **MHS** - Missouri Historical Society, **MOT** - Museum of Transportation, **PD** - St. Louis Post-Dispatch, **SLCW** - St. Louis County Watchman, **SLCWA** - St. Louis County Watchman-Advocate.

Even the Weather Bird imparted safety lessons to the streetcar riders. "The Post-Dispatch Weather Bird Learns the Disadvantage of Ill-Timed Haste," reads the title of the January 31, 1903 panel of illustrations showing the bird hurrying because February had only 28 days. Panel 3 of 6.

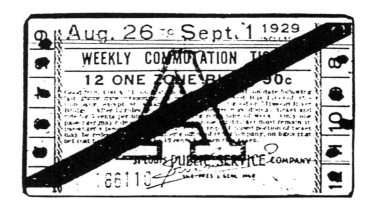

Public Service Company - 1929 Weekly Commutation Ticket - 12 one zone runs for 90 cents.